PAKISTAN'S FOREIGN POLICY 1947–2005

A Concise History

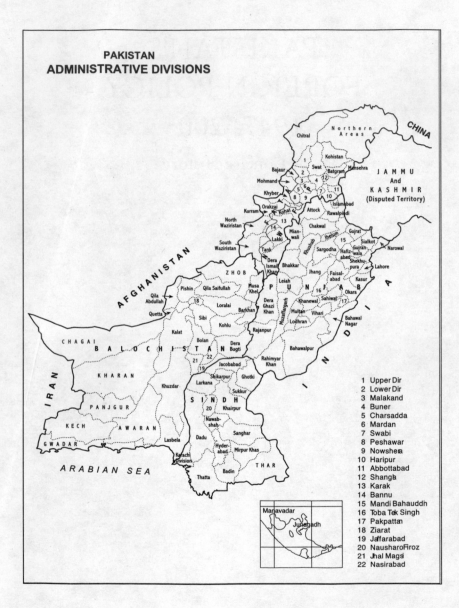

PAKISTAN
ADMINISTRATIVE DIVISIONS

1 Upper Dir
2 Lower Dir
3 Malakand
4 Buner
5 Charsadda
6 Mardan
7 Swabi
8 Peshawar
9 Nowshera
10 Haripur
11 Abbottabad
12 Shangla
13 Karak
14 Bannu
15 Mandi Bahauddin
16 Toba Tek Singh
17 Pakpattan
18 Ziarat
19 Jaffarabad
20 NausharoFiroz
21 Jhal Magsi
22 Nasirabad

PAKISTAN'S FOREIGN POLICY 1947–2005

A Concise History

ABDUL SATTAR

Foreword by
Agha Shahi

OXFORD

UNIVERSITY PRESS

OXFORD

UNIVERSITY PRESS

Great Clarendon Street, Oxford OX2 6DP

Oxford University Press is a department of the University of Oxford.
It furthers the University's objective of excellence in research, scholarship,
and education by publishing worldwide in

Oxford New York

Auckland Cape Town Dar es Salaam Hong Kong Karachi
Kuala Lumpur Madrid Melbourne Mexico City Nairobi
New Delhi Shanghai Taipei Toronto

with offices in

Argentina Austria Brazil Chile Czech Republic France Greece
Guatemala Hungary Italy Japan Poland Portugal Singapore
South Korea Switzerland Turkey Ukraine Vietnam

Oxford is a registered trade mark of Oxford University Press
in the UK and in certain other countries

ISBN 978-0-19-547167-0

Second Impression 2007

Typeset in Minion Pro
Printed in Pakistan by
Print Vision, Karachi.
Published by
Ameena Saiyid, Oxford University Press
No. 38, Sector 15, Korangi Industrial Area, PO Box 8214
Karachi-74900, Pakistan.

Contents

Foreword   ix

Preface   xi

1. **The Emergence of Pakistan**   1
   Historical Background

2. **Foreign Policy—Beginnings**   8
   The Founding Father's Vision
   Enduring Relevance of Principles
   The Shadow of Partition
   The Muslim World

3. **The Kashmir Question, 1947–57**   21
   The Dispute
   At the United Nations
   The Dispute Festers

4. **Search for Security**   33
   USSR
   Approaches to the USA
   Korean War
   Japan
   China

5. **Alliances**   41
   Four Alliances
   Reactions of India, China and the USSR

6. **Alliances—Costs and Benefits**   53
   The Costs of the Alliances
   Pakistan–US Cooperation Agreement, 1959
   The Benefits of the Alliances
   Swings of Opinion in the USA and Pakistan

7. **Relations with China and other Developments**   68
   China
   Pakistan–China Boundary Agreement, 1962
   Sino–Pakistan Entente
   Oman: Gwadar Retrocession

Indus Waters Treaty, 1960
India–China War, 1962
Pakistan–US Relations Corroded
Negotiations on Kashmir, 1962–63
Changing the Strategic Environment
Alliance under Strain
Ayub Khan's Visits to China and the USSR
Second Afro–Asian Summit
US Reaction
RCD and IPECC

8. **The Pakistan–India War, 1965**   88
Clash in Kutch
Operation Gibraltar
Escalation to War
Stance of Foreign Powers
The Tashkent Declaration
Bilateralism

9. **Policy Ups and Downs: 1965–71**   105
China
USSR
USA
Kissinger's Secret Visit to China
Organisation of the Islamic Conference

10. **1971 Disaster**   112
Bhutto's dynamic role, 1972–73

11. **Shimla Agreement: Negotiating Under Duress**   124
Opening Gambit
Principles of Relations
Withdrawal from Occupied Territory
Jammu and Kashmir
Dénouement
Assessment
Secret Understanding?
Normalisation with Bangladesh

12. **The Nuclear Programme
and Relations with the USA**   144

13. **The Afghanistan Crisis**   154
Revival of the US Alliance
Geneva Accords

14. **Kashmir: The Struggle for *Azadi***   169

15. **The Afghanistan Civil War, 1990–1998**   177
The Rise of the Taliban
Proxy War
Fatal Blunders
Retrospect

16. **Pakistan–India Disputes and Crises**   187
Sir Creek
Siachen: A Dispute within a Dispute
Salal, Wuller, Baglihar and Kishenganga Projects
Consular Missions
Indian Plan for Attack on Kahuta, 1984
Consular Missions
The Brasstacks Crisis, 1986–87
Re-entry to the Commonwealth
War Averted, 1990
Disarmament Issues

17. **Nuclear Tests**   201
Tests
Nuclear Restraints
Impact on Security
Issues and Non-Issues
Ballistic Missiles: The Threat of Destabilization

18. **Increasing Isolation, 1990–2001**   225
US Sanctions Again
Support for the Taliban
Declining Prestige
Nuclear Tests
Pakistan–India Dialogue, 1997–99
The Kargil Crisis, 1999
Coping with Isolation
The Agra Summit

19. **Post–9/11 Policy**   240
Policy Planning by Pakistan
US Policy
Consultation with Opinion Leaders
Economic Cooperation and Assistance
New Afghanistan

20. **Terrorism** 256
    Islam Targeted
    Terrorism and Religion
    State Terrorism
    The Need for a Comprehensive Strategy

21. **Pakistan–India Relations, 2001–05** 266
    Retrospect
    Developments
    Peace in Kashmir
    Prospects

22. **The UN and International Cooperation** 275
    The Millennium Summit
    Reform of the United Nations
    Human Rights
    International Financial Institutions (IFIs)
    SAARC–South Asian Association for Regional Cooperation
    ECO–Economic Cooperation Organisation

23. **Policy in a Changing World** 294
    'End of History'
    The New Power Structure
    Setbacks to an Emergent Era of Peace
    War on Iraq
    A Better Future

Appendices
    I.   The Shimla Agreement, 1972 304
    II.   Composite Dialogue, 1997–98 313
    III. Lahore Declaration, 1999 315
    IV.   Agra Declaration, 2001—Draft Agreement 317
    V.   Presidents, Prime Ministers and Foreign Ministers of Pakistan 319

Bibliography 321
Index 323

Foreword

Gaining independence by the exercise of the principle of self-determination, the nascent state of Pakistan wished, as its founding father repeatedly said, to build friendly and cooperative relations with its neighbours. Idealistic in inspiration, the state's foreign policy had soon to come to grips, however, with the reality of the challenge to its right to peaceful coexistence. The failure of its own efforts and those of the United Nations for the settlement of disputes in the wake of Partition, in conformity with the principles of international law and justice, illustrated the tyranny of power disparity in the region.

In order to ameliorate the situation, Pakistan did what many other states in a similar predicament had done and began to look outwards for friends and allies to support its own efforts to safeguard the independence, strengthen the security and build the economic sinews of the infant state. Resistance to hegemony in the regional context complemented Pakistan's policy of opposition to the Soviet policy of expansionism and subversion, although Pakistan was not motivated by Cold War or ideological considerations, as illustrated by its policy to develop friendly cooperation with the People's Republic of China, disregarding the objections and sanctions by its partners in military alliances led by the United States of America.

The failure of the allies to come to Pakistan's assistance and the powerlessness of the United Nations to restrain India from intervention and aggression in East Pakistan in 1971, convinced Pakistan's leaders of the need to develop nuclear capability for the purpose of deterrence—an aim the Pakistani leadership pursued with single-mindedness in the face of discriminatory sanctions and pressures, the nation willingly bearing the burdens and sacrifices resulting from the cut off of foreign assistance.

Through diligent research Ambassador Abdul Sattar has recapitulated the rationale of these and other major policy decisions, including that of opposition to Soviet intervention in Afghanistan in 1979, in order to write what he calls 'a plain history'. He has delineated the objective strategic considerations on the basis of which the government and its leaders made the fateful decisions. He draws also on personal knowledge as an official in the ministry of foreign affairs in the 1980s when the Geneva Accords were negotiated for the withdrawal of the Soviet forces from Afghanistan, and as foreign minister when Pakistan decided on a policy reappraisal in the wake of 9/11.

The scholarly work he has produced accomplishes his laudable purpose of writing an objective history of Pakistan's policy. The book provides an authoritative account for students of foreign policy, observers and analysts to understand the past and benefit from its lessons in formulating effective strategies for the realisation of the aims and objectives of the state: to strengthen security and accelerate economic and social progress to achieve a position of dignity and self-respect in the comity of nations.

I commend *Pakistan's Foreign Policy* to students and scholars at home and aboard, as well as to members of the security and foreign policy establishment in Pakistan, as it will facilitate a deeper understanding of the strategic compulsions that have driven decision-making in Pakistan's national security and foreign policy. It will also serve to inculcate a sense of history in the younger generation of Pakistanis and heighten the consciousness of their national identity.

Agha Shahi
(former Foreign Minister of Pakistan)

Preface

Emulating the example of worthy predecessors like Ambassador S. M. Burke, who wrote the first book on Pakistan's foreign policy, I have tried, in this recapitulation, to contribute to the transfer of knowledge acquired, at times, through participation in policy implementation and formulation, but more continuously by osmosis, during my association with the Ministry of Foreign Affairs for over forty years.[1] My assignments at the Foreign Office and in missions abroad provided useful opportunities to form perspectives on key foreign policy issues.

I have put together a plain narrative, faithfully recalling the facts and constraints of the time when the policy decisions had to be made, and their rationale, as far as possible in the words of the policy-makers. This book is not a critique but I hope it will provide a factual basis for objective appraisal and help identify lessons useful to future policy makers.

The chapter on the Shimla conference, with a detailed account of the difficult but purposeful negotiations by able and sophisticated diplomats, will be of particular interest to students of diplomacy, as an example of step-by-step adjustment of positions to the realities of the situation manifest in the changing drafts by the Pakistani and Indian sides. Also, the chapter on Post-9/11 policy will provide insights into the process of planning and preparing a realistic policy for optimum results at another crucial juncture in our history.

The reader may be intrigued to find that, in recalling the views of Pakistani decision makers with regard to our policy towards the United States, I have more often quoted foreign sources than our own. The explanation is that the relevant references are available in the released records of foreign governments whilst ours, if they exist, lie scattered, so that even one with official access would find the task of locating the relevant papers as onerous as finding a book in a library without a catalogue.

The task of a Pakistani researcher suffers from multiple handicaps, perhaps common to developing countries; antiquated secrecy laws are just one of the hurdles. Where records do exist, adequate personnel are lacking for sifting and declassification. The foreign office has started the exercise but the task is time-consuming and current issues always take the first claim on the time of senior officials. Particularly difficult to reform is the tendency of leaders and high officials to talk with foreign leaders and diplomats, especially on more sensitive issues, in one-to-one conversations, and at times on the telephone, without keeping notes for the record. The oral culture of decision-making makes reconstruction of policy a daunting exercise. Fortunately, books written by officials and scholars with access to leaders or their papers provide invaluable material and these sources have been consulted for this book.

Histories of foreign policy often suffer from a one-dimensional focus on political aspects of relations with foreign countries to the detriment of other determinants. Pakistan's foreign policy has been especially dominated by security and development concerns, and the requirement for foreign military and economic assistance. An attempt has been made to include these aspects in this book.

I am grateful to Foreign Minister Agha Shahi for reading through the entire text of the manuscript, and for his valuable suggestions. For me, and for two generations of Pakistani diplomats, he has been an icon, dedicated to the service of our nation.

My wife Yasmine, and daughters Simeen and Sarosh, encouraged me over the years to write and to them I dedicate this book with love and affection.

Abdul Sattar
Islamabad

NOTES

1. At the time of the 1965 war I was deputy high commissioner in New Delhi. In 1972 I was a member of the Pakistan delegation at the historic Shimla conference. Later, I served at the India desk in the ministry of foreign affairs, as ambassador in New Delhi, and then as additional secretary and foreign secretary in Islamabad. For some thirteen of my thirty-nine years in the foreign service I was directly associated with the conduct of Pakistan's tortured relations with India. I met national leaders as well as a variety of people in different parts of that vast and variegated country.

CHAPTER 1

The Emergence of Pakistan

Historical Background

The late nineteenth century marked the beginning of a seminal transformation in the political evolution of South Asia with the penetration of modern ideas of nationalism and self-rule. Until then, different parts of the vast geographical region inhabited by indigenous people and settlers of diverse races and religions were ruled by whoever conquered their lands. More often the region was an aggregation of kingdoms and princely states, with kaleidoscopic boundaries expanding and contracting with the rise and fall of dynasties.[1] Over the millennia, the rulers were as often local as foreign. Some came with waves of migrations, others as invaders, and most who came from Central Asia settled in the land.

Following Alexander's invasion across the Sulaiman Range in 325 B.C., Chadragupta Maurya,[2] conquered the Indus and Gangetic plains. His descendant, Asoka (273–232 B.C.), built a great empire that extended from Afghanistan to Kalinga (Orissa), and after his conversion to Buddhism, spread the new religion throughout the land. In 200 BC, Greek Bactrians occupied the Gandhara region and two centuries later were supplanted by Central Asian Kushans who ruled the region from Peshawar, as their capital, till the fifth century. Kanishka (AD 120–162), the greatest of the Kushans, extended the realm from Kabul to Kashgar and Kashmir in the north, to Sindh in the south, and the Gangetic plain in the east. The Gandhara region became a meeting place of Buddhist and Hellenist arts and cultures, leaving a legacy of glorious sculptures. After the raiding forays of White Huns in the fifth century, the region was conquered by the Gupta rulers of central India, who unleashed a Brahminical reaction that wiped out Buddhism from the land of its birth.

The Arabs penetrated South Asia via the Indus delta in the eighth century. After pirates along the Sindh coast pillaged ships carrying Muslim pilgrims, the Governor of Basra sent a force under Mohammad bin Qasim in 711 to Debul. Two years later Multan became the first Muslim province in South Asia. In the late twelfth century Muhammad Ghori, a Turkic ruler of Ghazni, extended his realm eastwards to Delhi. His successors, Iltutmish and Balban, ruled the northern plains during the thirteenth century. The Delhi Sultanate was taken over by Khilji and Tughlak dynasties until the end of the fourteenth century. Amir Timur marched his army through Afghanistan into Punjab, and plundered and sacked Delhi before returning to Samarkand in 1399. The Sayyids and the Lodhi Afghans subsequently re-established the Delhi Sultanate. In 1526 Babar led his army from Kabul to supplant the last Lodhi Sultan.

Zaheeruddin Babar, a descendant of Amir Temur, and heir to the small fief of Ferghana, aspired to revive the empire of his fourteenth century ancestor. He captured Samarkand twice but was defeated and driven across the Hindukush to Kabul. Receiving an invitation from the Governor of Punjab, he marched down the passes to capture the Delhi Sultanate in 1526, and from his new capital at Agra he extended his realm, laying the foundation of the great Mughal Empire that rose to its zenith under Shah Jehan in the seventeenth century. After Aurangzeb the dynasty went into decline in the eighteenth century. Its fall was hastened by European empire-builders who scrambled to pick up the pieces. Defeating France and Portugal, Britain put the pieces together to rule the expanding realm through the East India Company, before assuming direct imperial rule after a coalition of the aggrieved local elite tried to wrest power back from the company in the name of the Mughal titular emperor in 1857. Calling it mutiny, the British suppressed the challenge in a savage manner. The last Mughal emperor was exiled to Burma and Britain then assumed the reins of government directly until 1947.

The Central Asian people who came with the waves of migrations over the centuries mixed with local people and developed a syncretist culture with Persian as the court language. Immigrant scholars preached the message of Islam and Sufi saints won a cross-religious following by their exemplary piety, noble conduct and service to humanity. The Muslim rulers did not impose their religion on local inhabitants nor did they exclude local allies from positions in the army and administration, though like others before them they gave preference to their kin and clansmen. After the British took control, Muslims became suspect and were not only supplanted by loyal non-Muslims but also subjected to suppression, exclusion and expropriation. They were further marginalised, because of their refusal to reconcile and adjust to the loss of power.

Syed Ahmad Khan, a social reformer and political visionary, discerned the dangers confronting his community, and embarked on a campaign to awaken and inspire the Muslim people to abandon the boycott of the foreign rulers and to acquire contemporary education. He also founded a school that grew into the Aligarh Muslim University where learned academics, some of them from England, were employed to teach modern subjects and prepare the youth for gainful opportunities in the professions and participation in the expanding political and economic life and institutions of the land.

As contemporary ideas of self-government and nationalism began to stimulate political thought in the latter part of the nineteenth century, different ethnic and religious communities projected their futures in terms of their interests. The Muslim community, comprising a quarter of the population in British India, awoke to its predicament, characterised by economic disparities and social exclusion. The future looked bleak as they faced the prospect of a powerless 'permanent minority'. British India, Syed Ahmad Khan argued in 1883, was 'a continent in itself inhabited by vast populations of different races and different creeds' which lacked 'the community of race and creed [that] make the English people one and the same nation.'[3] The idea of nationhood captured the imagination of the Muslim community as its leaders discerned the looming danger of political domination across the religious and social fault line. At first they sought legal and constitutional safeguards to secure and ensure an equitable share in social and political institutions.

The rift began to widen after the founding of the Indian National Congress in 1886 with Allan Octavian Hume, a British ex-official, as its first president. Dominated by the Hindu elite, the Congress attracted few Muslims as their leaders advised them to keep aloof from this nominally secular party that sought to supplant the British in positions of power and influence. To protect and promote the rights of the Muslim community, the leaders with modern education and political vision established the Muslim League in 1906. The issues were joined in 1909, when the Congress opposed the proposal for separate electorates that would ensure representation for Muslims in the government. The two communities had also clashed earlier, in 1905, when the Congress opposed, and the Muslims supported the British government's decision to create the new province of East Bengal and Assam, which brought to the Muslim majority some relief from domination and exploitation by West Bengal. More enduring, and in the end insoluble, were constitutional issues, as the League proposed, and Congress opposed, safeguards for Muslims.

Mohammad Ali Jinnah, a brilliant barrister with impeccable anti-colonial credentials, successfully promoted a compromise package for the future constitution. The package known as the Lucknow Pact, after its approval by both the Congress and the League in 1916, included separate electorates, provincial autonomy, a one-third share for Muslims in the central assembly, and safeguards in respect of legislation affecting any of the religious communities. The Indian National Congress, however, went back on its commitment in 1928, when it adopted the Motilal Nehru Report, recommending replacement of separate electorates with a joint electorate and the curtailment of provincial autonomy, thus striking a fatal blow to any prospect of harmonious politics.

The Muslim League's struggle evolved through four stages. At first it sought an equitable share in political and social life. During the second stage, the League's emphasis was on constitutional safeguards for Muslims in provinces where they were a minority. As political thought progressed, they sought autonomy for Muslim-majority provinces and then finally raised their sights to an independent state. A profound grasp of the history and aspirations of the Muslim people led the influential poet-philosopher Muhammad Iqbal to conclude, as early as 1930, that the formation of a Muslim state amalgamating the Punjab, North-West Frontier Province, Sindh and Balochistan, 'appears to me to be the final destiny of the Muslims.'[4] He also urged Mohammad Ali Jinnah, then living in London, to return, as he was 'the only Muslim in India today to whom the community has a right to ask for safe guidance.'[5]

The cleavage between the League and the Congress widened following the elections in early 1937. The Congress exploited its triumph by excluding League members from participation in governments in the provinces, adopting symbols of the Hindu raj and promoting the replacement of Urdu with Hindi. Muslim leaders, realising the consequences of disunity and factional politics before the election, now closed ranks under Jinnah's leadership. He galvanised Muslims by laying before them a lucid vision of political salvation. Eminent Muslims and the Muslim media began to call him Quaid-i-Azam, Great Leader.[6] In 1938 he was authorised by the League to explore the possibility of a suitable alternative political structure which would completely safeguard the interests of Musalmans and other minorities in India.'[7] The Sindh Muslim League recommended the devising of a scheme for Muslims to attain full independence.

The Second World War accelerated the political evolution. 'The British wanted to win the war first and transfer power afterwards; the Congress demanded power at once, and a Hindu–Muslim settlement afterwards; the Muslims insisted on a Hindu–Muslim settlement first.[8] On 23 March 1940, the Muslim League, at its Lahore session, adopted the historic resolution demanding, 'that the areas in which Muslims are numerically in a majority, as in the North-Western and Eastern zones of India, should be grouped to constitute Independent States in which the constituent units shall be autonomous and sovereign.[9] It was to go down in history as the 'Pakistan Resolution.'[10] Muslim students in England had first suggested the name in 1932.[11]

Enfeebled by the war, the British announced their intention to depart. The Congress demanded transfer of power, claiming the right of succession as the largest political party. The Muslim League reiterated its 'divide-and-quit' demand, asking the British to first agree to the creation of Pakistan in regions where Muslims constituted a majority. In a last attempt to realise their dream of preserving the unity of their Indian empire, the British Cabinet Mission, in 1946, proposed a constitutional plan based on the division of British India into three autonomous zones with the powers of the centre to be limited to foreign affairs, defence and communications. The League first accepted the plan but later rejected it, because the Congress leader, Jawaharlal Nehru, asserted his party 'regarded itself free to change or modify the Cabinet Mission plan as it thought best.'[12] With the plan thus undermined by the Congress refusal to guarantee the autonomy of the zones, the League reverted to the demand for the partition of British India into sovereign states.

The British government then proposed the Partition Plan. After hectic consultations and negotiations, it was accepted by the leaders of the Muslim League as well as the Indian National Congress, and announced on 3 June 1947. Pursuant to the agreement, Pakistan was established through the exercise of self-determination by the people of the Muslim-majority provinces and parts of provinces of the British Indian Empire, either in popular referenda or by the votes of the elected representatives of the people.

The Congress grudgingly agreed to the partition, and some of its leaders projected the economic collapse of Pakistan. No one epitomised the contradictions in the Congress more strikingly than its spiritual leader Mahatama Gandhi. He agreed that partition was 'inevitable' but also declared, 'So long as I am alive, I will never agree to the partition of India'.[13] The Congress leadership accepted the June 3 plan but the highest organ of the party, the All-India Congress Committee, quibbled in endorsing the decision. Its resolution professed that the Congress 'cannot think in terms of compelling the people in any territorial unit to remain in the Indian Union' but in another sentence harked back to its view that 'the unity of India must be maintained.'[14] While emphasizing the 'unity of India', the Congress tried to undermine the unity of Pakistan by suggesting that 'the referendum in the North-West Frontier Province should provide for the people voting for independence.'[15]

Apart from the difficult and divisive legacy of pre-independence political rivalry, adversarial perceptions of history, differences of religions and cultures and the clash of political ideologies, deep bitterness was engendered by communal rioting. This led to the massacre of hundreds of thousands of innocent people and the exodus of some fifteen million people who moved from the country of their residence to seek refuge in the other. Further worsening of relations, and the perpetuation of tension, was owed, in particular, to the failure to resolve the disputes that arose after Independence.

The 3rd June Plan gave only seventy-two days for transition to independence. Within this period three provinces had to be divided, referenda organised in North-West Frontier Province and the Sylhet division of Assam, civil and armed services personnel given the opportunity to decide which country they would serve, and assets apportioned. The telescoped timetable prepared at the behest of Governor General Mountbatten seemed tailor-made to create formidable problems for Pakistan, which, unlike India, inherited neither a capital with a functioning secretariat nor the resources to establish and equip the administrative, economic and military institutions of the new state. More daunting problems soon arose in the wake of Partition.

NOTES

1. 'Sometimes all India was a patchwork quilt of states; sometimes empires as that of the Guptas prevailed over great areas.' H. G. Wells, *The Outline of History*, The Macmillan Company, New York, 1921.

2. He was 'helped in his intrigue by an astute Brahmin of the name of Chanakya or Kautilya.' Rawlinson, H. G., *India*, Frederick and Praeger, New York, 1952, p. 65.

3. Speech in the Legislative Assembly, extract cited by Chaudhri Muhammad Ali, *The Emergence of Pakistan*, Columbia University Press, p. 11.

4. In his address to the annual session of the Muslim League at Allahabad, 1930, Iqbal said, 'I would like to see the Punjab, North-West Frontier Province, Sind and Baluchistan amalgamated into a single State. Self-government within the British empire or without the British empire, the formation of a consolidated North-West Muslim State appers to me to be the final destiny of the Muslims, at least of North-West India.' Shamloo, *Speeches and Statements of Iqbal*, Lahore, 1948, pp. 11, 12.

5. Letter of Iqbal to Jinnah.

6. Although admiring Muslims and media called him by this honorific earlier, the Muslim League first used the title in 1937. Sharif Al Mujahid, *Quaid-i-Azam Jinnah*, Quaid-i-Azam Academy, Karachi, 1981, p. 41.

7. Resolution of the Muslim League, December 1938.

8. Chaudhri Muhammad Ali, *The Emergence of Pakistan*, Columbia University Press, New York, 1967.

9. The resolution states that: 'no constitutional plan would be workable or acceptable to Muslims unless it is designed on the following basic principle, namely that geographically contiguous units are demarcated into regions which should be so constituted, with such territorial adjustments as may be necessary, that the areas in which the Muslims are numerically in a majority as in the north-western and eastern zones of India should be grouped to constitute independent States in which the constituent units shall be autonomous and sovereign.' Text quoted in Chaudhri Muhammad Ali, op. cit., p. 38.

10. The ambiguity was clarified by the Quaid-i-Azam. When asked whether the resolution asked for one or two States, he said 'one'. The next day newspapers referred to it as the 'Pakistan Resolution.' Stanley Wolpert, *Jinnah of Pakistan*, Oxford University Press, New York, 1984, p. 185.

11. The signatories of the pamphlet *Now or Never* were Mohammad Aslam Khattak, President Khyber Union, Choudhury Rahmat Ali, Inayatullah Khan (of Charsadda), and Sheikh Mohammad Sadiq of Mongrol, Kathiawar. They conceived the name Pakistan by combining P for the Punjab, A for Afghania (a synonym then for land of Pathans), K for Kashmir, S for Sindh and TAN for Baluchistan. Mohammad Aslam Khan Khattak, *A Pathan Odyssey*, Oxford University Press, Karachi, 2004, pp. 15 & 264.

12. Ibid., p. 67.

13. Abul Kalam Azad, *India Wins Freedom*, Orient Longman, Delhi, pp. 185 and 187.

14. The *Encyclopaedia of the Indian National Congress*, Moin Zaidi and Shaheda Zaidi, S. Chand & Co., New Delhi, Vol. 13, p. 111.

15. Government of India records quoted in Chaudhri Muhammad Ali, p. 152.

CHAPTER 2

Foreign Policy—Beginnings

Pakistan emerged onto the world stage on 14 August 1947, after a two-pronged struggle; first, for independence from colonial rule, and secondly, freedom for the people of Muslim-majority areas from the looming threat of economic, social and political domination by another people manifestly dismissive of their urge to preserve their separate identity. Neither British nostalgia for maintaining the unity of the 'Jewel in the Crown' nor the ambition of the Indian National Congress to step into the shoes of the departing colonial power, conformed to the imperatives of the dawning era of self-determination and self-rule. The Muslim League had to wage a long, and at times bitter, political battle, but the issue was ultimately resolved through agreement. The British and the Congress leaders conceded the League's demand for the creation of two independent states to succeed the Indian Empire. Pakistan came into existence through the explicit exercise of the right of self-determination. The people of Muslim-majority parts of British India voted directly in referenda or through their elected representatives to join the new state.[1]

The foreign policy of Pakistan was to be moulded in the crucible of interaction with its neighbour India, but it was imbued from the start with the idealistic vision of the state's founding fathers. Quaid-i-Azam[2] Mohammad Ali Jinnah, the first head of the new state, was a man of ideals and integrity, committed to the principles of peace with faith and confidence in human capacity to resolve differences through the application of logic and law. Another exemplar was Liaquat Ali Khan, a barrister who became secretary general of the Muslim League in the 1930s and first prime minister of Pakistan. He believed, like Jinnah, that Pakistan should be a progressive, democratic polity founded on Islamic principles of social welfare, religious tolerance and the equal rights of all citizens. The first foreign minister, Zafrullah Khan, was a jurist of repute and throughout his tenure sought to promote the resolution of international disputes in conformity with the principles of the United Nations Charter.

Quaid-i-Azam Mohammad Ali Jinnah

Choudhary Sir Zafrullah Khan (first Foreign Minister of Pakistan)

The nation's mentors were dedicated, practical men, with implicit faith in the Muslim community's capacity to end stagnation and build a better future. An early titan was Syed Ahmad Khan who believed in the acquisition of 'education in its modern sense' to promote 'equal and proportionate progress' for all people. Mohammad Iqbal, a humanist scholar with profound insights into Islamic as well as western history and philosophy, rejected the concept of predestination and advocated constant human striving to shape a better destiny for mankind. His inspiring poetry, widely read in the early twentieth century, sought to inculcate the spirit of dynamism in society. Holding out the vision of Islam as a progressive faith, Iqbal argued in favour of revival and the active use of the Islamic doctrine of *Ijtihad* as a means of adaptation of temporal laws to resolve the social dilemmas arising from progress in science and industry.[3]

The Founding Father's Vision

In the one year he lived after the establishment of Pakistan, Jinnah laid the foundations of so many institutions, and proclaimed principles of enduring value in so many diverse affairs of state ranging from administrative, fiscal and economic to constitution-making and formulation of foreign policy, that people marvel at his genius as well as feel more acutely the sense of loss at the all-too-brief time Providence allowed him to guide the new state.

Manifest in the views Jinnah articulated is a modern intellect with a firm commitment to fundamental principles indispensable for the maintenance and promotion of international peace, progress and prosperity of humankind, illustrated in the following excerpts from his speeches:

> There lies in front of us a new chapter and it will be our endeavour to create and maintain goodwill and friendship with Britain and our neighbourly dominion, Hindustan, along with other sisterly nations so that we all together may make our greatest contribution for the peace and prosperity of the world.[4]
>
> Our foreign policy is one of friendliness and goodwill towards all the nations of the world. We do not cherish aggressive designs against any country or nation. We believe in the principle of honesty and fair play in national and international dealings and are prepared to make the utmost contribution to the promotion of peace and prosperity among the nations of the world. Pakistan will never be found lacking in extending its material

and moral support to the oppressed and suppressed people of the world and in upholding the principles of the United Nations Charter.[5]

There is nothing that we desire more ardently than to live in peace and let others live in peace, and develop our country according to our own lights without outside interference, and improve the lot of the common man.[6]

Jinnah's concept of Pakistan as a Muslim, liberal, democratic and modern nation-state naturally predisposed him in favour of close relations with democratic countries. During the Second World War the Muslim League decided, under his leadership, to support the Allies against the Fascist powers. Jinnah paid special tribute to the United States as having 'acted as a beacon of light and had in no small measure served to give inspiration to nations who like us were striving for independence and freedom from the shackles of foreign rule.'[7] Equally warm were his words for the French ideals of liberty, fraternity and equality.

The Soviet Union's record of rapid economic progress and its foreign policy of opposition to colonialism and imperialism impressed all educated people. The Soviet system, however, was unattractive to League leaders because of its restrictions on freedom, atheist ideology and sponsorship of subversion in other countries.

Pakistan was at first averse to becoming involved in the ideological contest between the emergent blocs led by the United States and the Soviet Union. As Liaquat Ali Khan said, the State started 'without any narrow and special commitments and without any prejudices in the international sphere.'[8] It was 'neither tied to the apron strings of the Anglo-American bloc nor was it a camp-follower of the communist bloc.'[9] Foreign Minister Zafrullah Khan echoed the same thought saying Pakistan followed the principle of 'Friendship towards all states, but with regard to each individual question, standing on the side of fairness and subject to that, to help and succour the weak.'[10]

Sharing an overarching sense of community with other Muslim peoples of the world, Pakistan remained true to the tradition of solidarity of the Muslim people of British India with the just causes of fraternal nations. Records of the Muslim League since the early twentieth century are replete with resolutions voicing deep concern over the injustices done by European powers to the Ottomans and the Arab countries, and extending support to the causes of the people of Turkey and Palestine. An admirer of Mustafa Kemal Ataturk, after Independence, Jinnah recalled the 'deep sympathy and interest' with which the fortunes of Turkey were followed 'right from the birth of political consciousness among the Muslims of [British] India.'

Preoccupied with developments in South Asia, the Quaid did not allow the political conflict of the pre-Independence period to cloud his vision. He transcended the bitter legacy and looked with hope and anticipation to future relations with Britain and India.

Proud of having achieved Pakistan 'peacefully by moral and intellectual force'[12] Pakistani leaders hoped that law and reason would govern relations between Pakistan and India. Jinnah expressed the hope that both countries would adhere to the principles of equity and justice, and build peaceful and cooperative relations to the mutual benefit of their people. He said:

Our object should be peace within and peace without. We want to live peacefully and maintain cordial and friendly relations with our immediate neighbours and with the world at large... We stand by the United Nations Charter and will gladly make our full contribution to the peace and prosperity of the world.[13]

In another statement, Jinnah said:

It is of vital importance to Pakistan and India as independent, sovereign states to collaborate in a friendly way to jointly defend their frontiers, both on land and sea against any aggression. But this depends entirely on whether India and Pakistan can resolve their own differences. If we can put own house in order internally, then we may be able to play a very great part externally in all international affairs. The Indian Government should shed their superiority complex and deal with Pakistan on an equal footing and fully appreciate the realities.[14]

The bonds of geography were of obvious importance in relations with other neighbours. Iran was a friend and brother; so was Afghanistan. Despite Kabul's challenge to the boundary agreement it had signed with the British Indian government as far back as 1893, Jinnah hoped that Pakistan and Afghanistan would soon 'secure and strengthen' the goodwill and friendship between the two fraternal nations. Similarly, he expressed 'warmest goodwill' towards Sri Lanka.

Enduring Relevance of Principles

The thread that runs through the statements of Pakistani leaders—and which has a timeless value—is that the interests of Pakistan are best served by upholding the universally recognised principles of international law codified in the Charter of the United Nations. Their observance by all states, large or small, more or less powerful, is indispensable for the preservation of international peace and the promotion of cooperation among nations, to their mutual benefit.

Just as an individual cannot achieve fulfilment in isolation from the nation to which he or she belongs, a state too has to seek its destiny in cooperation with the world community. The successes as well as the failures of our foreign policy can be traced to whether or not it earned the nation a place of respect in the international mainstream. A policy that leads to isolation is inimical to the interests particularly of middle and small powers.

Friendship between states, as between individuals, is dependent on reciprocity, mutual goodwill, and respect for equity and justice. It cannot be promoted by attempts on the part of one to dominate or impose unilateral preference on the other. The UN Charter calls for peaceful settlement of disputes consistent with the principles of justice and international law. The Quaid reiterated that principle in offering friendship and collaboration with India.

In the catalogue of enduring principles enunciated by the Quaid-i-Azam, it is necessary also to mention his views on human rights, the state's responsibility towards citizens, and the obligation of citizens to be loyal to their state. In a speech to the Constituent Assembly on 11 August 1947, he said, 'You may belong to any religion, caste or creed—that has nothing to do with the business of the State. We are starting with the fundamental principle that we are all citizens, and equal citizens of one State.'[15] Remarkable for its perspicacious recognition of the implications of the transition from his role as leader of a political party to that of head of state, the speech symbolised an intellectual leap: so far his primary concern had been the future of the Muslim people; now it would be all citizens of the state. The nation henceforth was all the people of Pakistan, irrespective of their religion.

Characteristically, Jinnah was consistent in giving the same message to Muslims who remained in India. Four months later, at the last session of the Muslim League as its leader, he endorsed the bifurcation of the party. The meeting decided: 'It is obvious that the Musalmans of Pakistan and India can no longer have one and the same political organisation.' The Muslims of India would no longer be guided from any source outside and they would aspire to equal rights and obligations as loyal citizens of India.

Giving Muslims of minority provinces the credit for the establishment of Pakistan, Jinnah told the session, 'Pakistan is going to be a Muslim State based on Islamic ideals. It is not going to be an ecclesiastical State. In Islam there is no discrimination as far as citizenship is concerned.'[16] In affirming the principle of equality of citizens, Jinnah emulated the precedent set by the first Islamic state in the *Misaq-i-Madinah* that provided for equal rights for all people, Muslims as well as Jews, Madinites as well as those who migrated from Mecca.[17]

Jinnah's vision of human rights anticipated the Universal Declaration of Human Rights. Adopted a year later, it proclaimed the principle:

> Everyone is entitled to all the rights and freedoms set forth in this Declaration, without distinction of any kind, such as race, colour, sex, language, religion, political or other opinion, national or social origin, property, birth or other status.

From the very beginning Pakistan's foreign policy upheld the fundamental principles of international law, especially respect for independence, non-aggression and non-interference in internal affairs as an indispensable condition for peace and progress. It extended goodwill towards all states and support for the legitimate causes of peoples, the cherishing of fraternal bonds with other Muslim nations and the desire for cooperation with all other states, especially its neighbours.

The Shadow of Partition

With the emergence of Pakistan and India as independent states, by mutual consent of the leaders of major political parties, old political controversies were relegated and the emphasis shifted instead to building peaceful coexistence and good-neighbourly cooperation, to the mutual benefit of the two people. Jinnah urged such a course, but the transition from checkered past to a beckoning future could not be achieved by Pakistan alone.

The Indian National Congress accepted the partition officially but the resolution adopted by the Central Working Committee declared, 'The picture of India we have learned to cherish will remain in our hearts and minds.' Sardar Patel was 'convinced that the new state of Pakistan was not viable and could not last.'[18] Three days before the 3rd June Plan, Gandhi had declared, 'Even if the whole of India burns, we shall not concede Pakistan' and then, changing his mind a few days later, said, 'the two parts of India would ultimately reunite!'[19]

As the leaders of Pakistan grappled with the monumental task of establishing the government of the new state in a new capital, in the midst of myriad challenges, they were sustained by the strength of their faith and the support of the nation. Meanwhile, the civil administration and armed forces of British India were still in the process of division and resources were meagre as India delayed or withheld Pakistan's share of financial and other assets. Complex partition problems were compounded by the unfair boundary award and the un-anticipated tide of millions of refugees fleeing communal riots of unprecedented magnitude. Relations between the two countries got off to an inauspicious start and tensions mounted as unforeseen disputes darkened the South Asian horizon.[20]

Agreement on the division of the assets and liabilities of British India provided for a 17.5 per cent share for Pakistan, but India stalled implementation. The transfer of cash balances amounting to Rs. 750 million was delayed for months, causing severe difficulties for Pakistan. Of the other assets, India 'dishonestly retained much of Pakistan's share.'[21] Of Pakistan's share of 165,000 tons of defence stores, India had transferred only 4,730 tons by 31 March 1948, and another 18,000 tons by 10 September 1949, expropriating the balance of 142,000 tons.[22] In contrast, Pakistan promptly transferred ninety fighter aircraft that were India's share. Indian leaders 'persistently tried to obstruct the work of partition of the armed forces.'[23] 'What mattered to them, above all else, was to cripple and thwart the establishment of Pakistan as a viable independent state.'[24]

Demarcation of boundaries in Punjab and Bengal was entrusted to the Boundary Commission headed by Cyril Radcliffe, a British jurist. Its mandate required it to do so 'on the basis of ascertaining the contiguous majority areas of Muslims and non-Muslims.' While it could also take into account 'other factors' it was expected to be just and impartial. But Radcliffe yielded to Governor General Mountbatten's pressure and awarded several Muslim-majority areas to India, including two *tehsils* (subdivisions) of Gurdaspur district, providing it access to the state of Jammu and Kashmir.[25] Jinnah called the award 'unjust, incomprehensible and even perverse' but urged, 'As an honourable people we must abide by it.'[26] Already in Nehru's thrall, Mountbatten had earlier helped promote Nehru's designs on Kashmir in his talks with the maharaja in Srinagar. He was now indebted to Nehru for retaining him as Governor General of independent India.

Apart from providing India with a road link to Kashmir via Jammu, the unjust boundary award, announced on 17 August, three days after

Pakistan's independence, added fuel to the raging fire of communal violence. Despite calls for the maintenance of peace by Jinnah and Gandhi, communal riots escalated as the partition was being effected. Although acts of savagery took place on both sides, the policy of the rulers of the princely states of Patiala and Kapurthala was particularly virulent. They unleashed local forces to kill and expel Muslim inhabitants. In a matter of weeks they liquidated the Muslim population of some 700,000. They also sent armed men to Jammu and Kashmir to assist the Dogra forces of this state in unleashing terror. Within weeks, a quarter of a million Muslims were 'systematically exterminated.'[27]

Suddenly, in April 1948, India cut off the water in the irrigation canals that flowed from headworks on the rivers Ravi and Sutlej, menacing agriculture in Pakistan. Ignoring principles of international law governing international rivers, it claimed 'seigniorage' charges for the water flowing to Pakistan. Facing the ruin of agriculture in the affected areas, Pakistan submitted under duress.

Tension between Pakistan and India built up as disputes between the two countries multiplied. Pakistan sought their resolution on the basis of law and equity, willing to accept impartial settlement. India, however, was intent from the start to impose its unilateral preferences. The divergence was aggravated by India's primordial inclination as a more powerful state to exploit power disparity to its advantage.

The Muslim World

For seven hundred years after the establishment of the first Muslim state in the seventh century, the dynamic Islamic civilisation contributed to unprecedented advances in all fields of human endeavour, achieving glorious heights in arts and architecture, and extending the frontiers of knowledge in philosophy and historiography, geography and astronomy, mathematics and medicine, trade and commerce. Expanding across the continents of Asia and Africa, it established its sway also in parts of Europe, and contributed to its renaissance. Following the devastating invasions of the Mongols, the Muslim power declined and by the eighteenth century large parts of its former territories were colonised by European empires.

Emerging as the largest Muslim state, Pakistan hoped to join other Muslim nations in the revival and reconstruction of the Muslim world, through cooperation in science and technology and rediscovering the path to progress. It also believed that by joining hands, the independent

Muslim states could protect mutual security, defend legitimate causes and promote freedom and international peace.

Upon independence, Pakistan developed close relations with most Muslim countries. Saudi Arabia, the cradle of Islam, wished 'the new Muslim State great prosperity and progress',[28] and ever since has remained a fraternal friend and constant supporter. Pakistan's championship of the Palestinian cause evoked appreciation in the Arab world. The Shahanshah of Iran was the first head of state to visit Pakistan and was given a memorable welcome by enthusiastic crowds. Turkey, aware of Pakistan's admiration of Kemal Ataturk, responded with cordiality. Indonesia was impressed by Pakistan's support for its struggle.

The start was promising. Pakistan hosted a number of conferences of representatives of Muslim peoples to deliberate on issues of common concern. While many appreciated the initiatives, others were less enthusiastic. Differences in policies emerged with the rise of Arab nationalism that emphasised the Arab bond virtually to the exclusion of non-Arab Muslim States. While Egypt leaned towards the Soviet Union for support against the UK and USA, Pakistan's security imperatives drove it into alliance with those powers. The Baghdad Pact provoked strong Arab denunciation on the additional ground that Iraq's membership was divisive of Arab unity. Pakistan's role at the first London conference on the Suez crisis further antagonised Arab sentiment against Pakistan.

Afghanistan. As the British rule over India drew to close, the Afghan government decided to fish in the troubled waters by questioning the validity of the Durand Line boundary with Pakistan. Apparently the Afghan advocates of the irredenta were misled by Indian National Congress politicians who wishfully believed Pakistan was economically unviable. They were encouraged by the pro-Congress Red Shirts party in NWFP, led by Abdul Ghaffar Khan, an old and respected veteran of the anti-colonial struggle who sadly failed to keep pace with the sweeping political evolution in the 1940s. In June 1947 Afghan prime minister, Mohammad Hashim Khan stated, 'If an independent Pukhtoonistan cannot be established then the Frontier Province should join Afghanistan.' The Afghan government sought to justify the irredenta by (i) arguing the boundary agreement was concluded under duress, (ii) calling the boundary 'unnatural' because it divided the Pushtoon people who lived on both sides of the boundary, and (iii) professing sympathy with the 'miserable plight of the Pushtoons.' Actually, the Durand boundary agreement of 1893 was negotiated at the initiative of Amir Abdur Rahman of Afghanistan, who expressed full satisfaction with the agreement and reiterated its acceptance in the treaty of 1905. Also, in subsequent treaties of 1919 and 1921, at the time of Amir Amanullah Khan, reputed for his assertion of independence, the government of Afghanistan reconfirmed acceptance of the boundary. As for the nature of the boundary, commonalties of ethnicity, language and culture are a common feature of most international boundaries. Nor could the 'plight' of people on either side be said to be much better or worse than on the other.

Explaining that Pakistan's boundary with Afghanistan was disputed, the Afghan representative to the United Nations cast the solitary negative vote when Pakistan was admitted to the organisation on 30 September 1947. Three weeks later, the delegation of Afghanistan withdrew the negative vote. Speaking for Pakistan, Mr M.A.H. Ispahani expressed the hope that the latest Afghan statement 'reflects more accurately the feeling of friendship and good-neighbourliness which exists between Pakistan and Afghanistan.'

Although Kabul continued to nourish a movement to reclaim territory recognised as part of British India and supported the slogan for an independent 'Pakhtoonistan', raised by the Red Shirts' leader, Pakistan took Kabul's contrariness in its stride and maintained a consistent policy of friendship towards the Muslim neighbour, continuing to allow transit facilities to land-locked Afghanistan, in accordance with the principles of international law.

NOTES

1. The Sindh assembly and representatives of Muslim-majority districts in Bengal and Punjab assemblies voted to join Pakistan. In Balochistan a *Shahi Jirga* and members of the Quetta municipality decided unanimously to join Pakistan. In NWFP, Congress and Red Shirts boycotted the referendum but 289, 244 votes, representing 51 per cent of the total electorate, were cast in favour of Pakistan. Tribal *jirgas* declared in meetings held by Governor Cunningham, and confirmed in writing, that they were part of Pakistan. 'The Tribal Areas' in Chaudhri Muhammad Ali, *The Emergence of Pakistan*, Columbia University Press, New York, 1967, pp. 163-166.
2. The title given by the admiring nation during the freedom struggle means 'Great Leader.'
3. Allama Mohammed Iqbal's *Reconstruction of Religious Thought in Islam*, the key to his ideas on reformation, advocated that *Ijtihad* in modern times could be entrusted to elected members of parliament. Limited to temporal issues concerning *mu'amilaat* (worldly affairs) innovations would not relate to *ibadaat* (theological affairs). Javid Iqbal's lecture on Iqbal's anniversary, *Dawn*, Islamabad, November 10, 2004.
4. Mohammad Ali Jinnah—Speeches as Governor General, 1947–48, Ferozsons, Karachi, p. 11.
5. Ibid., p. 65.

6. Ibid., p. 62.
7. Ibid., p. 67.
8. Prime Minister Liaquat Ali Khan quoted in S. M. Burke & Lawrence Ziring, *Pakistan's Foreign Policy*, Oxford University Press, Karachi, Second Edition, 1990, from Sarwar Hasan, *Pakistan Horizon*, 4 December 1951.
9. S. M. Burke and Lawrence Ziring, *Pakistan's Foreign Policy*, Oxford University Press, Karachi, 1990, quoting from *Dawn*, Karachi, 9 March 1955.
10. Zafrullah Khan, Constituent Assembly Debates, 1948 (821).
11. Jinnah, Speeches, p. 32.
12. Radio broadcast, August 31, 1947. *Jinnah Papers*, ed. H. Zaidi, Quaid-i -Azam Papers Project, Islamabad, Vol. VI, p. 1.
13. Statement on 11 March 1948.
14. Speeches of Quaid-i-Azam Mohammad Ali Jinnah as Governor General of Pakistan, p. 45.
15. *Jinnah Papers*, Vol. VI, pp. 446-450.
16. Sharif Al Mujahid, *Dawn*, Islamabad, 26 December 2004.
17. Abul Kalam Azad, op. cit., 207.
18. *The Times*, London, of June 5, 1947, quoted in G. W. Choudhury, op. cit., p. 84.
19. For information on the partition period, the author greatly benefited from Chaudhri Mohammad Ali, *The Emergence of Pakistan*, Columbia University Press, New York, 1967; S.M. Burke and Lawrence Ziring, *Pakistan's Foreign Policy*, Oxford University Press, Karachi, 1990, and G. W. Choudhury, *Pakistan's Relations with India, 1947–1966*, Pall Mall Press, London, 1967.
20. Ian Stephens, *Horned Moon*, Chatto and Windus, London, J 954, p. 215.
21. G. W. Choudhury, op. cit., p. 62.
22. John Connell, *Auchinleck*, pp. 915-8. 10. Ibid., pp. 220-22.
23. Ibid., pp. 220-22
24. Others included Ferozepur, Zira and Fazilka which had a Muslim majority and most importantly included the Fazilka Headworks that controlled canals on the Sutlej which irrigated lands on the Pakistan side.
25. Jinnah, *Speeches*, op. cit., p. 32.
26. *The Times*, London, 17 October 1947.
27. Message from Prince Faisal bin Abdul Aziz Al Saud, *Jinnah Papers*, Vol. VI, p. 195.
28. *Jinnah Papers*, Vol. VI, p. 170.

CHAPTER 3

The Kashmir Question, 1947–57

The Dispute

The state of Jammu and Kashmir was one of some 500 quasi-autonomous princely states which exercised varying degrees of internal autonomy on the basis of treaties and agreements made during the period of colonial penetration, and recognised Britain as their suzerain. The British Indian Independence Act of 1947 affirmed the lapse of British suzerainty over the states. Theoretically, the states regained their sovereignty. The rulers of some of the larger ones nourished ambitions to independence but they did not receive much support. The British secretary of state for India announced, 'We do not, of course, propose to recognise any states as separate, international entities.'[1] Earlier, on 25 July 1947, Governor General Mountbatten had advised the princes to accede to Pakistan or India, and in doing so, he told them: 'You cannot run away from the Dominion government which is your neighbour any more than you can run away from the subjects for whose welfare you are responsible.'[2] This advice was consistent with the principle underlying the Partition Plan of 3rd June. On the basis of this principle the Indian National Congress had insisted on the partition of the provinces of Assam, Bengal and Punjab.

All the princely states except Hyderabad, Jammu and Kashmir and Junagadh followed the principle of partition and acceded to India or Pakistan. The Nizam of Hyderabad aspired to independence, but his state was invaded and occupied by India in 1948.[3] When the Muslim ruler of the Hindu-majority state of Junagadh announced accession to Pakistan on 15 August 1947, the Indian government protested, arguing that the decision by the ruler was 'in utter violation of the principles on which partition of India was agreed upon and effected.'[4] Pakistan offered to hold a plebiscite but India peremptorily invaded and occupied the state.

Two months later, however, the Indian government itself committed an 'utter violation' of the principles on which partition was based' when it accepted the offer of accession by the Dogra-Hindu Maharaja of the state of Jammu and Kashmir, even though 77 per cent of its four million people were Muslims.

The Maharaja's decision to accede to India followed events that testify to a pre-conceived design. In June 1947, two months before independence, Nehru betrayed his mind in a note to Mountbatten arguing: 'The normal and obvious course appears to be for Kashmir to join the Constituent Assembly of India,' falsely stating, 'This will satisfy both the popular demand and the Maharaja's wishes.'[5] Gandhi visited Srinagar in July and held talks with the maharaja. After the meeting the maharaja appointed a chief minister who openly advocated accession to India.[6] Mountbatten connived in the Indian design on Kashmir by influencing Sir Cyril Radcliff, the supposedly impartial chairman of the Punjab Boundary Commission, to award two Muslim-majority *tehsils* (subdivisions) of Gurdaspur district to India.

The ruler of Jammu and Kashmir, Maharaja Hari Singh, was notorious for his oppressive rule. Whilst decisions were being made on the partition plan, he incarcerated prominent leaders of the two major political parties, the All Jammu and Kashmir Muslim Conference, the most important Muslim party in the state and an ally of the Muslim League, and the National Conference, a secularist ally of the Indian National Congress.

Popular opinion in Jammu and Kashmir made its preference clear. The Muslim Conference adopted a resolution in July 1947 in favour of accession to Pakistan. Majority opinion, even in the National Conference, was also said to be of the same view, but it was decided to postpone a decision until its leader, Sheikh Abdullah could be consulted. No political party favoured accession to India. Pakistan's independence day was enthusiastically celebrated in Srinagar with flags. The maharaja ordered the flags torn down and closed down all pro-Pakistan newspapers.[7]

The maharaja had other plans. First, he delayed the decision on accession and offered to sign a 'standstill' agreement with Pakistan and India.[8] Prior to this, in late July, he had ordered Muslims to deposit any arms they possessed with the state authorities. He strengthened garrisons in areas where rebellion was suspected. Assisted by elements of state forces sent by the Sikh rulers of Patiala and Kapurthala, who had already acceded to India, plus armed volunteers of the militant Hindu RSS, the Dogra force of the maharaja 'wantonly plundered whole areas inhabited by Muslims and set fire to their homes.'[9]

Popular suspicion of the maharaja's intentions was corroborated by his actions. Demonstrations were held in Poonch and Mirpur, and on

17 August, Sardar Abdul Qayyum Khan and a few of his companions declared a revolt. Soon, 60,000 ex-soldiers who had served in the British army during the Second World War joined the revolt. In September, a freedom movement was launched by Sardar Mohammad Ibrahim Khan. It later established the Azad government of Jammu and Kashmir in the liberated territory.

In pursuit of his design, the maharaja singled out Sheikh Mohammad Abdullah for release from jail on 29 September in response to Nehru's repeated demand. Abdullah immediately started a pro-India campaign. Addressing a public meeting he was permitted to hold in Hazaribagh on 5 October, he said, 'We will naturally go to that dominion where our own demand for freedom receives recognition and support.' That dominion, he left no doubt, was not Pakistan.[10]

Meanwhile, the maharaja's forces embarked on a campaign of massacres and mass evictions, evidently designed to reduce the Muslim majority in the state. More than half a million people were driven out across the border towards Pakistan. In Jammu province, where Muslims were 61 per cent of the population, 200,000 Muslims were exterminated and in some of the districts the majority was reduced to a minority.

The plight of the Muslims evoked strong sympathy in Pakistan. The government of Pakistan sent strong protests to the maharaja but with little effect. To save their Kashmiri brethren from extermination, Afridi and Mahsud tribesmen from Tirah and Waziristan formed a *lashkar* and entered Kashmir on 22 October. Although they made short shrift of the state forces, they unfortunately displayed poor discipline, and killed a number of Christian missionaries in Baramula. By 26 October they were on the outskirts of Srinagar but were diverted by looting.

New Delhi reacted instantly. The Indian Defence Committee had already met on 25 October and decided to rush arms aid to Kashmir. On Governor General Mountbatten's advice it decided to first secure the state's accession. Secretary V. P. Menon flew to Kashmir and claimed to have obtained the signatures of the maharaja on the document on 26 October. At the same time, the maharaja set up an interim government and asked Sheikh Abdullah to join the state prime minister to carry out the responsibilities. On 27 October Mountbatten accepted the accession. On the same day, the Indian air force flew paratroops to Srinagar. Pakistan lacked military strength to counter the Indian use of force, as India had withheld the transfer of Pakistan's entire share of the ordnance.

In an attempt to camouflage the 'utter violation' of the principles of the partition, the Indian government erected a smokescreen of promises to the people of Kashmir and the government of Pakistan, Mountbatten stated in the letter of acceptance of the maharaja's offer of accession:

> Consistently with their policy that, in the case of any state where the issue of accession has been the subject of dispute, the question of accession should be decided in accordance with the wishes of the people of that state, it is my Government's wish that as soon as law and order have been restored in Kashmir and her soil cleared of the invader, the question of the state's accession should be settled by a reference to the people.

Also on the same day Nehru sent a telegram to Liaquat Ali Khan:

> I should like to make it clear that the question of aiding Kashmir in this emergency is not designed in any way to influence the state to accede to India. Our view which we have repeatedly made public is that the question in any disputed territory or state must be decided in accordance with the wishes of people and we adhere to this view.[11]

The circumstances clearly pointed to a preconceived design and the Pakistan government did not give credit to the hypocritical proviso or Nehru's assurance. On 27 October the Quaid-i-Azam ordered General Gracy, the acting commander-in-chief of the Pakistan army, to send troops to counter the Indian attack, but he demurred and instead sought instructions from the Supreme Commander, Field Marshal Auchinleck, in New Delhi.

Another part of the Indian design to annex Kashmir under a cloak of legitimacy was the appointment of National Conference leader Sheikh Abdullah as administrator of the state. Meanwhile, the Muslim Conference was silenced and its leaders Ghulam Abbas and Mirwaiz Mohammad Yusuf remained in detention. (Months later, in early 1948, they were released but, barred from political activity, they decided to cross over to Azad Kashmir.)

Upon receiving news of accession the people of Gilgit were outraged and on 30 October the Gilgit Scouts, the agency's force, ousted the maharaja's governor, who had been appointed after the British government's lease of the territory expired on August 15. At the request of the Scouts, Pakistan took over the administration of the agency.

On 30 October, the Pakistan government issued a public statement declaring that the maharaja's accession to India was based on 'fraud and violence.' Pakistan would never recognise the accession which was 'fraudulent inasmuch as it was achieved by deliberately creating conditions with the object of finding an excuse to stage the 'accession'...(which) was against the well-known will of an overwhelming majority of the population and could not be justified on any grounds whether moral or constitutional, geographical or economic, cultural or religious.'[12]

On 16 November, Liaquat Ali Khan proposed a request to the United Nations to send its representatives to stop the fighting and the repression in Kashmir. On 21 November Nehru replied it was not clear to him what the UN could do. Meanwhile, the Indian forces met with stiff resistance by the people as they proceeded to occupy the state and drive out Kashmiris.

At the United Nations

On 1 January 1948, India filed a complaint with the Security Council against Pakistan, under Article 35 of Chapter VI of the Charter, and asked the Council to call upon Pakistan to stop giving assistance to the invaders. In an attempt to reassure the Council of its own *bona fides*, the Indian complaint stated:

> In order to avoid any possible suggestion that India had taken advantage of the State's immediate peril for her own political advantage, the Dominion Government made it clear that once the soil of the State had been cleared of the invader and normal conditions were restored, the people would be free to decide their future by the recognised democratic method of plebiscite or referendum which, in order to ensure complete impartiality, may be held under international auspices.

The Security Council started consideration of the question on 15 January. By then Pakistan had also filed a counter-complaint, charging India with genocide and refuting the validity of the maharaja's accession. Pakistan requested the Security Council to (a) call upon India to desist from acts of aggression, and (b) appoint a commission to investigate its charges against India.

During the debate in the Security Council, foreign minister Zafrullah Khan spoke for five hours. After refuting the allegations made by the Indian representative, he concluded with the question 'What is to be done?' and suggested, 'Everyone who has gone into

Kashmir should get out,' including Sikh bands, RSS volunteers, tribesmen, and Indian troops.

Acting under Chapter VI—Pacific Settlement of Disputes—and with the consent of both parties, the Security Council decided on 20 January 1948 to establish the UN Commission for India and Pakistan (UNCIP) in order to investigate the facts and exercise mediatory influence. Comprising selected members of the Council, the Commission visited Pakistan and India. On its recommendation, the Council adopted the first substantive resolution on 21 April 1948. Referring to the Indian complaint 'concerning the *dispute* over the state of Jammu and Kashmir' (emphasis added), and Pakistan's 'counter-complaints', and 'Noting with satisfaction that both India and Pakistan desire that the question of the accession of Jammu and Kashmir to India or Pakistan should be decided through the democratic way of a free and impartial plebiscite, 'the Security Council accepted UNCIP's recommendation for measures 'appropriate to bring about cessation of the fighting and to create proper conditions for a free and impartial plebiscite to decide whether the State of Jammu and Kashmir is to accede to India or Pakistan.'

Ignoring the Security Council's call to both sides to refrain from any action that might aggravate the situation, India embarked on a large-scale offensive in the spring. General Gracy then submitted to the Government of Pakistan his appreciation that the operation would lead to another serious influx of refugees from Kashmir into Pakistan and recommended that the Indian advance needed to be stopped. Pursuant to his advice, the government of Pakistan decided to send limited forces to hold defensive positions in the state. When UNCIP came to Pakistan in July, Zafrullah Khan informed the representatives that three brigades had been sent to reinforce the defence lines held in Azad Kashmir in May, as Pakistan could not sit back passively unmindful of the danger of the Indian army's invasion of Pakistan territory.

India seized upon the Pakistani decision to allege aggression. Both sides hotly debated the issue in the commission. Finally, on 13 August 1948 UNCIP adopted an elaborate three-part resolution providing for a ceasefire order by India and Pakistan, a truce agreement and plebiscite. Pakistan was to withdraw its troops, as their presence in Jammu and Kashmir 'constitutes a material change in the situation' and territory vacated by them would be administered by the local authority under the surveillance of the commission. Also, the Indian government 'would begin to withdraw the bulk of its forces from Kashmir after the Commission had notified them that the tribesmen and Pakistani nationals had withdrawn and that the Pakistani troops were being withdrawn.' The resolution also contained the following key paragraph:

> The Government of India and the Government of Pakistan reaffirm their wish that the future status of the State of Jammu and Kashmir shall be determined in accordance with the will of the people and to that end, upon acceptance of the Truce Agreement, both Governments agree to enter into consultations with the Commission to determine fair and equitable conditions whereby such free expression will be assured.

On 5 January 1949, following the entry into force of the ceasefire, UNCIP adopted another resolution incorporating supplementary principles accepted by India and Pakistan about a truce, the appointment of a plebiscite administrator and arrangements for the plebiscite. The resolution reiterated: 'The question of the accession of the State of Jammu and Kashmir to India or Pakistan will be decided through the democratic method of a free and impartial plebiscite.'

Although the British role in the Security Council was pro-India, most members brought an impartial and salutary approach to deliberations on the Kashmir Question rooted in the norms of international law, in order to promote a solution consistent with the ethics of justice and the right of self-determination. Unfortunately, this spirit soon suffered attrition and some of the key members of the Security Council later adopted stilted positions on the basis of self-interest rather than the merits of the dispute, with India exploiting the Cold War to gain the support of the Soviet Union by using or threatening the use of the USSR veto.

Having occupied the bulk of the state, India set about consolidating its control over it. Sheikh Mohammad Abdullah was installed as prime minister. At the same time India also began attempts to wriggle out of its solemn pledges and commitments to the people of Kashmir, Pakistan and the United Nations. It alleged non-compliance by Pakistan with one part of the Security Council resolutions or another regarding arrangements for a plebiscite, but rejected proposals by UN mediators for impartial arbitration on differences of interpretation. A suggestion by the US State Department, urging flexibility on legal points, drew a rigid and rude response from Nehru. He 'would not give an inch. He would hold his ground if Kashmir, India, and the whole world would go to pieces.'[13] A joint appeal by President Truman and Prime Minister Attlee on 31 August 1949 for arbitration on differences of interpretation of the UNCIP plan elicited a similarly truculent response.

Proposals[14] made by UNCIP for a reduction of forces on both sides of the ceasefire line prior to the plebiscite were rejected by India.[15] The Security Council decided in March 1950 to replace UNCIP with a Representative, to assist the two countries towards demilitarisation. The first Representative, Judge Owen Dixon of Australia, discussed arrangements for the plebiscite but India refused to concede temporary authority to the UN Administrator. Instead, Nehru tried to divert the focus by calling for condemnation of Pakistani 'aggression.' Dixon pointed out that the Security Council had made no such declaration and such a question had 'nothing to do with the... fairness and freedom of a... plebiscite.'[16] Dixon came to the conclusion that India's agreement 'would never be obtained to demilitarization' in any such form as would permit the plebiscite to be conducted in conditions sufficiently guarded against intimidation and other forms of influence and abuse. He then decided to propose either four 'regional plebiscites' or partition conceding 'some areas' to Pakistan, 'some' to India, and limiting plebiscite only to 'the Valley of Kashmir and perhaps some adjacent country.' Nehru indicated interest, calculating that Abdullah could manipulate the plebiscite. Liaquat Ali Khan pointed out that the proposals departed from the Security Council resolutions which envisaged that the 'destiny of the state of Jammu and Kashmir as a whole should be decided by a single plebiscite taken over the entire state.'

The Dispute Festers

The Security Council then appointed Frank P. Graham as its Representative. He took up the question as to the number and character of forces to be retained by India and Pakistan consistent with the holding of a free plebiscite. In his report of 23 December 1952, Graham proposed that Pakistan should reduce the forces on its side to between 3,000 and 6,000, and India to between 12,000 and 18,000. Pakistan accepted but India rejected the proposal. Graham continued his efforts and made five more reports during his tenure until 1958, but with no result.

Meanwhile, observing that Abdullah's National Conference recommended determination of the future affiliation of the state by the Constituent Assembly, the Security Council adopted a resolution on

30 March 1951 affirming that 'any action that assembly might attempt to determine the future shape and affiliation of the entire State or any part thereof would not constitute a disposition of the State in accordance with the above principle.' The Council also reiterated the principle that 'the final disposition of the State of Jammu and Kashmir will be made in accordance with the will of the people expressed in the democratic method of a free and impartial plebiscite conducted under the auspices of the United Nations.' (All seventy-five members of the 'Constituent Assembly' were 'elected' by the vote of fewer than five per cent of the electorate in 1951without opposition. All belonged to Abdullah's own party.)

In June 1953, Prime Minister Mohammad Ali Bogra opened a dialogue with Nehru in the hope of settling differences bilaterally. After a meeting in New Delhi in August, the two leaders agreed that the Kashmir question 'should be settled in accordance with the wishes of the people of that State' and 'the most feasible method of ascertaining the wishes of the people was by fair and impartial plebiscite'. The dialogue was soon called off by Nehru, taking the position that the contemplated military pact between Pakistan and USA 'will affect the major questions... more especially, the Kashmir issue.' He did not care to explain what the connection was between such a pact and the right of the Kashmiri people to determine the future of their state. Instead, he continued to put forward irrelevant arguments, making convenient use of absurd press reports such as the one that conjured up expansion of the Pakistan army to 'a million men.'[17]

Realising that his friend Nehru had duped him by solemn promises of plebiscite, in 1953 Sheikh Abdullah sought to retrace his steps declaring that he had supported only conditional accession to India 'despite our (i.e. Kashmiris') having so many affinities with Pakistan.' In a meeting with Adlai Stevenson, presidential candidate of the United States, in Srinagar, he expressed views in favour of independence for the state. He had also done so earlier in meetings with foreign visitors.[18] Sheikh Abdullah was dismissed in August 1953 because he 'was on the point of demanding that the Indian Army leave the soil of Kashmir.'[19] He remained imprisoned for a decade. The people of the state cursed him for selling out their interests and allowing himself to be used as an instrument in the Indian design.

When the United States began consideration of a defence pact with Pakistan in 1953, India came up with another specious argument to renege on its commitments on Kashmir. It declared that such arrangements would constitute 'a qualitative change of circumstances' relating to the Kashmir question. Of course, Pakistan's alliance with other countries could neither absolve India of its obligations under UN resolutions nor prejudice the recognised right of self-determination of the people of Kashmir.[20]

India's argument that Pakistan's defence pact with the United States represented 'change of circumstances' releasing India from its obligation under the UN resolutions was totally inadmissible in law and logic. Bad faith was also writ large on India's plea that a decision by Kashmiris in favour of Pakistan would prejudice India's secular character and political unity. This was entirely an afterthought. The law does not permit a state to disown an international obligation. According to Article 25 of the United Nations Charter, 'The Members of the United Nations agree to accept and carry out the decisions of the Security Council in accordance with the present Charter.'

When Pakistan learned that the so-called 'Constituent Assembly' in Srinagar was to ratify the maharaja's accession, it brought the matter to the attention of the UN Security Council, and on 24 January 1957, the council reminded 'the Governments and Authorities concerned of the principle... that the final disposition of the State of Jammu and Kashmir will be made in accordance with the will of the people expressed through the democratic method of a free and impartial plebiscite conducted under the auspices of the United Nations' and reaffirming that any action taken by the assembly 'would not constitute a disposition of the State in accordance with the above principle.'[21]

As India attempted to wriggle out of its obligations under the UN resolutions, it exploited the Soviet unhappiness with Pakistan's decision to conclude a defence agreement with the United States in order to gain Soviet support for India's position on the Kashmir question. At first the USSR abstained but later it threw its powerful weight behind India and its statements endorsed the Indian position on Kashmir. The Security Council was henceforth prevented from dealing with the Kashmir question impartially or to act with determination to secure implementation of its own resolutions.

One after another obstacle was thus raised by India to prevent a settlement of the Kashmir question. The dispute itself was—and remains—quite simple. So, too, is its solution. All that it required is the implementation of the pledge in the UN resolutions, accepted by India as well as Pakistan, and to let the people of the state decide the question of the state's accession in a free plebiscite. If it had become complicated it is because India had made it so.

India's later claim that the Maharaja of Kashmir had the right to decide the question of accession is not congruent either with its stance in respect of Junagadh and Hyderabad, the conditional acceptance of the maharaja's accession, the pledges of Jawaharlal Nehru to the people of Kashmir or India's commitment in the Security Council resolutions that the question of accession would be decided by the people of the state in a free and impartial plebiscite.

Similarly, India's subsequent argument that implementation of the UN resolutions was subject to the condition of withdrawal of Pakistani troops ignores the record of negotiations. Pakistan was prepared to reduce its forces to the bare minimum but India refused the UN mediator's suggestion to reduce its forces sufficiently to permit the Kashmiri people to exercise their right of self-determination without fear of duress.

NOTES

1. S. M. Burke, op. cit., p. 16.
2. Chaudhri Muhammad Ali, op. cit., p. 226, quoting Alan Campbell-Johnson, *Mission with Mountbatten*, pp. 51-56. On another occasion, Mountbatten repeated the same advice in the following words: 'Normally geographical situation and communal interests and so forth will be the factors to be considered.' S. M. Burke, op. cit., p. 16.
3. British foreign secretary Ernest Bevin expressed regret that 'a warlike spirit has developed' in India. Quoted by G. W. Choudhury, op. cit., p. 79.
4. S. M. Burke, op. cit., p. 17.
5. Quoted from *Transfer of Power*, Vol. XI, No. 229, in Alastair Lamb, *Kashmir—A Disputed Legacy*, p. 109. Nehru's assertion that the maharaja wished to join India either evidenced a preconceived conspiracy or, if the maharaja wanted to remain independent, it was a deliberate lie.
6. Josef Korbel, op. cit., p. 60.
7. Ibid., p. 63.
8. Pakistan signed the agreement on 15 August; India did not respond.
9. Premnath Bazaz, *The History of the Struggle for Freedom in Kashmir*, p. 325, quoted in G. W. Choudhury, op. cit., p. 73.
10. Josef Korbel, op. cit., p. 71.
11. Quoted in Chaudhri Muhammad Ali, op. cit., p. 288 from K. Sarwar Hasan, *Documents on the Foreign Relations of Pakistan: The Kashmir Question*, p. 104.
12. Liaquat Ali Khan quoted in S. M. Burke, op. cit., p. 27, from K. Sarwar Hasan, op. cit., p. 100.
13. Quoted in McMahon, op. cit., p. 24.
14. For summaries of the various proposals and discussion of their merits, see Lamb, pp. 170-179.
15. US Secretary of State Dean Acheson sent a message to Nehru recommending acceptance of McNaughton's 'realistic approach to the demilitarization issue' and observing that if India did not 'it will be the third consecutive time India will have refused impartial proposals.' Nehru 'exploded' and called the message 'unfriendly.' Quoted in McMahon, op. cit., p. 60.
16. Quoted in S. M. Burke, op. cit., p. 35.

17. Nehru's letter to Bogra dated 9 December 1953, quoted from *Negotiations between the Prime Ministers of Pakistan and India regarding the Kashmir dispute (June 1953-September 1954)* published by Government of Pakistan, Ministry of Kashmir Affairs, Karachi, 1954, quoted in Lamb, p. 228.

18. In 1950, according to US Ambassador Loy Henderson, 'in discussing the future of Kashmir, Abdullah was vigorous in restating his opinion that it should be independent.' US Department of State, Foreign Relations of the United States, 1950. Vol. V. The Near East, South Asia and Africa, Washington, D.C., 1978, pp. 1433-35, quoted in Lamb, pp. 189-190.

19. Akbar, M.J, *Nehru—The Making of India*, Penguin Group, London, 1988, p. 452.

20. Retired Justice M.V. Tarkunde of India, a respected advocate of respect for human rights, said that 'The offer of plebiscite was not in the nature of a concession made by India to Pakistan, but was a recognition of the right of self-determination of the people of Jammu & Kashmir.' Quoted from 'The Radical Humanist', March 1990, in Bahauddin Farooqi, *Kashmir Holocaust*, pp. 26-27.

21. The UN Security Council first dealt with the matter on 30 March 1950, after observing that a constituent assembly was sought to be created in Srinagar. It reminded the governments and authorities concerned of its earlier resolutions incorporating the principle of disposition of the state on the basis of plebiscite and affirmed that 'any action that assembly might attempt to take to determine the future shape and affiliation of the entire State or any part thereof would not constitute a disposition of the State in accordance with the above principle.'

CHAPTER 4

Search For Security

On almost every issue that arose in relations with India, Pakistan found itself faced with New Delhi's refusal to resolve the differences on the basis of principles of law and justice. Whether it was the transfer of Pakistan's share of the assets inherited from British India, accession of princely states, or continued flow of river waters, India sought to impose its own will, in disregard of the principles of the partition agreement between the two countries. Exploiting power disparity, India dismissed reason and equity in negotiations, spurned resort to impartial peaceful means of resolving differences, and did not hesitate to use force or threat of force to impose its own preferences. India's military intervention in Jammu and Kashmir, and its refusal to hold a plebiscite as agreed in Security Council resolutions, injected a sense of urgency to the fledgling state's search for ways and means to bolster its capacity to resist dictation.

Pakistan's response to the objective problem posed by the tyranny of power imbalance, and the agony and humiliation of dictation, was in classical style. As other states have done throughout history when faced with a more powerful neighbour intent on exploiting disparity to achieve its inimical aims, Pakistan embarked upon cultivation of sympathy and support wherever it could be found. It sought friends and allies, and assistance to strengthen the 'sinews of statehood'[1] and to preserve its sovereignty and security. The contours of Pakistan's foreign policy were thus shaped by the desperate need for arms to ensure the security of the new state and for funds to finance its economic development.

For economic and defence assistance Pakistan first approached Britain, the only Western country Pakistani leaders knew at first hand. Britain was, however, too exhausted and debilitated following the Second World War to render help. Also, the Labour government was antipathetic to Pakistani leaders, whom it simplicistically blamed for wrecking the British hope of maintaining the unity of their Indian empire—'the Jewel in the Crown.' Clement Attlee, prime minister at

the time, 'never liked Jinnah' and too many British Labour Party
members thought in terms of 'a progressive Congress and a reactionary
Muslim League.'

USSR[2]

As Pakistan looked for economic and military cooperation, the Soviet
Union was not an option. Having borne the brunt of Nazi Germany's
powerful war machine in Europe, with 25–30 million people killed and
its economy devastated, it was hardly in a position to provide
assistance. Politically, too, the Soviet system was unattractive to
Pakistani leaders who were committed to democracy. Moreover, the
communist ideology was considered antithetical to Islam. Also, the
Soviet leadership looked with little favour upon Pakistan (or India).[3]
Moscow perceived the partition as having 'facilitated British
domination in both dominions.'[4]

Relations between the two countries got off to an inauspicious start,
as the USSR did not even send a customary message of felicitations on
Pakistan's independence. Alone among major countries to manifest
such discourtesy, the Soviet Union also did not take an initiative to
establish an embassy in Pakistan.

On the Pakistan side, too, inherited and inherent factors prejudiced
Pakistan against the Soviet Union. The Pakistani administrative elite,
nurtured in the British strategic view, suspected that the Soviet state
cherished the czarist aim of carving out a land access to the warm
waters of the Arabian Sea, and therefore, posed a danger to Pakistan's
security. They also considered communism a secretive and revolutionary
movement subversive of law and order. However, Pakistan was by no
means hostile to the USSR and in the early years had no interest in the
emergent power blocs.

The Soviet record of rapid economic progress evoked admiration
and its foreign policy of opposition to colonialism and imperialism
made a ready appeal. Progressive artists and littérateurs lauded
communist ideals of egalitarianism and full employment, sang paeans
to socialist ownership of means of production and denounced
capitalism for colonial domination and exploitation of labour for the
benefit of the rich. Few spoke or were even aware of Soviet repression
at home and its annexation of territories of neighbouring states and
imposition of communism over East European countries.

Invitation to Liaquat Ali Khan. An episode that aroused much attention at the time and later, involved the invitation to the Pakistani prime minister to visit the Soviet Union, which was accepted but not honoured. The known facts are that President Harry S. Truman's invitation to Nehru to visit the United States was announced in May 1949. At a reception held during Liaquat Ali Khan's visit to Tehran, Ambassador Ghazanfar Ali told the Soviet chargé d'affaires of the prime minister's desire to visit the USSR. Moscow responded within five days. Josef Stalin's invitation to Liaquat Ali Khan was delivered at the Pakistan Embassy in Tehran on 4 June. Liaquat Ali accepted it immediately. Each side then suggested visit dates for August, which the other found inconvenient. It was then decided to defer the visit for two months, during which the two sides agreed to establish resident embassies. Follow-up action met further delays. Pakistan designated an ambassador but Moscow took its time to give *agrément* while failing to nominate its own ambassador. According to an informed Pakistani account, neither side acted with any sense of urgency.[5]

The question as to why the visit to USSR did not take place has remained intriguing. It has been surmised that pique at Truman's invitation to Nehru provoked Liaquat Ali's initiative to solicit an invitation from Moscow. Conversely, it has been suggested that Moscow's immediate response was prompted by a desire to cultivate Pakistan to balance Washington's courting of Nehru. While no evidence is available to corroborate either conjecture, it is known that the US invitation to Nehru, but not to Liaquat Ali, was a disappointment to the Pakistanis, and that announcement of Liaquat Ali's acceptance of Stalin's invitation served to awaken Washington to its omission. Overnight, reported Ambassador Ispahani from Washington, Pakistan began to receive serious notice and consideration.[6] The 'desirability of offsetting the impact of Liaquat's anticipated travel to the Soviet Union, along with balancing Nehru's state visit to the United States, were the main arguments for the invitation to the Pakistani leader.[7] Washington wanted to reassure Pakistan that there was no change in its policy of 'objectivity, impartiality and friendly interests in both India and Pakistan.'

There is little evidence to suggest that the US invitation to Liaquat Ali caused Moscow to lose interest in his visit to the Soviet Union. Perhaps, the cooling of Moscow's interest was due to Pakistan's harsh anti-communist rhetoric, and official discouragement of contacts with the Soviet Union. Pakistan refused passports to poets and writers who wanted to visit the Soviet Union.

Approaches to the USA[8]

The United States was the only promising source of assistance. Emerging from the Second World War with its economy intact, it was the wealthiest nation in the world, accounting for over 40 per cent of global production. Also, its democratic system was congenial. It was, however, preoccupied with Soviet expansion in Eastern Europe and the need to stabilise Western Europe through economic and military assistance. US interest in South Asia was rather cursory. However, Pakistan's location next to the Middle East, with its petroleum resources, provided a strategic link of benefit to Pakistan's search for cooperation.

The US was not then alive to the threat in the Middle East, nor was it favourably disposed toward the Pakistan movement. The demand for a state in the name of Islam was difficult for secular America to comprehend.[9] Motivated by wartime priorities and anti-colonial predilections, President Franklin D. Roosevelt believed a free India could make a useful contribution towards the war effort. When Prime Minister Winston Churchill refused to concede the Congress demand for self-government, Roosevelt sent him a strongly worded protest.'[10] Apparently unaware of the cooperation the League extended to the Allies by encouraging Muslims to join the armed forces in the war against fascism, Washington considered the Congress as the leading party, and supported a united India. In December 1946, Acting Secretary of State Dean Acheson endorsed the Cabinet Mission Plan.[11] The League tried, within its limited means, to educate opinion in the United States. In 1946 it sent two prominent leaders, M. A. H. Ispahani and Begum Shah Nawaz, to Washington. They met Dean Acheson but received little more than a polite audience.

The Pakistani leadership carried no grudge against the United States, however. In May 1947, Mr Jinnah received the US chargé d'affaires in New Delhi and explained to him that Pakistan's foreign policy would be oriented towards the Muslim countries of the Middle East, and they 'would stand together against possible Russian aggression and would look to the U.S. for assistance.'[12]

After Pakistan emerged, the United States showed a friendly predisposition towards the new state. President Truman sent a warm message on Pakistan's independence on 14 August 1947, saying, 'I wish to assure you that the new Dominion embarks on its course with the firm friendship and goodwill of the United States of America.'[13] A high US State Department official, Assistant Secretary Philips Talbot came to Karachi in August. A month later Truman gave a 'sympathetic' response to Ambassador Ispahani's statement about Pakistan's need 'to balance our economy, to industrialise our country, to improve health and education and raise the standard of living.'[14]

Constrained by its desperate needs, Pakistan hurriedly sounded out the US chargé d'affaires for financial assistance. In October 1947, the government sent Mir Laik Ali to Washington to seek a loan of two billion dollars for economic development and defence purchases over five years in order to 'attain a reasonably independent position and... to make a fair contribution to the stability of the world order.'[15] To impress Washington, he emphasised compatibility of Pakistan–US interests, on the one hand, and Pakistan's strategic location, on the other, referring to 'the proximity and vulnerability of western Pakistan to Russia.'[16] The US showed little interest, however. Apparently taken by complete surprise at the amount of the aid request, the US politely turned it down, saying it did not have funds of that magnitude. The first rather fumbling request drew a blank, but Pakistan did not give up hope.

Pakistan did not take the US 'no' for an answer and continued to emphasise the commonality of interests. In December 1947, Firoz Khan Noon, a prominent leader and future prime minister, drew an American official's attention to Pakistan's significance as 'the eastern bastion against communism as Turkey is the western bastion.'[17] This point was stressed at the government level as the hostile relations between the USA and the USSR froze into the Cold War. In a meeting with Secretary of State Marshall in Paris, in October 1948, Liaquat Ali Khan said it was 'unthinkable that Pakistan could fall prey to communism' and urged the US to provide economic help to Pakistan and the Muslim nations of the Middle East.[18]

Liaquat Ali Khan visited the USA in May 1950. President Truman received him on arrival in Washington. During his three-week visit, he seized every opportunity to emphasise the commonality of values and interests between Pakistan and the United States. Among these he mentioned democracy, fundamental human rights, right of private ownership, equal citizenship of all whether Muslim or non-Muslim, equality of opportunity, equality before law, and the moral responsibility of those fortunate in wealth and knowledge towards the unfortunate. He described Pakistan and the United States as 'comrades' in the quest for peace and in translating dreams of democracy into reality. He underlined Pakistan's strategic location 'in relation to communications to and from the oil-bearing areas of the Middle East.' In his speech to

Congress he declared 'no threat or persuasion, no material peril or ideological allurement' could deflect Pakistan from its chosen path of democracy. Though he avoided pointed criticism of Soviet policy, he made frequent references to the communist threat.[19]

Liaquat Ali's statements of desire to enlarge cooperation with the United States impressed the Americans, but the official response to his suggestions for aid was unenthusiastic. Considering South Asia a region of 'secondary importance', the State Department brief for the Pakistani leader's visit simply noted that Pakistan's economic or military requests for assistance had so far 'seemed impracticable.'[20] That appraisal was to come under reconsideration following the Korean War, but it took two years and a change of administration in Washington to formulate a new policy.

Korean War

North Korean forces moved across the 38th parallel on 25 June 1950. Pakistan promptly issued a statement denouncing the attack as 'a clear case of aggression.'[21] Liaquat Ali, who was still in the United States, endorsed the US decision to invoke the UN Charter provisions for collective security. Pakistan voted for the General Assembly resolution authorising the UN operation for the defence of South Korea. But when the United Nations called upon members to contribute to the UN action, Pakistan decided against sending a military contingent and limited its contribution to supply of 5,000 tons of wheat for South Korea. Pakistan was willing to send an army brigade but only if its own security was assured in the event of Indian aggression. The United States balked at the suggestion for such a commitment.

Pakistan's position, combining principle with manifest constraints of security, was generally well understood at home and abroad. Its low-key policy was seen by the Western countries to contrast favourably with that of India, which sought to exploit the crisis for advancing its own foreign policy objectives. Its support for the UN operation was limited to sending an ambulance unit, but India sought to play a hyperactive mediatory role and presented proposals for settlement of the crisis which were warmly endorsed by Moscow, but resented in Washington.

Pakistan's decision against sending forces to Korea proved a blessing. Otherwise, Pakistani troops could have been involved in fighting against the Chinese forces which entered Korea after the UN decided, under American influence, to extend the war into North Korea.

Pakistan's hopes for assistance from the United States continued to be frustrated for the next two years. Meanwhile, political instability increased following the assassination of Liaquat Ali Khan, and deterioration of economic conditions, as prices of cotton and jute plummeted after the end of the Korean War. Former foreign secretary M. Ikramullah was sent to Washington at the head of a military mission in October 1951 to press for aid. The US response was again discouraging. It agreed only to sell arms for $10 million and provide technical and economic development assistance under the Point Four Programme. Another such mission headed by Mir Laik Ali was sent by Prime Minister Nazimuddin in July 1952 to ask for an immediate credit of $200 million. The US response was both hesitant and meager. It agreed only to provide $15 million for wheat purchase. But the US policy toward Pakistan was under steady if invisible review in the light of the changing situation in Asia, and especially, the Middle East.

Japan

Pakistan supported the conclusion of a Peace Treaty with Japan and attended the San Francisco conference convened in 1951 to sign the treaty. On the question of China's representation, Pakistan supported participation by the People's Republic. When the majority voted against, Foreign Minister Zafrullah Khan voiced regret over the absence of China whose people had suffered the most at the hands of Japan's erstwhile oppressor regime.

Pakistan's policy on issues in East Asia was appreciated by China, Japan and South Korea and laid the foundation for friendly relations with these important states. It also served to embellish Pakistan's image in the United States as a moderate and cooperative country. The New York Times was so impressed as to praise Pakistan editorially as America's 'one sure friend in South Asia.'[22]

China

Although cultural contacts between the people of Pakistan and China have ancient roots,[23] the two lands remained generally cut off by the Himalayas for most of history. Mindful of China's importance, Pakistan was among the first countries to extend diplomatic recognition to the new government soon after[24] the People's Republic was proclaimed on

1 October 1949, and a year later opened a diplomatic mission in Beijing. Differences of ideology did not obstruct the development of friendly relations between the two neighbours as both conducted bilateral relations strictly in conformity with the principles of non-interference in internal affairs. With bitter experience of foreign domination, China evinced understanding and sympathy for the struggle of other countries of Asia and Africa to maintain their independence and develop their economies. Particularly engaging was China's treatment of small and medium countries on the basis of sovereign equality eschewing big power chauvinism and condescension.

NOTES

1. W. Howard Wriggins, *Pakistan: The Long View*, p. 304.
2. For comprehensive factual and analytical treatment of the subject, see Hafeez Malik, *Soviet-Pakistan Relations and Post-Soviet Dynamics, 1947–92*.
3. A Soviet spokesman dubbed Gandhi and Nehru as 'lackeys of imperialists' and Stalin considered the leaders of the governments in South Asia as 'stooges.' For Soviet attitude toward India and Pakistan during 1947-53 period, see Maqbool A. Bhatty, *Great Powers and South Asia*, pp. 100–105.
4. *Great Soviet Encyclopaedia*, published in 1953, quoted in Maqbool A. Bhatty, p. 103.
5. Sajjad Hyder, Reflections of an Ambassador, p. 14.
6. Quoted in McMahon, p. 70.
7. Dennis Kux, Estranged Allies, p. 32.
8. The account of the evolution of Pakistan–US relations has benefited greatly from Robert J. McMahon, *The Cold War on the Periphery, America-Pakistan Relations—Documents*, ed. K. Arif, and and research by Dennis Kux for his forthcoming book on the subject.
9. Robert J. McMahon, op, cit., p. 65. According to McMahon, American experts feared that 'the establishment of an independent Muslim state might balkanize the subcontinent.'
10. Dennis Kux, Estranged Democracies, p. 6.
11. Bhuttom op. cit., p. 38, quoted from *Indian Annual Register*, vol. 2, p. 88.
12. Dennis Kux, *Disenchanted Allies*, p. 13, quoting from US documents.
13. *Documents*, ed. K. Arif, p. 3.
14. Z. H. Zaidi, *M. A. Jinnah Ispahani Correspondence*, p. 538.
15. Memorandum given by Mir Laik Ali Khan, America–Pakistan *Relations—Documents*, ed. K. Arif, p. 5.
16. Documents, ed. Arif, p. 5.
17. Quoted from US released records in McMahon.
18. Dennis Kux, Estranged Allies, p. 28.
19. Liaquat Ali Khan, Pakistan: *The Heart of Asia*, (Harvard University Press, 1950).
20. Dennis Kux, Estranged Allies, p. 34.
21. *Documents*, ed. Arif, pp. 33, 35.
22. *New York Times*, 14 September 1951.
23. The Kushan kingdom with Peshawar as capital included Chinese Turkistan. Fa Hian came to Gandhara in AD 401 and Hiuen Tsang (alias Yuan Chuang) came for pilgrimage to Taxila in AD 630.
24. Recognition was announced on 4 January 1950.

CHAPTER 5

Alliances

Rising security concerns due to India's exploitation of its military and economic dominance and recurrent threats were the determining factor that impelled Pakistan to search for foreign defence cooperation. Britain was unsympathetic because of the priority it attached to relations with the larger India. For the same reason, the United States was reluctant to respond to Pakistan's efforts for provision of military assistance. For several years after the Second World War, the United States expected Britain to ensure the defence of the West's interests in the region East of Suez and followed its advice.

Defence analysts in the United States had begun to recognise the value of Pakistan's geographic location as early as March 1949, when the US Joint Chiefs of Staff noted the strategic importance of the Karachi–Lahore area 'as a base for air operations' against the Soviet Union and 'as a staging area for forces engaged in the defence or recapture of Middle East oil areas.'[1] Others highlighted Pakistan's position as the world's largest Muslim state with the best army in the Middle East, its proximity to the Soviet Union and the oil fields of the Persian Gulf, and even warned that it would be prejudicial to US interests to develop an India policy without taking into account Pakistan's legitimate interests.

Pakistani leaders lost no opportunity to project the country's strategic importance. Speaking to a visiting assistant secretary of state in October 1949, Finance Minister Ghulam Mohammad stressed the 'importance to the United States... of the establishment of a bloc of (Islamic) nations... as a check to any ambitions of USSR.'[2] Ambassador George McGhee, impressed by the directness of Pakistani leaders and their willingness to support any US-backed efforts to prevent communist encroachments in South Asia, recommended limited American military aid to Pakistan.[3]

Interest in defence cooperation with Pakistan mounted after the Korean War. Analysts in Washington concluded that the North Korean attack, which took place less than a year after the triumph of the

Chinese liberation struggle, evidenced an expansionist Soviet design. They were particularly concerned about the security of the Middle East, especially the vital Persian Gulf region with the world's richest petroleum reserves. The rise of the nationalist Mohammed Mossadegh in Iran and nationalisation of the Anglo-American Oil Company heightened concerns over upheavals in the Middle East and lent urgency to the need for insulating the region against Soviet political penetration and 'stemming any military advance towards the Persian Gulf and in the Near East generally.'

A meeting of US ambassadors to South Asian countries held in Colombo in February 1951 'favoured the idea of Pakistani participation in the defence of the Middle East.'[4] In April 1951, American and British officials agreed that Pakistan's contribution would probably be the decisive factor in ensuring defence of the area.[5]

Pakistan came to be viewed as a valuable asset. But even though sympathetic, Washington remained indecisive 'lest arming Pakistan ensnare the United States in India–Pakistan disputes.'[6] Pakistan's arms procurement missions led by former foreign secretary Ikramullah in late 1951, and by Mir Laik Ali in July 1952, proved infructuous.

Washington's reluctance to make the leap was reinforced by British officials with whom Americans held regular consultations. Considered experts on South Asia, they long opposed American arms supply to Pakistan because, they argued, that would antagonise politically and economically the more important India, foreclose prospects for a Kashmir settlement and spoil prospects of improved relations between Pakistan and India.[7] In effect they uncritically endorsed Indian arguments, ignoring the fact that the Kashmir dispute arose because Pakistan was militarily weak and denial of arms to it could hardly improve prospects of a fair settlement. The British were in effect conceding India a veto over arms supply to Pakistan, an objective India has pursued ever since. Mountbatten was not alone in seeking to promote Indian domination.

In May 1952, Paul Nitze, the Director of the State Department's policy planning staff, wrote a paper deploring Western fragility in the Middle East and recommending direct US involvement in the defence of the region because British capabilities were 'wholly inadequate.' He envisaged assistance to Pakistan to increase its capability to contribute to the defence of the Middle East.[8] By the end of 1952, the Truman administration endorsed the idea of a Middle East Defence Organization (MEDO) that was conceived by London to shore up its sagging position. The problem, however, was that Gamal Abdel Nasser and Nehru opposed the suggestion. British influence in the region had suffered manifest decline.

The post-Korean War perceptions in Washington finally began to crystallise into a search for a new policy. Even before the presidential elections, the US realised it had to take the lead. But the task of launching a major initiative fell to President Dwight D. Eisenhower who took office in January 1953, and his Secretary of State, John Foster Dulles.

'Northern Tier'. As the British idea of MEDO proved a non-starter, the US began to search for an alternative. To that end, Secretary Dulles undertook a tour of the Middle East and South Asia in May. Nowhere did he receive a warmer welcome or was more impressed than in Pakistan. Governor General Ghulam Mohammed, Prime Minister Mohammed Ali Bogra, who had replaced Khawaja Nazimuddin a month earlier, and Foreign Minister Zafrullah Khan 'all stressed their allegiance to the anti-communist cause and emphasised Pakistan's desire to join the free world's defence team.'[9] Army Commander-in-Chief General Ayub Khan, convinced that the threat to Pakistan's security could be contained only with the support of a powerful ally, argued that the United States needed to fill the vacuum created by the British withdrawal.[10] His strategic assessment of the threat of a Soviet drive to the warm waters of the Arabian Sea, and Pakistan's potential for opposing it, made a most favourable impact. In a cable to Washington, Dulles said the feeling of friendship in Pakistan 'exceeded to a marked degree that encountered in any country previously visited on this trip.' He was struck by the 'spirit and appearance' of the Pakistani armed forces and their leaders, and had a 'feeling that Pakistan is one country that has [the] moral courage to do its part in resisting communism.'[11] Testifying before the House Foreign Affairs Committee on his return to Washington, he praised the courage and determination of Pakistanis.

Even before Dulles came to Pakistan, the US demonstrated its goodwill, reflecting appreciation of Pakistan's potential importance and friendly disposition. A Pakistani request for the supply of a million tons of wheat to avert a food crisis was processed with exceptional speed. Assistant Secretary of State Byroade recommended prompt action. A US delegation was sent on a study mission to Pakistan in April. Eisenhower approved speedy action. Dulles personally testified before a congressional committee. Within two weeks Congress gave bipartisan approval and Eisenhower signed the bill in July. The wheat, valued at $74 million, was delivered free at Karachi.

Sensing the new administration's positive disposition toward Pakistan, India mounted a barrage of criticism, arguing that supply of arms to Pakistan would disturb the 'natural balance' in South Asia. Ignoring international law and practice, India's blind opposition to military aid or sales to Pakistan was obviously motivated by the perverse desire to exploit the existing power disparity to impose its malign agenda on Pakistan.

An even stronger antagonist was US Ambassador to India, Chester Bowles, who believed with missionary zeal that India was a democratic counter-model to communist China in the ideological crusade for the mind of the emergent nations. He warned of 'catastrophe' if the US supplied arms to Pakistan, which, he said, would provide the Soviet Union with a golden opportunity to enhance its position in South Asia. The American embassy in India warned that aid to Pakistan would change the course of US relations with India for a long time to come. State Department officials dealing with India agreed: 'India is the power in South Asia. We should seek to make it our ally rather than cause it to be hostile to us. Pakistan is distressingly weak.' Joining the chorus of opposition, Afghanistan made a *demarche* conveying apprehension that the aid might be exploited by a 'foreign ideology.'

Weightier was the British step to convey consternation, repeating its set warning that aid to Pakistan would antagonise India, wreck negotiations on Kashmir, mar prospects of improved relations between India and Pakistan, and undermine Pakistan's limited capacity to play a valuable role in western defence plans. Foreign Secretary Eden even spoke to Dulles who, however, dismissed the British argument, saying India could not claim a right to prevent other nations from lining up with the West.

Dulles publicly spoke of the idea of a defence arrangement of 'northern tier' countries—Turkey, Pakistan, Iraq and Iran. In July, the proposal was considered and adopted by the National Security Council. Eisenhower approved the proposal. Washington decided in principle to go ahead with the alliance idea but Pakistan's request for military aid was still obstructed by fear of the consequences. Ayub Khan went to Washington in September and Governor General Ghulam Mohammed in November 1953, but were disappointed because they received only assurances of sympathy. Dulles counselled patience, and assured them that Pakistan would get aid regardless of India's attitude.

Neither Eisenhower nor Dulles was dismissive of the India factor, however. They abhorred displeasing India. In the hope of preempting Indian objections, Washington informed New Delhi, in 1953, of its

intention to provide assistance to Pakistan. Nehru denounced the
intention and promptly exploited it to renounce India's pledge of a
plebiscite in Kashmir. He made daily speeches against the US policy.
The Indian 'public campaign verged on hysteria' with Nehru declaring
that aid to Pakistan would be a step, not only toward war, but even
world war. A veteran foreign observer saw through the Indian design:
'A cardinal underlying Indian purpose was to keep her smaller
neighbour weak and isolated for eventual re-absorption...'[12]

The decision was still pending when Vice President Richard Nixon
came to Karachi (and New Delhi) in December 1953. He found Ayub
Khan 'seriously concerned about the communist threat.'[13] On his
return he made a strong recommendation in favour of aid. Finally, in
January 1954, Eisenhower 'agreed in principle to [US] proceeding with
military aid to Pakistan.'

Before announcing the US decision, Eisenhower asked the State
Department to make a conciliatory approach to India and explain that
the US was not trying to help Pakistan against India, that the arms for
Pakistan were part of a regional security package, and offered a similar
pact to India. On 24 February 1954, he wrote a letter to Nehru,
assuring him that if the aid to Pakistan was misused for aggression the
United States would immediately take 'appropriate action, both within
and without the United Nations, to thwart such aggression.' He also
offered his 'most sympathetic consideration' of a request for military
aid by India.

Disconsolate, Nehru gave a point-by-point rebuttal, adding a new
argument that the arms supply to Pakistan could trigger Hindu–
Muslim tensions in India. Composed in meetings with the US
ambassador, Nehru seethed in briefing Indian officials: the US, he said,
wanted to check India's power in the region and outflank neutralism.

In the end, India's bluster 'backed the US administration into a
corner.'[14] The US Congress was annoyed by the self-serving arguments
of Nehru and Krishna Menon. If it did not go ahead with the idea, it
concluded, not only would that abort its new proposal, it would be
tantamount to giving Nehru a veto over US policy in Asia. Nixon, a
vocal proponent of arms for Pakistan, warned it would be a fatal
mistake to back down.

Four Alliances

1. Mutual Defence Assistance Agreement, 1954. Pakistan and the United States signed the first defence agreement on 19 May 1954. The US undertook to provide defence equipment to Pakistan 'exclusively to maintain its internal security, its legitimate self-defence, or to permit it to participate in defence of the area.' The assistance was to be made available under US legislation—the Mutual Defence Assistance Act of 1949 and Mutual Security Act of 1951 relating to the defence of the free world. On its part, Pakistan undertook to cooperate with the United States in measures to restrict trade with nations 'which threaten the maintenance of world peace.' Prime Minister Mohammad Ali Bogra lauded the Pakistan–US agreement. The two countries, he said, 'have a great deal in common' They shared convictions regarding freedom and democracy and spiritual strength to fight the totalitarian concept.[15]

2. SEATO, 1954. The idea of a South East Asia Treaty Organization came up in 1954 after the French defeat at Dien Bien Phu. It was conceived by the United States in order to create deterrence to communism in general and Vietnam in particular. Dulles did not envisage the inclusion of South Asian countries but Anthony Eden thought that inclusion of only Thailand and Philippines from the region would make the pact a Western undertaking, and besides, association with India, Pakistan and Ceylon would provide local military backing. He sent a message to these countries on 18 May inviting them to join talks on the defence of the region. Prime Minister Bogra replied in June that Pakistan should be involved. Acting Foreign Secretary Agha Hilaly told an official of the British High Commission in Karachi that Pakistan would wish to participate in discussions on the defence of south east Asia, East Pakistan being a part of the region, Ambassador Amjad Ali, talking to an official of the department of State in Washington, observed that Pakistan would require equipment to contribute to the defence of the region. Foreign Minister Zafrullah Khan told the American under secretary of state even earlier, in July, that Pakistan would definitely join if asked.[16]

Pakistan was invited to attend the Manila Conference in September 1954 to discuss the plan for the defence of South East Asia. In his response, Prime Minister Bogra was, however, careful to inform Eden that participation in the conference did not 'imply acceptance of any scheme that might emerge from the discussions in the meeting.' The chief reason for Pakistan's sudden reservations about SEATO was disappointment with the small amount of assistance the United States allocated for Pakistan. Ambassador Amjad Ali told the State Department that Ayub Khan was 'dejected and broken-hearted,' even regretting that Pakistan had joined in a defence agreement with the United States. Dulles thought that Pakistani expectations of US aid were 'self-stimulated.' He asked the US ambassador in Karachi to clarify to the Pakistan government that the US capabilities were limited and that while it would provide equipment to enable Pakistan to play an effective role in the Middle East, Pakistan itself would have to bear the cost of maintaining its forces. Similarly, the US was not in a position to provide massive economic aid. Dulles believed that it was in Pakistan's interest to join SEATO but he said it should not do so to oblige the United States. He also considered it imperative to clarify to Pakistan that the treaty aimed at defence against communist aggression, and excluded involvement in Pakistan–India disputes.

The message could only add to Pakistan's reservations about SEATO. The government was not satisfied with the first draft of the treaty which would cover only East Pakistan. Unlike NATO, it provided only for consultations, not joint action, in the event of aggression against one of its members. Nor did the treaty envisage the provision of defence and economic assistance. Keen not to offend China, it did not want the treaty to refer to communism or even appear to permit its possible extension to Formosa.

During discussions in Manila, the conference agreed to a redraft so as to cover the entire territories of the Asian parties. In Article IV each party recognised that aggression against any of the parties would endanger its own security. However, the United States remained adamant in appending to the treaty the reservation that its obligations would apply only in the event of communist aggression. The treaty did not cover Pakistan against Indian aggression so far as the United States, its most powerful member, was concerned.

In the circumstances, the brief required the Pakistani delegation to first consult the government before accepting the document. However, upon urging by Dulles, Foreign Minister Zafrullah Khan decided to sign the treaty nevertheless. The Pakistan cabinet was surprised and displeased and some of its members were critical of the foreign minister. Zafrullah Khan offered to resign. On reflection, the cabinet quietly acquiesced in his judgement.

Much has been made in Pakistan of Zafrullah's decision to exceed his brief but not enough attention has been given to the consequences of a refusal to sign the treaty. Having insisted on an invitation to participate in the conference, it would have been counter-productive to withhold signature. It would have offended other participating states, antagonised opinion in the United States and thus jeopardised the aid Pakistan so desperately sought. The obvious consequences were clearly unacceptable to the government, which hummed and hawed for four months but, in the end, ratified the treaty in January 1955, after receiving an assurance from Dulles that in the event of non-communist aggression against Pakistan, the US 'would be by no means disinterested or inactive.'

SEATO members did not consider the 1965 War or the 1971 Indian military intervention in Pakistan to come under the purview of the treaty. After East Pakistan was severed, Pakistan withdrew from the organization, in November 1972.

3. **Baghdad Pact, 1955**. Turkey and Iraq laid the foundation of the Baghdad Pact, signing a Pact of Mutual Cooperation for 'security and defence' in February 1955 in the Iraqi capital. It was not an auspicious start. In the first place, Turkey was unpopular in the Arab world for having recognised Israel. Secondly, Egypt, which was considered by Britain as the key to a defence arrangement in the Middle East, denounced the Baghdad Pact.

On receiving an invitation from Turkey and Iraq to join, Pakistan was not enthusiastic. Disappointed with the amount of US aid, Pakistan was no longer keen to undertake further military commitments in the Middle East. Ayub Khan, then defence minister as well as commander-in-chief of the army, whose opinion was decisive in security matters, was sceptical about the worth of the pact unless the United States also joined. Prime Minister Bogra did not make a commitment when the ambassadors of Iraq and Turkey met him. This position was, however, difficult to sustain. The bilateral agreements Pakistan had signed with Turkey and the United States were conceived as steps leading to a defence arrangement for the 'northern tier.' Pressures mounted from the USA as well as Britain, which wanted a regional arrangement, not so much for the defence of the countries of the region as to shore up its prestige after the setbacks it suffered in Iran, and to protect its interests in oil and the Suez Canal.

In June, Ayub Khan was invited to Turkey. Prime Minister Nuri Said of Iraq was also there. He and the Turkish premier Adnan Menderes succeeded in convincing Ayub of the advantages of joining the pact, explaining that the United States could be counted upon to support the regional members, and that, in any case, the pact involved no additional commitments. Ayub agreed to recommend adherence by Pakistan. Within days the Pakistan cabinet approved accession to the Baghdad Pact. Formal action was delayed, first, because Pakistan wanted to reserve its position in order to limit defence commitments in case of a war involving Turkey as a member of NATO, and then, on account of major changes in the leadership in Pakistan in August. The new prime minister, Choudhri Muhammad Ali, entertained reservations about joining the pact but he was over-ruled by President Iskander Mirza.

On 23 September 1955, Pakistan signed the Pact of Mutual Cooperation in Baghdad; it the other regional members included Iran, Iraq and Turkey. Britain also joined it but the United States did not become a full member. The US Congress was concerned about the implications of the treaty in the event of a war involving Israel. Instead, the US decided to become an observer and agreed to association with its defence and political committees. Since that did not satisfy Pakistan, the US later signed another defence agreement with Pakistan.

The royal regime in Iraq was not popular to begin with. President Nasser's denunciation of the Baghdad Pact in general, and of the Iraqi government in particular, for breaking rank with the Arab world, made it more vulnerable to criticism. In 1958, the Iraqi regime was overthrown in a bloody coup and the country pulled out of the pact named after its capital. Consequently, it was renamed the Central Treaty Organization (CENTO) in 1959.

Pakistan did not see eye to eye with London or Washington on issues in the Middle East. It was historically supportive of the Palestinian cause, friendly with Iran, no less under Prime Minister Mohammed Mossadegh than under the Shahanshah, and sympathetic toward Egyptian aspirations despite incipient reservations about the Neguib–Nasser government's emphasis on Arab nationalism, seemingly downgrading solidarity with non-Arab Muslim countries. Pakistan enjoyed especially close relations with Saudi Arabia, Jordan and Iraq. There could be no question of Pakistan joining the West against the interests of Muslim nations in the Middle East. At the same time it hoped for understanding of Pakistan's own security constraints.

Badaber Base. Meanwhile, during his visit to the United States in July 1957, Prime Minister Suhrawardy informed President Eisenhower of Pakistan's agreement to the establishment of a secret intelligence base at Badaber near Peshawar and for permission for US aircraft to use the

Peshawar airbase. Ayub Khan was said to have made the decision in the light of his assessment of Pakistan's security imperatives and its economic and military aid needs. Also, Pakistan was interested in the early delivery of B-57 bombers.

Describing the base as a 'Communication Centre' the US did not disclose its exact purpose. Given extra-territorial rights, it operated the base with some 1,200 military and technical personnel, all from the United States. No Pakistani was ever admitted to the base and its purpose was indicated in general terms to a very few high Pakistani officials, that it was for electronic eavesdropping on the Soviet Union.

Meanwhile, the Peshawar airbase was used by high-level U-2 'spy in the sky' surveillance aircraft for illegal flights over the Soviet Union for photographic intelligence. The base enabled the US to complete a ring of similar bases around the Soviet Union. It was not only the most concrete and strategic benefit the US derived from the alliance, but exponentially increased Pakistan's importance in the eyes of the strategic community. The Pentagon, which had played virtually no part in the formation of the CENTO alliance, became its main protagonist. Pakistan did not learn until years later that the facility was also used for the same purpose against China.

For a decade the base remained an anchor of US military and economic aid to Pakistan. It was also an important factor in restraining Washington from selling modern weapons systems to India.

4. **Pakistan–US Agreement on Cooperation, 1959**. More important than SEATO or CENTO, the 1959 agreement was negotiated to specifically assure Pakistan of US support in the event of aggression. In years to come, Pakistan spoke of the alliances with the West as 'the sheet anchor of Pakistan's foreign policy.'[17] America, too, was appreciative of Pakistan as a 'wholehearted ally' which undertook 'real responsibilities and risks' by providing facilities 'highly important to (US) national security.'[18] Pakistan invoked this agreement in 1971 but the US did not honour its obligation to come to Pakistan's assistance. (For more details, see page 57).

Reactions of India, China and the USSR

Learning that the US was considering signing a defence assistance agreement with Pakistan, India poured out shrill criticism, despite the fact that it had itself signed a Mutual Defence Assistance Agreement with the US in 1951 under which it received military equipment, and another Technical Cooperation Agreement in 1952.

China understood Pakistan's reasons for joining alliances. At the Bandung Conference in April 1955, Prime Minister Bogra asked to meet Prime Minister Zhou Enlai to explain Pakistan's rationale for joining SEATO. The response was beyond expectations: Zhou replied he would come himself to call on Bogra that afternoon. During the meeting he manifested effusive warmth, promptly accepted Pakistan's rationale for its alliance policy, and neither then nor ever again cast doubt on its intentions. Zhou invited Bogra and accepted the latter's invitation to visit Pakistan.

In contrast, the Soviet Union's reaction was furious. Moscow rejected Pakistan's explanation that its decision to join alliances was solely for its security. It not only criticised Pakistan but also decided to court India by exploiting Indian resentment. On a visit to India in November 1955, Marshal Bulganin and Nikita Khruschev declared in Srinagar that Kashmir belonged to India. Similarly, they visited Kabul and announced support for the Afghan *irredenta* against Pakistan.

In subsequent years, the USSR abused its veto in the Security Council to prevent adoption of every resolution on Kashmir. To Pakistan's dismay, the United States rewarded India by diluting its support for Security Council resolutions on Kashmir.

President John F. Kennedy adopted a policy of befriending India in 1961, but he remained sensitive to Pakistan's concerns. The joint communiqué issued after President Ayub Khan's visit to the United States in July 1961, reaffirmed: 'The Government of the United States regards as vital to its national interest and to world peace the preservation of the independence and integrity of Pakistan.' Kennedy also 'affirmed the desire of the United States to see a satisfactory solution of the Kashmir issue.' In conversations with the Pakistani president, he added that settlement of Kashmir was 'a vital US interest' as the Indians kept diverting the economic aid that the US was pouring into India to build armaments. He gave the assurance that he would try to bring Nehru round to a peaceful settlement of Kashmir and if he failed Pakistan could bring the matter to the UN Security Council where the US would support Pakistan. The US kept this promise when the Kashmir issue came before the UN Security Council in May 1962. It joined six other members in support of a resolution that reminded India and Pakistan of earlier Security Council resolutions. The resolution was, however, vetoed by the USSR.

Neither in 1965 nor in 1971 did CENTO consider rendering assistance to Pakistan. Still it remained marginally useful and Pakistan continued its association until March 1979 when it decided to seek membership of the Non-aligned Movement.

NOTES

1. *Documents*, ed. Arif, p. 15.
2. Ibid., ed. Arif, p. 25.
3. McMahon, pp. 60–75.
4. Dennis Kux, Disenchanted Allies, p. 45.
5. McMahon, p. 132.
6. Dennis Kux, op. cit., p. 47.
7. For quotations from the now public US records of British leaders including Prime Minister Winston Churchill and Foreign Secretary Anthony Eden, opposing arms supply to Pakistan, see Robert J. McMahon, *The Cold War on the Periphery*, pp. 134, 144, 149, 167, 170, 171 etc.
8. Quoted in McMahon, p. 145.
9. Kux, p. 55.
10. M. Asghar Khan, p. 84.
11. Ibid.
12. Ian Stephen, Pakistan, Earnest Benn, London, 1967, pp. 220–221.
13. *The Memoirs of Richard Nixon*, p. 163.
14. Dennis Kux, Estranged Democracies, p. 109.
15. *Documents*, ed. Arif, p. 107.
16. Bajwa, op. cit. p. 106.
17. Statement by Foreign Minister Manzur Qadir on 11 March 1960, op. cit., ed. Arif, p. 184.
18. US Assistant Secretary of State G. Lewis Jones, quoted in Dennis Kux, op. cit., p. 169.

CHAPTER 6

Alliances—Costs and Benefits

No sooner had Pakistan joined the alliances than second thoughts arose on the wisdom of the policy. Particularly corrosive was the harsh criticism of the Baghdad Pact by influential Arab countries. Pakistan's initial policy in the Suez Crisis caused an outrage even at home. Also, Pakistan was suddenly isolated in the kindred community of African–Asian nations, who were suspicious of the West and looked upon the Soviet Union as a supporter of the struggle for emancipation from colonial domination and exploitation. Even more concrete were the costs of the furious Soviet reaction. Assured of the Soviet veto in the Security Council, India exploited Pakistan's decision to join the alliance to renounce its obligation for a plebiscite in Kashmir.

The Costs of the Alliances

Arab Criticism. Egypt was quick to take umbrage. Concerned about the implications of the alliances for Arab unity, and Egypt's aspirations to leadership of the Arab world, it denounced the alliance proposal. Radio Cairo said a Turko–Pakistan alliance would be 'a catastrophe for Islam... the first stab in our back. The next one will probably occur when Iraq joins the plot.'[1] The Saudi radio echoed the Arab Voice from Cairo, when Pakistan joined the Baghdad Pact, calling the decision 'a stab in the heart of the Arab and Muslim states.'[2] Coming from a country that is the cradle of Islam, this made Pakistanis ashamed. The Saudi Kingdom invited Nehru to visit. On arrival he was greeted with banners saying 'marhaba, rasool al salam.' Even its literal meaning 'Welcome messenger of peace' indicated unconcern for the sentiments of Pakistan towards which Nehru's message was seldom of peace. Moreover, the slogan was deeply hurtful to sentiments of Pakistanis because they reserve the word 'rasool' only for the Prophet.

M. Ayub Khan (President of Pakistan, 1960–69).

The Suez Crisis, 1956. President Gamal Abdel Nasser's sudden decision to nationalise the Suez Canal Company in July 1956 was provoked by the American decision to withdraw support for the building of the Aswan High Dam. Revenues from the canal were expected to provide an alternative source of funds. The decision outraged Britain and France, who owned the company. It also worried the United States and other Western countries. Though mistaken in retrospect, they imagined that Egypt's exclusive control over the maritime highway would jeopardise their vital trade interests. Pakistan, too, was similarly misled, on the ground that more than half of Pakistan's trade passed through the Suez Canal. Perhaps that was no more than a rationalisation; Ceylon, India and Indonesia, too, depended on the Suez Canal for trade but they recognised the political roots of the issue.

Relations between Pakistan and Egypt had suffered on account of the clash between their policies on alliances with the West. Nasser evinced even less comprehension of Pakistan's security dilemmas than the Pakistan government did of Nasser's aim of uniting the Arab world for the defence of its dignity against Israel and its Western supporters. Pakistan disliked Nasser's emphasis on Arab nationalism and relegation of the Islamic bond. The two came into collision over the Baghdad Pact. Iraq's decision to join it was denounced by Egypt as a treacherous blow to Arab solidarity. Its emotional propaganda branded non-Arab Iran, Pakistan and Turkey as agents of imperialism. Particularly offensive to Pakistan was Nasser's partiality to the Indian stand on Kashmir, failing to take cognisance of the right of self-determination of the Muslim people of the state.

Yet Pakistan was torn by a fundamental contradiction: its national commitment to solidarity with the causes of Muslim nations demanded support for Egypt. Loyalty to allies called for concession to their concern. No other issue in Pakistan's short history posed a sharper and more excruciating dilemma. The government decided on an expedient compromise. Lacking roots in the people, it failed to win credibility for the policy it thought best served the national interest. The people of Pakistan, who were wholly and uncritically supportive of Egypt, denounced it. The government had to correct its course but only after Pakistan's name had suffered much damage.

Prime Minister Chaudhri Mohammad Ali decided on an objective and balanced approach, upholding Egypt's sovereign right to nationalise the canal, opposing the Anglo–French threat of use of force to resolve the dispute, and also recognising the interests of Pakistan and many other nations 'vitally concerned with the maintenance of the freedom of navigation.'[3] The policy did not meet with popular approval. The masses, the media and revered veterans of the Pakistan movement of the stature of Fatima Jinnah and Sardar Abdur Rab Nishtar wanted unqualified support for Egypt. Worse, Pakistan's approach lost balance and its diplomacy credit as it came under pressure.

On the way to London to attend the conference of major users in mid-August, Foreign Minister Hamidul Haq Chowdhury personally assured Nasser of Pakistan's support for Egypt's right to ownership and control of the canal. At the conference, however, he succumbed to pressure and decided, apparently without clearance from the prime minister, to join eighteen (out of twenty-two) countries in supporting the suggestion for an international board to supervise the canal. Apparently, he did not think such international supervision detracted from Egypt's sovereignty.

The Pakistan delegation's vote not only provoked a charge of betrayal by Nasser, which was orchestrated by media throughout the Arab world, it also raised a political storm in Pakistan. Pained by the obloquy Pakistan incurred in the Muslim world, political parties including the ruling Muslim League censured the government's policy. Leaders from East and West Pakistan denounced the alliances. The masses came out to protest. Foreign Minister Chowdhury's attempt to explain the vote failed to carry conviction. The press subjected him to harsh censure.

For disconnected internal political reasons, Prime Minister Muhammad Ali resigned in September and Huseyn Shaheed Suhrawardy became prime minister. He steered the government out of the storm. Chastened by the blunder at the first London conference, Pakistan made amends at the second, held in September. Foreign Minister Firoz Khan Noon was the only delegate to speak out against the proposal to set up a users' association. Instead, he advocated negotiations with Egypt. This did not please the sponsors; Dulles was especially unhappy. But Egypt was delighted by 'the return of the prodigal.' Nasser promptly sent an invitation to Noon to visit Cairo.

Although Suhrawardy retrieved Pakistan's self-respect, the Suez episode confirmed the view of those who regarded alliances as a liability, as Pakistan was seen to have obliged ally Britain and supported its imperialist aim at the cost of a Muslim country with a just cause, and thus allowed itself to be stood in a corner of shame and isolation. He would have been more kindly remembered had he not given gratuitous offence by venting his views, however logical they must have appeared to him, when, asked by a journalist in December 1956 why

Muslim countries did not band together instead of getting tied to the West, he said, 'My answer is that zero plus zero plus zero is after all equal to zero!'[4]

Soviet Fury. Pakistani leaders were not enamoured of communism, and some military analysts thought also of the historical Soviet drive towards the warm waters of the Arabian Sea. But the severity of the Soviet reaction went beyond their calculation. Discarding its neutral stance in Pakistan–India disputes, Moscow threw its powerful weight behind India. Promising 'all help' to make India industrially strong,[5] the USSR announced aid for a big steel plant. On a visit to India in December 1955, Nikolai Bulganin and Nikita Khrushchev spited Pakistan by declaring they were 'grieved that imperialist forces succeeded in dividing India into two parts.' The *Hindi–Roosi bhai bhai'* relationship was reflected also in their reference to Kashmir as 'one of the states of India.' The Soviet leaders also visited Afghanistan and demonstrated their hostility toward Pakistan by announcing support for Pushtoonistan.[6] They also extended a credit of $100 million to Afghanistan, to which they later added $85 million for the Kushk–Kandahar road and the Shindad military airfield.

Pakistan–US Cooperation Agreement, 1959

Although the costs of the alliances were high, Pakistan did not—could not afford to—abandon the policy. Guarantees against the ever-present security threat constrained reappraisal. In fact, Pakistan went on to strengthen the alliance with the United States by signing another defence agreement in April 1959.

In the new Cooperation Agreement, the United States went further than before in declaring, in Article I, that it 'regards as vital to its national interests and to world peace the preservation of the independence and territorial integrity of Pakistan.' It further stated that 'in case of aggression against Pakistan... the United States of America... will take such appropriate action, including the use of armed forces, as may be mutually agreed upon and as is envisaged in the Joint Resolution to Promote Peace and Stability in the Middle East, in order to assist Pakistan at its request.' In Article II, the United States pledged 'to assist the Government of Pakistan in the preservation of its national independence and integrity and in the effective promotion of economic development.'[7]

Records are not available to indicate that the Pakistani side comprehended the significance and implications of the reference to the Joint Resolution. The US commitment in this agreement to assist Pakistan in the event of aggression seemed more specific and responsive than any contained in SEATO or CENTO. But when Pakistan tried to invoke the agreement in 1965, the US pointed out that the Joint Resolution on the Middle East limited the US obligation to come to Pakistan's assistance in the event of aggression by a communist state.

The Benefits of the Alliances

Pakistan's purpose in joining the alliances was primarily to contain the Indian threat in which the US had little interest. Deterred by the predictable repercussions on its relations with the larger and more influential India, the US did not at first 'dare'[8] to give military assistance to Pakistan. The need to strengthen security in the Middle East with its strategic oil resources impelled the US and Britain to harness Pakistan. With its location close to the Persian Gulf, its military manpower and its friendly predisposition, it was a 'real bulwark,' as Dulles said. But even then the US remained excessively sensitive to Indian preferences. Eisenhower sent a letter of explanation to Nehru assuring him that the arms given by the US to Pakistan would not be allowed to be used for aggression, and offering to supply arms to India as well.

Benefits were initially meagre. The military aid announced by the United States for 1954, amounting to only $29.5 million, greatly disappointed even the protagonists of the alliance. Stunned, a 'broken hearted' Ayub Khan said, 'It would be better for Pakistan not to be involved in defence arrangements with the United States.' Prime Minster Bogra told Dulles he would be 'derided.' It was argued that the aid did not compensate Pakistan for the additional risks it assumed by openly allying itself with the United States.

Washington did not expect Pakistani leaders to protest so vociferously. Having first pressed the United States for an alliance they now seemed to imply it was being forced on them, and that as a result Pakistan was a target of Soviet hostility and therefore entitled to adequate aid to make it secure. If Pakistanis cited the analogy of a man leading a girl up the primrose path and then abandoning her, the Americans compared the Pakistani attitude to that of the girl chasing a man down the aisle and then complaining of gunpoint marriage.

Chaudhri Muhammad Ali gave the apt example of 'a man asking for a gun to shoot a mad dog and being given a needle and thread to repair a hole in the trouser!'[9]

Pakistan's concerns were not dismissed in Washington, however. The US increased economic assistance to $106 million for 1954 and boosted military aid for 1955 to $50 million. More significantly, the US soon gave a commitment to equip four infantry divisions, one armoured division and another armoured brigade, to provide modern aircraft for six squadrons for the air force and supply twelve vessels for the navy over the coming years.

Despite Indian protests, US economic and military aid for Pakistan rapidly increased. Annual allocations were doubled after 1959. Altogether, over the 1954–1962 period, US economic assistance amounted to $3.5 billion.[10] In addition, the US provided $1,372 million for defence support and purchase of equipment.[11] From an antiquated, poorly equipped force in 1954, Pakistan's armed forces became a powerful defence machine, with heavy armour and artillery, the latest aircraft and ships, confident of its self-defence capability. Speaking in the National Assembly in February 1957, Suhrawardy expressed satisfaction over the 'dividends' of the country's foreign policy. In the United States Pakistan had 'a friend and an ally.'[12]

The grievance over the amount of aid was substantially rectified but Pakistan still considered the aid level incommensurate with the liabilities the alliance was perceived to entail. Its second thoughts continued to grow because of criticism by friends and penalties by adversaries.

Pakistani grievance was no longer so much about the quantity of American aid as about the quality of its political support. The United States' desire to maintain friendly relations also with India was understandable but not so a policy that downgraded an ally to a level of parity with a nominally neutral state with a pro-Soviet tilt. With both the USA and the USSR competing for its favours, India was rewarded for hunting with the hounds and running with the hare.

The seeds of disaffection were inherent in the ambiguous bargain. The alliance lacked the bond of a common adversary. Pakistan was focused on the threat from India. The US premise was that Pakistan would play a major part in the defence of the Middle East. Neither side gave enough thought to the glaring contradiction. Having first sought the alliance, Pakistan soon felt it was doing the United States a favour, exaggerating its costs and undervaluing the benefits. Still the mismatch was accepted. Current imperatives prevailed over seemingly remote risks. In 1959, Pakistan entered into another agreement with the United States.

At the popular level Pakistani dissatisfaction was articulated in the cultural context that expects a friend to be constant and loyal, supportive and self-sacrificing. Having thrown in its lot with the West, it also threw caution to the winds by proudly joining the fight against 'the totalitarian concept.'[13] The 'great disappointment' was particularly due to the American failure to throw its weight behind a just settlement of the Kashmir dispute.[14]

The imperative of national security is primordial. Lacking adequate means to ensure defence against the ever-looming Indian threat, it was perfectly rational for Pakistan to look for alliances to compensate for the glaring power disparity. Opposition to the policy of alliances increased over the years because it cut across other aims and aspirations of the people. Foremost among these was the deep-seated desire of the people for solidarity with other Muslim peoples. They felt they were a part of the *umma*, the global Muslim community. If the state allowed security policy to clash with the national aspiration for support of the cause of a Muslim nation, the people of Pakistan felt torn, and the more open the contradiction, the greater was the popular opposition. Nowhere did the opposing priorities clash more glaringly than in the Suez crisis and nowhere else did they mesh so perfectly as in the Afghanistan crisis a quarter of a century later.

The contradiction could have been reconciled as it was in the final stage of the Suez crisis. A government in tune with public opinion might have done it sooner but those in power at the time contributed instead to widening the gulf by flouting popular sentiments and antagonising the Egyptian leader.

Popular views in Pakistan about the United States and the Soviet Union were not as clear-cut as those of the government. Political opinion was ranged against the United States and Britain from the beginning because of their support for the creation of a Zionist state in Palestine at the expense of its predominantly Muslim population. The resentment built up as Israel pursued a policy of genocide, depriving the Palestinian people of their national homeland, killing tens of thousands and driving hundreds of thousands into forced exile. The capitalist system was considered abominable, its exploitative nature manifest in the striking gulf between the rich and the poor. By contrast, despite the official heritage of suspicion of Russian expansionism and subversive communism, the popular view admired the Soviet Union for achieving rapid development and redistribution of wealth on an equitable basis. Opinion was swayed by progressive writers and poets with their idealist depiction of socialism, totally oblivious to the reality of Stalinist repression with millions liquidated or terrorised by a brutal and ruthless state machinery invested with arbitrary powers of arrest, torture to extract confessions and summary justice, condemning dissidents to death or slave labour in Siberian exile. The Soviet suppression of religion, prohibition of public prayers and the demolition of all but a few hundred of the 27,000 mosques and 80,000 churches that existed during the czarist period remained unknown because the carefully selected Pakistani visitors were rarely interested in seeing, much less publicising, the seamy side of their socialist paradise.

The US policy was to change dramatically after the Sino-Indian border clash in 1962. But even before that, opinion in the United States began to change in favour of India.

Swings of Opinion in the USA and Pakistan

Pakistan was not alone in having second thoughts about the policy of alliances. Opinion in the United States, too, began to swing within a few years, illustrated by the radical change in evaluation of neutralism. At first allies were admired and rewarded, neutral states criticised and penalised in allocation of economic assistance. In 1954, influential Republican Senator William Knowland opposed the policy of 'rewarding neutralism' and in 1956 Dulles denounced neutralism as 'an immoral and shortsighted conception.'[15] By 1957, neutralism acquired a mantle of respectability, indeed a position of privilege. Eisenhower endorsed India's neutrality and in internal discussions became critical of his own administration's 'tendency to rush out and seek allies.' He called the alliance with Pakistan 'a terrible error.'[16] As the USSR began assistance to non-aligned India, opinion in the Democratic party and academia in the USA began to advocate increased economic assistance to India. Professors Walt Rostow and Max Milliken of MIT called for aid to India and other countries faced with 'the revolution of rising expectations' in order to enable them to achieve 'take off' under democracy.[17] Adlai Stevenson, Averell Harriman and former ambassadors to India Chester Bowles and Senator Cooper became massive-aid-to-India advocates. Calling India 'the hinge of fate of Asia' Senator John F. Kennedy advocated maximum support to India's development in February 1959, warning 'If China

succeeds and India fails... the balance of power will shift against us.'
He even defended Indian neutrality recalling that during its formative
period in the nineteenth century America, too, followed non-
involvement.[18]

Opinion in Pakistan was deeply agitated by the change in US policy.
While Pakistan was 'taken for granted' by its allies and penalised by
the Soviet Union, neutral India was courted by both the US and the
USSR. The West was becoming lukewarm in its support for Pakistan
on the Kashmir question. The Pakistan government was placed on the
defensive. It seemed to have made a bad bargain politically, if not also
materially. While Pakistan suffered loss of esteem due to its alliance
with the West, neutralism enhanced India's prestige, with the Soviet
Union and the United States competing for India's goodwill and giving
it aid and assistance. Under pressure of criticism in the National
Assembly, Prime Minister Firoze Khan Noon exploded in frustration
on 8 March 1958: 'Our people, if they find their freedom threatened
by Bharat, will break all pacts and shake hands with people whom we
have made enemies because of others.'[19]

General Ayub Khan, during his visit to the United States as army
commander-in-chief in April 1958, also emphasized to US officials and
military chiefs that 'a definite ground swell' was developing in Pakistan
against alliances, because Indian attitudes towards Pakistan had
hardened as US aid enabled it to divert its own resources to the
purchase of military equipment. Hearing this from one of the architects
of the alliance, the US administration was impressed. Secretary of State
John Foster Dulles explained that strategic compulsions necessitated
aid to India but, he assured Ayub, the American relationship with India
was on an intellectual level whereas that with Pakistan was 'more from
the heart.'[20]

Assessing that the military threat of communist expansion had
abated, and the threat now centred on the contest for economic
development, the United States decided to focus on economic
assistance, overlooking the distinction between allied and non-aligned
countries. Even before embarking on a collision course with China on
the border issue, India was flaunting itself as a counter-model to China.
The world was supposed to be watching 'who would win—India under
democracy or China under communism.'[21] Senator John F. Kennedy
foresaw apocalypse: 'If India collapses, so may all of Asia.' In 1958, he
joined with Republican Senator John Sherman Cooper to sponsor a
resolution for enhanced aid to India. Deterioration in India's relations
with China due to disagreement over the boundary, and India's support

for the secessionist Dalai Lama in 1959, provided a further fillip to burgeoning US support for India. It was proclaimed a 'key country'[22] in the West's struggle against communism. The Eisenhower administration, which had started by cutting aid to India, now swung to the other extreme, increasing the amount from $ 93 million in 1956 to $365 million in 1957[23] and a record $822 million in 1960. In addition, the US decided, in 1960, to provide $1,276 million under PL 480 (US Public Law 480 relating to the Global Food Aid Programme) for the export of 12 million tons of wheat to India over the next four years. President Eisenhower also interceded with other Western leaders and the president of the World Bank to enhance economic support for India.

Reacting to the new trends, Pakistan also sought to normalise relations with the USSR. In December 1960, Pakistan signed an agreement with the Soviet Union for exploration of petroleum resources that marked the beginning of an improvement in bilateral relations.

The wooing of India became even more pronounced after John F. Kennedy became president. Although he was not unaware of 'Nehru's talent for international self-righteousness'[24] he regarded India as 'the key area' in Asia. In his inaugural address he paid high tribute to 'the soaring idealism of Nehru' and placed ardent Indophiles in key positions.[25] The administration provided $1 billion for aid to India in its first budget. Soon, the United States also decided to provide a 400 megawatt nuclear power plant to India.

Pakistan welcomed the opportunity provided by Vice President Johnson's visit in May 1961 to get its message across to the new US administration. He was impressed by the case made by President Ayub Khan for the resolution of the Kashmir dispute and provision of American military equipment.

Ayub Khan's Visit to the USA. Kennedy decided to ask President Ayub Khan to advance his visit from November to July 1961 'to exchange views on matters of immediate concern.' In his welcoming speech he expressed concern over the 'misunderstandings' that had arisen. He was evidently aware of Pakistan's perception of declining US support. During talks, Ayub Khan gave an account of India's stonewalling on Kashmir. Kennedy recognised the urgency of settling the Kashmir dispute and said that it was 'a vital interest of the United States.' He promised to speak to Nehru, and if unsuccessful, to support Pakistan at the United Nations.

When Ayub Khan expressed apprehension over the possible US supply of weapons to India, Kennedy replied that the US did not intend to do so but 'if a Sino-Indian conflict ever erupted, and India asked the United States for military aid, he would first consult with Ayub before making a commitment.'[26] He also gave an unequivocal assurance that Pakistan had the right to use American equipment freely in defence of its borders.

Ayub Khan told Kennedy he was going to publicly advocate the restoration of the rights of the People's Republic of China in the United Nations. Kennedy commented, 'Let them have it!' Ayub Khan did so during the NBC's 'Meet the Press' and ABC's 'Editors' Choice' TV programmes.

In a 50-minute extempore speech Ayub Khan told a joint session of the US Congress 'You have great obligations (and) you cannot hide from them.' While it was 'easy to get tired' of the foreign aid programme, he suggested, 'you had better not get tired at this point.' He assured the congressmen, 'The only people (in South Asia) who will stand by you are the people of Pakistan provided you are also prepared to stand by them.' He received a standing ovation. The previous evening he had been taken by decorated launches down the Potomac to President Washington's historic house, Mount Vernon, for a glittering banquet, personally planned by Mrs Kennedy. He 'charmed everybody' in Washington.[27] Vice President Lyndon Johnson hosted a reception in the Pakistani president's honour for 600 prominent guests at his Texas ranch.

In the joint communiqué issued on 13 July, 'President Kennedy affirmed the desire of the United States to see a satisfactory solution of the Kashmir issue and expressed the hope that progress towards a settlement would be possible at an early date.' The two leaders also reaffirmed 'the solemn purpose of the bilateral agreement (of March, 1959)' and 'the value of existing security agreements as an instrument against aggression.'

Kennedy's Efforts to Promote a Kashmir Settlement. Four months later Nehru visited Washington. Kennedy entertained high hopes of the Indian leader, but after talks he felt disappointed. When Kashmir was discussed, Nehru was rigid and dogmatic, ruling out any solution other than perpetuation of the division of the state. Talking to Nehru, Kennedy said after the talks, was 'like trying to grab something in your hand, only to have it turn out to be just fog.'[28] Nehru would answer questions with indifference or lapse into silence. It was partly because at seventy-one his energies were depleted but partly, too, it was his self-centred focus.[29] Like President Truman and Secretary of State Dean Acheson before him,[30] Kennedy found Nehru's sense of superiority 'rather offensive.' Their meeting was a 'disaster.' Nehru's visit was 'the worst' state visit Kennedy had ever had.[31]

Washington was further disillusioned when, in December 1961, India invaded defenceless Goa. 'The contrast between Nehru's incessant sanctimony on the subject of non-aggression and his brisk exercise in *Machtpolitik* was too comic not to cause comment. It was a little like catching the preacher in the hen-house.'[32] Kennedy professed, 'shock.' Adlai Stevenson, the US representative to the UN, soared to heights of eloquence in concluding that, 'if the United Nations was not to die as ignoble a death as the League of Nations, we cannot condone the use of force in this instance and thus pave the way for forceful solutions of other disputes.' However, neither disappointment with Nehru nor admiration for Ayub Khan had much influence on American policy of support for India in the context of their relations with China.

The United States made an attempt to promote settlement of Kashmir. On 3 January acting Secretary of State George Ball said the US was 'very serious about it' and would take 'a very strong position.' The next morning Kennedy told the same thing to the Pakistani ambassador, saying he was conscious of the importance of settling this dispute, as resources of both India and Pakistan were being wasted on 'diversionary arms build-ups.' That afternoon Kennedy announced that he proposed to appoint World Bank president, Eugene Black, to lend his good offices to India and Pakistan to settle the Kashmir dispute. Pakistan accepted the offer but Nehru rejected it.

Kashmir Back at the Security Council. In the meantime, Pakistan decided to move the Security Council to take up consideration of the Kashmir dispute. Contrary to Kennedy's commitment to Ayub Khan, the US administration was hesitant to extend support. On 11 April, Dean Rusk told Ambassador Aziz Ahmed and Zafrullah Khan, then representative to the UN, 'If we are to be helpful in settling this matter in both capitals, then for us to reaffirm our position in the Security Council will affect our ability to be of use. This is our dilemma.' Zafrullah Khan asked Rusk to determine what was holding up progress. and who could do what, so that the block could be removed. Assistant Secretary of State Talbot asked if Pakistan would go back to the resolutions of the Security Council. When Zafrullah Khan replied there was no other way, Talbot commented that India was of the view it was not feasible to implement the resolutions as so much time had elapsed. Zafrullah asked him, 'Is the right of self-determination subject to a time limit?'

The Security Council took up discussion of Kashmir on 28 April 1962. India repudiated its commitment to a plebiscite and Krishna Menon said, 'There has been no commitment at any time by the Government of India that they would take a plebiscite in Kashmir.' (sic) Recalling Nehru's statement of 5 March 1948 reiterating India's 'unilateral declaration that we would abide by the will of the people of Kashmir as declared in a plebiscite or referendum', *The Washington Post* called Menon's statement 'a brilliant piece of double think.'[33]

The Security Council continued to debate the question over two months. Under pressure from India, members from non-aligned countries were reluctant to move a resolution. Finally in June, the Republic of Ireland agreed, after Kennedy's personal intercession with its president, to sponsor a resolution that reminded India and Pakistan of past resolutions of the Security Council calling for a plebiscite in Kashmir. Seven out of the Council's nine members supported the resolution but it was vetoed by the Soviet Union.

NOTES

1. Quoted from *Dawn* of 22 February 1954 in Burke, op. cit., p. 202.
2. Quoted from *Dawn* of 26 September 1955 in Burke, op. cit., p. 204.
3. Statement issued on 14 August 1956, quoted in S. M. Burke, op. cit., p. 185.
4. *Documents*, ed. Arif, p. 125.
5. Burke, op. cit., p. 209.
6. Taking note of the Soviet statements, the SEATO council declared at its meeting in Karachi on 8 March 1956 that 'sovereignty of Pakistan extends upto the Durand Line' and the treaty area included territory up to that line. Documents, ed. Arif, p. 116–117.
7. Text of the agreement in *Documents*, ed. Arif, pp. 156–159.
8. John Foster Dulles's briefing to Senate Foreign Relations Committee on 3 July 1953, extract in *Documents*, ed. Arif, p. 78.
9. Farooq Bajwa, *Pakistan and the West*, p. 87.
10. The table below illustrates the level of US economic assistance to Pakistan, including both grants and soft loans. The data for 1953–70 is from *Effectiveness of Aid to Pakistan*, March 1990, Economic Affairs Division, Government of Pakistan, and from 1971 from *Economic Survey*, 1995–96, Finance Division, Islamabad. It illustrates how the aid level rose and fell during the period. (Also see footnote 295).

    (Figures are in US $ million)

1953	1954	1955	1956	1957	1958	1959	1960	1961	1962	1963	1964	1965	1966	1967
45	89	114	93	365	305	367	758	668	755	151	140	95	182	223

1968	1969	1970	1971	1972	1973	1974	1975	1976	1977	1978	1979	1980	1981
162	123	28	15	129	110	100	107	108	133	78	79	82 .	57

11. *Documents*, ed. Arif, pp. 285–86, statement by James Noyes, Deputy Assistant Secretary for Defence, on 20 March 1973. Part of the aid was used to build Multan and Kharian cantonments and Sargodha air base.

12. *Documents*, ed. Arif, p. 127.

13. Prime Minister Bogra's broadcast to the nation, 1 October 1954. Extract in *Documents*, ed. Arif, p. 102.

14. Firoz Khan Noon's Memoirs, extracts in *Documents*, ed. Arif, p. 163.

15. Quoted from the *New York Times* of 10 June 1956 in Dennis Kux, op. cit., p. 128.

16. Report of National Security Council meeting of 3 January 1957 quoted in Dennis Kux, op. cit. p. 154.

17. Dennis Kux, op. cit., p. 144.

18. Arthur M. Schlesinger, Jr., *A Thousand Days*, p. 482.

19. Quoted from *Dawn* of 9 March 1958 in Altaf Gauhar, *Ayub Khan*, pp. 113–114.

20. Altaf Gauhar, op. cit., p. 119.

21. India's ambassador Chagla, quoted in McMahon, op. cit. p. 260.

22. Walter Lippman quoted in Robert J. McMahon, op. cit., p. 261.

23. In contrast US aid to Pakistan increased marginally from $162.5 million in 1956 to $170 million in 1957.

24. Schlesinger, op. cit., p. 483.

25. Chester Bowles, who as ambassador to India advocated the ditching of Pakistan, was given the No. 2 slot in the State Department as under secretary. Phillips Talbot, an India specialist, became Assistant Secretary of State for the Near East and South Asia, and a Harvard professor known for his sympathy for India, John Kenneth Galbraith was appointed ambassador to New Delhi.

26. Quoted from US documents, McMahon, op. cit, p. 280.

27. Ayub 'charmed everybody' during his visit to the USA, 'ingratiated' himself with Mrs Kennedy and 'shone' at a gala dinner. Quoted in McMahon, op. cit., p. 280. Vice President Johnson described Ayub as a 'seasoned' leader and a 'dependable' ally. US records, quoted in McMahon, op. cit. pp. 278–79.

28. Schlesinger, op. cit., p. 485.

29. He 'displayed interest and vivacity only with Jacqueline.' When reminded of this, Kennedy remarked, 'A lot of our visiting statesmen have that same trouble.' Schlesinger, p. 485.

30. According to US document 690D/760.02, Central File, quoted in Farooq Naseem Bajwa, *Pakistan and the West*, p. 15, President Truman told Avra Warren, US ambassador to Pakistan, that he had a 'disagreeable' time with Nehru, Nehru's attitudes on disputes with Pakistan were 'silly' and he did not observe 'any inclination on the part of Nehru to be reasonable on the Kashmir dispute.' Truman's Secretary of State Dean Acheson described Nehru as 'one of the most difficult men with whom I have ever had to deal.' McMahon, op. cit. p. 56.

31. Quoted from *Robert Kennedy in His Own Words*, and Arthur Schlesinger, *A Thousand Days*, in McMahon, op. cit., p. 281.

32. Schlesinger, p. 487.

33. Dated 26 May 1962.

CHAPTER 7

Relations with China and other Developments

China

Pakistan recognised the People's Republic of China in 1950 soon after the revolution. Relations were amicable and remained on an even keel despite Pakistan's criticism of communism and its increasing cooperation with the United States, as well as tension in Sino–US relations. Even after Pakistan joined SEATO, China criticised the alliance but not Pakistan. Unlike the Soviet Union, it understood that Pakistan's motivation was the need for security against the Indian threat, and not any hostility toward China or any other nation.

More impressive for Pakistan was China's scrupulous avoidance of any partisan pronouncement on Pakistan–India disputes. It did not seek to strengthen relations with India at Pakistan's expense. Even during a visit to India at the height of the 'Hindi-Chini bhai bhai' phase in June 1954, Premier Zhou Enlai did not criticize Pakistan.

Pakistan was less careful in its anti-communist rhetoric. At a conference in Colombo in May 1954,[1] Prime Minister Mohammad Ali Bogra spoke of international communism as 'the biggest potential danger to democracy in the region.' At India's insistence the conference communiqué was more balanced. It called for resistance to interference by 'external communist, [as well as] anti-communist or other agencies.'

Premier Zhou Enlai told the departing Pakistani ambassador that he was hurt by Pakistan's statement, because he regarded Pakistan as a friend. Still, he said he 'fully understood' Pakistan's circumstances.[2] He expressed the hope that Pakistan would follow principles of peaceful coexistence.[3]

Pakistan did not fail to notice Chinese forbearance and henceforth followed a more balanced policy. At the Afro–Asian summit conference in Bandung in April 1955, Bogra asked for a meeting with the Chinese premier; Zhou Enlai insisted on coming over himself. The meeting was remarkably friendly. Zhou readily accepted Bogra's explanation that Pakistan's membership of SEATO was not directed against China.

In the summit conference, the Pakistani prime minister stated that China 'is by no means an imperialist nation and has not brought any other country under her heel.' He especially praised Zhou who 'has shown a great deal of conciliation.' Zhou, playing the role of the statesman that he was, helped to reconcile the differences among participants on the question as to whether the communiqué should refer to colonialism only by the Western powers or by both Soviet and Western powers, by suggesting that it refer to 'colonialism in all its manifestations.'[4]

The Bandung Conference provided an opportunity for Bogra and Zhou to also discuss bilateral relations. Zhou publicly acknowledged Bogra's statement in conversation with him, that Pakistan was not against China, had no fear that China would commit aggression and, further, that if the United States should take aggressive action under SEATO, Pakistan would not be involved, adding that 'through these explanations we achieved a mutual understanding.'[5]

Prime Minister Zhou's visit to Pakistan in December 1956 led to further development of bilateral understanding. The joint communiqué recorded the shared view of the prime ministers that 'the divergence of views on many problems should not prevent the strengthening of friendship between their two countries... They are happy to place on record that there is no real conflict of interests between the two countries.'[6]

Despite better mutual understanding, US pressure on Pakistan at times led to anomalous stances. On the one hand, Pakistan recognized the People's Republic of China and supported its government's claim to China's seat in the UN. On the other, it did not oppose a resolution sponsored by the United States for the postponement of the consideration of the question of China's representation, and instead abstained in 1952 and 1957, and supported the US manoeuvre for several years up to 1960. Similarly, in October 1959, Pakistan voted for a UN General Assembly resolution calling for 'respect for the fundamental human rights of the Tibetan people and for their distinctive cultural and religious life.'[7]

At other times, offence was gratuitous. In April 1959, Ayub Khan made the extraordinary proposal of joint defence with India. Even after Nehru ridiculed the offer by rhetorically asking, 'Joint defence against whom?', Ayub Khan persisted, forecasting that South Asia would become militarily vulnerable in five years to major invasions from the north.[8] To leave no doubt that he meant both China and the Soviet Union he issued yet another statement.[9] Perhaps he 'genuinely believed'[10] that Pakistan and India needed to cooperate to forestall the danger. Perhaps he hoped to convince Nehru to realise the desirability of resolving the Kashmir issue in the interest of defending the region. Or perhaps he was trying to humour Washington.[11] Whatever his reasons, Ayub Khan's statements were incongruent with emergent strategic realities and Pakistan's interests.[12]

It is a tribute to the wisdom and foresight of Chinese leaders that Beijing continued to show extraordinary forbearance, overlooking Pakistan's aberrations. Fortunately, these lapsed into limbo. After 1959, friendship and cooperation between the two countries followed a steady and unswerving path and became a crucial factor for peace in South Asia. No other country has been as comprehending of Pakistan's constraints as China.

By 1960 the Sino–Soviet split began to surface. The United States was already hostile to China, with its naval and air power operating close to China's seaboard. Resolutely resisting both superpowers, China was now concerned also about India, which was giving encouragement to separatist elements in Tibet and evincing an imperious attitude on the boundary issue. Beijing understood even better than before the difficulties Pakistan confronted at the hands of India, backed by the Soviet Union. Sharing adversity, the two countries drew closer.[13] By no means so presumptuous as to enter the contest of giants, Pakistan demonstrated the courage to resist the political and economic pressures of its American ally in grasping China's hand of friendship across the Karakorum Range and breaching the ring the USA, the USSR and India sought to build around China.

Pakistan–China Boundary Agreement, 1962

Pakistan approached China in November 1959 with the proposal for demarcation of the border between the two countries. It was desirable to do this in order to pre-empt any problems. Pakistan was encouraged by China's eminently reasonable posture, manifest in its boundary agreement with Myanmar, in January 1960, to their complete mutual satisfaction. Its boundary agreements with Nepal and Thailand were also amicably negotiated. In March 1961, Pakistan sent a formal note to China proposing negotiations on the boundary. Beijing was still hesitant because the matter involved Kashmir territory and it did not want to have another argument with India. This problem took time to resolve but a formula was found whereby the boundary to be demarcated would be between Xinjiang and the contiguous areas 'the defence of which was under the control of Pakistan' thus by-passing the question of sovereignty over the territory. On 4 May 1962, the two countries announced agreement to begin negotiations.

Started on 12 October 1962, the talks were conducted in a friendly spirit of mutual accommodation, and within two months Pakistan and China reached an agreement (nine days before the Sino–Indian clash).[14] The boundary followed the Karakorum watershed, crossing over K-2, the world's second highest peak. It involved no transfer of territory from the control of either country to the other. Pakistan remembers with gratitude an extraordinary gesture by Premier Zhou Enlai: after the alignment was agreed, the Pakistan government belatedly realised that some grazing lands along the Murtagh River in the Shimshal Pass on the other side of the watershed were historically used by inhabitants of Hunza. It then appealed for an exception to the watershed principle to save hardship to the poor people. Zhou generously agreed to the amendment of the boundary so that an area of 750 square miles remained on the Pakistan side.

The Indian allegation that Pakistan ceded a part of Kashmir territory to China was unfounded. Since a recognised boundary historically did not exist, there could be no question of any such give-away. Pakistan did not transfer any territory that was under its control.

The boundary agreement was motivated by a desire to preclude any controversy between the two neighbours. It was, however, misunderstood by Washington as a tactic of pressure in the context of Kashmir, and considered yet more evidence of 'Pakistan's drift toward Communist China.'[15]

Not too many years later the USA saw that it was mistaken in its biased assumption of a monolithic communist bloc, its distorted view of China as an expansionist state, and its analysis of the Sino–Indian border clash as a defining moment in the history of democracy's crusade against communism. In the early 1960s, however, Washington was intent on isolating China, and pulling India into its orbit was a dominant passion of the time. Pakistan was seen to be an obstruction, and the United States had no hesitation in pulling levers of pressure in its attempt to bring Pakistan into line.

Sino–Pakistan Entente

A unique characteristic of China's policy toward Pakistan was to observe implicit respect for Pakistan's sovereignty. The Chinese leaders did not even proffer unsolicited advice. During exchanges of views with their Pakistani counterparts, they would describe their own experiences and let Pakistanis draw the conclusion if they so wished. When Pakistan embarked on improvement of relations with the Soviet Union in 1960, the Chinese leaders did not try to hold Pakistan back although Beijing–Moscow relations had begun to sour, and even expressed understanding of Pakistan's reasons.

Relations between Pakistan and China continued to deepen in the wake of the boundary agreement and especially after Pakistan defied Anglo–American pressures to join their policy of support for India against China during the Sino–Indian border war. Pakistan also demonstrated a firm independent stance when, despite sanctions imposed by the United States, it established air links with China, breaching the American strategy aimed at containment and isolation of China. Contacts between the leaders of the two countries became frequent. On their way to countries of the Middle East, Africa and Europe, Chinese leaders transited through Pakistan, which provided opportunities for achieving closer sympathetic understand of each other's concerns. In multilateral fora, Pakistan defended Chinese interests.[16]

During his visit to China in March 1965, Ayub Khan was accorded an effusive welcome. Chairman Mao Zedong expressed warm appreciation for Pakistan's support. In the joint communiqué, Pakistan joined China in denouncing the 'two Chinas' policy of the United States. Also 'the two parties noted with concern that the Kashmir dispute remains unresolved and considered its continued existence a threat to peace and security in the region. They reaffirmed that this dispute should be resolved in accordance with the wishes of the people of Kashmir as pledged to them by India and Pakistan.'

Oman: Gwadar Retrocession

In the nineteenth century the Gwadar territory on the Balochistan coast had been given to the Sultan of Oman by the Khan of Kalat on the occasion of his daughter's wedding. It was an obvious anachronism in the post-colonial era. Pakistan sought its return and reunion by amicable negotiation through the UK government. An agreement was reached in 1958 by which the fraternal sultanate ceded the territory to Pakistan. Apart from a modest payment, Pakistan agreed to allow continued recruitment of personnel for the sultanate forces from Gwadar. The peaceful transaction ensured the maintenance of friendly relations between Pakistan and Oman as well as continued enjoyment of benefits of employment in Oman by the people of Balochistan.

Indus Waters Treaty, 1960

As Egypt is said to be the gift of the Nile, Pakistan is the gift of the Indus. Of the thirty-seven million acres of land irrigated by canals from the Indus River and its tributaries, in 1947 over thirty million acres were in Pakistan—an area equal to the irrigated lands in Egypt and Sudan. The Indus and its major tributaries rise in or beyond the Himalayas and flow through Indian-held Kashmir or India. Partition gave India a stranglehold over the rivers flowing south into Pakistan. In 1948, India decided unilaterally to cut off supplies to the canals flowing from headworks under its control, ignoring Pakistan's rights under international law. It also embarked on the construction of the Bhakra Dam on the Sutlej, in order to divert the entire water supply of the river.

In 1950, Pakistan proposed arbitration but India refused. As David Lilienthal, former chairman of the Tennessee Valley Authority wrote in an article: 'No armies with bombs and shellfire could devastate a land so thoroughly as Pakistan could be devastated by the simple expedient of India's permanently shutting off the source of waters that keep the fields and people of Pakistan green.'[17] In 1952, World Bank president Eugene Black offered his good offices for a solution of the dispute that would provide India additional supplies of water without damage to Pakistan, which the two countries accepted. Negotiations over the highly technical issues took eight years to resolve. The Indus Waters Treaty was signed on 19 September 1960. It allocated the waters of the three eastern rivers (Ravi, Beas and Sutlej) for use by India, and the waters of the western rivers (Indus, Jhelum and Chenab) for use in Pakistan, except for (a) domestic and non-consumptive uses of the river waters in the areas under Indian control, and (b) for agriculture, subject to specified limits.

The compromise conceded to India what it wanted, but the World Bank raised the requisite funds for the construction of two large dams at Mangla on the Jhelum and Tarbela on the Indus, and 400 miles of link canals from the western rivers in Pakistan to replace the loss due to diversion of waters of the eastern rivers by India. (Three of the seven link canals carry ten times as much water as the Thames and twice as much as the Potomac). Of the estimated expenditure of $1.3 billion on replacement works, the treaty required India to pay $170 million while the United States contributed over $500 million and the rest was donated largely by Australia, Britain, Canada, Germany and New Zealand.

The Indus Waters Treaty was also farsighted in anticipating problems that might arise in interpretation and implementation of the complex agreement. World Bank experts in law, economics, construction and engineering foresaw as many contingencies as were likely to arise, so that the treaty provides a self-executing mechanism for their peaceful resolution in a professional manner. In the first place, the Permanent Indus Commission, comprising high-level technical representatives of the two sides, has the responsibility to resolve differences of interpretation and ensure smooth implementation. In case the commission is unable to agree on a 'question' of interpretation, the matter can be taken up at the level of government; and if governments also cannot agree, the 'difference' can be referred to a 'neutral expert' to be appointed by the parties or, if they fail to agree, by the World Bank. The decision of the neutral expert is binding. If the difference does not fall in the mandate of the neutral expert or the neutral expert rules that it should be treated as a 'dispute', it has to be submitted to a court of arbitration whose award is final.[18]

India–China War, 1962[19]

Rooted in contested historical claims to territories along almost the entire length of the Sino–Indian border from eastern and northern India and the disputed state of Jammu and Kashmir, the boundary dispute surfaced in 1958 when the Indian government came to know of the Tibet–Xingiang road along Ladakh. India protested that the road was built 'through indisputably Indian territory,' basing this assertion on the McMahon Line drawn in 1914 pursuant to discussions between Henry McMahon and a representative of Tibet whose claim to sovereignty was contested by the Chinese government. China maintained, 'Historically, no treaty or agreement on the Sino–Indian boundary has ever been concluded between the Chinese central government and the Indian government.'[20] It suggested the observance of the line of actual control pending negotiations to delimit the boundary, taking into account both the historical background and the existing realities. India, however, insisted on the acceptance of the McMahon Line. Emboldened by Soviet military supplies and the Kennedy administration's stepped-up economic assistance, while China was under increasing Soviet pressure, in addition to continuing US hostility, India adopted a 'forward policy', hoping to negotiate from a position of strength. Its forces undertook aggressive patrolling and built military posts in the disputed area. The easy conquest of Portuguese ruled Goa in December 1961 made Indian leaders even more reckless. In February 1962 an Indian minister publicly threatened to 'drive out the Chinese forces.' In September India sent a brigade to Thagla Ridge in the northeast.

On 11 October 1962, Nehru gave a call for battle, declaring 'Our instructions are to free our territory. I cannot fix the date; that is entirely for the army.' China repeatedly warned India to desist from military adventurism. Fighting broke out on 20 October. Each side accused the other of firing the first shot. The Indian forces suffered severe losses. General Maxwell Taylor, Chairman, US Joint Chiefs of Staff, said in testimony before a congressional committee that India might have started the war.[21] On 24 October, China, for the third time proposed mutual withdrawals to twenty kilometers from the line of actual control, to be followed by talks. Nehru again rejected the offer.

Nehru appealed to the Western countries as well as the Soviet Union for support and assistance against China. Moscow, despite its growing differences with China, was reluctant to side with India in the border dispute. Britain and the United States responded readily, perceiving in the border clash a golden opportunity to pull India into the West's orbit. On 29 October Kennedy wrote to Nehru offering, 'support as well as sympathy.' The US ambassador in New Delhi, John Kenneth Galbraith, had already embarked on efforts, more pathetic than comic, to coax a request for military aid from Nehru himself, playing on his vanity by telling him that 'he is loved in the US as no one else in India' and assuring him that the request would not imply a military alliance. Once Nehru agreed, Galbraith gleefully reported that Indians were 'pleading for military association.'[22] Forgetting his non-aligned professions, Nehru 'reversed policy 180 degrees to seek military assistance from the United States.'[23]

Promptly, USA and UK started sending planeloads of weapons every day, the former on terms to be negotiated later and the latter gratis.

Israel, too, responded to Nehru's request by sending a shipload of heavy mortar.[24]

Emboldened by the West's support and assistance, India decided, on 14 November, to mount a division-strength attack in the northeast, leading to large-scale hostilities in which the Indian force was routed. Although the fighting was still limited to the border, a frightened Nehru flew into a panic. In a radio address he bade goodbye to Assam. Ignoring the nature of the Himalayan terrain and the approaching winter, when snow would block the passes, New Delhi projected a general war, imagining that the Chinese forces would descend into the Gangetic plane. 'In this mood of crisis, the Prime Minister sent off two startling letters to President Kennedy.'[25] The texts of the two letters have not yet been declassified, apparently to spare embarrassment to the memory of 'the father of nonalignment',[26] but officials then working in the Kennedy administration have variously described one of the two as 'a hysterical letter, a silly letter asking us to bomb China,' a desperate appeal for help 'forgetting the virtues of non-alignment.'[27] Nehru asked the United States to send a dozen squadrons of fighter aircraft to protect India's major cities and two squadrons of B-47 bombers with American pilots to attack Chinese positions.[28]

Kennedy decided to dispatch an aircraft carrier, the USS *Enterprise*,[29] to the Bay of Bengal. To India's, and America's, utter surprise, however, on 21 October China announced a unilateral ceasefire and withdrawal of its forces back to pre-war positions, twenty kilometers behind their claimed boundary, returning to India 'practically all the territory their army gained in the east.'[30]

Pakistan–US Relations Corroded

From its own experience of Indian policy, Pakistan saw that Nehru's tactics regarding the boundary problem with China were of a piece with his postures on Kashmir. He refused to acknowledge the existence of a dispute, claiming the disputed territory was an integral part of India. He spurned Premier Zhou's offers of negotiations and rejected his proposals for mutual withdrawals. He simply wanted China to acquiesce in his interpretation of where the boundary lay.

Pakistan viewed the border conflict as a limited and local affair, precipitated by Indian provocation. The United States and the United Kingdom implicitly accepted, indeed encouraged, Nehru's exaggeration of the Chinese threat and the projection of a border conflict as an invasion and war threatening occupation of India. Ignoring secret testimony by the chairman, of the US Joint Chiefs of Staff, President Kennedy wrote to Nehru saying, 'Our sympathy in the situation is wholeheartedly with you.' When Nehru approached the US for military aid, Washington seized the opportunity with alacrity and agreed to provide arms to India.

Contrary to the pledge of prior consultation Kennedy gave to Ayub Khan a year earlier, he merely informed the Pakistan president of the US decision by letter on 28 October, saying the arms provided to India would be 'for use against China only.'[31] Kennedy went on to suggest Ayub 'signal to the Indians' that Pakistan would not embarrass them. Such a gesture, he said, would do more to bring about a sensible resolution of Pakistan–India differences than anything else.[32]

In his letter of 5 November, Ayub Khan's reply was statesmanlike. While pointing out that Pakistan could not alter its defensive deployments, as 80 per cent of Indian's armed forces remained poised against Pakistan—the bulk of them on Pakistan's borders—he agreed not to take advantage of the situation.[33] The answer, he suggested, lay in the settlement of Kashmir.[34]

Meanwhile, in an aide memoir of 5 November 1962, the United States embassy in Karachi reaffirmed America's 'previous assurances that it will come to Pakistan's assistance in the event of aggression from India against Pakistan.'[35] The communication was obviously drafted rather cleverly to create an illusion of assurance without going any further in defining what coming to Pakistan's assistance meant.

As the US and the UK rushed arms to India, opinion in Pakistan was outraged. People felt betrayed, realizing that the arms would enhance India's offensive capability to the detriment ultimately of Pakistan. Speaking 'in anguish and not in anger,' Foreign Minister Bogra said, in the Pakistan National Assembly, that the US failure to consult Pakistan before deciding to rush arms to India was 'an act of gross unfriendliness.' As for the border clash with China, India 'was making a mountain of a molehill.' Keeping the bulk of its forces poised on Pakistan's border, 'India has adopted a strange method of resisting the Chinese.' If friends of Pakistan and India wanted to see good relations between the two countries and settlement of disputes between then 'Time for reliance on words and assurances has gone.'[36]

Kennedy said he was bewildered as to why Pakistanis were so bitter toward a nation that had done so much to help them.[37] At the same time he said he understood Pakistani concerns and agreed to launch joint efforts with Harold Wilson to promote a Kashmir settlement.

Negotiations on Kashmir, 1962–63

Ambassador Averell Harriman and British Commonwealth Secretary Duncan Sandys were charged by their governments to undertake efforts for a Kashmir settlement. They persuaded Nehru to agree, on 29 November, to a joint statement with Ayub Khan for 'a renewed effort to resolve the outstanding differences... on Kashmir and other related matters.'[38] But Nehru then made complete nonsense of the statement by declaring that 'an upset of the present arrangement would be very harmful to the people of Kashmir as well as to the future relations of India and Pakistan.'[39] As a result, the proposed negotiations were almost aborted, but Duncan Sandys rushed to New Delhi and obtained a clarification from Nehru that he did not intend to limit the scope of the scheduled negotiations.

Six rounds of meetings were held between December 1962 and May 1963 with Zulfikar Ali Bhutto, Minister for Industries, leading the Pakistan side, while Swaran Singh, Minister for Railways, was leader of the Indian side.

At the first meeting, which was held in Rawalpindi, India wasted much time on protesting against the Sino-Pakistan boundary agreement, the conclusion of which had been announced the previous day. After the two sides settled down to business, Pakistan proposed discussion should focus on building on the existing agreement contained in the Security Council resolutions and reports of the UN mediators McNaughton and Dixon, who had suggested regional plebiscites implementing the pledge of a plebiscite. India merely explained why a plebiscite could not be held.

At the second round, in New Delhi in January, the Indian side took the position that they did not consider old proposals of any value. Swaran Singh refused to consider any solution that involved ascertaining the wishes of the people, putting forward a new excuse that if Kashmiri Muslims voted in Pakistan's favour, the Hindus of India would consider their vote as proof of disloyalty to India, and their safety and security would be in danger. India would be bathed in blood. On the basis of this argument, amounting to the use of Indian Muslims as hostages to blackmail Pakistan and the Kashmiri people, he proposed a 'political settlement', implying partition of the state. Pakistan was willing to probe the idea, provided a division was based on the composition of the population and was acceptable to the people of the state, apart from safeguarding economic and strategic interests, defence requirements and control of rivers.

The 'political settlement' idea was further discussed at the third round in February and the fourth round in March. The Indian side suggested division of the state along a boundary broadly corresponding to the ceasefire line, with minor adjustments and modifications. It maintained an adamant position on the Kashmir Valley. The Pakistan side indicated a willingness to consider division along the Pir Panjal watershed in northern Jammu, giving Pakistan the districts of Riasi, Mirpur and Poonch. As India contended the Srinagar–Leh road was essential for defence of Ladakh against China, Pakistan offered to postpone implementation. It further proposed ascertainment of the wishes of the people six months after withdrawal of Indian forces, placing the valley under international control in the interim.

A similar suggestion was made earlier by Ayub Khan through Duncan Sandys. It envisaged placing the valley under international control for 5–10 years as an interim arrangement. Nehru was reported to have turned the idea down.[40] Ayub Khan told an American envoy that any compromise would be unpalatable to many people on both sides. He envisaged a settlement that safeguarded 'honour, security and economic interests.'[41] The idea was, however, soon lost. As the danger of a further flare-up on the border with China receded, Nehru had no incentive in giving even an impression of interest in a settlement with Pakistan.

No progress was achieved at the fifth and sixth rounds in April and May. Instead of narrowing differences, the positions of the two countries became divergent. Before the breakdown of talks, the two sides reverted to their original positions.

President Kennedy was keen to promote a Kashmir settlement and tried to persuade Nehru to join in the effort. However, the priority he attached to this objective suffered as accelerating evolution in the strategic environment opened up opportunities of greater importance to the United States. India emerged as an important factor in the global power and ideological contest, and the value of the regional alliances in Asia was progressively diminishing.

Changing the Strategic Environment

The Sino–Indian border conflict in 1962 coincided with the Cuban missile crisis and emergent differences between USSR and China. Kennedy called it 'a climactic period' and 'a new era in history.' The United States saw in the Sino–Indian border clash an opportunity to court and wean India away from neutrality and the Soviet orbit, into the West's embrace. The time also seemed opportune to intensify pursuit of the other objective of building non-communist India as a rival to communist China and an example to other newly independent countries.

At first the US sought to assure Pakistan that aid to India would not be at the expense of Pakistan's security or the aim of promoting a Kashmir settlement. Kennedy said on 2 November that the US help to India 'in no way diminishes or qualifies our commitment to Pakistan.' Harriman said Kashmir is the most important single question.' On 12 December, Ambassador McConaughy told journalists in Pakistan, 'Washington viewed the Kashmir problem as a matter of extreme urgency.' On 20 December Dean Rusk told Ambassador Aziz Ahmed in Washington, the United States had 'a great interest' in a Kashmir settlement'. Despite these reassuring declarations, it was evident that the primary US objective now was to strengthen India against China.

On 20 December President John Kennedy and Prime Minister Harold Wilson announced the decision to provide $120 million for military aid to India, and help to enable India to raise six additional divisions. Seeking to mollify Pakistan, in a letter dated 22 December, Kennedy assured Ayub Khan the US would 'take any one-sided intransigence on Kashmir into account as a factor in determining the extent and pace of our assistance.' However, other US officials were singing a different tune. Contradicting the president, US ambassador to India, Galbraith said, on 28 December, 'The American assistance is in no way contingent on an India–Pakistan agreement on the Kashmir problem.'

Galbraith played a major part in the failure of the Kashmir talks, by advising Washington it should not allow the Kashmir issue to cause the US to miss the opportunity to win over India. In view of Nehru's role in the grab for Kashmir it is doubtful if he would have considered it a reasonable stance, but he must have been emboldened in his obduracy, by signals from Washington, to harden the posture in negotiations with Pakistan.

By March 1963 little doubt was left about the change in US policy. A committee headed by General Lucius Clay recommended that 'in the interest of our own and free world security, economic and military assistance to India, as well as Pakistan, must continue under present circumstances.' Galbraith's successor, Chester Bowles, declared in May that the United States was 'very anxious to help India' build up military strength against China, adding, 'The only thing to be determined was the amount of military aid that the Indians can absorb.' The joint communiqué issued after talks between President Kennedy and President Radhakrishnan in June stated, 'Both the Presidents recognised the vital importance of safeguarding the freedom, independence and territorial integrity of India for peace and stability not only in Asia but in the world.' On 20 July Kennedy and Macmillan decided to provide a United States–Commonwealth umbrella to India, to familiarize the Indian air force with supersonic fighter-bombers and plan for further military aid to strengthen India against China.

The United States seemed to believe India could successfully compete with China for leadership of Asia. Its strategic thinkers failed to see that few countries in Asia would accept India's leadership so long as it sought to pursue a hegemonic goal. The Indian proclivity to exploit power disparity in order to impose its own preferences on neighbours was responsible for vitiating its relations with them. Had India played fair on a basis of universally recognised principles of inter-state relations, Pakistan could have been a natural friend. American thinkers deliberately exaggerated the Chinese threat. They completely ignored the unilateral ceasefire and withdrawal of forces by China within days of the border clash, falsifying their premise of Chinese expansionism. The United States was to pay a high price for that assumption in Vietnam. Similarly incorrect was the US belief that US withdrawal from Vietnam would have a domino effect.

As the US policy was changing, so also, it should be added, was that of Pakistan. Whilst its relations with China were amicable from the start, Pakistan took timely steps to remove possible irritants and enhance cooperation with this important neighbour, resisting and defying US pressures and sanctions. As early as 1959 Pakistan proposed demarcation of the Sino–Pakistan boundary and an agreement was concluded in 1962. The two countries also agreed to commence air services, and for years PIA enjoyed a virtual monopoly on the new corridor to China. Pakistan extended an effusive welcome to Premier Zhou Enlai in February 1964. Enormous crowds lined his route and many stood on rooftops. His talks with President Ayub Khan were marked by convergent views. In the joint communiqué the Chinese Premier 'expressed the view that the Kashmir dispute would be resolved in accordance with the wishes of the people of Kashmir as pledged to them by India and Pakistan.' The two leaders agreed that an early settlement of the border dispute between China and India 'was necessary in the interest of world peace and the well-being of the peoples of Asia.'

Also, Pakistan took initiatives for normalisation of relations with the Soviet Union. On 1 October 1963, Pakistan allowed transit rights to the Soviet airline via Karachi. Appreciating the gesture, Moscow proposed bilateral talks for improving relations. These began two months later and laid the foundation for President Ayub's visit to USSR in 1965.

Alliance under Strain

The increasing US lurch towards India disturbed Pakistan. The military aid was not very large, but its significance was exaggerated by describing it as 'massive.' If Pakistan–US relations did not deteriorate more than they did it was partly because Pakistan valued the assistance the US provided and partly because the US attached importance to the intelligence facilities in Peshawar.[42]

President Kennedy was philosophical when he received the new Pakistan ambassador, G. Ahmed on 11 August 1963, saying, 'We are conditioned by our history. I can well understand your reaction to our extending military aid to India, but allowance must be made for the special circumstances which occasioned our assistance.' George Ball, who was to visit Pakistan as Kennedy's emissary, spoke with less understanding. He told the Pakistani ambassador that the Pakistan–China relationship was 'very dangerous.' A year after ceasefire on the Sino–India border, he still assumed China was intent on attacking India. He wanted Pakistan and India to join in 'common defence' against China. With that thought in mind, he asked Ayub Khan, on 4 September, what exactly Pakistan had in mind in its relations with China. Ayub Khan said it was normalisation and Pakistan wanted to reduce its political and military commitments, especially in view of the US aid to India.

The US attitude towards Pakistan further stiffened after Lyndon Johnson succeeded John Kennedy. He took a tough line with Pakistan with regard to its developing relations with China. When he met Foreign Minister Zulfikar Ali Bhutto, who went to Washington to attend Kennedy's funeral, Johnson sternly warned that Premier Zhou Enlai's upcoming visit to Pakistan would jeopardize US economic and military aid to Pakistan.[43] The warning was repeated through General Maxwell Taylor, Chairman of Joint Chiefs of Staff, who visited Pakistan in December 1963. Johnson wanted Ayub Khan to know that 'Pakistan's flirtation with China was rapidly approaching the limits of American tolerance'[44]

The US increased aid to India for 1963–64 to $100 million. Its confrontation with China was growing as war in Vietnam reinforced trends in US policy in South Asia. Washington became keener to build up India militarily against China, while Pakistan's entente with China contradicted the US plan for building a coalition of Asian countries against China. De Gaulle's decision to recognise the People's Republic on 27 January 1964 increased Washington's sense of isolation on its China policy. The proposal for a second summit of African and Asian countries placed the US on edge as it apprehended criticism of its Vietnam policy. It considered Pakistan's support for the second Bandung Conference as anti-American. Washington, once opposed to neutrality, now supported a summit of non-aligned countries where China would be absent.

Taylor also informed Ayub Khan that US aid to India would be modest—about $60 million a year. 'This was a worthwhile price,' he said, 'for detaching India from the communist bloc.'[45] The United States actually decided on a $500 million, 5-year programme of military aid for India. Ayub Khan was concerned about the enhanced threat to Pakistan from India, which was engaged in a military expansion programme. In a letter to Johnson on 7 July 1964, he protested against the decision that, he said, 'would oblige Pakistan to reappraise CENTO and SEATO'. Johnson's response was even more curt, warning that the US, too, would be obliged to re-examine its relations with Pakistan if it continued to develop its relations with China. The warnings had little effect. Pakistan continued to strengthen cooperation with China. The United States proceeded to 're-examine its relations with Pakistan.'

Ayub Khan's Visits to China and the USSR

Ayub Khan visited China in March 1965. The welcome accorded to him was described as 'magnificent, enthusiastic, elaborate and colourful.' He held cordial meetings with Chairman Mao and Premier Zhou and spoke of 'lasting friendship and fruitful cooperation' with China. The joint communiqué stressed adherence to the Ten Principles of Peaceful Coexistence, and condemned colonialism and racial discrimination. It reaffirmed that the Kashmir dispute should be resolved in accordance with the wishes of the people of Kashmir as pledged to them by India and Pakistan. At Pakistan's request, no mention was made of Vietnam. The gesture did not impress Washington, however.

A month later, Ayub Khan visited the USSR—the first visit ever by a Pakistani head of state. He held talks with Leonid Brezhnev and Alexei Kosygin. Foreign Minister Gromyko also participated in the talks. The Pakistan delegation included both Foreign Minister Z. A. Bhutto and Foreign Secretary Aziz Ahmed. The Soviet leaders evinced great interest in Pakistan–India relations. They showed understanding for Pakistan's view on Kashmir. They could not explain why they were supplying arms to India if these were not intended for use against Pakistan. In a separate meeting Kosygin agreed to consider Pakistan's request for military equipment. Although the joint communiqué did not mention Kashmir by name, it declared 'resolute support for the peoples who are fighting for the right to determine their future in accordance with their own will' and further stated 'that in order to promote universal harmony, international agreements should be implemented.' At Pakistan's behest, the communiqué was moderately worded, and refrained from referring to Vietnam.

Second Afro–Asian Summit

The idea of convening a second Afro–Asian summit had been under discussion among several countries of the region since 1960. It was strongly supported by China, Indonesia and Pakistan. Even the USSR expressed interest in attending the conference, claiming it was also an Asian country. The conference was to be held in Algiers from 29 June 1965. As the date approached, apprehensions mounted in Washington that the conference, in which North Vietnam would participate, would criticise US policy. In mid-April, a preparatory meeting of eighteen countries was held in Jakarta. Most of the speakers condemned the US bombing of North Vietnam. Foreign Minister Bhutto's statement was moderate but there could be no doubt of Pakistan's sympathy. Pakistan had earlier declined to send even a token military contingent to join the US armed forces in South Vietnam. The Algiers summit was aborted because of overthrow of Ahmed Ben Bella and a bomb blast at the conference venue in Club des Pins.

US Reaction

Neither the scrupulous moderation of communiqués issued following President Ayub Khan's visits to China and the USSR, nor even his extraordinary statement in Beijing, suggesting recognition of US 'legitimate interests' in Asia, made any impression on Washington. Instead, the administration was angered by the success of the Pakistan president's visits. It showed no interest in taking advantage of his contacts to open the door to negotiations for a Vietnam settlement. President Johnson was in a truculent mood. On 17 April 1965 he declared the US objective was 'an independent South Vietnam', forgetting, as Walter Lippman said, 'This was not our original position.'[46]

Reputed as a go-getter and wheeler-dealer inclined to use strong-arm methods, and under tremendous stress because of a failing war in Vietnam, President Johnson decided to punish Pakistan. First he cut off a loan for upgradation of Dhaka airport. On 16 April he announced unilateral postponement of Ayub Khan's visit to the United States, due to begin nine days later. In early July the United States advised the World Bank to defer the meeting of the Pakistan Consortium to pledge aid to Pakistan. First it wanted Pakistan to discuss the political issues. The Pakistan government did not bend in the face of the US pressure. Instead it began to consider refusal to renew the lease for the US base at Badaber.

RCD and IPECC

Allies in CENTO, Iran, Pakistan and Turkey, began to feel the need to supplement and enlarge their one-dimensional military contacts. At a meeting in Istanbul on 22 July 1964 the heads of the three states agreed to promote cooperation in economic and cultural fields, and to that end formed an organisation—Regional Cooperation for Development (RCD). A number of industrial projects were later established by two or all three agreeing to share in investment and production. Although the joint projects were relatively small, RCD symbolised the aspiration of the people of the three countries for closer cooperation.

A similar sentiment grew between Pakistan and Indonesia. They both looked upon African–Asian solidarity as a better alternative to the formation of the non-aligned group, which excluded not only Iran, Pakistan, Philippines, Thailand, etc. but also China, the world's largest and most important developing country. India's motivation in keeping China out was transparent. As Soekarno well remembered, Zhou Enlai had out-shone Nehru as a statesman and leader of great acumen and sagacity at the Bandung Afro–Asian summit in 1955. By keeping China out, India wanted to retain the limelight on itself. Pakistan as well as Indonesia realized, moreover, that India nourished hegemonic ambitions. They cooperated closely in preparations for the second Afro–Asian summit. Such multiple commonalties of interest led the two countries to decide on the formation of Indonesia–Pakistan Economic and Cultural Cooperation (IPECC) in August 1965. IPECC, like RCD, has continued to provide a forum for the promotion of cooperation despite changes in the two countries.

NOTES

1. Convened to support de-colonisation of Indo-China, the summit conference was attended by India, Indonesia, Myanmar, Pakistan and Sri Lanka. Burke, op. cit., p. 174.
2. *Hindu*, Madras, of 27 November 1954 quoted in Burke, op. cit., p. 214.
3. *People's China*, 16 October 1954 quoted in Burke, op. cit., p. 214.
4. Quoted from George McT. Kahin, *The African Asian Conference*, in Burke, op. cit., p. 178.
5. Ibid.
6. Burke, op. cit., p. 215.
7. Quoted from UN records in Burke, op. cit., p. 198.
8. *Times of India*, 24 October 1959.
9. On 9 November 1959, *Reuter* reported Ayub to have said Chinese activities in Tibet and road building in Afghanistan posed a serious threat from the north.
10. Gauhar, p. 197.
11. In an article in *Foreign Affairs* of July 1960, Ayub Khan said: 'I can see quite clearly the inexorable push of the north... in the direction of the warm waters of the Indian Ocean. This push is bound to increase if India and Pakistan go on squabbling with each other.'
12. Prime Minister Z. A. Bhutto said in an article in *Foreign Affairs* in October 1976 that Ayub Khan's joint defence offer was 'humiliating...(and) dangerous...(as) he was serving a notice to China of Pakistan's hostility.' Extracts in *Documents*, ed. Arif, p. 325.
13. Mohammad Yunus, op. cit., 131–32.
14. For all these dates see Altaf Gauhar, op. cit., p. 234.
15. US Embassy, Karachi, press release of September 1963, quoted in Gauhar, op. cit., p. 245.
16. At the Commonwealth summit in 1964, Pakistan opposed a move to declare opposition to 'the Chinese threat.' Bhatty, op. cit. p. 165.
17. The article 'Another Korea in the Making' published in *Colliers*, August 1951, quoted in G. W. Choudhury, op. cit., p. 157.
18. World Bank statement clarified the procedure following Pakistan's reference of the Baglihar issue, *Dawn*, Islamabad, 20 January 2005.
19. Neville Maxwell, *India's China War*; and Stevan A. Hoffman, *India and the China Crisis*, are two well-known works on Sino-Indian relations.
20. Quoted in Maqbool A. Bhatty, *Great Powers and South Asia*, p. 105, from Maxwell.
21. Revealed a year later in *The New York Times* of 29 April 1963; quoted by Aziz Ahmed, manuscript, chapter IX.
22. Quoted from John Kenneth Galbraith, *Ambassador's Journal*, in Gauhar, op. cit., p. 207.

23. Dennis Kux, op. cit., p. 204.

24. Quoted from Maxwell, op. cit., p. 410, in Gauhar, op. cit., p. 504.

25. Dennis Kux, op. cit., p. 207.

26. Sudhir Ghosh, *Gandhi's Emissary*, pp. 326–338, quoted in Altaf Gauhar, op. cit., p. 500.

27. Altaf Gauhar, op. cit., pp. 497–517

28. Kux, op. cit., p. 207, based on Hoffman, op. cit., pp. 206–208.

29. Ironically, the same ship was considered by India as a symbol of US hostility when it was sent by Nixon in December 1971.

30. Kux, op. cit., p. 208.

31. Kennedy's letter of 28 October 1962 to Ayub, quoted in Kux, op. cit., p. 205.

32. Ayub Khan, *Friends not Masters*.

33. Some of the president's colleague, including Z. A. Bhutto, thought that his decision was a mistake. Ambassador Aziz Ahmed was of the view that it would have been out of character for Pakistan to stab India in the back; also that would have left an intensely bitter trail, besides antagonising the big powers.

34. The assurance from Pakistan sought by the Western powers was given, though not in so many words.' Quoted from Pakistan's *White Paper On the Kashmir Dispute*, Yusuf Buch suggested in his paper 'Kashmir and the Big Powers' presented at the International Seminar on Fifty Years of Kashmir Dispute, at Muzaffarabad on 24 August 1997.

35. US National Security Archives, NEA/PAB: R K McKEE:gn, dated 23 May 1977, quoted by Altaf Gohar in *Ayub Khan*, p. 196, Footnote 1.

36. Mohammad Ali Bogra, statement of 22 November 1962, *Documents*, ed. Arif, pp. 213–215

37. US Memo of Kennedy–Shoaib meeting, October 9, 1963, quoted in McMahon, op. cit., p. 303.

38. A statement to that effect by Ayub and Nehru was announced on 29 November 1962, ref. Gauhar, op. cit., p. 217.

39. Gauhar, op. cit., p. 219.

40. *New York Times* of 11 February 1963 quoted in G. W. Choudhury, op. cit., p. 73.

41. Gauhar, op. cit., p. 230.

42. Kux, op. cit., p. 213.

43. Bhutto was 'deeply upset and disturbed' at the discourtesy shown to him, gleefully noted Talbot. A White House aide thought 'Bhutto was asking for it.' McMahon, op. cit., p. 307.

44. McMahon, op. cit., p. 314.

45. Quoted by Gauhar, op. cit., p. 249.

46. *Washington Post*, 17 April 1965, quoted in Aziz Ahmed, mauscipt, p. 276.

CHAPTER 8

The Pakistan–India War, 1965

The Pakistan–India 'Kashmir' war in 1965 was the culmination of a process of the rise and fall of expectations of a peaceful settlement of the Kashmir dispute, popular agitation and state repression in the India-held state, jingoism triggered by border clashes in the Rann of Kutch, a limited operation born of frustration and desperation conceived by the Pakistan government to draw international attention, and unintended escalation. In the perspective of history, leaders on both sides seemed to have lost control over actions decided under pressure, provoking like reactions and allowing the build-up of momentum that pushed them into an unwanted war neither side had planned.

The fundamental cause of tensions lay in the failure to settle the festering Kashmir dispute. The ceasefire in the state was defined in the 1949 Security Council resolution as the first step toward the holding of a plebiscite under UN auspices to determine the question of the accession of the state. Accepted by Pakistan as well as India, the resolution constituted an international agreement requiring implementation by the parties. But India concocted one pretext after another to evade its obligation. Agreement on the quantum of troops India could retain in the state proved impossible. Even before Pakistan signed a defence assistance agreement with the United States, Prime Minister Nehru began using the assistance Pakistan might receive as representing a change in the situation, though how that could affect the rights of the people of the state defied logic. Then India invented the argument that if the Muslims of Kashmir opted to accede to Pakistan that would trigger a Hindu backlash and massacre of Indian Muslims. Another pretext for refusal to implement the resolution was that continued hold over Kashmir was a necessity for maintaining the integrity of India, otherwise, its unity would be destroyed.[1] In the process, the pledge to the people of the state and to the United Nations was relegated, as India sought to freeze the status quo and perpetuate its occupation of two-thirds of the state. This was unjustified in law and unacceptable to Pakistan.

Rise and fall of hopes. Expectations rose in 1962, as a result of American and British intercession with India during the Sino–Indian border clash, that purposeful negotiations with Pakistan for a peaceful settlement of the festering Kashmir dispute would be held. If Pakistan first thought India might be serious about settling the dispute to avert a two-front situation, it was disabused soon after the negotiations began. India stalled earnest negotiations. Although the panicky perception of the border clash as a Chinese invasion aimed at conquering and occupying India was soon proved incorrect, India continued negotiations with Pakistan merely to keep the eager allies against China in tow. Meanwhile, with India in tow they too, lost interest. Their strategy focused not on promoting a Kashmir settlement, but on drawing neutral India away from its bias in favour of the USSR towards their own orbit. After the border war ended and India received large quantities of weapons, it reverted to its rigid position on Kashmir, refusing to consider a solution in conformity with the plebiscite principle. As six rounds of fruitless talks collapsed, opinion in Pakistan blamed Ayub Khan for having missed the opportunity to promote decisively a peaceful settlement.

Pakistani disappointment over the failed talks was soon followed by anger when, in October 1963, India initiated legal manoeuvres to erode the disputed status of Kashmir. The puppet prime minister of the state, Bakhshi Ghulam Mohammad, who was installed by New Delhi and sustained in power through rigged elections, announced changes in the constitution of the state designed to bring Kashmir on a par with the states of India. The designation of *sadr-i-riyasat* (president of state) would be abolished, and the title replaced with 'governor'. Also, the head of government of Jammu and Kashmir would no longer be called prime minister but chief minister. Nehru announced in November that a 'gradual erosion' of the special status of Kashmir was in progress. Pakistan protested, denouncing the proposed changes as 'clearly illegal' and a 'flagrant violation of India's commitments'.

Deeply disturbed by New Delhi's moves, evidencing once again the Indian design to annex the state against their will, the Kashmiri people launched an agitation which assumed massive proportions following the theft of *moo-e-muqaddis* (holy hair of the Prophet) from the Hazratbal shrine. Attributing the crime to Indian authorities, the Kashmiri people poured out in a spontaneous eruption. Demonstrations of unprecedented proportions were held in cities and towns across the occupied valley. Even after the Indian authorities announced the recovery of the relic, the agitation did not cease. Instead, it took a political direction with the Kashmiri people demanding an opportunity to exercise heir right of self-determination. In the months following December 1963, Kashmir was in the grip of a crisis, with the administration in collapse and India resorting once again to repression against the unarmed Kashmiri people. Pakistan appealed to the UN Security Council, which held lengthy debates in February and May 1964, but was prevented by the threat of a Soviet veto not only from taking any effective action but even from reaffirming its previous resolutions on the Kashmir question. This failure on the part of the apex organ of the United Nations was yet another blow to prospects of peace between Pakistan and India. A proverbial 'unkindest cut' was the remark, by the US ambassador to the UN, Adlai Stevenson, in a conversation with Foreign Minister Bhutto, that the US felt Pakistan kept bringing Kashmir to the Security Council merely for 'internal propaganda.' Clearly, the United States was becoming unsympathetic.

Hopes rose again in April 1964, when Nehru decided to release Sheikh Mohammad Abdullah, the dismissed and imprisoned former prime minister of Indian-occupied Jammu and Kashmir. Called the 'Lion of Kashmir' for leading popular protests against the oppressive rule of the maharaja in the 1930s, he was once again considered a leader of stature capable of bringing peace to the troubled state. His popularity had declined in 1947 when he allowed himself to be duped to endorse Indian military intervention and paraded internationally as proof of Kashmiri preference for India, but it had recovered after he reminded India of its plebiscite pledge and suffered a decade of incarceration for upholding the right of the Kashmiri people to self-determination.

Whether Nehru wanted only to use Abdullah again merely to pacify the Kashmiri people and divert international opinion, or whether, by now old and sick and possibly penitent for the excesses he had ordered against his friend and ally, Nehru had come round to realize that there was no escaping a settlement acceptable to the Kashmir people, remains unclear. Abdullah, however, believed that Nehru wished for a resolution that might satisfy the Kashmiri people.

The assessment that India was inclined to settle the Kashmir question was encouraged by the public stance taken by Jayaprakash Narayan, a leader respected in India for his advocacy of morality in politics. In a courageous article[2] he exploded some of the myths India had fostered. The highly suspect elections held by India in Kashmir, Narayan argued, did not represent a vote for integration with India. He ridiculed the argument that self-determination by the people of

Kashmir would trigger countrywide communal rioting and prove a prelude to the disintegration of India. He argued that it was not only silly but implied that India was held together by force. In essence, Narayan advocated that India should rethink its position in the light of not only its own interests but also those of Pakistan. The two countries, he said, could prosper only if they cooperated.

In this hopeful atmosphere, Sheikh Abdullah came to Pakistan in May 1964. He led Ayub Khan to believe that Nehru and India were sincere in wanting a settlement. After extended discussions of an exploratory nature he suggested that Ayub should visit New Delhi for a meeting with Nehru. Ayub agreed. The next day, 27 May, Nehru died, and with him perished yet another hope.

The new Indian prime minister, Lal Bahadur Shastri publicly pledged to continue Nehru's policy but he did not follow up Abdullah's suggestion for Ayub Khan's visit to India. A brief meeting between Shastri and Ayub Khan at Karachi airport on 12 October 1964 went off without promise of progress. Not only that, in December 1964 the Indian government resumed moves aimed at the merger of Kashmir with India through the application of the Indian constitution enabling it to impose presidential rule and extend Indian laws to Kashmir. Here again was another proof of Indian treachery, speaking of negotiations but acting unilaterally in pursuit of its illegitmate design.

Clash in Kutch

The boundary in the Rann of Kutch, a low-lying marsh wedged between the province of Sindh and the Indian state of Gujarat that floods during the monsoon season, was the subject of dispute a dating to before 1947 between the princely state of Kutch and the British government. Although the boundary was not demarcated, an area of about 3,500 square miles north of the 24th parallel was contested. After Independence, India claimed the entire territory and in 1956 sent its forces to seize the Chhad Bet high ground. Pakistan protested but India did not begin negotiations until 1960. Meanwhile, the two countries agreed to maintain a ceasefire. In violation of the agreement, the Indian forces advanced to the north in January 1965, and tried to establish new posts and obstruct Pakistani patrols in the disputed area. Pakistan sent in forces to stop India from solving the dispute unilaterally by force. As both sides strengthened their forces in the Rann, fighting flared up in April. The Pakistani forces surrounded the Indian contingent and could have captured it but President Ayub ordered restraint. The danger of further escalation was averted partly due to the approaching monsoon. More importantly, the British government persuaded the two sides to agree to a ceasefire on 1st May.

Indirect but intense negotiations were then held through British high commissioners, Maurice James in Islamabad and John Freemen in New Delhi. Foreign Secretary Aziz Ahmed ensured that the agreement, signed on 30 June 1965, provided for a time-bound, self-executing mechanism for settlement of the dispute peacefully. The agreement gave two months for the two sides to try to resolve the issue through bilateral negotiation. If that failed they would submit the dispute to arbitration by a tribunal, to be constituted within four months, with the UN Secretary General designating its chairman. Both sides further agreed that the tribunal's award 'shall not be questioned on any grounds whatsoever,' that it would be implemented as soon as possible, and until then the tribunal would remain in being.

Relying on evidence as to where the traditional boundary was, the tribunal awarded 350 square miles to Pakistan, a mere 10 per cent of the territory under dispute.[3] Interestingly, Pakistan was satisfied that the dispute was honourably resolved. India got 90 per cent of the disputed territory but was still indignant. Always wanting to settle disputes on its own terms, it vowed never again to accept third-party mediation or impartial adjudication.

The demonstrated inefficacy of negotiations where one party seeks to impose its own preferred solution on the other has been illustrated over and over again in Pakistan–India disputes, even in comparatively minor disputes including that involving the residual issue of Sir Creek at the western terminus of the boundary in the Rann. Officials of the two countries have held innumerable meetings over three decades but failed to agree on the boundary in the creek, entailing endless suffering for poor fishermen from both sides. Hundreds of them are arrested in recurrent cases of trespass and spend long periods in prison losing their boats to confiscation.

In normal circumstances the agreement to settle the Kutch dispute peacefully might have contributed to improvement of Pakistan–India relations. But circumstances between Pakistan and India are seldom normal. India fumed over what it perceived to be a reverse in the Rann of Kutch. In a statement on 29 April, Prime Minister Shastri threatened that India would fight Pakistan at a time and place of its own choosing. Only Jayaprakash Narayan, who later came to be revered in India as Sarvodaya leader, had the vision and the wisdom to commend the

Kutch agreement 'as an object lesson in peace-keeping' which should be applied to all disputes 'including that of Kashmir.'[4] Most Indian politicians and commentators considered the arbitration agreement humiliating and denounced it in Lok Sabha in 'extremely bellicose' speeches.[5] In effect, the Kutch clash, by making India want to settle a score and Pakistan over-confident, proved to be one further stumble toward war, which came within five months, as the Kashmir cauldron came once again to the boil.

At the same time as domestic opinion was fired up by clashes and jingoistic statements, international restraints were weakened. US diplomacy allowed itself to be placed on the defensive during the Kutch crisis. While both sides used American arms, India was vehement in protest against the use of American weapons by Pakistan though it felt free to use Soviet as well as American weapons against Pakistan. Washington announced an embargo on the further supply of arms or spare parts. Apparently even-handed, the decision was weighted against Pakistan because almost all of its equipment was of US origin while the restriction had little impact on India, whose arsenal was mainly of Soviet origin. President Johnson also ordered discontinuation of any additional US aid or loans. Here again the decision worked to Pakistan's detriment; the World Bank Consortium for India had already met and the US had pledged aid, while the meeting of the Consortium for Pakistan, which was scheduled for later, had to be postponed, contributing to the build up of a mood of desperation in Pakistan. Americans, Ayub exploded, were 'power drunk.' Pakistan, he said on another occasion, was seeking 'new friends, not new masters.'[6]

Tension built up further when India took additional steps to integrate occupied Kashmir. Abdullah and his colleague, Mirza Afzal Beg, leader of the Plebiscite Front, were arrested in May 1965 on their return from abroad, having had meetings with leaders of Muslim countries during Haj and with Premier Zhou Enlai in Cairo. The Indian moves triggered another popular upsurge in Kashmir with Mirwaiz Mohammad Farooq, leader of the Awami Action Committee, joining the Gandhi-style non-violent disobedience movement. India unleashed its forces to crush the struggle in the state.

Operation Gibraltar

Recurrent popular uprisings in occupied Kashmir and their brutal repression by India, and the rise and fall of hopes for a settlement through peaceful means, fostered mounting frustration in Pakistan. Official thought in the latter part of 1964 turned to what else might be done to thaw the situation and jolt the world community into recognizing the urgency of fulfilling the pledge given by India, Pakistan and the United Nations to let the Kashmiri people themselves determine their future. Some in positions of influence believed it was morally incumbent on Pakistan to do something to press for a Kashmir settlement, before India's burgeoning military expansion aggravated power disparity as a result of growing supplies by USA and the concessional sale of the latest MIG aircraft, armour and artillery by the USSR.

President Ayub Khan, too, was exasperated by India's refusal to agree to a peaceful settlement of the Kashmir question. He was moved by the heroic struggle of the people of Algeria and Vietnam, and his and the army's confidence grew after the encounter in the Rann of Kutch, though he was still averse to war. However, he appointed a group of high-ranking officials to suggest appropriate means. Chaired by Foreign Secretary Aziz Ahmed it was called the Kashmir Publicity Committee. It reported directly to President Ayub Khan. Although controversy surrounds its precise recommendations, Ayub Khan agreed to the preparation of a plan by the GHQ.

The plan named Gibraltar, prepared by Major General Akhtar Hussain Malik, was approved. Calling for incursions by Kashmiri volunteers into India-held Kashmir, it was based on three assumptions–people in Kashmir would rise to support the guerillas, a large-scale Indian offensive against Azad Kashmir was unlikely, and the possibility of attack across the international border could be ruled out–all of which turned out to be wrong.[7]

Escalation to War

The volunteers entered Kashmir in August. Poorly equipped for survival in the cold and desolate conditions in the high mountains on the way, they were not joined by the Kashmiri people, who had not been informed or prepared for an uprising. Nevertheless, the guerillas inflicted heavy damage on the Indian forces. To cope with the situation the Indian authorities decided to mount a major offensive across the ceasefire line and occupied a large territory in the Kargil area in the north and the Haji Pir Pass between Uri and Poonch, posing a threat to Muzaffarabad, the capital of Azad Kashmir. Now the Pakistani side had no alternative but to respond. It decided to launch an attack in the Chamb area from Pakistan territory. As the force commanded by Major General Akhtar Malik advance toward Akhnur, a nodal point on the transport and supply link between Jammu and the Kashmir Valley, India decided to up the ante by launching an offensive across the international border. Actions and reactions thus led step by step inexorably, to a war neither side had planned.

The Indian forces crossed the international boundary before dawn on 6 September. Their offensive aimed at the capture of Lahore, Pakistan's second largest city, twenty miles from the Indian border. The Pakistan army was caught unprepared but legendary acts of heroism and sacrifice halted the Indian thrust.

The small but highly professional Pakistan air force went on the offensive and attacked a number of Indian bases on the evening of 6 September, inflicting severe losses. The Indian air force launched a counter-attack on 8 September but was checkmated. Particularly bold was the initiative taken by the out-numbered contingent in East Pakistan. It not only rose in defence but took the battle into enemy airspace, bombing targets in India in retaliation for the Indian bombing of Dhaka and Chittagong. Over a few days, the PAF shot down seventy-five Indian aircraft for the loss of nineteen of its own, clearing the Pakistani airspace. The Indian air force then receded to a passive role. Even Pakistan's tiny navy made an audacious foray into Indian territorial waters to attack Dwarka, a naval base 200 miles from Karachi. It captured almost a hundred coastal ships. The Indian navy did not join the battle.

On 9 September, the Pakistan army launched a major offensive in the Khem Karan area towards Amritsar. The armoured division made good progress but then became bogged down as the Indian forces flooded the countryside by breaching an irrigation canal. The Indian armour then counter-attacked in the Sialkot area. The biggest tank battle of the war was fought in the Chavinda area, containing the Indian advance aimed at cutting off Wazirabad, a communications nodal point.

Considering the disparity of size and resources between the two countries and their force levels, the Pakistani armed forces can be legitimately proud of their performance in the war. Pakistan made marginally larger territorial gains[8] but the war ended in a stalemate. Neither side achieved any decisive break-through.

The UN Security Council adopted its first resolution on 4 September, calling for a ceasefire and withdrawal of all armed personnel to the positions held by them before 5 August, the date on which, according to UN's information, armed men began to cross the ceasefire line. Neither this nor the resolution of 6 September was acceptable to Pakistan. In reply to Secretary General U. Thant's letter asking for implementation of the ceasefire, Ayub Khan said that a 'purposeful' resolution must provide for a self-executing arrangement for settlement of the Kashmir dispute. India, on its part, was willing to order a ceasefire but not to withdraw from areas in Kashmir.

China took the lead in relieving Indian pressure on Pakistan. On 27 August, Beijing issued a strong protest against Indian 'acts of aggression and provocation' along China's border. Rejecting India's denial, China demanded, on 8 September, an end to India's 'frenzied provocation activities.' On 16 September, China delivered an ultimatum. Unless India dismantled its military structures on the Chinese side of the border, stopped incursions into China and returned livestock and kidnapped civilians 'within three days' it would have to bear 'full responsibility for all consequences.' On 19 September, China extended the ultimatum by three days.[9]

The threat of expansion of the war served to inject a sense of urgency into the deliberations of the Security Council. It passed a resolution on 20 September which went beyond earlier resolutions. Besides demanding a ceasefire and withdrawals it promised to consider 'what steps could be taken to assist towards a settlement of the political problems underlying the present conflict.' This resolution was accepted by Pakistan and India on 22 September. Not all of Ayub Khan's advisers agreed but the armed forces, running short of ordnance and spares, favoured immediate acceptance.

In accepting the resolution, Pakistan attached weight to the promise given by the premier organ of the United Nations, that it would go beyond a mere return to the *status quo ante* and contribute to the building of permanent peace by promoting a settlement of the 'underlying', that is, the Kashmir, dispute. The hope thus generated was, however, to prove illusory. In making this pledge, the Council was not moved by Pakistani negotiating strength or the inherent logic of the proposition. The great powers were concerned about the danger of expansion of the war, with China issuing one warning after another to India in the context of the Sino–Indian border problems as well as statements of support for Pakistan.

Stance of Foreign Powers[10]

China's Support. In the 1965 crisis, China extended full support to Pakistan, both directly and implicitly. Foreign Minister Chen Yi and the Chinese foreign ministry used vivid language to manifest their friendship. In transit through Karachi on 4 September, Marshal Chen expressed support for 'the just action taken by Pakistan to repel Indian armed provocations.' On 7 September, China condemned India's 'criminal aggression' against Pakistan and charged India with trying to 'bully its neighbours, defy public opinion and do whatever it likes.'[11] It further declared on 12 September that its non-involvement in the Kashmir dispute 'absolutely does not mean that China can approve of depriving the Kashmiri people of their right of self-determination or that she can approve of Indian aggression against Pakistan.'

China responded generously to Pakistan's request for assistance. Apart from providing munitions and spare parts, China was prepared to fly in the material by fighter aircraft. Ayub Khan, apprehending adverse reaction from the United States, asked for their supply by sea.

Allies. The available record does not indicate that Pakistani leaders gave any advance consideration to the applicability of the alliances in the event of war with India. One obvious explanation for the omission could be that they did not anticipate Indian aggression, projecting the conflict to remain confined to the state. Evidently not sanguine about assistance by the allies, they made a belated and half-hearted attempt to invoke the alliances, realising that not all the allies agreed that India was the aggressor. The SEATO council did not meet even for consultations and CENTO could not be activated. The UK backtracked after India raised a storm over Prime Minister Wilson's criticism of Indian aggression.

USA. The US response to the outbreak of war between Pakistan and India was one of frustration. Finding its policy in South Asia in a shambles, with Pakistan and India using US-supplied arms to fight each other rather than against its enemies, the US adopted a neutral, hands-off stance, leaving it to the Security Council to promote an end to the war. On 8 September, the US decided to stop the supply of arms to Pakistan and India. When the Pakistan foreign minister protested that the US decision to cut off defence supplies amounted to punitive action against an ally, the US ambassador said he considered Pakistan to have provoked the war. Ayub Khan felt 'let down.'

The US view that it was not bound to come to Pakistan's assistance provoked a predictable Pakistani reaction of betrayal. The 1959 bilateral defence agreement had stated, 'the US regards as vital to its national interest and to world peace the preservation of the independence and integrity of Pakistan.' The Ayub–Kennedy communiqué of 13 July 1961 reaffirmed commitment to 'the preservation of the independence and integrity of Pakistan', and the US embassy aide memoir of 5 November 1962 assured assistance to Pakistan 'in the event of aggression from India.' Washington did not interpret the Indian attack as aggression.

'The seeming even-handedness was deceptive,' as Henry Kissinger later noted, because 'the practical consequence was to injure Pakistan, since India received most of its arms either from Communist nations or from its own armouries.'[12]

Washington's hopes of balanced relations with both Pakistan and India proved fallacious, and finding itself reviled in both countries by governments as well as the public, the US sought to wipe the whole slate clean. President Johnson did not respond to Ayub Khan's public appeal, on 13 September, to play a role to establish peace in the region; what stirred Washington a few days later was China's ultimatum to India. The US and Britain then began to play an active role in the Security Council in order to secure a ceasefire, promising that they would promote an urgent settlement of the Kashmir question.[13]

Other Friends. President Soekarno of Indonesia extended memorable assistance, readily agreeing to provide some MIG aircraft. It sent two submarines and four missile boats. By the time they reached Karachi, Pakistan had agreed to a ceasefire. Iran and Turkey provided planeloads of arms and ammunition, though the two CENTO allies could not send equipment imported from the United States because of American restrictions on transfer to another country. The United States embargoed the supply of defence equipment, including spare parts, that constrained Pakistan because most of its war weapons were of US origin.

No country blamed Pakistan for its attempt to thaw the festering Kashmir dispute, whilst a large number of countries criticised India for aggression across the international border and several provided memorable assistance to Pakistan. President Nasser, though he often favoured non-aligned India, echoed sympathy for Pakistan and endorsed the Arab summit's communiqué, which called upon India and Pakistan to resolve the Kashmir dispute 'in accordance with the principles and resolutions of the United Nations.' Prime Minister Kosygin 'took exception to India's crossing the international border,' reflecting a change in its erstwhile blanket support to India. Prime Minister Harold Wilson was 'deeply concerned' when the Indian forces 'attacked Pakistan territory across the international frontier.' Only Yugoslavia sided with India, and the Malaysian representative in the Security Council, a person of Indian origin, made remarks so offensive as to provoke Pakistan to cut off diplomatic relations.

Ceasefire. Pakistan was at first averse to a ceasefire without a UN commitment to promoting a settlement of the Kashmir question. But soon it came under pressure from its allies, the USA and the UK. Also, its capacity to wage a long war was limited. President Ayub Khan decided to accept the resolution adopted by the Security Council on 20 September. 'Convinced that an early cessation of hostilities is essential as a first step towards a peaceful settlement of the outstanding differences between the two countries on Kashmir and other matters,' the Council 'decided' to consider 'what steps should be taken to assist towards a settlement of the political problem underlying the present conflict' as soon as the ceasefire took effect.[14] Not for the first time did the Security Council fail to pursue its decision, however.

The Tashkent Declaration

With both the Unites States and the UK loath to take an initiative, the field was left open for Soviet diplomacy to promote a post-war settlement. Prime Minister Kosygin offered his good offices to work for a settlement between Pakistan and India. Pakistan was initially reluctant, entertaining misgivings on account of the Soviet Union's pro-India policy ever since Pakistan joined the western alliances. But it decided to accept the Soviet proposal not only because there was no alternative on offer but also because, in recent years, Moscow was less partisan. Ayub Khan's visit to Moscow the previous April ended on a positive note, with the Soviet leaders pleased to be told that Pakistan intended to terminate the lease for Badaber. Also, Moscow now had a stake in ensuring disengagement between Pakistan and India, and thus prevent a dangerous polarisation between China and the Soviet Union, one backing Pakistan and the other India.

Before going to Tashkent, Ayub Khan visited London and Washington in December. Johnson told him that the alliance between the United States and Pakistan was over.[15] The United States might provide economic aid to Pakistan in future, but that would hinge on Pakistan's willingness to curtail its ties with China. It became evident that Washington had decided to lower its profile in South Asia.

The Pakistan delegation to the Tashkent Conference, 4-10 January 1966, was internally divided on how far to go in pressing for settlement of the Kashmir dispute. The Security Council resolution envisaged some effort to this end. It was not illogical to hope that the Soviet Union would work for progress in that direction. Some believed Pakistan could get India to agree to the creation of a mechanism for settlement. Others were of the view that neither did the stalemated war permit Pakistan to adopt a strong negotiating posture, nor could the Soviet Union be expected to pressurise India to agree to settle the Kashmir dispute. Ayub Khan himself was clear about the priority need for disengagement.

The Tashkent Declaration provided for the withdrawal of forces to positions held on 5 August 1965, repatriation of prisoners of war, and return of high commissioners to their posts. The declaration provided for further meetings between the two sides 'on matters of direct concern to both countries.' It made no direct reference to the crucial Kashmir question. Pakistan's effort to include a provision for compulsory settlement of the dispute was opposed by India. Prime Minister Shastri, though he recognised the desirability of a settlement, told Ayub Khan that as a 'pygmy succeeding a giant' his position did not permit him to change India's stance. The Soviets, too, considered the Kashmir question too 'complicated' and the Pakistani demand impractical. Kosygin had to work hard to evolve the ambiguous formulation that the two sides 'will continue meetings both at the highest and at other levels on matters of direct concern to both countries.' Ayub Khan's agreement to this formulation, though eminently rational under the circumstances, was to spark a bitter controversy in Pakistan.

Official propaganda during the war had built up an impression of Pakistani forces having gained great advantage, if not victory, over India. Not for the first time did state propaganda delude its own people. It was difficult enough to understand why Pakistan accepted the ceasefire when Pakistan was doing so well. Even more baffling was the failure to secure any advance toward a settlement of the Kashmir dispute. The Tashkent Declaration came as an anti-climax to the high hopes that propaganda had built up. It exposed Ayub Khan to baseless accusations of squandering at the negotiating table what the armed forces had won on the battlefield. Bhutto later exploited this myth to considerable political advantage.

The provision for bilateral meetings in the Tashkent Declaration papered over the gulf between the two sides on the purpose of such meetings. The cover was torn apart at the first meeting held between their foreign ministers at Rawalpindi in 1966. The Pakistani side interpreted the declaration as requiring recognition of the 'special importance of reaching a settlement of the Jammu and Kashmir dispute.' The Indian side did not agree, joining only in the statement that 'all disputes' should be resolved. According to Z. A. Bhutto, this meant India was willing to hold discussions for settlement of the Kashmir dispute. Sardar Swaran, however, said India was willing to discuss any dispute including Kashmir, but India's sovereignty over Kashmir was not negotiable. What then was the purpose of negotiation? The stalemate illustrated the futility of further meetings which were, therefore, not held.

The hiatus in India's logic was obvious also to the people of Kashmir. Just as Pakistan's policy of alliances in the 1950s could not detract from Nehru's pledges and the UN resolutions recognising the right of the people of Kashmir to self-determination, neither the 1965 war nor the Tashkent Declaration could be a valid reason for depriving them of their inalienable right. Their restlessness was demonstrated in recurrent outbreaks of protests and agitation.

Kosygin was disappointed at the lack of progress in Pakistan–India relations. In 1968 he exhorted the two countries to resolve their disputes, as that would 'meet the vital interests of the two countries as well as of universal peace.' Not for the first time, India ignored an earnest and reasonable appeal.

Post-War Controversy. 'Victory finds a hundred fathers but defeat is an orphan.' The aphorism[16] was illustrated once again after the 1965 war. Controversy continues to envelop history in a fog that has only thickened with contradictory claims and disclaimers by former officials. The records of the period have not been released and it is even doubtful they exist.

A cautious military leader, Ayub Khan initially rejected the plan for sending armed volunteers into Indian-held Kashmir because it involved unacceptable risk.[17] Although he later agreed, he still believed the incursions would not trigger a war. That he did not anticipate war is also corroborated by his decision to allow a change of command of the Pakistan air force. Air Marshal Asghar Khan who had led the air force for eight years was allowed to retire on 23 July, two weeks before incursions began across the ceasefire line, even though his successor, Air Marshal Nur Khan, had been away from the force for six years, seconded to Pakistan International Airlines. Neither the air force nor the navy was informed of Operation Gibraltar and the fact that the army did not prepare for the contingency of war is further evidence of his anti-war intentions.

From Asghar Khan's account, Ayub Khan emerges as 'kind, intelligent and shrewd' but not logical. Even as late as 4 September, when war was imminent, 'Ayub Khan did not feel that the Indians would react so decisively,' and 'there was nothing to worry about' as he was assured by Foreign Minister Bhutto, 'Pakistan's incursions into Azad [sic] Kashmir would not provoke the Indians to extend the area of hostilities along the Indo–Pakistan border.'[18]

Zulfikar Ali Bhutto advocated an activist policy, believing it was morally incumbent on Pakistan to do something to press for a Kashmir settlement. But he, too, does not emerge as a farsighted strategist and some of his critics go to the extent of thinking he was devious. They accuse him of deliberately misleading Ayub Khan to believe that in the existing global and regional situation the conflict would remain confined to Kashmir.[19] According to Asghar Khan, Ayub Khan said Bhutto had 'assured' him Gibraltar would not lead to a general war. Other critics attribute the blunder to 'foreign affairs experts' who were alleged to have given a similar assessment.

Assuming that such assessment was, in fact, given, not only those who gave it should be faulted; acceptance of the assessment at face value and calling it 'assurance' projects Ayub Khan as well as his apologists as naïve analysts.

The inescapable fact is that the decision to send armed volunteers across the ceasefire line, however limited its scope, was bound to provoke a reaction. If Bhutto and 'foreign affairs experts' failed to foresee the consequences, they were not the only ones to do so. Nor is it clear whether or not they had access to the details of the plan. Foreign Secretary Aziz Ahmed told the author at the time of the war that he was taken aback by reports in the press on 9 August. Not only did he not know the date for the beginning of the operation, the number of armed men who were reported to have crossed the ceasefire line particularly surprised him. Quantity made a qualitative difference.

Certainly hubris fostered by the battle victory in Kutch misled some to believe the Indian political leadership was not bold enough to pick up the gauntlet.[20] Whatever preparations were made for the contingency of war were too little, too late. Not until June was approval given for an additional budgetary allocation of 900 million rupees (then equal to 200 million dollars) to augment ammunition and spare parts reserves. Still another month passed before it was decided to raise one additional infantry division. Some blamed the finance minister, Mohammad Shoaib, for 'myopic' opposition to the army's proposal for two divisions, though it is unclear if he was privy to the decision to send armed volunteers. If not, he was not the only one. Commanders in-chiefs of the air force and navy were not even informed of the fateful decision.

Few in the army were aware of the danger of war. Not only were mines not laid on the border with India, but those laid during the Kutch crisis were removed. It was later said influential retired or serving generals with lands in the area complained that the mines were obstructing agricultural operations on their lands, ironically given to them on the assumption they would contribute to the requirements of defence on the dangerous frontier.

Bilateralism

Disappointment at the failure of Western allies during the war hastened the process of reappraisal of Pakistan's policy of alliances, which had been in progress since 1960, when Pakistan embarked upon efforts for the normalisation of relations with China and the Soviet Union. The attempt by the United States and Britain to use the alliances to advance their own interests during the Sino–Indian border clash in 1962 had also served to disillusion Pakistan. Proceeding from the realistic premise that Pakistan had neither the capacity nor any reason to get mixed up in the wrangling of the great powers, it now decided on a policy of lowering its profile in the Cold War. Termed 'bilateralism,' the new policy in effect sought to distance Pakistan from the West and open windows to the East. The idea was different from non-alignment mainly to the extent that Pakistan did not intend to repudiate SEATO and CENTO or denounce the 1959 agreement of cooperation with the United States. Pakistan also resisted the anti-West bias of some of the prominent non-aligned countries, thus hoping to cultivate new friends without offending the existing ones. After he became prime minister,

Z. A. Bhutto tried to elaborate this idea and make it into a doctrine in international relations but, as often happens, artificial innovations pass away with their authors.

NOTES

1. An Indian official spokesman '*Hamara sheeraza bikhar jaiga*' (i.e. Our unity would be destroyed), said Atal Bihari Vajpayee in a conversation with the author in 1980.
2. Summarised from *Hindustan Times* of 20 April 1964 in Alastair Lamb, *Kashmir—A Disputed Legacy*, pp. 248–50.
3. The award allocated to Pakistan narrow—up to eight miles deep—stretches of land that surface after the flood season along the northern edge of the Rann while India received the rest, mostly marshy area.
4. Quoted from *Hindu Weekly* of 26 July 1965 in Burke, op. cit., p. 326.
5. Lamb, op. cit., p. 256.
6. Statement of 14 July 1965 quoted in McMahon, op. cit., p. 326.
7. M. Asghar Khan, pp. 75–76.
8. Pakistani forces captured 1,617 square miles of Indian territory and 201 sq. miles in Kashmir while India gained 446 sq.m. in Pakistan and 740 sq.m. in Kashmir.
9. China demand the return of four Chinese inhabitants, 800 sheep and 59 yaks that India had kidnapped.
10. For details and references see Burke, pp. 338–3357, and Gauhar, pp. 340–41 & 347–53.
11. Gauhar, op. cit., pp. 347–8.
12. Henry Kissinger, op. cit., p. 846.
13. The UK high commissioner in Pakistan gave a 'firm promise' to President Ayub, 'We and others are now determined to settle it.' UN under-secretary Ralph Bunch told the Pakistan ambassador: 'How can you possibly believe that after the war we will forget the Kashmir dispute, as we did earlier.' White Paper, op. cit. p. 59.
14. UN document S/Res/211 in *Documents* Vol. Two, ed. Arif, pp. 115–116.
15. McMahon, p. 345.
16. Count Galeazzo Ciano: 'As always, victory finds a hundred fathers but defeat is an orphan.'
17. This account, and much of the information here about official discussions during the period, is based on *Ayub Khan* by Altaf Gauhar, *The First Round* by Air Marshal M. Asghar Khan, Manuscript by Aziz Ahmed, and conversations with senior foreign office officials.
18. M. Asghar Khan, op. cit., p. 6.
19. Gauhar holds the view that Ayub Khan was influenced by Foreign Minister Z. A. Bhutto and Foreign Secretary Aziz Ahmed. All three were dead before *Ayub Khan* was published in 1993. Aziz Ahmed told the author in 1965 that he was taken completely by surprise when he read newspaper reports on 9 August to the effect that a large number of armed volunteers had crossed the CFL. Apparently, he expected the number to be smaller.
20. Surprisingly for so well experienced a soldier, Ayub Khan held the bigoted notion that 'Hindu morale would not stand more than a couple of hard blows at the right time and place.' Gauhar, op. cit., p. 329.

CHAPTER 9

Policy Ups and Downs, 1965–71

China

Pakistan's acceptance of the Security Council's demand for a ceasefire surprised Chinese leaders, but after Ayub Khan explained Pakistan's constraints[1] they, as usual, showed understanding of Pakistan's decision even though their own view was different. An engaging characteristic, which has distinguished Chinese leaders, has been their respect for the right of Pakistan, as also other countries, to determine what is in their own interest.

China's support of Pakistan in the 1965 crisis made a deep impression on the Pakistani people. President Liu Shao-chi's visit to Pakistan in March 1966 was a memorable occasion. In Lahore, Karachi and Dhaka, his welcome by enthusiastic multitudes was on a scale rarely seen since Independence. His description of Sino–Pakistan relations as *mujahidana dosti* (friendship in righteous struggle) aptly translated the sentiments of the Pakistani people and boosted their morale. Here was a friend the nation could trust and rely on. This friendship, forged in the heat of the war, developed in succeeding years.

To help Pakistan's defence capability after the United States embargoed military sales, China agreed, in 1966, to provide equipment for two divisions of the army as well as MIG aircraft for the air force. It also gave $60 million for development assistance in 1965, a further $40 million in 1969 and $200 million for the next five-year plan. For China, itself a low-income developing country, this assistance was generous. Also, China placed emphasis on the transfer of technology to help Pakistan achieve self-reliance. The Heavy Mechanical Complex, the Heavy Rebuild Factory, the Kamra Aeronautical Complex and several other industrial plants were later established with Chinese assistance. To provide a land link, the two countries decided, in 1969, to build a road across the Karakorum.[2] China played a major part in the construction of the spectacular Karakorum Highway linking Gilgit in the Northern Areas with Kashgar in Xinjiang, over the second highest mountain range in the world and through the 15,800-foot high Khunjerab Pass. Speaking at the UN General Assembly in October 1970, President Yahya Khan described friendly cooperation with China as the 'cornerstone' of Pakistan's policy. In the communiqué issued after his visit to China the following month, the Chinese reiterated support on Kashmir; and Pakistan reaffirmed that 'Taiwan was an inalienable part of China'.

USSR

Pakistan's policy of normalisation of relations with the Soviet Union gathered momentum after the 1965 War. The Soviet Union provided credit for development projects in Pakistan. Trade expanded. Pakistan sent a military delegation to Moscow in 1966 to probe the purchase of military supplies from the Soviet Union, and although no agreement was concluded, Moscow did not reject the idea. Ayub Khan visited Moscow in 1967, and before Kosygin returned the visit in April 1968, Pakistan informed the United States of its decision not to renew the lease for the Badaber electronic base upon its expiry in July 1968. Moscow appreciated Pakistan's decision. In 1968, Kosygin announced Soviet assistance for building a steel plant. Later that year the Soviet Union agreed to sell a small quantity of military equipment to Pakistan. Kosygin visited Pakistan again in May 1969 for a meeting with Yahya Khan, the new military ruler. The Soviet Union committed over a billion dollars in soft loans for thirty-one development projects.[3] Predictably, India raised a howl over this 'unexpected' development. Acquiescing in Indian pressure, Moscow discontinued the further supply of military equipment in 1970, illustrating to Pakistan the limits of bilateralism. In the East Pakistan crisis, Soviet priority reverted to one-sided support for India, leading to a breakdown of the developing links with the Soviet Union.

USA

Already under increasing strain since 1962, the Pakistan–US alliance broke down after the outbreak of Pakistan–India hostilities in the Rann of Kutch and war over Kashmir five months later. The US was antagonised by Pakistani allegations of betrayal. Lyndon Johnson told

Ayub Khan in December that the alliance between the United States and Pakistan was over. Military aid was discontinued. Any further economic aid was made conditional on Pakistan curtailing its close ties with China. That was unacceptable to Pakistan.

Neither Washington nor Islamabad renounced the 1959 Cooperation Agreement, however. The US still valued the Badaber base, and Pakistan, not wanting to further antagonise the US superpower, decided to wait till 1968 when the base agreement would expire.

The alliance was torn apart because of the divergent pulls of state interests in a changing world situation. In early 1960s the US did not decide to downgrade Pakistan but the opportunity of pulling India into its own orbit was irresistible in the context of global strategic power and ideological confrontation. Similarly, Pakistan was compelled by its own security interests to improve its relations with China and the USSR.

In retrospect, the damage to friendly cooperation between Pakistan and the United States might have been contained had both sides lowered expectations of each other in the light of the evolution in the strategic environment. Kennedy was right, in his observation in 1962, that 'allowance must be made for the special circumstances' but his successor made no such allowance. Pakistani spokesmen unnecessarily emotionalised an objective situation, a tendency that culminated in accusing the US of 'betrayal' in 1965, a charge that could not stand scrutiny. The US was committed under the 1959 agreement to come to Pakistan's assistance in the event of aggression but it did not accept such an interpretation of the Indian attack across the border. Instead, it held Pakistan responsible for provoking the war. The Gibraltar Operation was Pakistan's own decision and it was illogical to expect US support in consequential escalation. An ally, especially an unequal one, cannot compel another to underwrite objectives not envisaged in the alliance agreement; the US did not endorse, much less support, the Anglo–French–Israeli attack on Egypt in 1956.

The alliance with Pakistan was conceived by the United States in the context of the threat of communist aggression. The Manila Pact did not identify any source of aggression, and even if aggression was recognised to have occurred, it entailed only the obligation to consult together to agree on measures for common defence. Even that obligation was limited by the United States through a reservation in the treaty to the event of communist aggression. CENTO provided generally for cooperation for security and defence without creating any specific obligations in the event of aggression. When the United States joined the military committee it clarified that its participation 'related solely to the communist menace.'[4] Britain, too, declared that it promised to defend the region against communist aggression only.[5]

Pakistani failure to consult the US in advance of its high-risk policy in Kashmir and the US failure to assist Pakistan after Indian aggression widened the gulf between the two countries that had opened up as a result of their divergent policies towards China and the increasing US assistance to India after its border clash with China in 1962.

Still Ayub Khan realised the necessity of mending fences with the United States. Also, tempers cooled down in Washington as some people in high places recognised Pakistan's potential for contributing to better understanding between the US and China. In April 1966, Secretary of State Dean Rusk even asked Foreign Minister Bhutto for Pakistan's help to arrange a meeting with the Chinese foreign minister for discussions on Vietnam.[6] The idea was not, however, pursued. Bhutto, increasingly on the defensive for his role in policies leading to alienation of the United States, was asked to resign. On 12 April 1967, the US announced termination of military assistance to Pakistan (and India), exempting only cash sales of spare parts for the previously supplied equipment on a case-by-case basis.

US–Pakistan relations improved after President Richard Nixon took office in 1969. An advocate of close relations with Pakistan since the 1950s and appreciative of its role as an ally, he also did not view Pakistan–China relations in a frozen inimical perspective. Cognisant of the sea change in China's position following the Sino–Soviet split and the border tensions between them, he was among the first leaders in America to detect a 'dimly perceived community of interests between the United States and China'.[7] Pakistan's close relations with China no longer needed to be viewed from the jaundiced eyes of the previous administration. On the contrary, the Nixon administration considered Pakistan an asset for opening communications with China.

The upbeat tone of Pakistan–US relations was manifest in the strong support the US gave for aid to Pakistan at the World Bank's consortium meeting in May 1969. In August, Nixon paid a visit to Pakistan. In early 1970 Pakistan agreed to Nixon's request for the opening of a secret channel of communication between Washington and Beijing via Islamabad. In October 1970 the US relaxed the ban on military supplies, allowing the sale of a limited number of B-57 and F-104 aircraft.

Kissinger's Secret Visit to China

Before the White House activated the secret channel in October 1970 for negotiations with Beijing, the Nixon administration had already been engaged for a year in cautious diplomacy aimed at making 'a new beginning' in relations with China.[8] Following China's split with the Soviet Union, Nixon and his National Security Council advisor, Henry Kissinger, appraised China to be confronted with the 'nightmare of hostile encirclement' in which it might welcome 'strategic reassurance' from improved relations with the United States. Tentative probes were initiated in the fifteen-year old ambassador-level contacts in Warsaw. In January 1970, the US offered to send a representative to Beijing to consider ideas to reduced tension. The Chinese response was affirmative. To signal serious intent, Nixon started to dismantle obstacles to better relations by relaxing restrictions on travel and trade. Kissinger, well known for his preference for secret diplomacy, used personal friends for confidential contacts with the Chinese embassy in Paris, in order to prepare the ground for a positive outcome of the proposed direct dialogue.

In October 1970, Nixon asked Yahya Khan, in a meeting in New York, to inform the Chinese leaders, during his visit to China in November, that Nixon considered rapprochement with China 'essential.' Upon his return, Yahya Khan conveyed the Chinese response in an elaborately confidential manner. Kissinger was fascinated by Ambassador Agha Hilaly's insistence on dictating the message at slow speed, which he had to take in long hand. For four months thereafter, messages were passed on this Kissinger–Hilaly–Yahya Khan channel to Beijing in utter secrecy. Pakistan was equally helpful in arranging Kissinger's secret trip for talks in Beijing, 9-11 July 1971. The world was stunned when Nixon announced the breakthrough simultaneously with a similar announcement from Beijing about an invitation to Nixon to visit China.

Moscow's reaction to the development was both angry and quick. Taking advantage of the spiraling crisis between Pakistan and India, it concluded a Treaty of Peace, Friendship and Cooperation with India. Its article IX committed the two countries to mutual consultation in the event of an attack or threat of attack, in order to remove such threat and to take 'appropriate effective measures' to ensure their peace and security. Not so specific as to appear an alliance, its purpose was unmistakably strategic. The Soviet Union, in effect, provided India with an umbrella against intervention by China, allowing it to execute its design with impunity. The Soviet object was 'to humiliate China and to punish Pakistan for having served as an intermediary.'[9]

Organisation of the Islamic Conference

Israeli aggression against Egypt, Jordan and Syria in 1967 evoked strong condemnation in the world. The Muslim peoples were stirred, as never before, because of the Israeli occupation of Jerusalem, the first *qibla* of Islam. Mammoth demonstrations were held in Pakistan. Ardent solidarity with the victims of aggression was made manifest not only in words but also in concrete ways. Pakistani military deputations in these countries volunteered their services and participated in action. Pakistan's ambassador to the United Nations, Agha Shahi, made an effective contribution to the Arab cause. In reasoned speeches he supported resolutions in the General Assembly calling for respect for international law and for the rights of the people of occupied territories pending Israeli withdrawal. The resolution declaring invalid the measures imposed by Israel to change the status of Jerusalem was piloted by him.

On 21 August 1969, arson inflicted extensive damage on Al Aqsa Mosque, which is associated with the Prophet's Ascension. It triggered a tidal wave of anguish and outrage among Muslims throughout the world. Arab and non-Arab Muslim states joined the first Islamic summit conference held in Rabat, on 22-24 September 1969. It adopted a moving declaration reflecting the profound distress of Muslim peoples, agreed to coordinate action to secure Israeli withdrawal from all Arab territories occupied in 1967, and affirmed full support to the Palestinian people in their struggle for national liberation. Also, recognising that a common creed constituted a powerful bond between Muslim peoples, the leaders decided to institutionalise the conference and established the Organisation of the Islamic Conference (OIC) with a permanent secretariat to be located in Jeddah pending the liberation of Jerusalem.

Criteria for membership of the OIC were defined against the background of India's 'pathetic importuning'[10] for an invitation to attend the Islamic summit, justifying its inclusion on the grounds of its large Muslim population. Recognising the historic and abiding concern of the Muslim community in South Asia for the welfare of their co-religionists throughout the world, Pakistan—itself being an heir to that legacy—agreed to accord representation to the Muslims of

India at the conference. But when, by sending a non-Muslim envoy, India failed to observe the distinction between Muslims of India and India as a state, Pakistan raised an objection which was upheld by the conference. If the size of a state's Muslim population was the criterion for membership, many other states such as the USSR and China should have been invited to participate; their Muslim minorities were larger than the population of some of the participating Muslim states.

NOTES

1. Ayub Khan secretly visited Beijing for this purpose on 20 September. Gauhar, op. cit., pp. 351–3.
2. A jeepable road was completed in 1971, an asphalt road in 1978. The Karakorum Highway, crossing the Khunjerab pass, at 15,800 ft. (4800 m) was opened to adventure-traveling in 1986.
3. Quoted from *Asian Recorder*, 1957, in Burke, op. cit., p. 171.
4. Quoted from *Dawn* of 13 February 1959 in Burke, op. cit., p. 171.
5. Z.A. Bhutto's note for Ayub Khan, extract in *Documents*, ed. Arif, p. 250.
6. Hafeez Malik, op. cit., p. 202.
7. Henry Kissinger, *The White House Years*, Little Brown, 1979, p. 685.
8. Henry Kissinger, *The White House Years*, p. 684.
9. Kissinger, op. cit., p. 767.
10. *Statesman Weekly*, 27 September 1969, quoted in Burke, p. 374.

CHAPTER 10

1971 Disaster

Shared interest in the protection of cultural, economic and political rights brought the Muslim people of British India to a common platform, with leaders of Bengal playing a seminal role in the formation of the Muslim League and the formulation of the demand for Pakistan. After the state came into existence, the unity of its two wings, separated by a thousand miles, came under strain as a result of several factors, some of which were inherent in demography and differential colonial legacy and resource endowment, while others arose from narrow and shortsighted politics.

Differences with the distant centre's views began to surface in East Pakistan soon after Independence. A group of students protested when the Quaid-i-Azam said, in a speech in Dhaka in 1948, that Urdu alone would be the national language. Expectations of the people for visible self-rule were disappointed. Few of the senior administrative personnel inherited by Pakistan were from East Pakistan, and some of those who were appointed to East Pakistan did not win the confidence of the people.[1] East Pakistan did not have a sense of participation in the government in distant Karachi. In 1950, the East Pakistan Muslim League asked for 'maximum autonomy'. After elections in East Pakistan in 1954, the Muslim League was eclipsed. The United Front, which won 223 out of 237 seats, asked for 'complete autonomy according to the Pakistan Resolution.'[2] This reversion to the ambiguous text of the 1940 resolution depicted the sea change that had taken place in political opinion after Independence. It ignored the fact that in 1946 the most representative body of elected Muslim League legislators[3] had adopted a unanimous resolution declaring that Pakistan would be 'a sovereign independent State,' thus clarifying the ambiguity of the 1940 resolution, which spoke of 'autonomous and sovereign' constituent units in 'independent States' in the Muslim-majority north-western and eastern regions. The central government's manipulation to deny power to the elected majority in East Pakistan added to the accumulating grievances. Delays in constitution-making and holding of national elections exacerbated East Pakistan's sense of exclusion.

East Pakistan's isolation during the 1965 War and its lack of self-defence capability gave a fillip to the existing demand for autonomy. In March 1966, the Awami League leader Sheikh Mujibur Rahman put forward Six Points[4] calling for a new constitution under which the federal government would be responsible 'only for defence and foreign affairs', for which purpose it would be 'provided with requisite revenue resources' by the federating units. Ayub Khan's highly centralised government equated the demand for autonomy with secessionism. A process of polarisation set in with West Pakistani opinion looking at East Pakistanis as dupes of Indian propaganda, and Bengali elites ascribing motives of domination and exploitation to West Pakistanis. Ayub Khan said, 'They are not going to remain with us.'[5]

Alert to the brewing trouble and growing alienation in East Pakistan, India encouraged the separatist sentiment. Operatives of its secret service agency, Research and Analysis Wing (RAW), intensified subversion. In 1966 they met with a group of extremists in Agartala to plan sabotage.[6] A raid on an armoury led to the arrest of twenty-eight people including a few low-level civilian and armed forces personnel in January 1969. The case against them was not without substance but the government also implicated Mujibur Rahman, though he was in custody during the Agartala Conspiracy period. Trial by a special tribunal robbed the proceedings of credibility. Opinion in East Pakistan concluded that the case was concocted for political persecution.

Nature too seemed to collude in the tragedy. A cyclone of ferocious intensity in November 1970 left death and devastation in its trail. A quarter of a million people were drowned. The federal government was charged with indifference to the plight of the people of East Pakistan. In the election in December, the Awami League, led by Sheikh Mujibur Rahman, swept the polls in East Pakistan winning 167 out of 169 seats from the province, sufficient for an absolute majority in the 313-member National Assembly. The Pakistan People's Party led by Z. A. Bhutto emerged with the second largest number of seats, all from West Pakistan, and sought a share in power. The focus first was on constitutional issues. Although Sheikh Mujibur Rahman had earlier told Yahya Khan the Six-Point demand was negotiable, after the electoral triumph he became a prisoner of his own extremist rhetoric and lost control over hawks in the party who wanted independence. He declined Yahya Khan's invitation to visit Islamabad for talks. When the President went to Dhaka he found Mujibur Rahman was in no mood for a compromise. Yahya Khan then convened the Assembly for 3 March, hoping the political leaders would settle the issues among themselves.

Now Bhutto announced that his party would boycott the Assembly unless the constitutional issues and power sharing were first resolved. Yahya Khan then postponed the Assembly meeting and again went to Dhaka in mid-March. Whether his purpose was to hold talks with Mujibur Rahman or prepare for imposition of martial law remained unclear. The talks broke down on 23 March when the Awami League proposed Pakistan should be made a confederation. Martial law was imposed on 26 March.

'Almost all nations will fight for their unity, even if sentiment in the disaffected area is overwhelmingly for secession', observed Henry Kissinger, adding, 'So it was during our Civil War, with Nigeria toward Biafra and with Congo toward Katanga.'[7] But Yahya Khan's decision to use force was a gamble with the dice loaded against Pakistan. Not only was use of military force against compatriots unconscionable, it was foolish to hope 42,320[8] West Pakistani troops could suppress 75 million people in East Pakistan, with India determined to obstruct and prevent the effort through instigation, abetment and military intervention.

India had started planning to exploit the internal situation in Pakistan years earlier. The Agartala operation instigated by RAW has been mentioned above. On 30 January 1971, an Indian Airlines plane named *Ganga,* on a Srinagar–Delhi flight, was hijacked to Lahore by two Kashmiri youths. They were lionised as freedom fighters on arrival at Lahore airport. Let alone popular opinion, even the usually alert Z. A. Bhutto applauded the 'brave freedom fighters'.[9] Their leader set the plane on fire. New Delhi made furious protests, demanding compensation and immediate surrender of the criminals. Struck by this bolt from the blue, Islamabad was paralysed, too proud to concede to peremptory Indian demands and too weak to control the emotional outburst of popular opinion. Before it knew what was happening, India suspended overflight rights of Pakistan's planes. Subsequently, a Pakistani inquiry tribunal discovered the facts: the leader of the 'hijackers' was a recruit of Indian intelligence, trained and coached for the mission; the 'weapons' given to him and his innocent accomplice were toy pistols and wooden grenades; and the *Ganga* was the oldest plane in the airline's fleet. Pakistan had walked into a clever trap.

After Yahya Khan ordered the crackdown in East Pakistan, the Indian government moved into higher gear. India saw in the crisis an 'opportunity of the century' to cut Pakistan into two.[10] RAW operatives smuggled out Tajuddin Ahmad, an Awami League leader, escorted him to a border village to proclaim the independence of Bangladesh and installed him as head of the provisional Bangladesh government in Mujibnagar, a house in Calcutta rented by RAW.[11] On 31 March the Indian parliament adopted a resolution assuring the East Pakistani insurgents that 'their struggle and sacrifices will receive the wholehearted support of the people of India'.[12] Indira Gandhi reassured parliament that she would make timely decisions about the developing situation. Within days, the Indian border police started operating inside East Pakistan. India embarked on an emergency training programme for Bengali army officers and provided military equipment for armed resistance.[13] First secretly, and later openly, India began building up a rebel force called the Mukti Bahini. An estimated 100,000 men were trained in guerrilla skills.[14]

Public opinion and the media in the US and Western Europe were outraged by the Pakistani military crackdown. The excesses committed by Pakistani forces were reported at great length, and the number of refugees who entered India was wildly exaggerated. Few bothered to take notice of Indian interference or its rejection of proposals for impartial international inspection. To ease India's burden on account of the refugees, the United States provided $350 million in aid but that did not dissuade Indira Gandhi from her preconceived purpose. 'The opportunity to settle scores with a rival that had isolated itself by its own shortsightedness was simply too tempting'. All efforts by the international community to promote a political solution were resisted as India 'insisted on terms that escalated by the week'.[15] President Nixon read the Indian design clearly, but the State Department was swept off its feet by popular reaction. He acquiesced in the State Department's decision to embargo delivery of arms to Pakistan.

Pakistan learnt from its own sources, as did the United States 'from sources heretofore reliable that Mrs Gandhi had ordered plans for a lightening 'Israeli-type' attack to take over East Pakistan.'[16] Only its implementation had to be deferred in the light of Chief of Staff General Manekshaw's view that the army needed six to seven months to prepare for war.[17] 'The Indian commanders insisted, at a minimum, on waiting until November when weather in the Himalayas would make Chinese intervention more difficult.'[18]

Indo–USSR Friendship Treaty. Washington learnt in June that the Soviet Union 'had informed India of its approval of guerilla operations into East Pakistan and had promised protection against Chinese reprisals.'[19] On 9 August the USSR concluded a Treaty of Friendship with India, providing for consultations 'on major international problems' of concern to the two sides and requiring each to refrain from giving assistance to any third country taking part in an armed conflict with the other. The treaty 'was bound to eliminate' fears of Chinese intervention.[20] With the Soviet shield in place, and the veto in its pocket to stymie the UN Security Council, India issued orders to the armed forces to prepare for operations.[21] Other preparations, too, were 'excellent'.[22] A policy planning committee was established to ensure political and military coordination at home and the buildup of international opinion through propaganda and high level visits.

In contrast, conditions in Islamabad were confused and chaotic. The army was said to be operating largely on its own.[23] Yahya Khan 'was oblivious to his perils'; Pakistan's military leaders were 'caught up in a process beyond their comprehension'.[24] Yahya Khan did not inform others in the government of his role in providing a secret channel between Washington and Beijing, and did not anticipate the strong reaction it was bound to provoke in Moscow. The importance of the Indo–Soviet Treaty was not correctly assessed; some thought the Soviet objective was only to restrain India.

Indira Gandhi rejected Washington's suggestion for UN monitoring of the border in order to curb guerrilla activities from its territory. By October, Yahya Khan informed Washington that he was willing to grant full autonomy to East Pakistan. A month later he was even agreeable to a unilateral withdrawal of forces. Any such decision would have been better than the fate that befell the country. Unaccountably, Yahya did not act on these ideas.

Before moving in for the 'kill', Indira Gandhi undertook an international tour. She visited Washington on November 4–5, mainly for the purpose of influencing public opinion. Nixon was not unsympathetic to India. During the two years of his administration, the United States had given $1.5 billion in aid to India.[25] But he detested the condescension Indira Gandhi exuded, like her sermonizing father,[26] and he was opposed to her designs against Pakistan. His conversation with Indira Gandhi was 'a classic dialogue of the deaf' and he 'was disturbed by the fact that although Mrs Gandhi professed her devotion to peace, she would not make any concrete offers for de-escalating the tensions'.[27] She 'denied that she was opposed to [Pakistan's] existence but her analysis did little to sustain her disclaimer'.[28] In fact, she argued that Pakistan should not have come into being. As Nixon later recorded in his diary, Indira Gandhi 'purposely deceived me in our meeting'[29] having 'made up her mind to attack Pakistan at the time she saw me in Washington and assured me she would not'.[30] In retrospect, Nixon further lamented: 'how hypocritical the present Indian leaders are' and how 'duplicitous' Indira Gandhi.

Pakistan protested on 21 November that India 'without a declaration of war, has launched an all-out offensive.' By 22 November Henry Kissinger 'had no doubt that we were now witnessing the beginning of an India–Pakistan war and that India had started it.' While 'Pakistani repression in East Bengal had been brutal and shortsighted,' in his view, and Nixon's, 'it was India's determination to use the crisis to establish its prominence on the sub-continent.'[31]

'From 21 to 25 November several Indian Army divisions, divided into smaller tactical units, launched simultaneous military actions.'[32] Troops, tanks and aircraft were used to assist the Mukti Bahini occupy 'liberated' territory. Nixon sent another letter to Indira Gandhi informing her of Yahya Khan's offer of unilateral withdrawal, and he also wrote to Kosygin to intercede with her. She was implacable. On 29 November she told the US Ambassador, 'We can't afford to listen to advice which weakens us.'

On 2 December, Yahya Khan invoked the 1959 agreement asking for US assistance. The State Department argued that the agreement did not oblige the US Government to give a positive response. This view, Kissinger said, 'ignored all other communications between our government and Pakistan.'[33] For, the 'plain import (of the agreements) was that the United States would come to Pakistan's assistance if she was attacked by India.' As Kissinger concluded: 'The image of a great nation conducting itself like a shyster looking for legalistic loopholes was not likely to inspire other allies who had signed treaties with us or relied on our expressions in the belief the words meant approximately what they said.'[34]

In the event, the White House was stalled by the State Department. Not even a statement was issued. Meanwhile, the military situation in East Pakistan grew desperate by the day. 'Yahya chose what he considered the path of honour', and ordered a retaliatory attack across the border from West Pakistan on December 3. This decision, like the others Yahya Khan made, proved ineffectual and merely helped India advance its military plan which was to commence operations on 4 December.[35]

Despite Indian propaganda, the United Nations took a principled position. On 4 December the Security Council voted 11 to 4 in support of a resolution calling for a ceasefire and withdrawal of forces, but it was killed by the USSR veto. On 7 December the General Assembly, acting under the Uniting for Peace procedure, recommended a ceasefire and withdrawal of forces to their own territories and the creation of conditions for the voluntary return of refugees. As many as 104 member States voted for the resolution, only ten voted against and eleven abstained. The overwhelming vote of the world community had no effect on India, however, as it persisted on its ruthless course of aggression in violation of the principles of the Charter.

China was supportive of Pakistan, and Premier Zhou recognised that India was guilty of 'gross interference' in Pakistan's internal affairs. China continued to supply military equipment under existing agreements and extended political support to the Pakistani position in the United Nations. At the same time, it was circumspect and did not make any promises to Pakistan that it could not fulfil.

The United States upheld the principles of international law and while it did not fulfill its alliance commitments to help maintain Pakistan's unity and territorial integrity, it reviewed its posture on learning that Indira Gandhi was determined to continue fighting 'until the Pakistani army and air force were wiped out'.[36] On 9 December Kissinger called in the Indian ambassador to warn against such a course. On 10 December, Nixon sent a message to Leonid Brezhnev saying if Indian military operations continued, 'we must inevitably look toward a confrontation between the Soviet Union and the United States. The Soviet Union has a treaty with India; we have one with Pakistan.'[37] The crisis now involved high stakes, and the threat of great power confrontation loomed on the horizon as the USSR encouraged New Delhi in its design, promising that it would initiate military moves if China threatened India. Washington decided it could not allow Moscow to intimidate Beijing if it wanted its China policy to retain credibility. On 10 December Kissinger met China's representative to the UN, Huang Hua, and briefed him on the steps the US had taken to help Pakistan.

On 9 December Nixon authorised the dispatch of a task force of eight ships, including the aircraft carrier *Enterprise* from the Pacific to the Bay of Bengal. The 'objective was to scare off an attack on West Pakistan...[and] to have forces in place in case the Soviet Union pressured China'.[38] He stressed upon the Soviets, who had 'proceeded to equip India with great amounts of sophisticated armaments', to restrain India. On 12 December he sent a 'hot line' message to Leonid Brezhnev saying, 'I cannot emphasize too much that time is of the essence to avoid consequences neither of us wants.'[39] To make the point more concretely, the Soviet authorities were also informed of fleet movements. Evasive at first, Moscow finally responded on 13 December to say that they were conducting 'a clarification of all the circumstance in India'. Kuznetsov was sent to New Delhi to work for a ceasefire. On 14 December at 3 a.m. the Soviet ambassador in Washington delivered a message reporting 'firm assurances by New Delhi that India has no intention of seizing West Pakistani territory'.

At this stage, Poland proposed a resolution in the Security Council which called for the immediate transfer of power to the elected representatives in East Pakistan, and a ceasefire and troop withdrawals by both sides. Presumably it had Soviet support and could have, even at this eleventh hour, saved Pakistan from further humiliation. But, as often happens in a crisis, the rush of events overtakes human capacity to make timely decisions. To India's relief, the resolution was not pressed to a vote.

Under mounting US and Soviet pressure, Indira Gandhi offered an unconditional ceasefire on 16 December. Speaking in parliament, she was reported to have said she had defeated Pakistan, and avenged several centuries of Hindu humiliation at the hands of Muslim sultans and emperors. 'Delirious with joy' the members of parliament gave her a 'thunderous ovation'.[40]

Nixon could credibly claim that his diplomatic signals and the dispatch of the US naval fleet persuaded the Soviet Union to join in pressurising India, thus saving West Pakistan from India's evil design. Nixon not only demonstrated his long-standing goodwill towards Pakistan but also manifested a profound understanding of the implications of India and the Soviet Union succeeding in destroying Pakistan. That would have encouraged the Soviet Union 'to use similar tactics elsewhere... (and) change the balance of power in Asia... A victory of India over Pakistan would be the same as a victory of the Soviet Union over China.'[41] Nixon's decision to improve relations with China was a part of the same global vision.

It is a sad commentary on the American system that it precluded a statesman from fulfilling US obligations under the alliance with Pakistan and from acting as a superpower and permanent member of the Security Council, which could have retrieved the situation. Failing to grasp the strategic dynamics, the American Congress and media, not to mention South Asia 'experts' in the State Department, opposed Nixon's policy and thus became accomplices in the Indian crime against peace and international law. Of course, that does not mitigate the blunders and follies of Pakistani leaders over the years, manifest in the neglect of East Pakistan and its exclusion from due share in power.

Political autonomy for East Pakistan would have been consistent with the vision of the founders of Pakistan.

Pakistan suffered a disaster. The country was divided and diminished. The dream of the founding fathers was wrecked. The nation was demoralised. The people were bewildered and distraught, their pride in the armed forces destroyed, their leadership exposed as self-centred and incompetent. Over 93,000 soldiers and civilians were taken prisoner after the Pakistani contingent in East Pakistan was overwhelmed. Indian forces seized 5,139 square miles of territory in West Pakistan and a million people were dislocated. A dark shadow hovered over the prospects of the state.

Bhutto's Dynamic Role, 1972–73

In this tortured and turbulent situation, Z. A. Bhutto assumed office as president of residual Pakistan. His government had to 'pick up the pieces', bring the nation to grips with the new reality, and rebuild morale and confidence. Above all, it needed to rehabilitate Pakistan in the world community and re-orient failed policies both at home and abroad. To rescue Pakistan in this predicament he decided first to turn to friends for sympathy and support.

Even before returning to Pakistan from New York, Bhutto visited Washington and met President Nixon on 18 December 1971, and told him that Pakistan was 'completely in the debt of the United States during the recent trying days' and that he now wanted good relations[42]—a rather belated realisation, considering that in the 1960s he had advocated 'normalisation' of the 'abnormal' relations with the United States,[43] and was responsible for the myth of American betrayal in 1965. President Nixon promised that the US would do 'all within its power'[44] to help Pakistan and that 'The cohesion and stability of Pakistan are of critical importance to the structure of peace in South Asia.'[45]

The first country Bhutto visited after becoming President was China, in January 1972. As always, China extended diplomatic support and economic and military assistance. Bhutto also undertook a whirlwind tour of Islamic countries in the Middle East and Africa which upheld the principles of law for the unconditional release of Pakistani prisoners and the withdrawal of Indian forces from occupied territories.

Z. A. Bhutto (Prime Minister of Pakistan, 1973–1977).

Britain was unsympathetic. It not only recognised Bangladesh precipitately but also persuaded several countries of Western Europe, Australia and New Zealand to do so simultaneously. In disgust, Bhutto decided to quit the Commonwealth.

Little was expected of the Soviet Union. When Bhutto visited Moscow in March 1972, in the hope of moderating its hostility, the Soviet leaders suggested recognition of Bangladesh and negotiations with India for a 'realistic' solution of the post-war problems. It indicated no interest, however, in playing a role. Like the United States, it seemed exhausted by its diplomatic efforts to avoid the threat of a confrontation between them during the December war.

Pakistan was left to itself to solve the problems of prisoners of war and recovery of territory occupied by India.

NOTES

1. Of 101 top civil and police officers who opted for Pakistan on Partition only 18 were Bengalis. Though the number of those who belonged to areas of West Pakistan was also small (35), the issue was politicised so that any non-Bengali was dubbed a 'Punjabi'.

2. The resolution adopted by the Muslim League at its meeting in Lahore on 23 March 1940, demanded that contiguous Muslim-majority units in the north-western and eastern zones should be grouped to constitute 'independent states in which the constituent units shall be autonomous and sovereign.' The popular intent was later clarified by the Muslim League representatives elected by the Muslim masses in a resolution that left no doubt that Pakistan was to be 'a sovereign independent State.' For the texts of the resolutions, see Syed Sharifuddin Pirzada, *The Pakistan Resolution*, Pakistan Publications, Karachi. 1968.

3. The 1946 resolution was adopted unanimously by elected Muslim League legislators who had won 446 out of the 495 seats at stake.

4. For texts of the original and revised formula see Siddiq Salik, *Witness to Surrender*, Oxford University Press, Karachi, 1977, pp. 215–17.

5. Altaf Gauhar, op. cit., p. 411.

6. Asoka Raina, *Inside RAW*, Vikas Publishing Co., Delhi, 1981, p. 49.

7. Henry Kissinger, op. cit., p. 852.

8. Siddiq Salik, op. cit., p. 101. This figure did not include local risings and para-military formations.

9. Alastair Lamb, op. cit., p. 288.

10. K. Subramaniam, Director of the official Indian Institute of Defence Studies and Analyses said on 31 March 1971, 'What India must realise is the fact that the break-up of Pakistan is in our interest, an opportunity the like of which will never come again.' He was also reported by The *Hindustan Times*, New Delhi, of saying 'a chance of the century'. Quoted in Siddiq Salik, op. cit., p. 97.

11. Asoka Raina, op. cit., p. 54.

12. *Bangaldesh Documents*, Government of India, Vol. 1, p. 672, quoted in Siddiq Salik, op. cit., p. 97.

13. Asoka Raina, op. cit., p. 57.

14. Siddiq Salik, op. cit., p. 100.

15. Henry Kissinger, op. cit., pp. 857 & 861.

16. Ibid., p. 856.

17. Richard Sisson and Leo E. Rose, *War and Secession—Pakistan, India and the Creation of Bangladesh*, University of California Press, Berkeley, CA, 1990, p. 209.

18. Henry Kissinger, p. 857.

19. Ibid., p. 860.

20. Ibid., p. 867.

21. Richard Sisson and Leo E. Rose, p. 209.

22. V. Langer, *The Defence and Foreign Policy of India*, Sterling Publishers, New Delhi, 1988, p. 205.

23. The visiting US official Maurice Williams was so informed by Pakistani officials in August. Dennis Kux, op. cit., p. 197.

24. Henry Kissinger, op. cit., p. 861.

25. Henry Kissinger, op. cit., p. 848.

26. Nixon was not alone in finding Nehru insufferable. Secretary of State Dean Acheson said he was 'One of the most difficult men with whom I have ever had to deal.' Quoted from Acheson, *Present at the Creation*, pp. 439–40, in Robert McMahorn, op. cit., p. 56. Truman considered Nehru 'disagreeable' and Kennedy, who publicly praised Nehru's 'soaring idealism' found his sense of superiority 'rather offensive'.

27. *The Memoirs of Richard Nixon*, Vol. I, Warner Books, New York, 1978, p. 651.

28. Henry Kissinger, op. cit., p. 880.

29. Nixon, op. cit., p. 652.

30. Ibid., p. 658.

31. Henry Kissinger, p. 885.

32. Sisson and Rose, op. cit., p. 213.

33. Henry Kissinger, op. cit., pp. 895–6. In footnote 7 on p. 1488, he further says, 'Assurances were given by the Kennedy and Johnson administrations, including a letter from President John F. Kennedy to President Mohammad Ayub Khan on 26 January 1962; an aide-memoir presented by the State Department on 17 November 1962; and an oral promise by President Lyndon Johnson to Ayub Khan on 15 December 1965.'

34. Henry Kissinger, p. 895.

35. General Manekshah made this statement in an interview with BBC. Dennis Kux, op. cit., p. 199.

36. Henry Kissinger, op. cit., p. 901.

37. White House Memorandum of conversation between President Nixon and Soviet Minister of Agriculture Vladimir Matskevich, quoted in Dennis Kux, op. cit., p. 201.

38. Henry Kissinger, op. cit., p. 905.

39. Ibid., p. 910.

40. V. Langer, op. cit., p. 215.

41. Memorandum of conversation with President Pompidou, 13 December 1972, quoted in Denis Kux, op. cit., p. 203.

42. Dennis Kux, op. cit., p. 204, quoting Memorandum of Conversation of Nixon-Bhutto meeting, 18 December 1971, President's Office Files, NPMP, NA.

43. Z. A. Bhutto, op. cit., p. 158.

44. Memorandum of Nixon–Bhutto meeting, quoted in Dennis Kux, op. cit., p. 204.

45. Statement of Policy for the 1970s, issued on 3 May 1973, Documents, op. cit., p. 207.

CHAPTER 11

Shimla Agreement:
Negotiating under Duress

For over four months after the ceasefire of 17 December no foreign power offered to mediate a peace settlement nor did Pakistan or India take the initiative to call for a bilateral meeting. Then India sent Union Minister D. P. Dhar to Islamabad for preliminary talks preparatory to a peace conference. The talks were held in Murree from 26–29 April 1972. Pakistan had a glimpse of the demands India had in mind at the meeting. Dhar proposed that the peace conference should aim at eliminating once and for all the sources of antagonism between the two countries, and focus on the determination of 'elements of durable peace'. He did not mention Kashmir and made eloquent disclaimers of any intention to impose a solution on Pakistan, but the assurance rang hollow: India was not prepared to release the prisoners of war and withdraw from occupied territory without conditions. The message came through loud and clear. India wanted to dictate a settlement of the Kashmir question. Pakistan, on its part, wanted the peace conference to address issues generated by the war.

The Murree meeting did not resolve the question as to whether immediate postwar issues or the establishment of durable peace (i.e. settlement of the Kashmir question) should receive priority at the summit conference. Dhar and Secretary General Aziz Ahmed agreed to place both the items on the agenda for simultaneous consideration. The compromise was to prove illusory.

The Shimla conference, even more than the Murree meeting, seems in retrospect a veritable drama in which superb diplomats played skillful roles using words and gestures that masked, but did not conceal, the real aims and intentions of each side from the other. President Z.A. Bhutto and Prime Minister Indira Gandhi, the twin-directors of the drama without a script, were also the principal actors. The chief executives, however, dominated the centre of the stage even when they were not on it, and kept strategic control of the direction in their own hands, letting the officials determine negotiating tactics to suit the evolving situation.

Zulfikar Ali Bhutto, a leader of exceptional intellect and percipience, also excelled in rhetoric and eloquence. A proud man, he had the misfortune to come to the helm when Pakistan lay prostrate in defeat. He must have hated having to negotiate from a weak bargaining position, but comprehended the country's predicament and the traumatised nation's need to be spared further humiliation. His legal education and superb knowledge of the English language stood Pakistan in good stead at the Shimla conference. He proposed the 'no-prejudice' clause in the Shimla Agreement, which Indira Gandhi accepted, protecting Pakistan's position on the Kashmir question from compromise. His party colleague and able lawyer, Rafi Raza later disclosed that he had suggested the idea.

Indira Gandhi, petite and seemingly frail in body but robust in mind, was deceptive also in her inarticulate speech. The words at her command did not do justice to the clarity and depth of her thought, but no one could miss the thrust of her remarks. She seemed engagingly shy but was entirely self-confident and unwavering in resolve. A rare leader with a capacity to view her role in history from a vantage point in the future, she spoke and acted with a sense of accountability to her country. The 'iron lady' was also intensely nationalistic and probably never felt happier and more self-fulfilled than on the day when India humiliated Pakistan. Yet she was capable of discerning the limits beyond which the adversary could not be pushed or squeezed, as she demonstrated by reducing the demands in the final draft in order to prevent collapse of the peace conference.

Aziz Ahmed, Pakistan's secretary general for foreign affairs, was a senior and reputable civil servant, with experience at top levels of diplomacy, having served as ambassador to Washington and foreign secretary. He was widely respected as much for his ability and integrity as for his patriotism. Stern of mien and single-minded in pursuit of the national interest, he probably did not win the sympathy of his Indian interlocutors but even they could not grudge him credit as a dour negotiator and a hard bargainer.

India's D. P. Dhar, on the other hand, was a charmer. Courteous and sophisticated, he won the trust of his counterparts—which is half the battle in negotiation—by a positive and empathetic approach, often presenting the demands in his brief as requests and recommendations. Although capable of holding his own in argumentat, he seldom sought to score points. When debate became sterile and unpleasant, threatening to derail negotiations, he diverted attention to the common ground between the two sides and brought discussion back onto a constructive course.

P. N. Haksar, secretary general in the Indian prime minister's office, became the leader of the Indian official delegation at the conference after D. P. Dhar was taken ill. Without a peer in knowledge and erudition, he was also blessed with lucidity of expression to match the clarity of his thought. He seemed to relish saying: 'Only the Devil knows what is in your mind; I can only go by the words you use.' But the chuckle at his own wisecrack instantly reassured every one that he meant no offence. No one could doubt his desire for a positive outcome of negotiations, which cannot be said about T.N. Kaul, the Indian foreign secretary, whose unctuous speech contrasted vividly with unmistakable hostility towards Pakistan.

Rafi Raza, an able barrister and special assistant to president Bhutto, was a senior member of the Pakistan delegation both at the Murree and Shimla meetings. He seldom intervened in discussions across the table, but used the weight of his position as a confidant of Bhutto to good effect in informal negotiations with senior Indian officials.

Opening Gambit

Despite formal politeness and courtesies characteristic of conversations between diplomats, and despite the mildness of their words that at times camouflaged harsh intent, the wide gulf between the Pakistani and Indian positions was manifest in the opening round of negotiations at Shimla on 28 June. It was reflected more vividly in the initial drafts tabled by India on 29 June and by Pakistan on 30 June. Concise and cold in their content, the drafts were bare of the overlay of protestations of goodwill and noble intentions.

Leaving aside the preambular parts, pledging mutual respect for independence, sovereignty and territorial integrity, the Pakistani and Indian drafts diverged fundamentally in concepts about the outcome of the Shimla conference. India proposed an elaborate treaty that already comprised eleven articles, with more to be added later to incorporate a Kashmir settlement. It was comprehensive in every aspect of interest to India but, rather surprisingly for the Pakistani side, did not include a word about either withdrawals from occupied territories or release of prisoners, which were, unsurprisingly, the main focus of the unpretentious but pragmatic draft presented by Pakistan.

The two drafts presented an interesting contrast in their selection of principles for the conduct and regulation of relations between the two countries. Whilst the Indian selection betrayed intent to construct a rather peculiar and particularistic framework of principles, with not even a mention of the United Nations Charter, Pakistan emphasised the universally recognised principles of relations between sovereign states. Of course, the most substantive difference between the two drafts centred on Jammu and Kashmir. While India proposed discussion on the Kashmir question and inclusion of the envisaged agreement in the suggested treaty, Pakistan omitted any reference to it because, in its view, the purpose of the Shimla conference was limited to resolving the problems resulting from the December war.

In the negotiations that followed, both sides tried to give the impression of accommodation, each toning down its own formulations and incorporating portions of the other's draft, but there was little progress on core issues. By 1 July a sense of gloom set in, which was reflected in the second Indian draft. Premised on the failure to bridge differences on substantive issues, it envisaged an interim agreement, leaving the substantive issues for settlement at a subsequent summit. Pakistan declined to join such a charade that would create an illusion of success. Faced with the collapse of the Shimla conference, India changed tack again. On 2 July it presented Pakistan with a final draft. That, too, was unacceptable, to Pakistan. A detailed account of the discussions on various issues is necessary for clarification of the obstacles.

Principles of Relations

The omission of any reference to the United Nations Charter from the selection of principles included in the Indian draft was rather peculiar. More than surprising the Pakistani side, it served to bare a design in India's mind to circumscribe and restrict the applicability of some of the Charter principles to relations with Pakistan. Pakistan's approach was, of course, directly the opposite. Its draft emphasised the UN Charter and universally recognised principles of relations between sovereign states, including in particular the fulfilment in good faith of the obligations assumed by them in accordance with the Charter—a pointed reminder that India had failed to implement the obligations arising from the Security Council resolutions on Kashmir.

When the Pakistan side pointed to the flaw in the Indian draft, Haksar explained the omission by arguing that the two countries did not need to invoke 'foreign ideas.' A high-flyer in logic, and a loquacious man, even he found himself flapping in thin air in arguing that the two 'civilised nations should rely on their own wits.' Perhaps unconvinced themselves, the Indian luminaries were unconvincing in their attempt to justify the exclusion of a mention of the UN Charter, which incorporates accepted principles of international law representing the accumulated experience and distilled wisdom of the community of states. Realising the hiatus in their logic, the Indian side gave up their stand, and reference to the Charter was not only incorporated but also given pride of place as substantive point (i) in paragraph 1 of the agreement.

India agreed to make formal deference to the Charter, but resisted Pakistan's suggestion, based on Article 33 of the Charter, that any dispute between the two countries 'will be settled by peaceful means such as negotiation, conciliation, enquiry, mediation, or, should these methods prove unavailing, by arbitration or judicial settlement.' The Indian side suggested that the two countries agree to 'undertake to settle all issues between them bilaterally and exclusively by peaceful means.' Pakistan argued long and hard in favour of retaining the Charter formulation and would have insisted on it were the circumstances normal. But considering the dire situation, it tried to reduce the damage. It suggested amendment of the Indian text so that differences would be settled 'by peaceful means through negotiation or any other peaceful means.' India, however, had the last word and added the qualification 'mutually agreed upon between them.' This version became subparagraph 1(ii) in the agreement.

Arguments on principles of relations and means of settlement of differences, even presented in the abstract, barely concealed their real object. India sought to use its strong bargaining position to compromise and curtail Pakistan's sovereignty and to secure its acquiescence in India's preferences. Pakistan, on the other hand, struggled because, and in spite of, the constraints of the situation, to safeguard its rights under law as an independent member of the world community. This contest of wills was more vividly illustrated in the discussions on the release of prisoners of war and, especially, on Jammu and Kashmir.

Release of Prisoners. India made the release and repatriation of Pakistani military and civilians prisoners contingent on the concurrence of Bangladesh. India was honour-bound, said Indian interlocutors, to consult and associate with the Bangladesh government over the decision regarding their release. Dhar said he did not 'plead' for recognition of Bangladesh but in his 'personal opinion' recognition was the key to resolving not only the question of prisoners of war but also 'a number of other matters.' He did not need to elaborate what these other matters were. It was plain from published reports in the Delhi and Dhaka newspapers that Bangladesh would use the prisoners as a lever to pressure Pakistan into agreeing to its demands. Dhaka claimed a share of Pakistan's assets (gold and foreign exchange reserves, aircraft of the national airline, etc.) without reference to its debt and other liabilities. Also, it wanted Pakistan to accept the transfer of all those Urdu-speaking residents of former East Pakistan who had declined to accept its citizenship.

Both Dhar and Haksar told the Pakistan side that India wanted Bangladesh to relent and that it had, in fact, used 'whatever little influence' it had with the government of Bangladesh in favour of forbearance but, they added, Sheikh Mujibur Rahman was an 'emotional' man. They might have believed in what they said, but the Pakistani side could see that India itself was not averse to using the prisoners as a bargaining counter. Dhar's statement that India did not want to use the Pakistani prisoners for any objective of its own was implicitly contradicted by the Indian minister for external affairs three days later. When Aziz Ahmed asked him whether the release of prisoners was linked to settlement of the Kashmir question, Sardar Swaran Singh replied: 'Yes and No.' He wanted these and other issues to be settled as a package.

India seemed to believe that the Pakistani prisoners were a valuable bargaining chip in negotiations because some of them were related to high officials of the armed forces. It calculated that their families would pressure Bhutto's fledgling government to secure their release obliging it to pay the price India demanded. Bangladesh, too, proceeded on the same assumption, either on its own or on Indian instigation. India's pledge, that the prisoners would not be released without the concurrence of Bangladesh, further encouraged Dhaka to adopt a hard stand. Nor could New Delhi have failed to see that Dhaka's attempt to use the release of prisoners would add to the bitterness already existing between Dhaka and Islamabad, and vitiate the prospects for early normalisation of relations between them. Some in the Pakistan delegation believed that New Delhi's policy was actually based on such a calculation.

The Indian side did not, of course, know that, anticipating the exploitation of prisoners to extract concessions, Pakistani policy planners had decided in advance not to fall into the trap of bargaining over their release. They realised that a willingness to do so would expose Pakistan to blackmail, as no price could then be too high for the ransom of the unfortunate soldiers and civilians. Accordingly, the Pakistan side took the position that the release of prisoners of war was an obligation that the custodian state had to discharge in accordance with the principles of international humanitarian law. Consistent with the strategy, it did not respond to initiatives from the Indian side to link the prisoners to any other issue between either Pakistan and India, or Pakistan and Bangladesh.

Withdrawal from Occupied Territory

Security Council Resolution 307 of 21 December 1971 demanded the withdrawal of all armed forces 'to their respective territories and to positions which fully respect the ceasefire line in Jammu and Kashmir supervised by the United Nations Military Observers Group in India and Pakistan.' The first Pakistani draft at the Shimla conference called for compliance with this resolution. India, however, did not even refer to this matter either in its first draft of 29 June or in the second draft of 1 July. Even its final draft referred to and provided for withdrawal of forces to the international border, but not to the 1949 ceasefire line in Jammu and Kashmir. The Indian formulation about observance of respect for the 17 December 1971 ceasefire line was designed to compromise Pakistan's position on Jammu and Kashmir.

Jammu and Kashmir

Aware of the constraints on negotiations, the Pakistani side would have liked to eschew any discussion on the Kashmir question at Shimla. It soon became obvious, however, that India would not let Pakistan off the hook. It was determined to try to utilise the leverage it then enjoyed in the negotiations in order to secure Pakistan's acquiescence in a settlement of India's preference—legalisation of the status quo in Kashmir. This suggestion emerged not only from the statements of Indian interlocutors in the negotiations but also from their drafts.

During the verbal fencing in the negotiations, the Indian side initially avoided direct reference to the Kashmir question. Even the first Indian draft mentioned the subject only in a note at the bottom of the last page. Perhaps Dhar and Haksar were too courteous to raise the issue directly, much less in an abrasive manner. But foreign secretary T. N. Kaul could not restrain himself.

As the negotiating session on 30 June was drawing to a close, Kaul, with a smirk on his face, intervened in the discussion and remarked in unctuous Urdu: *Baqi sub kuch to theek hai laiken aap yeh to farmaeey Kashmir kay mutallaq moaheday main kia kaha jana chaheeye*? (Everthing else is all right but please tell us what should be said about Kashmir in the agreement?). Aziz Ahmed, who was leader of Pakistan's official delegation and a minister of state, and was reputed for being status conscious and haughty (his pride acquired in colonial Britain's elitist civil service), ignored not only the question but also Kaul, a mere secretary, and continued to talk to Haksar, his counterpart. Kaul, too proud to be thus snubbed and dismissed, persisted with his question, pointedly addressing 'Aziz Ahmed sahib.' On Kaul's second or third attempt, Aziz Ahmed turned a withering glance toward him and replied in cold and calculated cadence: 'If you must, you can say that the Kashmir question will be resolved in accordance with the Security Council resolutions.' Kaul, his face flushed in anger, shut his notebook, its clap echoing in the hushed room, and stood up from his seat to leave as if Aziz Ahmed's reply made further negotiations futile. Surprisingly for a diplomat of his long experience, he forgot that, not being the leader of the Indian delegation, he could not terminate the conference. Haksar had to virtually pull Kaul down by his coat tail to continue the meeting. Never again during the following two days did Kaul venture another intervention.

There was no escape, however, from the Indian suggestion contained in the note at the bottom of the first Indian draft, which envisaged not only separate discussions on Jammu and Kashmir, but an agreement on the question to be included as an integral part of the treaty to be signed at Shimla. Even otherwise, the Indian draft implicitly treated Jammu and Kashmir as part of Indian territory while the Pakistani draft, premised on the disputed status of the state, referred to Jammu and Kashmir only in the context of withdrawal of forces to the 1949 ceasefire line.

Haksar himself took up the subject of Kashmir in the context of India's suggestion for bilateral settlement of differences between the two countries. Recalling Aziz Ahmed's reference to the UN resolutions, he gave his 'preliminary assessment' that if the two countries 'were not capable of making a frontal attack' to settle this question, then India would find it extremely difficult to negotiate with 'anybody else.' The United Nations, he argued, had not led the two countries 'anywhere in the past,' of course omitting to add that this was so because India had turned down each and every proposal by UN mediators to facilitate the implementation of the Security Council resolutions of 1948 and 1949, envisaging a plebiscite by which the people of Jammu and Kashmir were to decide whether their state should accede to India or Pakistan.

Again omitting to recall that India had not only accepted the UN resolutions of 13 August 1948 and 5 January 1949 for a plebiscite, but also given a pledge to the people of Kashmir that they would be given an opportunity to decide the future of their state, Haksar went on to declaim that India did not accept the concept of self-determination.

The discussion on Kashmir exposed the contradiction in India's stance, manifest from its dual posture. On the one hand it asserted that the state was constitutionally 'a part and parcel of India' and on the other it formally proposed discussions with Pakistan for an agreement on the Kashmir question, acknowledging that the status of the state remained disputed. Not only that, Haksar went so far as to declare that there could be no durable peace between India and Pakistan until there was 'some agreement on some principles' on which the question of Kashmir could be settled. Pakistan could readily agree with the linkage between durable peace and settlement of the Kashmir question, but it would not reopen discussion on principles of settlement—the principle had been agreed and affirmed in UN resolutions.

India's effort to secure an agreement on Kashmir was at a dead end, but it was not abandoned. In the context of the discussion on withdrawal of forces from occupied territories, the Indian side took the position that the line to which the forces were to withdraw must have the same sanctity 'all the way from the Arabian Sea to the Himalayan heights.' In essence, India suggested conversion of the new ceasefire line in Jammu and Kashmir into an international boundary, that is, partition of the state. The Indian side even offered 'minor' territorial adjustments. This idea was, however, a non-starter because Pakistan was resolved not to barter the Kashmiri right of self-determination. Finding that a meeting ground between the two sides did not exist on the Kashmir question, India acted more or less as Kaul had done—it virtually terminated negotiations. The second Indian draft, tabled on 1 July, much shorter than the first, was limited in content to principles of relations and progressive normalisation measures; 'the question of Jammu and Kashmir, repatriation of prisoners of war and civilian internees, withdrawal of all armed forces to their respective territories and the resumption of diplomatic relations' would be deferred till another meeting. The Pakistani side was not prepared, however, to sign such an agreement that settled none of the postwar issues.

On 2 July the Indian side suddenly decided to delink withdrawals to the international boundary from a settlement of Jammu and Kashmir. Its final draft, given to the Pakistan side in the early afternoon, proposed withdrawal of forces to the international border. As for Jammu and Kashmir, it provided that 'the line of control resulting from the ceasefire of 17 December 1971, shall henceforth be respected by both sides as a Line of Peace.'

Although the offer of withdrawals to the international border was attractive, the final draft was loaded with formulations designed to convert the 'Line of Peace' in Jammu and Kashmir into an international boundary. Faced with a take-it-or-leave-it choice, Pakistan decided to leave it and so informed the Indian side at about 3 p.m. The conference had reached a dead end.

Dénouement

Addressing a crowded press conference at about six in the afternoon of 2 July, President Zulfikar Ali Bhutto announced that his delegation would depart the following morning. The expectant audience may have been disappointed but the officials were not surprised. Not only were they aware that India's final draft of the proposed agreement had been rejected earlier by Pakistan, they also knew that the gulf between the positions of the two countries after five days of intensive negotiations was very wide, with fundamental issues like Kashmir and even sovereignty at stake.

Suddenly, two hours later, near-failure turned into success. Around eight in the evening a breakthrough was achieved. During the Pakistani president's farewell call on the Indian prime minister, Indira Gandhi agreed to the following deletions and amendments to the Final Draft:

— Paragraph 1(vi) was amended with the addition of the words: 'That in accordance with the Charter of the United Nations they will refrain from the threat or use of force against the territorial integrity or political independence of each other.'

— Paragraph 4(ii) was amended to include a no-prejudice clause so as to read: 'In Jammu and Kashmir, the line of control resulting from the ceasefire of December 17, 1971, shall be respected by both sides without prejudice to the recognised position of either side. Neither side shall seek to alter it unilaterally...' Also the words 'as a Line of Peace' were deleted from the Indian draft which had initially suggested that the line of control 'shall henceforth be respected by both sides 'as a Line of Peace.'

— Paragraph 4 was further amended to delete the following subparagraphs: '(iii) Minor adjustments to the Line of Peace in Jammu and Kashmir or the rest of the international border considered necessary by both sides to make the border more rational and viable, may be made by mutual agreement;' and (iv) 'A joint body composed of an equal number of representatives, nominated by each Government, shall be appointed to establish ground rules and to supervise effective observance of the Line of Peace and the rest of the border between the two countries.'

After the Pakistani negotiating team was informed of the agreement, Aziz Ahmed met with P. N. Haksar to clean up the language of the agreed amendments. Ashok S. Chib, joint secretary in the Indian ministry of external affairs, and Abdul Sattar, director general, prepared the final documents. Bhutto and Gandhi signed the agreement. The date had already turned but 2 July remained unchanged in the agreement, which was signed past midnight between 2 and 3 July 1972.

The import of the deletions and amendments that Indira Gandhi conceded cannot be exaggerated by anyone aware of the issues arising from the conflicting aims and objectives of India and Pakistan at the Shimla conference. Thus,

— India's suggestion for the creation of a bilateral supervisory body, introduced for the first time in the final draft, was an attempt to salvage at least in part its aim to secure Pakistan's acquiescence in the status quo in Jammu and Kashmir. It wanted to pave the ground for a call for the withdrawal of the United Nations Military Observers Group in India and Pakistan (UNMOGIP), which had been mandated by the Security Council to discharge specific functions in Jammu and Kashmir, and thus to undermine the validity of the Security Council resolutions. By securing the deletion of the Indian proposal, Pakistan checkmated India's move. If India decided, nevertheless, to refuse cooperation with UNMOGIP, it could not cite the Shimla Agreement to justify its wilful violation of an international obligation.

— Even the addition of the clause 'in accordance with the Charter of the United Nations' in the subparagraph on non-use of force was of considerable if esoteric interest against the background of the history of the no-war declaration proposal. Bhutto did not want to be seen to have given up Pakistan's historical position, which sought to link a no-war pledge to a self-executing mechanism for the resolution of disputes. It also served to strengthen the emphasis on the principles of the UN Charter as the arbiter of relations between Pakistan and India, thus undercutting the Indian aim of roping Pakistan into a non-universal framework of principles that would circumscribe its rights as a sovereign state.

Assessment

Why did Indira Gandhi decide to concede the changes Bhutto sought in India's final draft? Did she think that having cut Pakistan into two and thus neutralised the 'threat' it presented, India should turn to building durable peace in South Asia? Was she under pressure from the Great Powers to conclude a peace treaty? Did she want to appease the world community which was aghast at India's blatant aggression? Was she concerned that the elected leader of Pakistan should not return empty-handed? Or was she beguiled by Bhutto's eloquence and promises?

The Pakistan side could not know what explanations she gave to her cabinet colleagues and officials for reducing India's demands below the rock-bottom level spelt out in the final draft. From the account Bhutto gave to his delegation it appeared that she was keen to salvage the Shimla conference from collapse, and decided to accept the changes without which, he told her, the people of Pakistan would reject the agreement. The presence at Shimla of several leaders of Pakistani political parties may have lent weight to this argument.

While only Indira Gandhi could give an authoritative answer, speculation as to why she agreed to dilute the final draft misses the important point that even in the signed text of the Shimla Agreement India extracted a substantial price. Pakistan would not have agreed to some of its provisions were it not for the constraints and pressures under which it was obliged to negotiate in the aftermath of defeat.

Exploiting the 'opportunity of a century', India cut Pakistan into two, first by instigating and aiding separatism in East Pakistan and finally by military intervention. A visceral antagonism towards Pakistan was not yet satisfied, however. Indian diplomacy continued to wage war by other means. Using occupation of territory and prisoners of war as instruments of duress in the post-war negotiations, it set itself three objectives: (1) legitimisation of the status quo in Jammu and Kashmir, (2) construction of a bilateral framework for relations with Pakistan to circumscribe its rights under the UN Charter, and (3) securing Pakistani recognition of Bangladesh. Pakistan's objectives were rather simple: to recover territories and obtain the release of prisoners of war, at the lowest cost to its national interests.

To take point (3) first, no progress whatsoever was made at Shimla on the question of recognition of Bangladesh. Pakistan's refusal to bargain over the release of prisoners weakened what both India and Bangladesh considered a lever of pressure. The miscalculation was to cause considerable embarrassment to India as continued incarceration of these unfortunate soldiers and civilians in violation of international humanitarian law incurred worldwide criticism. Bangladesh was disappointed at the time but, in the longer run, both it and Pakistan benefited. The delay in Pakistan's extension of recognition until after Bangladesh consented to the release of all the prisoners helped avoid the added bitterness that would have resulted from the attempt to use the prisoners for bargaining, and thus saved the prospect of cooperative relations between the two countries.

Subparagraph 1(ii) of the Shimla Agreement, providing for peaceful settlement of differences, was projected as a triumph of Indian diplomacy. India unilaterally interpreted the provision to mean Pakistan could no longer seek 'third party intervention,' nor raise Pakistan–India issues in the United Nations or any other international forum, nor invoke any peaceful means other than bilateral negotiations without India's concurrence. Pakistan did not then or later accept the Indian interpretation of so-called 'bilateralism'. It maintained that the text of the agreement did not compromise Pakistan's rights under the UN Charter. Firstly, the attempt to interpret one provision in isolation from others is untenable in law. Subparagraph (ii), which makes resort to peaceful means other than negotiations subject to mutual agreement, cannot be read in isolation from the preceding subparagraph (i), which explicitly affirms that the UN Charter 'shall govern the relations between the two countries.' Under the Charter, a state has the right to bring to the notice of the General Assembly or the Security Council any matter which threatens the maintenance of international peace and security. Also relevant is Article 103 of the UN Charter, affirming that obligations under the Charter prevail over conflicting obligations under any other international agreement. In practice, too, Pakistan has not allowed the Indian interpretation to affect its decisions from time to time to bring differences with India to the attention of the organs and agencies of the United Nations. For instance, it filed a petition with the International Court of Justice in 1973 charging India with violation of international humanitarian law in delaying the release of prisoners of war. The Shimla Agreement was no bar to the admission of that petition. Also, Pakistan has continued to exercise its right to raise differences with India in international fora. Pakistan has thus sought to underline the fact that the subparagraph does not prejudice Pakistan's rights under international law. That does not however gainsay the fact that, had the negotiating field been level, Pakistan would not have accepted the Indian formulation.

Pakistan's own suggestion for a self-executing mechanism for the resolution of disputes has manifest advantages. It would provide an incentive to the parties to settle the differences through bilateral negotiation, which is the cheapest means of resolving differences. If they fail to settle between themselves, they could agree to invite intercession by a mutually acceptable third party. If that, too, proves unavailing, the dispute would be referred either by common consent to an arbitration tribunal or by either of the parties to a judicial tribunal. The usefulness of mediation was demonstrated in the successful outcome of the World Bank's efforts in promoting the Indus Waters Treaty, and the efficacy and expeditiousness of arbitration in the matter of the boundary dispute in the Rann of Kutch. In contrast, negotiations between the two countries have a dismal record of failure even in relatively less complicated issues such as the Wullar Barrage and the Sir Creek disputes.

Impartial determination of differences is a necessary component of the strategy for the peaceful settlement and the prevention of use of force. All civilised polities do not merely forbid the use of force but also provide effective means for the peaceful settlement of disputes, so that an aggrieved party can bring the recalcitrant to court for compulsory adjudication of a dispute that they fail to settle between themselves. Regrettably, the community of states has yet to attain that state of civilisation. Powerful states prefer instead the present 'state of nature' in which they can exploit power to impose their own will and deny justice to less powerful neighbours.

Firm Stance on Kashmir. On the crucial Kashmir question, Pakistan did not accept the Indian demand for either legitimisation of the ceasefire line or an agreement on some new principles for settling the issue. On its part, India refused to withdraw forces to the 1949 'ceasefire line in Jammu and Kashmir supervised by the United Nations Military Observers Group for India and Pakistan' as was required under Security Council Resolution 307(1971).

India's refusal to return to the 1949 ceasefire line was ascribable to transparent political motivation. It sought to convey the message that if Pakistan did not agree to a settlement of Kashmir on its terms, then India felt free to retain the territorial gains it made in war. Otherwise the gains in Jammu and Kashmir in 1971 were not large. India took more, but mostly uninhabited mountainous land in the Kargil area, while it lost Chamb which supported an agricultural population of 10,000 people.

Pakistan had no means of compelling India to withdraw to the 1949 ceasefire line. As a result of its refusal to do so, India continues to bear the onus of non-compliance with yet another resolution of the Security Council, thus violating Article 25 of the Charter according to which it is committed 'to accept and carry out the decisions of the Security Council'.

As a consequence of the Indian refusal to withdraw to the ceasefire line it became necessary for the two sides to keep to the positions they held at the time of ceasefire on 17 December 1971. The term 'Line of Control' was accepted by Pakistan after India agreed to the 'without prejudice' clause. Its design thus nullified, India did not, in the immediate wake of the Shimla Agreement, project the Line of Control as anything more than an interim arrangement. The Indian minister for external affairs stated on 10 October 1972 that the Line of Control was 'obviously a new ceasefire line.' Any other interpretation would compromise India's declared position, claiming the whole of Jammu and Kashmir as an integral part of its territory.

The clause 'Line of Control resulting from the ceasefire of 17 December 1971' could not be deemed to alter the status of Jammu and Kashmir as an outstanding question. The same sentence in the Shimla Agreement that refers to the Line of Control contains also the key 'without prejudice' clause. Obviously, it cannot compromise Pakistan's recognised position that the Kashmir question has to be resolved in accordance with the relevant resolutions of the Security Council. Also, the Shimla Agreement itself reaffirms, in paragraph 6, that 'a final settlement of Jammu and Kashmir' was one of the outstanding questions, and further, that the establishment of durable peace between the two countries remained contingent on the resolution of this question.

Not much has been said here about the conversations between President Bhutto and Prime Minister Indira Gandhi. This is by no means an attempt to overlook their role or contribution which was, in fact, crucial to the outcome of the Shimla conference. They were not only the leaders of their delegations but determined the strategy and directed the tactics of the negotiators. Without their eleventh-hour intervention the Shimla conference had been doomed to failure.

What they said to each other in one-to-one meetings is not, however, a part of the record. Neither Bhutto nor Gandhi said much publicly about their conversation. The government of Pakistan and the government of India know only what their then leaders chose to tell them. Neither ever said they had secretly agreed to a settlement of the Kashmir question. When Foreign Minister Vajpayee claimed in 1978, that Bhutto and Gandhi had reached a secret understanding on Kashmir at Shimla, the latter publicly rejected the claim as baseless.

Secret Understanding?

Professor P. N. Dhar, who was one of the secretaries of Indira Gandhi in 1972, claimed in an article in *Mainstream* of 15 April 1995 that the change of nomenclature to Line of Control was 'the core of the Indian solution to the Kashmir problem: the *de facto* line was to be graduated to the level of *de jure* border.' Dhar alleged that 'Bhutto was personally inclined to accept the status quo as a permanent solution of the Kashmir problem', but he said he could not do so because his 'political enemies at home, and especially, the army bosses would denounce him for surrendering what many in Pakistan considered their vital national interest.' In effect, according to Dhar, Bhutto contradicted in private meetings with Gandhi the views he voiced in public and was prepared, in effect, to betray the Kashmir cause. Invited by the *Mainstream* editor[1] to respond to Dhar's account, the author, a member of Pakistan's delegation at the Shimla conference, wrote an article that was published in a subsequent issue of the journal.

In the first place, Bhutto made no such remark in any meeting with Gandhi at which members of their delegations were present. As for the one-to-one meeting they held on 2 July, Dhar's account was hearsay. If Indira Gandhi told Dhar that Bhutto had made the statement, it is not uncommon for negotiators to claim self-reconstructed accounts of conversations to embellish their own performance and denigrate that of the adversary. Incredible to those in Pakistan who heard Bhutto express his views on Kashmir in the inner councils of the government before, during and after the Shimla conference, Dhar's statement that he gave a secret understanding different from what is contained in the agreement amounts to an allegation of hypocrisy and betrayal against a deceased leader unable to set the record straight, which was, to say the least, in bad taste. Dhar knew that Indira Gandhi had refuted Vajpayee's claim in 1978 to the existence of a secret understanding between her and Bhutto at Shimla. The allegation was, besides, wholly pointless. No obligation devolves upon a state from an adversary's claim of a secret and oral understanding allegedly given by a functionary, however high his rank. Only agreed minutes of meetings are of any worth as evidence for interpretation of treaties. What binds the parties is the text of the agreement as ratified by them. The Shimla Agreement explicitly regards Jammu and Kashmir as an outstanding question.

Implications of Duress. Aside from the alleged secret understanding, the validity of even an agreement signed under duress is morally if not legally doubtful. The Shimla Agreement was negotiated under circumstances characterised by coercion and blackmail. India used occupied territory and prisoners to constrain Pakistan into submitting to its demands. Under domestic law a contract dictated under duress is not considered binding. International law has not yet risen to that civilised level. Still the moral validity of such an agreement is dubious. History records instances of repudiation of treaties after the power equation changed. When Germany denounced the Treaty of Versailles, even those who had dictated it did not insist on its observance. Scholarly opinion went further to blame Britain, France and the United States for the manifestly unfair *diktat* which provoked revanchism and led to the Second World War. Pakistan has not exercised that option.

Professor Dhar claimed that Indira Gandhi proposed to Bhutto that the two countries bury the hatchet and 'agree on the settlement of the Kashmir issue on the lines suggested by India', not by 'an immediate and formal acceptance of the status quo' but in the manner that 'the *de facto* Line of Control was to be graduated to the level of the *de jure* border.' Whilst there is no basis on the record for the claim, India did formally propose the conversion of the ceasefire line into an international boundary in one of its drafts. Those who argue that 'the whole of Jammu and Kashmir is an integral part of India' should remember that at Shimla the Indian government offered to 'give up' a part of the state. The Indian constitution can no longer be a credible excuse for denying the right of self-determination to the people of Jammu and Kashmir.

Finally, whilst opinions may differ as to which side did better in the negotiations, it is apparent that neither Pakistan escaped unscathed in safeguarding its interests nor did India succeed fully in securing its aims. India was persuaded, in fact, to scale down its aims and even the minimum it spelt out in its final draft was further curtailed as a result of negotiations between Bhutto and Gandhi.

Pakistan paid a high price for securing vacation of its territory. Under normal circumstances it would not, and could not, accept the provision regarding bilateral settlement of disputes. The gloom was relieved, however, by the thought that it held no bargaining counters whatsoever. An objective appraisal of the Shimla agreement cannot fail to marvel at the extent to which Pakistan managed to extricate itself from the clutches of duress. The credit for this achievement goes to the spirit of the Pakistani people who were defiant in adversity and did not want their government to capitulate. Their willingness to bear with the continued incarceration of their soldiers and civilians helped the leadership to set the priorities right. It was important to obtain withdrawals from occupied territories first, not only because this enabled a million displaced people to return to their homes but also because delay in withdrawals incurred the risk of prolonging occupation and distress to the refugees.

Unstinted tribute is due also to President Bhutto and officials such as Aziz Ahmed, who brought not only great ability and negotiating skill to their difficult task in an unenviable predicament, but also played their historical roles purposefully and with an inspiring and exemplary sense of commitment.

Normalisation with Bangladesh

The brutal separation of East Pakistan was a tragic fact. The government was aware that Bangladesh had to be recognised but it could not ignore the feelings of a traumatised nation. The government in Dhaka did not make the task easier. Miscalculation led it to believe that Pakistani prisoners of war could be used as a lever of pressure to secure satisfaction of its claim to a share of Pakistan's assets. It further spoke of its intention to try some of the prisoners on charges of war crimes. Indian officials disclaimed, during discussions at the Shimla conference, that they had encouraged Dhaka to adopt this policy of virtual blackmail. They said Mujibur Rahman was 'emotional.'

Pakistan had few options, but it was obvious that prospects of normalisation of relations in South Asia would be severely damaged if India transferred any of the Pakistani prisoners in its custody to Bangladesh for trials. It sought their unconditional release as required under international humanitarian law.

It took nearly two years for New Delhi and Dhaka to realise that the retention of Pakistani prisoners was a lever of diminishing value. Indeed, they became a liability for India, as world opinion became critical of their illegal detention in violation of international humanitarian law. Finally, in September 1973, India itself having obtained the concurrence of Bangladesh, agreed to release all Pakistani prisoners excepting 195 prisoners Bangladesh said it wanted to try on charges of war crimes. The agreement also provided for the transfer of Bengalis from Pakistan to Bangladesh. On humanitarian grounds, Pakistan accepted the transfer of a substantial number of non-Bangalis. Over 250,000 persons who had served in the government or had family connections were allowed to migrate to Pakistan. As many others, who were said to have 'opted' to leave the land of their settlement for Pakistan, remained stranded. Pakistan, on its part, did not expel Bengalis who wished to remain Pakistani citizens.

Nothing did more to convince Dhaka about the inadvisability of blocking the release of the Pakistani prisoners, or trying any of them, than China's decision to use its veto to bar the admission of Bangladesh into the United Nations. In retrospect, China did a great favour to both Bangladesh and Pakistan. Had Dhaka gone ahead with its intention to try Pakistani soldiers, prospects of normalisation of relations with Pakistan would have been obliterated for much longer.

Fortunately for the two countries, the Islamic summit conference in Lahore in 1974 provided an opportunity for common friends to persuade Bangladesh to abandon the idea of trying Pakistani captives. Pakistan promptly extended recognition to Bangladesh. Prime Minister Mujibur Rahman attended the Islamic summit.

The question of apportionment of assets and liabilities continued to obstruct development of normal relations between the two countries. Dhaka claimed a share in the assets of Pakistan. Pakistan denied that, as a part that was sundered by aggression, Bangladesh had a right under international law to any share in the patrimony. On that political ground, Pakistan declined to enter into any discussion on the substance of the issue. Had such a discussion been held, Dhaka would have realised that it was to its advantage to adopt the clean-slate principle, which allowed it to disown responsibility for a share of Pakistan's internal and international debt. An inter-departmental study in Islamabad led to the conclusion that Pakistan's liabilities being greater than its assets. Islamabad could have made out a case for Bangladesh to assume a share of the negative balance.[2]

OIC Summit. The Lahore Summit was a memorable event for the people of Pakistan as for the first time leaders of fraternal states met together to demonstrate mutual solidarity on all issues of common concern. The sagacious King Faisal bin Abdul Aziz captured the mood of Muslim people all over the world with tears of joy in his eyes as he offered Friday prayers along with the highest level congregation ever assembled at the Badshahi Mosque.

NOTES

1. Subhash Chakravartty was an eminently fair-minded journalist, and doyen of the Delhi corps, whom the author had the privilege to know during his assignments in New Delhi. Substantially the same article was later published, with texts of the agreement and various drafts added, in *Regional Studies*, Islamabad, August 1995.
2. The author chaired the study.

CHAPTER 12

The Nuclear Programme
and Relations with the USA

Pakistan's nuclear programme, started in the mid-1950s, aimed at acquiring scientific knowledge and technology for peaceful uses in agriculture and health. It also envisaged the construction of power plants in due course to meet the energy needs of its developing economy. The Pakistan Atomic Energy Commission obtained a small five megawatt research reactor from the United States in 1962 for the Pakistan Institute of Nuclear Science and Technology (PINSTECH), near Islamabad, under an agreement that provided for inspection and controls by the International Atomic Energy Agency. A few years later Canada agreed to extend cooperation to Pakistan for the construction of a 120 megawatt nuclear power plant. Completed in 1972, this plant, too, was placed under the safeguards of the International Atomic Energy Agency.

It became evident in the early 1960s that India was acquiring nuclear technology not only for peaceful purposes but also to develop weapons. While emphasising peaceful uses in public statements, it was establishing the entire nuclear fuel cycle facilities, including production of bomb-grade plutonium, that would give India the weapons option. Facts unmistakably pointed to the conclusion that Indian leaders 'sought to win for their country all the prestige, status and economic benefits associated with being a nuclear power, including the option of building "the bomb" if necessary.'[1] Taking cognisance of the emergent threat to Pakistan's security, and the potential for blackmail in an asymmetrical nuclear situation, Foreign Minister Zulfikar Ali Bhutto said in 1965, 'If India makes an atomic bomb, then we will also do so, even if we have to eat grass...an atom bomb can only be answered by an atom bomb.'[2] But his rhetoric was not matched with official action. Few leaders with influence favoured allocation of resources for PAEC to embark on an expanded programme, with a dual-use potential, for which nuclear equipment and technology was then not subject to stringent export controls or intrusive external inspection. In 1966, PAEC proposed purchase of a plutonium separation plant that France was willing to sell, but the ministries of finance and defence opposed the proposal and President Ayub Khan too, did not favour the idea.[3] Military leadership apparently believed that a strong conventional defence capability would suffice for deterrence.

Pakistan vested hope in the Non-Proliferation Treaty (NPT) and actively participated in efforts at the United Nations to promote its early conclusion. It joined multi-pronged efforts for a fair bargain between nuclear-weapons states and non-nuclear states that would provide for the progressive reduction and eventual elimination of nuclear weapons held by nuclear weapon powers, in exchange for the renunciation of the nuclear weapon by other states. At its initiative, a conference of non-nuclear states recommended that nuclear-weapon states should provide 'negative' and 'positive' guarantees pledging (a) non-use of nuclear weapons against non-nuclear states, and (b) assistance to a non-nuclear state threatened with nuclear weapons. Both proposals were conceded in principle, but the pledge on reduction of nuclear weapons in the NPT remained non-binding, and the resolution on security guarantees adopted by the Security Council, of which the five nuclear powers were permanent members, was far from reassuring. Pakistan nevertheless announced its readiness to sign the NPT, provided India did the same. India, however, refused to sign the treaty. Pakistan's reasonableness contrasted with intransigence on the part of India, which championed nuclear disarmament but at the same time persisted in a programme aimed at the acquisition of the weapons option.

The 1971 disaster compelled Pakistan to undertake the proverbial 'painful reappraisal' of its policy of nuclear abstinence. Pakistan's conventional defence capacity had proved inadequate to safeguard its territorial integrity, as East Pakistan was sundered by Indian military intervention to create Bangladesh. India's exploitation of Pakistan's internal political troubles, encouragement and assistance to separatism in East Pakistan, violation of the principle of non-interference in internal affairs, and aggression and military intervention, illustrated India's animus, the irremediable imbalance of power, the reluctance of allies to come to Pakistan's rescue and the powerlessness of the United Nations. Pakistan had to devise its own means to ensure its security and survival.

Soon after taking over the reins of government, President Zulfikar Ali Bhutto convened a meeting of nuclear scientists at Multan in January 1972, and later at Quetta, to review the nuclear programme. Participants included renowned nuclear physicist Professor Abdus

Salam, and Munir Ahmad Khan, a nuclear engineer serving at the IAEA. Already convinced of the necessity of acquiring the weapons option, Bhutto's main purpose was to discuss expeditious acquisition of fuel cycle facilities. To pursue the plan, he appointed Munir Ahmad Khan as chairman of the Pakistan Atomic Energy Commission, and allocated requisite funds for relevant projects.[4]

The decision to pursue the nuclear option was more easily made than implemented. Pakistan possessed neither fissile material nor explosion technology. Nuclear suppliers were already strengthening controls on nuclear technology transfer. The restrictions were further tightened after India, conducted the test explosion in 1974. Canada unilaterally cancelled the cooperation agreement with Pakistan even though, unlike India, it committed no violation of any agreement with Canada. The United States led other industrialised states in the Nuclear Suppliers Group to tighten restrictions on the export of nuclear technology.

To Pakistan's shock, few countries criticised India for the May 18 explosion. Washington's reaction to the Indian nuclear explosion was particularly muted. Secretary of State Henry Kissinger decided it was futile to fight the *fait accompli*.[5] India-apologists swallowed the pretext that the test codenamed 'Buddha Smiles', was peaceful, although they knew that a nuclear explosion causes irreversible contamination. For that reason both the USA and the USSR had virtually ruled out explosions for peaceful uses such as digging harbours or canals. The US state department was not too exercised. As far back as 1961 many of its officials recommended helping India acquire a nuclear explosive to 'beat Communist China to the punch.'[6]

Instead, the United States now focused its non-proliferation agenda on Pakistan. The first target was the reprocessing plant Pakistan was to build with French collaboration under an agreement signed in 1973, providing for application of IAEA safeguards. Moreover, the agreement prohibited Pakistan from replicating the technology for twenty years.

Meanwhile, Pakistan embarked on imaginative diplomacy to counter the pressures of the United States and other industrialised countries. In 1974 it proposed a resolution in the UN General Assembly for the establishment of a nuclear weapon-free zone in South Asia. The UN General Assembly approved the resolution, and support for it continued to increase year after year. India was cornered into virtual isolation, and although that made no dent in its resolve, Pakistan gained the moral high ground internationally and the US pressures on Pakistan were exposed as discriminatory. Also, Pakistan was able to exploit the opportunity to free-ride India's intransigence.

Relations with the United States, 1972-79. In November 1972, Pakistan withdrew from SEATO, but now keen to maintain good relations with the United States, did not withdraw from CENTO which was still valued by Washington in the context of its policy on the Middle East. Meanwhile, the Nixon administration continued to manifest understanding of Pakistan's economic and security problems. In March 1973, it authorised a 'one time exception' for delivery of 300 armoured personnel carriers Pakistan had purchased three years earlier.

Prime Minister Bhutto was invited to visit the United States in September 1973. Nixon said, in his banquet speech, 'The independence and integrity of Pakistan is a cornerstone of American foreign policy.' The US also resumed economic assistance, providing $24 million for wheat and $18 million as AID loan, and further agreed to seek congressional approval for $40-50 million as a rehabilitation loan. Also, the Ford administration lifted the embargo on arms sales to Pakistan and allowed purchase of arms and spare parts worth $160 million. India protested, although it received $1,273 million in arms aid from the Soviet Union during 1964–73.

The United States did not accept Pakistani professions of peaceful intent concerning its nuclear programme, Bhutto had made no secret of his views. He publicly said, 'It is vital for Pakistan to give the greatest possible attention to nuclear technology, rather than allow itself to be deceived by an international treaty limiting this deterrent to the present Nuclear Powers.'[7] In retrospect, the US assumption was not incorrect. But even more so was its acceptance of India's obviously hypocritical claim that its test explosion was for 'peaceful' purposes. Washington first tried to entice Pakistan by offering to sell 120 aircraft if Pakistan agreed to cancel the contract with France for the construction of a reprocessing plant. When Prime Minister Bhutto refused the proposal[8], the US pressured France to cancel the contract.

Providently, Pakistan had embarked on an alternative route for production of fissile material. A Pakistani metallurgist, Dr A. Q. Khan, was appointed by the government in 1976 to build a uranium enrichment plant at Kahuta. He and his team of dedicated scientists and engineers working at the Engineering Research Laboratories faced forbidding technological difficulties and obstacles, as the United States and other members of the nuclear suppliers group even refused export of non-nuclear components. But they succeeded in building the key centrifuges indigenously within a few years. By 1982, they achieved the capability to enrich uranium to the level required for building an explosive device.[9] PAEC was also charged with the responsibility for 'pre-and post-enrichment phases of research'.[10] It manufactured the first atomic device in 1983.[11] A tunnel had already been dug in Chagai Mountain. The government decided, however, to defer the test to avert political offence to Washington. PAEC scientists then used the time for research on 'different designs of the bomb, (and) conducted a number of successful cold tests to judge their performance.'[12]

The United States enacted legislation in 1977 and 1978—known as the Symington and Glenn Amendments to the Foreign Assistance Act—which provided for denial of economic aid and imposition of other sanctions and penalties against a country not party to the Non-Proliferation Treaty that imported equipment or technology for production of plutonium and enriched uranium. Nominally aimed at nuclear non-proliferation in South Asia, the law in practice singled out Pakistan; it had a built-in loophole to exempt India and Israel from their purview. Sanctions under the amendment were applied against Pakistan alone. Although India had imported nuclear technology for peaceful purposes and then diverted it to make nuclear explosive in violation of agreements with Canada and the United States, it got away scot-free.

At first, the Ford administration sought to persuade Pakistan to abandon the nuclear programme. Secretary of State Kissinger came to Pakistan in August 1976 and offered to recommend for congressional approval the sale of 110 A-7 aircraft. Bhutto thanked him but said 'No', after all senior officials urged the prime minister to decline.

Relations between Pakistan and the United States slid when Bhutto tried to divert attention from countrywide agitation following the rigged election in 1977, by projecting the United States as his adversary. He misinterpreted an intelligence intercept of a remark by an official of the US mission in Pakistan in April, saying, 'My source tells me the party is over' to mean Bhutto could no longer continue in power. (The officer later explained he was actually correcting an earlier message according to which Bhutto had been detained at a party.)[13] Bhutto, facing domestic protests against rigged elections, used the intercept to allege 'political bloodhounds were after him because of his opposition to US policies on a number of international issues.'[14] In response to Bhutto's accusation, Secretary of State Cyrus Vance sent a conciliatory letter refuting the charge. Bhutto projected it as an apology.

Until then the Carter administration had not reviewed the policy of the Ford administration. On April 28—the same day Bhutto accused the US of conspiring against him—the US navy transferred two destroyers to Pakistan under a long-term lease.

Soon President Carter's policy in South Asia became India-centric. Departing from the practice of his predecessors, Carter excluded Pakistan from his tour of Asian countries. Pakistan was concerned that National Security Adviser Zbigniew Brzezinsky's concept of 'regional influentials' would encourage and reinforce India's hegemonic ambitions. The slide in Pakistan-US relations accelerated after General Ziaul Haq took over in July 1977. The offer to sell A-7 aircraft was withdrawn. On April 1979, President Carter decided to apply sanctions against Pakistan: US aid to Pakistan of around $50 million a year was cut off. Noting that the US had taken no action against India even for exploding a nuclear device, Islamabad protested against this 'act of discrimination . . . (applying) different standards to different states.'[15] But it evoked no sympathy at the time. In August 1979, the US was reported to have even considered the option of destroying Pakistan's nuclear capability by an attack on Kahuta.[16] Although the state department issued a categorical denial, the report illustrated the dangerous deterioration in Pakistan-US relations.

Also, the United States continued pressure on France. In 1978, President Giscard d'Estaing decided to renege on the reprocessing plant contract, inflicting colossal damage to Pakistan's nuclear programme. By then Pakistan had already paid over a hundred million dollars to the French supplier of equipment. More than a decade later France agreed to partially compensate Pakistan for the losses.

US Embassy burned, 1979. On 21 November 1979, a mob of students from the Quaid-i-Azam University, infuriated by a false report broadcast by an unidentified radio alleging US occupation of the holy Kaaba, attacked the American embassy in Islamabad. Local police and a security contingent took four hours to come to the rescue. By then the premises were burnt and an American and two Pakistani staff members had perished in the fire. Pakistan accepted responsibility for failure to fulfil its obligation under international law to protect the diplomatic mission, and immediately agreed to pay compensation. (The students' protest cost the country $23 million.)

Steadfast pursuit of the nuclear programme. Meanwhile, Pakistan continued to make technological progress towards acquisition of the nuclear option. Overcoming obstacles and resisting discriminatory pressures, it succeeded not only in completing the Kahuta plant but also achieving explosion technology. Scientists at the Pakistan Atomic Energy Commission were able to master the design of the nuclear device. By the mid-1980s, Pakistan publicly acknowledged possession of the capability, although it disclaimed having produced nuclear weapons.[17]

Soon other strategic imperatives dictated a different priority to the United States, as a result of the Soviet military intervention in Afghanistan in December 1979. The Reagan administration, which came to office in January 1981, decided to join Pakistan in supporting and assisting the Afghan resistance against Soviet occupation. The nuclear sanctions were relegated, though only for the time being.

Indian plan of attack on Kahuta. After Indira Gandhi returned to power in January 1980, she manifested grave concern about the progress Pakistan had reportedly made towards acquiring nuclear explosion capability.[18] Whether under her direction or on its own, the Indian Air Force conducted a study in 1981 concluding that an attack on the Kahuta enrichment plant was feasible.[19] On December 20, 1982 *The Washington Post* reported that Indian military advisers had nine months earlier prepared a plan for strikes on Kahuta and PINSTECH.[20] New Delhi realised that the attack would result in Pakistani retaliation against nuclear power stations in Rajasthan and Trombay causing a disaster, as Munir Ahmad Khan, Chairman of PAEC, mentioned in a conversation with his Indian counterpart Homi Sethna in 1983.[21] But India did not abandon the idea. The notion of collaborating with Israel was then examined. It, too, was found unfeasible, as Pakistan warned it would presume Indian complicity. At the time, the USA was allied with Pakistan as the frontline state in assisting the Afghan Mujahideen against Soviet occupation. At Islamabad's request, the US ascertained Israel had no intention of joining in any such attack. In September 1984, reports appeared in the US press of Indian military planning for an attack on Pakistan's nuclear facilities.[22] Again, before the Brasstacks exercise in early 1987, Rajiv Gandhi considered a preemptive attack on Pakistani nuclear facilities, but he was dissuaded by defence analysts.[23]

By 1990, Pakistan was estimated to have accumulated enough enriched uranium for ten or more explosive devices.[24] By then India had built up a stockpile of weapon-grade plutonium for an estimated 100-plus Hiroshima-size bombs.[25]

India's dual-purpose programme.[26] In 1946 Homi Bhaba, an ambitious and brilliant Cambridge-educated physics professor at Bangalore, obtained approval for the establishment of the Atomic Energy Research

Committee at Mumbai. Jawaharlal Nehru, prime minister of the interim government, said: 'I hope India will use the atomic force for constructive purposes. But if India is threatened she will inevitably try to defend herself by all means at her disposal.'[27] Two years later, speaking in the Indian parliament Nehru said, 'I think we must develop [atomic energy] for peaceful purposes....Of course, if we are compelled as a nation to use it for *other purposes*, possibly no pious sentiment of any of us will stop the nation from using it that way.'[28] (Emphasis added.)

Taking advantage of the permissive environment for international cooperation, India embarked on a programme for acquisition of the entire range of fuel cycle plants. Under the Atoms for Peace plan, the USA provided training facilities for foreign scientists and engineers. Between 1955 and 1974 1,104 Indians trained at the Argonne Laboratory School of Nuclear Science and Engineering and 'mined' the declassified literature for design and operation of nuclear facilities. India built the first research reactor ASPARA in 1955 with the assistance of the UK which provided the heavy water. CIRUS, a 40 megawatt research reactor suitable for generation of bomb-grade plutonium was built with the assistance of Canada, which accepted the Indian statement that it would use the resultant fissile material for peaceful purposes only. On similar terms, the USA provided heavy water for the plant. In 1961 India began construction of the Phoenix plant for reprocessing plutonium. A US firm, Vitro International, was the contractor for preparing the construction blueprints, while technological assistance was provided by the British Atomic Energy Commission.[29] In 1963 the US decided to provide two reactors for the Tarapur power plant.

Vikram Sarabhai, although Bhaba's successor in 1966, was opposed to nuclear weapons on moral and economic grounds, a group of scientists led by Raja Ramanna, R. Chidambaran and P. K. Iyenger continued work on the project for a nuclear explosion. Meanwhile, the foreign policy establishment protected India's nuclear option in negotiations on NPT under the leadership of Trivedi, who opposed any prohibition on the transfer of nuclear technology for peaceful purposes, calling it 'nuclear apartheid.' Indira Gandhi's government decided not to sign the NPT in 1968. In 1972 she authorised preparations for a nuclear test.

Codenamed 'Buddha Smiles', the explosion on 18 May 1974 was termed a 'peaceful explosion.' Years later the Indian scientist who played a leadership role acknowledged it was actually a bomb test. Indian politicians and the media considered it a bomb test. 'Monopoly of Big

Five Broken', thundered the *Sunday Standard*. 'India Goes Nuclear at Last', crowed *Motherland*. Most parties were ecstatic. Jana Sangh called it 'a red letter day in Indian history'.

International sanctions and tightened export controls slowed down the programme, but India now had proven technology and all the requisite facilities for building a nuclear arsenal. It did not consider it necessary to conduct another test until the Bharatiya Janata party came to power. Under Prime Minister Atal Bihari Vajpayee's directive India, on 11 May 1998, tested three nuclear weapons and again two more two days later. The US condemned the tests publicly but once again accepted the reality. President Bill Clinton paid an unprecedented six-day visit to India in early 2000. In 2005, President George W. Bush agreed to extend technological cooperation to India for nuclear power plants, proposing an India-specific exception to US nonproliferation laws, as well as to the agreed restrictions of the Nuclear Suppliers Group. An equal criteria-based treatment was denied to Pakistan.

NOTES

1. George Perkovich, *India's Nuclear Bomb*, California University Press, Berkley, CAL, 1999, p. 13.
2. 'If India has the bomb, that does not mean we are going to be subjected to nuclear blackmail,' said Zulfikar Ali Bhutto, on 13 August 1966. See Stanley Wolpert, *Zulfi Bhutto of Pakistan*, p. 112. On another occasion Bhutto said:'[I]f India acquires nuclear status, Pakistan will have to follow suit...'
3. Iqbal Akhund, *Memoires of a Bystander: A life in Diplomacy*, Oxford University Press, Karachi, 1997, p. 264.
4. Former PAEC scientists who participated in a meeting in Islamabad on 29 April 2005 to commemorate the sixth death anniversary of Munir Ahmad Khan clarified that the Multan meeting did not discuss the question of making a bomb. Deserved tributes were paid for Munir's seminal role in developing the nuclear programme as PAEC chairman, as well as his extraordinary discretion in public statements, recognising the danger in flaunting the PAEC's great contribution to the success of the programme.
5. As recounted in Perkovich, op. cit., Kissinger rejected a draft prepared by a state department official (Dennis Kux) that criticised India for undermining nonproliferation efforts. Instead he decided that 'public scolding would not undo the event, but only add to bilateral Indo-US problems and reduce the influence Washington might have on India's future nuclear policy'.
6. Secret state department memorandum of 13 September 1961, quoted in Perkovich, op. cit., p. 52.
7. Z. A. Bhutto, *The Myth of Independence*, 1969.
8. To his credit, Air Marshal Zulfiqar Ali Khan advised against accepting the conditional offer of sale of aircraft because he believed acquisition of the nuclear option was more important in the longer perspective.
9. A. Q. Khan, Chairman, Khan Research Laboratories, 'The Journey to our Tests', *The News*, Islamabad, Special Issue, 28 May 1999.

10. Dr. Ishfaq Ahmad, Chairman, PAEC, 'Pakistan's nuclear capability', *The News*, Islamabad, Special Issue, 28 May 1999.

11. Interview on Radio Pakistan by Dr. Samar Mubarkmand, senior scientist of PAEC, reported in *The Gulf Today*, 19 May 1999.

12. *Ibid.*

13. Dennis Kux, op. cit., p. 229.

14. Prime Minister Bhutto's statement in parliament on 28 April 1977. *Documents*, ed. Arif, p. 329.

15. Statement by Pakistan Foreign Office, 7 April 1979. Documents, ed. Arif, p. 347.

16. *The New York Times* 12 and 15 August report, quoted in Dennis Kux, op. cit. p. 240.

17. A Pakistani spokesman reiterated on 24 August 1994, that Pakistan has the capacity to produce nuclear weapons but has not actually done so. Former Prime Minister Nawaz Sharif's statement that 'Pakistan possesses the atomic bomb' was described, also by a U.S. state department official, as having 'something to do with domestic politics.' *Reuters/AP* dispatches of 23 and 24 August 1994.

18. When the author, then ambassador to India, called on her after her election victory, she seemed obsessed about reports of Pakistan's nuclear programme.

19. Perkovich, op. cit., p. 240, quoting from a research paper by W. P. S. Sidhu.

20. Useful information on the subject is provided in Perkovich, op. cit., pp. 239-41.

21. Perkovich, op. cit., p. 241.

22. *The Times of India News Service* correspondent from Washington reported on 17 September 1984 that according to *The Washington Post* and *The New York Times* 'U.S. intelligence agencies recently briefed a senate subcommittee…that military advisers had suggested to (Indian Prime Minister) Mrs. Indira Gandhi that to prevent Pakistan from making the bomb, India should launch a pre-emptive strike on the Pakistani nuclear facility at Kahuta.' *The Times of India* published the report on 18 September 1984, under a slanted headline: 'U.S. false alarm to Pak of Indian pre-emptive attack.' Also see *The Indian Express*, 19 September 1984, report by H. K. Dua, entitled: 'India concerned over US signal to Pak on Jaguar deployment.'

23. Perkovich, op. cit., p. 280.

24. Lewis A. Dunn, *Containing Nuclear Proliferation*, Adelphi Paper No. 263 (London: International Institute for Strategic Studies, 1991), p. 17.

25. Ibid.

26. This section has benefited greatly from George Perkovich, *India's Nuclear Bomb*, University of California Press, Berkeley, 1999.

27. [27] Ibid., p. 14, quoting from Dorothy Newman, Nehru: *The First Sixty Years*.

28. [28] Jawaharlal Nehru, *Selected Works*, Second Series, Vol. 5, p. 27.

29. [29] Munir Ahmad Khan, 'Nuclearisation of South Asia and its Regional and Global Implications', *Regional Studies*, Islamabad, Autumn 1998.

CHAPTER 13

The Afghanistan Crisis

Few other countries are closer to Pakistan in culture and history than Afghanistan. The hope for friendly cooperation was, however, vitiated at the start. On the eve of the establishment of Pakistan, the Afghan government denounced the treaty Amir Abdurrahman had concluded in 1893, establishing the Durand Line as the boundary with British India. It launched a territorial claim, in the guise of support for 'Pushtoonistan', which it wanted to be carved out of Pakistan. Afghanistan was the only country to vote against Pakistan's admission to the United Nations. In the decades that followed, relations between the two neighbours remained strained though fortunately, tensions were kept under control. The Afghan government did not exploit Pakistan's vulnerability during the wars with India. When Sardar Mohammad Daoud assumed power on 17 July 1973, supplanting King Mohammad Zahir Shah, his cousin and brother-in-law, apprehensions of deterioration of bilateral relations rose in Islamabad, as he was a known Pakistan-baiter.

Aiming to use Soviet support to consolidate his power at home and pursue the irredenta against Pakistan, Daoud entered into close relations with the Soviet Union. He was no doubt pleased when Premier Alexei Kosygin exhorted Pakistan to improve relations with 'our friendly neighbour.' However, the embrace soon proved to be a bear hug. By 1976 Daoud appeared to have realised that the Soviets had an agenda of their own. They had penetrated the internal politics of the country, providing support and assistance to the revolutionary People's Democratic Party of Afghanistan (PDPA). To counterbalance the Soviet influence, Daoud embarked on efforts to improve relations with Pakistan, Iran and other Muslim countries. He and Prime Minister Z. A. Bhutto exchanged visits in 1976. Bilateral relations continued to improve after General Ziaul Haq assumed power in Pakistan in July 1977. Daoud's talks with Zia proved 'extremely useful.' He asked President Zia 'to give me time to mould public opinion in my country to effect a change... to normalise relations with Pakistan.'

Daoud's new policy did not please Moscow or the PDPA. He tried, too late, to control the revolutionaries at home. The contest culminated in a coup on 27 April 1978 that PDPA called the 'Saur Revolution'. Daoud and members of his family were murdered, the constitution was abrogated and a revolution proclaimed by a clique of communist intellectuals. Repeating Daoud's error, they too sought to exploit Soviet support for their own aims, and like him, suffered the same fate, proving the verity, 'Those who foolishly seek power by riding on the back of the tiger end up inside.'

Nur Muhammad Taraki assumed the office of president in the name of the PDPA. The party lacked a popular base. From the beginning the new regime was faced with opposition in the traditional and conservative Afghan society. Also the party was riven with rivalry between its predominantly rural and Pushto-speaking Khalq, and urban-based Persian-speaking Parcham, factions. Infighting led to Taraki's murder in September 1979. He was succeeded by Hafizullah Amin, whose radical reforms evoked even stronger opposition from the Afghan people. Headstrong and defiant of Soviet guidance, he was considered by his rivals in the party, and by the Soviets, to be endangering the stability of the revolution.

On 26 December 1979, the Soviet forces rolled into Afghanistan, eliminated Amin and installed Babrak Karmal, leader of the Parcham faction, as president in his place. The Soviet pretext of an invitation by the Afghan government for intervention by its forces was obviously false, as its target was none other than the head of that government.

The intervention provoked a deep sense of alarm in Pakistan. Suddenly the buffer disappeared and the Soviet superpower advanced to Pakistan's borders. The security strategists believed that if allowed to consolidate its hold, the Soviet Union could later leap down the Bolan and Khyber passes to fulfil the historical czarist ambition for access to the warm waters of the Arabian Sea.

Anxiety was enhanced by the realisation that Pakistan was deeply divided internally and isolated internationally. The rigging of elections by Prime Minister Bhutto in 1977, the countrywide agitation that brought the economy to the edge of ruin, Bhutto's overthrow in a military coup, and hanging in April 1979 upon conviction on a charge of murder, had polarised opinion at home as never before. General Ziaul Haq's decision to ignore appeals by foreign leaders and the media for clemency had antagonised the whole world.

Pakistan's reaction to the Soviet intervention was visceral, but in deciding policy it sought to exercise prudence.[1] It was 'fully conscious' of the risks of antagonising and pitting itself against a superpower. But it also realised that acquiescence in the *fait accompli* would entail even greater dangers. Apart from undermining the sacrosanct principle of inadmissibility of aggression, consolidation of Soviet power in Afghanistan would enhance the danger of Soviet collaboration with India for another military intervention, exposing Pakistan to the nightmare of an Indo-Soviet 'nutcracker'.

Zia's government took two days to decide on its public reaction. The carefully crafted statement did not even name the Soviet Union. Instead it referred to the 'induction of foreign troops' and described it as a 'serious violation' of the norms of peaceful coexistence and the principles of the UN Charter. Rather defensively, it explained Pakistan's 'gravest concern' in the context of its links of Islam, geography and non-aligned policy with Afghanistan, and concluded by expressing the hope that 'the foreign troops would be removed from the Afghan soil forthwith.' The element of caution was implicit in avoidance of condemnation.

Non-aligned Policy. Pakistan noted the strong reaction of the United States and West European countries[2] but, apprehensive of the possibly dangerous implications of involvement in the Cold War, it hitched its diplomacy to the hope of a political resolution of the crisis through the United Nations. It was assumed that Moscow, however cynical, could not dismiss the condemnation of the world, including the Western and especially Islamic and non-aligned nations.

At Pakistan's request, six non-permanent members, all non-aligned, sponsored a resolution in the UN Security Council. It strongly deplored 'the recent armed intervention in Afghanistan' and called for 'immediate, unconditional and total withdrawal of the foreign troops in order to enable its people to determine their own form of government and choose their own economic, political and social systems free from outside intervention, subversion, coercion or constraint of any kind whatever.' At Islamabad's request, the resolution neither named the Soviet Union nor used the stronger word 'condemnation'. It received thirteen votes in the fifteen-member Council but, as expected, it was vetoed by the USSR. The resolution was then taken up by the General Assembly under the 'Uniting for Peace' procedure and after a short debate, was adopted on 14 January 1980 by a majority of 104 votes in favour, eighteen against and eighteen abstentions. Foreign Minister Agha Shahi ably piloted these resolutions

The USSR suffered a severe blow to its image. Not only the Western bloc but also fifty-six out of ninety-two members of the Non-Aligned

Movement (NAM) voted for the resolution while most of the rest abstained. Even India was initially critical. In December, the Indian Prime Minister Charan Singh, issued a strong statement condemning the intervention. After his government lost the election in January 1980 the prime minister-elect, Indira Gandhi, adopted a pro-Soviet stance. The Indian statement in the General Assembly not only did not criticise the Soviet intervention but even accepted the Soviet explanation that its limited forces would be withdrawn after a limited period. Indira Gandhi mocked Pakistan's diplomacy of building moral pressure on the Soviet Union, rhetorically asking the Pakistani ambassador: 'Do you expect the UN resolution will force the Soviets to withdraw troops?'[3] Her cynical view was not surprising, as India itself had refused to comply with the UN resolutions on Kashmir. Soon India joined a coterie of Soviet apologists. In the NAM Coordinating Bureau, they sabotaged a resolution on Afghanistan. The outcome did not, however, damage the Afghan cause so much as it did the credibility of NAM itself.[4]

As part of a campaign to mobilise pressure of world opinion on Moscow, an extraordinary session of the Organisation of the Islamic Conference (OIC) foreign ministers was held in Islamabad on 29 January. Several members spoke in harsh terms. The resolution adopted by the meeting proclaimed a strong indictment of the Soviet intervention. It also suspended Afghanistan's membership of the OIC, and affirmed solidarity with the struggle of the Afghan people to safeguard 'their faith, national independence and territorial integrity.'

More critical to the outcome of the crisis than censure abroad was the opposition to the Soviet intervention inside Afghanistan. A traditional people with a sense of pride in their history, having challenged and defeated colonial Britain's invasions a century earlier, the Afghans were engaged in partisan resistance against the PDPA since it grabbed power in 1978. With the arrival of foreign troops to protect and perpetuate a regime with an alien ideology, the resistance was transformed into a people's war.

Pakistan was sympathetic to the Afghan cause, but caution and lack of resources limited the support and assistance it could provide to the Mujahideen. The Soviets were threatening in their warnings. Pakistan decided, nevertheless, to provide discreet help. Besides the motivation of solidarity with the Afghan people, self-interest was the clinching rationale of the decision. In fighting for their national survival, the Mujahideen would be fighting also for Pakistan's own security and independence.

Although the American CIA also began to provide some assistance to the Afghan resistance, Pakistan's decision to assist the jihad was made autonomously, without foreign instigation. Wary of the consequences, Pakistan was anxious to preclude any impression of acting at the behest of the United States or wanting to push Afghanistan into the Cold War.

The initial thrust of Pakistan's policy was diplomatic in orientation. To that end, it sought to build up greater political pressure on the Soviet Union at the regular session of the UN General Assembly in 1980. A group of like-minded non-aligned countries from Africa, Asia and Latin America coordinated by Kuwait, prepared an elaborate draft resolution that suggested the outlines of a political solution. The components included (i) immediate withdrawal of the foreign forces, (ii) preservation of the sovereignty, territorial integrity, independence and non-aligned status of Afghanistan, (iii) respect for the right of its people to determine their own form of government and economic system, free from outside intervention, subversion, coercion or constraint, and (iv) creation of conditions for the voluntary return of Afghan refugees to their homes in safety and honour. The resolution further provided for efforts by the UN Secretary General to promote a political solution that could include guarantees of non-use of force against the security of 'all neighbouring countries.' Similar resolutions, with updated text attracted even greater support over succeeding years, rising from 111 votes in 1980 to 123 in 1987. During the same period, negative votes and abstentions combined declined from thirty-six in 1980 to thirty in 1987.[5] Every year the world community administered a stinging blow to Soviet prestige.

Revival of the US Alliance

Pakistan's decision to oppose the Soviet intervention in Afghanistan was made at a time when its relations with the United States were strained because of the discriminatory sanctions imposed by the Carter administration in 1979.[6] Nor could Pakistan assume that the United States would join in opposing the Soviet intervention; Washington had remained quiescent following the communist coup in April 1978 and President Carter had hardly reacted to the murder of American ambassador Adolph Dubs.

The Soviet invasion appeared to shake the United States out of indifference, but hardly enough for Pakistan to conclude it could be

counted upon to review its policy toward Pakistan. Unknown to
Islamabad, US National Security Council adviser Zbigniew Brzezinski
had recommended to President Carter, 'This will require a review of
our policy towards Pakistan, more guarantees to it, more aid, and alas,
a decision that our security policy toward Pakistan cannot be dictated
by our non-proliferation policy.'[7] But Washington did not inform
Islamabad of what it contemplated with regard to security guarantees
or waiver of nuclear sanctions. Had consultations been held, Islamabad
would have sought a guarantee of American assistance in the event of
Soviet or a Soviet-backed Indian attack on Pakistan. To that end, it
needed the upgradation of the 1959 executive agreement on defence
cooperation into a binding treaty. As President Ziaul Haq later said,
the 'credibility and durability'[8] of American assurances was low,
founded in the widely held belief that at critical junctures, especially
in 1965 and 1971, the United States had betrayed a friend and ally.

Washington acted rather strangely. Without any consultation with
Islamabad the US President announced an offer of $400 million in
economic and military assistance for Pakistan over 18 months.
Islamabad believed that the defence component would enhance risks
of reinvolvement in the Cold War. Moreover, the aid package was
'wrapped up in onerous conditions' and these could affect Pakistan's
pursuit of the nuclear programme thus 'denuding (the offer) of
relevance to our defensive capacity.'[9] President Zia announced the
rejection of the offer, describing it as 'peanuts.' This word ridiculing
the amount of the offer gave the wrong impression that what Islamabad
wanted was larger aid. Actually, Pakistan was prepared to accept $200
million in economic assistance but not the other half for defence. It
was the United States that refused to de-link economic assistance from
the defence component. Pakistan's refusal to accept the US aid offer
did not affect its steadfast policy of opposition to Soviet intervention.
For more than a year it continued to support the Afghan resistance,
also providing it modest assistance out of its own meagre resources.

Non-acceptance of US aid in 1980 reduced the risk of plunging
Pakistan back into the orbit of the Cold War. It also helped in
projecting the Afghan cause in its genuine perspective of a liberation
struggle. It served, moreover, to save Pakistan's relations with Iran from
further strain. The Iranian media perception of Pakistan as a proxy for
US interests in the region was painful to Pakistanis, who value Iran as
a friend and a fraternal neighbour. The sincerity of Pakistan's solidarity
with Iran was illustrated again in April 1980 when it expressed 'shock
and dismay' at the US assault on Iran in an attempt to forcibly rescue

American embassy staff from captivity, and 'deplored this impermissible act which constitutes a serious violation of Iran's sovereignty.'

US Aid. After President Ronald Reagan succeeded Carter in 1981, Washington revived the offer of cooperation with Pakistan. Senior US officials visited Islamabad for talks. By April, the US decided on a new package, with loans and grants amounting to three billion dollars over five years.[10] The amount of $600 million a year for development and defence was a significant improvement over the Carter offer of $400 million for 18 months. The new offer still did not address Pakistan's concerns about defence against the Soviets or Soviet-aided Indian threat. These were taken up during negotiations. The US side explained that Congressional opinion was reluctant to support a formal security guarantee to Pakistan. The administration, however, evinced a reassuring understanding of Pakistan's vulnerabilities as a front-line state. As an earnest of US concern for Pakistan's security, it agreed to consider the sale of 40 F-16 aircraft. Also, the 5-year programme generated an aura of durability around the US commitment.

On the nuclear issue, the two countries maintained their formal positions, Pakistan reiterating its intention to continue research, and the US proclaiming its non-proliferation concern. But Washington turned the pressure off. Secretary of State Alexander Haig indicated that the nuclear was no longer the priority issue. Acknowledging past discrimination and expressing understanding of Pakistan's rationale,[11] Washington accepted Zia's assurance that Pakistan would not develop nuclear weapons or transfer sensitive technology.[12] Later, it secured Congressional approval for a waiver of the Symington prohibition. Senators and Congressmen who targeted Pakistan for discriminatory sanctions no longer commanded decisive influence.

Pakistan chose not to accept concessional loans for military sales, and instead opted to pay the market rate of interest, so as to safeguard its non-aligned credentials. Islamabad wanted to retain credibility as an independent actor in the hope of persuading the Soviet Union to agree to a political solution of the Afghanistan question outside the Cold War context. In the event, the sacrifice won no appreciation from either Moscow or New Delhi. They denounced Pakistan even though a year earlier India itself had signed a deal with the USSR for the latest MIG aircraft, T-72 tanks and warships, etc. for a give-away price of $1.6 billion on soft terms, though the market value was estimated at $6 billion. In retrospect, Pakistan's more-pious-than-the-Pope posture did not yield commensurate political advantage. Critics unmindful of non-aligned support considered it a costly pose.[13]

Geneva Accords[14]

UN efforts to promote a political solution began in earnest with the appointment of Diego Cordovez, a senior UN official from Ecuador, as the personal representative of the Secretary General in 1981. He found the situation rather bizarre. Before he could convene the first Geneva meeting, Iran declined to participate arguing that the Soviet withdrawal should be unconditional, and Pakistan was unwilling to meet with the Afghan regime which it did not recognize. Cordovez had to persuade Kabul to agree to indirect talks. The Soviet Union refused to join talks taking the position that its forces entered Afghanistan at Kabul's invitation and would be withdrawn when Kabul no longer wanted their presence, but it sent high-level officials to Geneva to be available for consultation.

Negotiations began in Geneva in June 1982 with exploration of the structure of a settlement that would integrate the components of the UN General Assembly resolution. An energetic, dedicated and persuasive diplomat of high calibre, Cordovez sidetracked controversy over the past by proposing an agreement on mutual non-interference and non-intervention between Afghanistan and its neighbours as a means of obtaining a Soviet commitment to withdrawal of forces. To satisfy the Soviet demand for American commitment to non-interference, he conceived the idea of guarantees by both super-powers. Negotiations were not, however, a serious undertaking at first. Moscow was confident that its mighty forces equipped with the latest weapons would rout the ragtag Mujahideen armed with antiquated rifles. It misjudged the situation, as it could not pin down the Mujahideen guerrillas who were supported by the Afghan populace and received sophisticated weapons from the United States for guerrilla warfare.

After the death of the hard-liner Soviet leader Leonid Brezhnev, in November 1982, hopes rose for a political settlement. In a meeting with Zia who visited Moscow for Brezhnev's funeral, Yuri Andropov, the new Soviet leader, gave a 'hint of flexibility.' UN Secretary General Perez de Cuellar and Diego Cordovez, who met Andropov in March 1983, received 'new encouragement' for pursuing UN mediation. Andropov counted out to them the reasons why the Soviet Union wanted a solution. Raising his fingers one by one he mentioned costs in lives and money, regional tensions, setback to detente and loss of Soviet prestige in the Third World.[15]

Buoyed by the positive signals, Cordovez successfully pressed the two sides in the 1983 April and June rounds of Geneva talks to agree on the components of a comprehensive settlement. These included an agreement on non-interference and non-intervention, guarantees by third states, and arrangements for the voluntary return of refugees. Discussions made good progress. Cordovez was optimistic and envisaged 'gradual withdrawal' of Soviet forces within a reasonable timeframe. But the Soviet–Kabul side dragged their feet, indicating that the hardliners were marking time as Andropov was ailing. After he died, they reverted to the policy of a military solution, which continued under Konstantin Chernenko and Mikhail Gorbachev till the end of the summer in 1987.

The struggle in Afghanistan was unequal but the Mujahideen demonstrated courage and resourcefulness in resistance, and did not wilt despite the increasing ferocity of Soviet pressure. Their sacrifices and stamina drew deserved praise and tribute. Assistance to them increased so as to neutralise the Soviet induction of more lethal artillery, helicopter gunships and bombers for savage and indiscriminate destruction of villages to interdict Mujahideen activities. The United States raised covert allocations for supply of arms to the Mujahideen, from $250 million in 1985, to $470 million in 1986 and $630 million in 1987.[16] The US aid was reportedly matched by Saudi Arabia. Also China, Iran and several other countries provided significant assistance. Pakistan calibrated the flow of assistance to the Mujahideen cautiously so as to minimise the risk of spillover of the conflict, but became bolder with time and experience. It realised that a super-power's forces could not be defeated militarily but also that attrition inside Afghanistan combined with blows to its prestige internationally offered the only hope of wearing Moscow down. Negotiations in Geneva and resolutions in OIC, NAM and the United Nations were a part of that strategy for increasing political pressure.

Diego Cordovez patiently kept the Geneva talks on track, however slow their pace. Altogether twelve sessions were held over six years. He and the Pakistani side occasionally discussed the question of a compromise between the Kabul regime and the Mujahideen, but this subject was not on the agenda. UN resolutions referred to the principle of respect for the right of the Afghan people to determine their own form of government and economic system, but this was not interpreted as requiring replacement of the regime installed by the Soviet forces.

Kabul and Moscow at first refused even to recognise the reality of internal resistance. They said 'everything comes from outside.'[17] USSR Foreign Minister Gromyko dismissed the idea of a broad-based government in Kabul as 'unrealistic phantasies.'

Cordovez himself realised the need for a compromise among the Afghans but as he said, correctly for the time, 'The UN is not in the business of establishing governments.'[18] In 1983, when Andropov indicated a desire for settlement, Cordovez was inclined to favour a role for former King Zahir Shah who offered to work to unite the Afghans. The idea received enthusiastic support from Afghan exiles. A poll organized by Professor Syed Bahauddin Majrooh, a prominent Afghan scholar who was editing a paper from Peshawar, found that 70 per cent of the Afghan refugees in Pakistan favoured Zahir Shah's return. But this view was rejected by the more powerful Mujahideen parties. When Majrooh was later assassinated, opponents of the king were suspected of having organised the crime.

By late 1986, the texts of the agreements having been all but finalised, Cordovez remarked: 'It (is) now true for the first time that the only issue remaining (is) the question of the timeframe (for the withdrawal of Soviet forces from Afghanistan).'[19]

Still evasive on the central issue in 1986, the Soviet side said its forces would be withdrawn four years after the conclusion of the Geneva Accords, while Pakistan asked for withdrawals to be completed in three months. By mid-1987 the Soviets wanted 18 months for withdrawal while Pakistan went up to seven months. The issue was not to be settled until after the failure of the Soviet military offensive in the summer of 1987. Mikhail Gorbachev then finally decided to abandon the misadventure. By then the imperatives of democratic and economic reforms at home necessitated an end to confrontation with the West.

In July 1987, Najibullah proposed a coalition offering twelve ministries and the office of vice president to the Mujahideen Alliance. Gorbachev endorsed the idea of national reconciliation to facilitate the process of 'constructing a new Afghanistan.' The Alliance leaders were, however, unanimous in rejecting a coalition with the PDPA. In September 1987, Cordovez put forward a 'Scenario Paper' envisaging a representative assembly comprising the seven Mujahideen Alliance parties, the PDPA and select Afghan personalities to form a transitional arrangement. Aware of the Alliance's views, Islamabad did not accord the idea much attention. When it was conveyed to them in early 1988, the Alliance leaders ruled out any dialogue with the PDPA. Engineer

Gulbuddin Hikmatyar, Professor Burhanuddin Rabbani and Maulvi Yunus Khalis also ruled out any role for the king. Pakistan did not pursue Cordovez's suggestion. Since resistance against the Soviets still commanded priority, it was considered inadvisable to press the Mujahideen lest that should divide and weaken the Alliance.

Gorbachev and Shevardnadze succeeded in winning the endorsement of the Politburo of the communist party for the policy of terminating military involvement in Afghanistan.[20] The costs of the policy in human and material resources and the obloquy it entailed, even in the Soviet Union's non-aligned backyard, were glaringly disproportionate to any benefits that continued hold over Afghanistan might yield. The new generation of communists no longer shared the pristine ideological fervour of the founders or faith in the inevitability of communism's victory. In fact, the Soviet system was faltering, the economy was in decline and the people were alienated. The cost of military confrontation and the arms race with the West, occupation of Eastern Europe, tension with China, and finally, intervention in Afghanistan had 'ruined'[21] the Soviet Union.

Gorbachev announced, at a press conference in Washington on 10 December 1987, that the Soviet forces would withdraw from Afghanistan within twelve months of the conclusion of Geneva Accords, and further, that during that period the forces would not engage in combat. Gorbachev also delinked the question of withdrawal from an internal settlement in Afghanistan. Though he reaffirmed support for 'a coalition on the basis of national reconciliation and the realities of the situation,'[22] Moscow was no longer prepared to allow the Alliance's rejectionist attitude to obstruct its decision to extricate the Soviet Union from the Afghan quagmire. Nor was it willing to undertake the removal of the Kabul regime and hand over the government to the Mujahideen Alliance.

Just as prospects for the conclusion of the Geneva Accords brightened, dark clouds suddenly appeared on the horizon in Pakistan. In January 1988, President Zia took the position that the conclusion of the Accords should be postponed until after agreement was reached on the formation of a government in Kabul with the participation of the Mujahideen. This took Pakistan's Prime Minister, Mohammad Khan Junejo, completely by surprise: heretofore Pakistan's refrain was that the only outstanding obstacle to the conclusion of the Geneva Accords was a reasonable timeframe for the withdrawal of Soviet forces. Besides, making the formation of a coalition government a precondition for the conclusion of the Accords seemed a recipe for delaying the withdrawal of the Soviet forces, because the Mujahideen Alliance was known to be averse to the idea of a coalition with the PDPA. Now the Soviets were no longer prepared to wait. When on 9 February, Zia pressed the visiting Soviet First Deputy Foreign Minister Yuli Vorontsov for postponement of the final Geneva round, his comment was withering to the point of insolence. He said: 'For eight years you have been asking us to leave Afghanistan. Now you want us to stay. I smell a rat!'[23]

The logic of Zia's eleventh-hour *volte-face* was never explained. Pakistan's foreign friends were as mystified as Prime Minister Junejo. His new policy reversed Pakistan's oft stated position, namely, that the only remaining obstacle to the Geneva Accords was an acceptable time frame for the withdrawal of Soviet forces. Zia's changed stance contradicted Pakistan's long-held position. Moreover, it was illogical because Moscow had decided to pull out of Afghanistan. Pakistan could block the Geneva Accords, but it could not prevent the Soviets from withdrawing from Afghanistan either unilaterally or pursuant to an agreement with the Kabul regime. In comparison with these alternatives, withdrawal under the Accords was decidedly more advantageous. The Soviet Union would be internationally bound to withdraw its forces completely, within a prescribed timeframe and under UN monitoring. It would be legally bound also to refrain from intervention in Afghanistan. Pakistan, too, would receive Soviet and US guarantees of respect for principles of non-interference and non-intervention. In contrast, unilateral withdrawal would entail no such commitments.

For Moscow, the residual consideration now was the manner of disengagement so as to avoid danger to their retreating forces and further humiliation for the Soviet Union. It prized the Geneva Accords because contained in them was a commitment to observe principle of non-interference and non-intervention. Pakistan and the United States would be under an obligation to discontinue assistance to the Mujahideen. That might save the Soviet friends in Afghanistan from massacre. No less important was their symbolic value. The UN-sponsored agreement would provide a fig leaf to cover the Soviet defeat. As for Pakistan, it could only gain by cooperating in sparing humiliation to the Soviet Union. That would open the possibility for Pakistan to improve relations with this superpower.

Gulbuddin Hikmatyar, an engineer by training but with an impressive grasp of law, contributed to the improvement of the Geneva texts. In a consultation meeting with Pakistani officials, he suggested two significant modifications. He pointed out that Pakistan's signature on an agreement with Afghanistan would constitute recognition of the Kabul regime. Secondly, the agreement would require discontinuation of arms supply to 'rebels' but not to the Kabul regime. He was right on both points.

In friendly conversations at the foreign office in February 1988, Vorontsov was informed that Pakistan would publicly state that the signing of the agreement would not constitute recognition of the Kabul regime. A diplomat of world class, confident in his understanding of his country's policy and decisive in negotiations, he instantly agreed not to make this matter an issue. Nor did he contest the logic of the view that peace in Afghanistan required all sides to discontinue arms supply. On the Soviet side, he convincingly explained, Moscow could not go back on its existing commitments to Kabul. 'Negative symmetry' was not feasible but when told that in that event 'positive symmetry' would ensue, and the Mujahideen, too, could continue to receive supplies, he did not make an issue of the matter. The discussion served to preclude subsequent misunderstanding between Islamabad and Moscow.[24]

The final Geneva round began on 2 March 1988. The talks proceeded in slow motion because the Pakistan delegation did not have authorisation to finalise the Accords. On their part, the Soviets conveyed their agreement to reduce the timeframe for withdrawal to nine months. The Kabul representatives still persisted in their objection to the phrase 'existing internationally recognised boundaries'[25] and suggested its substitution by the words 'international borders.' Pakistan considered it an artificial issue. The Geneva talks were not convened to debate the Durand Line. Pakistan had no difficulty in accepting the neutral phrase requiring the two states to refrain from the threat or use of force so as 'not to violate the boundaries of each other.'

The replacement of the Kabul regime was never a part of the Geneva negotiations but, as Diego Cordovez said in a statement issued on 8 April, 'it has been consistently recognised that the objective of a comprehensive settlement... can best be ensured by a broad-based Afghan Government' and to that end he agreed to provide his good offices. By that time Zia realised that the formation of such a government could not be made a precondition for the conclusion of the Accords.

The foreign ministers of Afghanistan, Pakistan, and the Soviet Union and the Secretary of State of the United States signed the Geneva Accords on 14 April 1988. Pakistan and the United States declared, on the occasion, that their signatures did not imply recognition of the Kabul regime. The US further declared that 'the obligations undertaken by the guarantors are symmetrical' and that it retained the right to provide military assistance to the Afghan parties, and would exercise restraint should the Soviet Union do so, too. Pakistan also made the same point, and underlined the right of the Afghan people to self-determination.

The Geneva Accords marked the first time for the Soviet Union to agree to withdraw from a 'fraternal' state. Gorbachev acknowledged that the intervention was a 'mistake.' A Soviet journal blamed 'an inner group of a few politburo members headed by Leonid Brezhnev (who), discounting the likely opposition of the Muslim world, China, the United States and the West, decided to take the fateful decision.'[26] Over 13,000 Soviet soldiers were killed and 35,000 wounded.[27] The financial drain was estimated at 100 billion rubles. A classic example of 'imperial over-stretch,'[28] the Afghanistan misadventure could well be considered the proverbial last straw that broke the camel's back. To say that, like the United States in Vietnam, the Soviet Union lost the war in Afghanistan due to pressures of domestic and international opinion is by no means to undervalue the courage and heroism of the Mujahideen, and the fortitude and sacrifices of the Afghan people.

NOTES

1. For an authoritative account of Pakistan's policy in the Afghanistan crisis, see Former Foreign Minister Agha Shahi, *Pakistan's Security and Foreign Policy*, Progressive Publishers, Lahore, 1988.

2. The US State Department issued a prompt condemnation of the 'blatant' Soviet intervention. President Carter called the intervention a 'grave threat to peace,' proclaimed a boycott of the Moscow Olympics and suspended arms limitation talks with Moscow. He expressed concern over the Soviet advance to 'within striking distance of the Indian Ocean and even the Persian Gulf...an area of vital strategic and economic significance to the survival of Western Europe, the Far East, and ultimately the United States.' West European, too, denounced the Soviet intervention but with restraint that reflected their desire not to vitiate detente in Europe.

3. The author was the ambassador.

4. Riaz H. Khan, *Untying the Afghan Knot*, Progressive Publishers, Lahore, 1933, 18–20.

5. For detailed table see Riaz M. Khan, op. cit., p. 40.

6. Also, Washington had remained quiescent following the communist coup by the PDPA in April 1978 and President Carter had hardly reacted to the murder of American ambassador Adolph Dubs in Kabul in February of that year. Now he was preoccupied with the hostage crisis in Iran.

7. Steve Coll, 'This Ghost War: The Secret History of the CIA, Afghanistan and bin Laden', quoted in *Dawn*,Islamabad, 19 November 2004.

8. President Zia in NBC-TV 'Face the Nation' interview with Walter Cronkite, 18 May 1980. *Documents*, ed. Arif, p. 394.

9. Statement by Foreign Affairs Adviser Agha Shahi, 5 March 1980. *Documents*, ed. Arif, p. 388-90.

10. The package included $150 million in economic aid for F'82 and $3 billion for economic assistance and military sales credits for the period F'83-F'87. The data below relates to the economic component. *Economic Survey*, 1995-96, Finance Division, Islamabad.

1981	1982	1983	1984	1985	1986	1987	1988	1989	1990
57	88	224	275	302	313	312	346	347	351

(US $ 100 million)

11. In testimony before a Congressional committee on 27 April 1981 Deputy Assistant Secretary of State Jane Coon acknowledged the injustice of past US policy, saying that sanctions were 'applied in the case of one country—Pakistan.' A few weeks later, Assistant Secretary of State James Buckley exuded understanding of Pakistan's perception that the threat to its security 'could not be met by conventional and political means.' For texts of statements, see *Documents*, ed. Arif.

12. US Department of State, 16 September 1981, *Documents*, ed. Arif, p. 457.

13. The package was carefully negotiated so as to increase the grant component for economic support funds. Still the interest differential on the defence component was initially 8%. As interest rates changed in subsequent years, the differential was reduced. The follow-up agreement remained in force only for three years until 1990 and provided for $700 million a year and the interest rate on military sales credits was reduced to below the market rate.

14. Riaz M. Khan, *Untying the Afghan Knot*, provides authoritative information on Pakistan's diplomacy and the UN-mediated negotiations leading to the Geneva Accords in April 1988.

15. Riaz M. Khan, op. cit., p. 107.

16. Selig Harrison, *Inside the Afghan Talks*, p. 31. Also, Bernett R. Rubin, *The Search for Peace in Afghanistan—From Buffer State to Failed State*, pp. 63-65, and slightly differene figures in Riaz M. Khan, p. 88.

17. Quoted by Diego Cordovez, Rubin, p. 40.

18. Rubin, p. 43.

19. Rubin, p. 77, based on press briefing by Diego Cordovez, 9 Decembr 1986.

20. Shevardnadze told Secretary of State George Shultz on 16 September 1987: 'We will leave Afghanistan... I say with all responsibility that a politial decision has been made.' Quoted from *Shultz, Turmoil* and *Tragedy*, p. 1090, in Rubin, p. 83.

21. Statement by Shevardnadze in a meeting of the Central Committee of CPSU in 1989, after cataloguing over 2,000 billion rubles spent by USSR on maintaining occupation of East European countries, creation of defence structure on the border with China, and in Afghanistan, reported in *Moscow News*, 1989. Author's memory.

22. Riaz M. Khan, p. 234.

23. This exchange took place on 9 February in the author's presence.

24. The author, then foreign secretary, had known Vorontsov for a decade. As ambassadors in New Delhi for four years around 1980 they established amicable relations of mutual trust.

25. This phrase was derived from the 1981 UN Declaration on the Inadmissibility of Intervention and Interference in the Internal Affairs of States.

26. *Literaturnaya Gazeta*, Moscow, 17 February 1988, quoted in Agha Shahi, p. 93.

27. K. M. Arif, p. 237, based on statements by General Alexei Lizichev and Prime Minister Nikolai Ryzhkov.

28. Paul Kennedy, *The Rise and Fall of Great Powers*. He ascribes the fall to 'imperial overstretch'.

CHAPTER 14

Kashmir: The Struggle For *Azadi*

Resisting Indian duress at the Shimla conference in 1972, Pakistan neither compromised its own position on the Kashmir question nor allowed any prejudice to the right of self-determination of the people of Kashmir. In speeches in the UN General Assembly, Pakistan continued to draw the attention of the world community to the festering issue. Neither Pakistan nor India took any initiative, however, toward implementation of the commitment in the Shimla Agreement to discuss 'a final settlement of Jammu and Kashmir.'

Meanwhile, groaning under occupation and suppression, the people of Indian-held Kashmir grasped every opportunity to protest against the denial of their fundamental right to self-determination. In 1973, the valley exploded in protest following the discovery of a book in a library in Anantnag with a drawing of the Prophet.[1] As disaffection continued to intensify, the Indian government installed Sheikh Abdullah as chief minister once again, to exploit whatever support he still had in order to pacify the people. Hankering for power after a long period in the political wilderness, he submitted to Indian terms. The people of Kashmir denounced him, and the government of Pakistan condemned him for this new perfidy.[2] For the few years he remained alive, he had to rely on protection by the Indian police.

In February 1984, a group of Kashmiris in England kidnapped an Indian consular official and killed him, after the Indian government refused to meet their demand for the release of a popular Kashmiri activist from jail in Delhi. The Kashmiri agitation gathered momentum as Indira Gandhi tried to suppress it by appointing a proven martinet as governor in Srinagar. Jagmohan Malhotra, who had demonstrated his ruthlessness during her authoritarian rule, used his sinister skills by playing Sheikh Abdullah's son-in-law, G. M. Shah, against Farooq Abdullah in 1984. When that did not work, Jagmohan imposed his own direct rule, in March 1986. With unrest becoming chronic, Rajiv Gandhi again tried Farooq Abdullah as chief minister but to little avail.

In September 1986, six months, prior to the election in Indian-held Kashmir (IHK), several popular political parties formed a United Muslim Front. Believing they could secure their political aspirations through the peaceful electoral process, the Front's young activists galvanised mass support. Over 75 per cent of the electorate turned out to vote. Always unwilling to accept popular opinion in the state, New Delhi panicked. The election held on 31 March 1987 was 'as unfree and unfair as any other.'[3] No one credited the result. The announcement that the United Front had won a token four out of seventy-six seats only added insult to injury. With hope in the peaceful process betrayed, the shocked and thoroughly disillusioned Kashmiri activists decided to resort to 'other means' to secure their fundamental rights.

A popular uprising was thus born. Called Tehrik (movement), it gathered rapid momentum. Peaceful to begin with, the Tehrik organised mass anti-India demonstrations and *hartals* (shutdowns of private business and transport).

As the Indian government responded with a heavy hand, its policy evoked strong condemnation in Pakistan. People demonstrated in cities and towns all over the country. The media condemned Indian atrocities. The government of Pakistan denounced India for its inhuman policy. Not only was the process of normalisation of Pakistan–India relations halted, much of the progress made since it began in 1972 was reversed.

In IHK, radical Kashmiri youth turned to militancy. An attempt was made to attack Chief Minister Farooq Abdullah in May 1987. Kashmiri youth banded together in armed groups. The largest among them was the Kashmiri Hizbul Mujahidden. Also active were Al Baraq, Al Omar and others. A Kashmiri politician of the Bharatiya Janata Party was killed in September 1989. In December, the daughter of the Indian Home Minister, Mufti Mohammad Sayeed, was kidnapped but freed unharmed after New Delhi agreed to the demand for the release of five Kashmiris from detention.

Determined to maintain occupation, the Indian government brought Jagmohan Malhotra back as governor in January 1990. During an earlier tenure he had demonstrated a savage streak. 'A rabid communalist,' he now beat 'all previous records of fascist regimes in the world in the matter of unleashing terror and oppression on the innocent people of the state.'[4] Jagmohan proceeded from the premise that 'Every Muslim in Kashmir is a militant today. All of them are for secession from India.' Believing that, 'The bullet is the only solution,'[5] he 'converted Kashmir into a free-fire zone' imposing 'continuous and indefinite curfews.' Local volunteers who tried to alleviate suffering were 'arrested and mercilessly beaten.' Even free kitchens to distribute food to people confined to their homes were not allowed. Correspondents of the foreign media were prohibited from entering Kashmir. Unseen by the world the Indian military and para-military forces, already given special powers and immunity from prosecution, now resorted to arbitrary arrests, searches of homes, rape and looting, and punitive destruction of houses.

Jagmohan was removed after months, less for what he did than for his embarrassing rhetoric. His successor, Girish Saxena, added even more ruthless techniques to crush the Kashmiri uprising. Captured militants were subjected to torture until they agreed to assist the armed forces. They were then told to rejoin the militants as embedded informants. The Indian government passed the Armed Forces Special Powers Act authorizing the use of lethal force and giving immunity from prosecution. Human rights organisations documented the widespread abuses. They published one report after another vividly depicting the inhuman repression by Indian police and armed forces in Kashmir:

Despite serious criticism, India is continuing its repressive policy against the Kashmiri people to crush their popular movement for right of self-determination....

Widespread human rights violations in the state since January 1990 have been attributed to the Indian army, and the paramilitary Border Security Force (BSF) and Central Reserve Police Force (CRPF). A 145,000 strong force of CRPF was flown into the state at that time. Cordon-and-search operations are frequently conducted in areas of armed opposition activity....Torture is reported to be routinely used during these combing operations as well as in army camps, interrogation centres, police stations and prisons. Indiscriminate beatings are common and rape in particular appears to be routine.

In Jammu and Kashmir, rape is practised as part of a systematic attempt to humiliate and intimidate the local population during counter-insurgency operations....

Amnesty International[6]

Indian forces in Kashmir have engaged in massive human rights violations including extra-judicial executions, rape, torture and deliberate assaults on health care workers....Such killings are carried out as a matter of policy. More than any other phenomenon, these deliberate killings reveal the magnitude of the human rights crisis in Kashmir.

Asia Watch and Physicians for Human Rights[7]

Rape is not uncommon and there is evidence of its employment as an instrument of terror.

Fédération Internationale des Droigts d'Homme[8]

Amnesty International repeatedly expressed grave concern about continuing reports of deaths in custody and of extra-judicial killings....

Amnesty International[9]

Serious human rights abuses, extra-judicial executions and other political killings and excessive use of force by security forces in Jammu and Kashmir and other northern states; torture and rape by police and other agents of Government, deaths of suspects in police custody, arbitrary arrests and in-communication detentions are rampant.

Researchers for Amnesty International and Human Rights Watch were not permitted to visit Jammu and Kashmir.

US Department of State[10]

The years of armed struggle have taken a heavy toll of lives lost, about which reliable figures are impossible to obtain. According to official (Indian) handouts 19,866 people have died in Jammu and Kashmir since January 1990....

The number of people who have 'disappeared' in Jammu and Kashmir is difficult to estimate because of widespread fear for relatives.... According to some observers the number could be as high as 2,000....

Amnesty International[11]

The figures [of those who 'disappeared'] vary between 700 to 2,000. However, the recent statement of Mushtaq Ahmad Lone in the state assembly substantiates the higher figure.... He said that the government is aware that 3,257 people are missing....

Economic and Political Weekly[12]

The Kashmiri freedom struggle faced a new obstacle after the collapse of the Soviet Union. An imaginary fear of Islam was built up in the West in the early 1990s. Considered an asset so long as it inspired opposition to Soviet expansion in Afghanistan, Islam was now projected as a threat to western civilization.[13] The word 'fundamentalism' came into sudden vogue to discredit political movements of Muslim peoples, even though their aims were freedom from alien occupation, respect for human rights and democracy. Exploiting this new environment of prejudice, India labelled Kashmiri activists as extremists, fundamentalists and terrorists. The United States, which had earlier imposed sanctions on

Pakistan because of alleged violation of the Pressler Law, considered placing Pakistan on its list of terrorist states.

To accelerate the favourable change in international opinion, the Indian government adopted a new posture of seeming willingness for political accommodation. It released some of the more prominent Kashmiri political leaders who were under prolonged detention in prisons in India. On returning to Srinagar they promoted the formation of the All Parties Hurriyat Conference (APHC) in February 1993, bringing together leaders of some thirty political parties and groups.[14] Mirwaiz Umar Farooq, young grandson of Mirwaiz Mohammad Yusuf who founded of the Muslim Conference in 1932, was elected as chairman. Recognising that the question of whether Kashmir should accede to Pakistan or become independent was premature; APHC emphasised the priority objective of ending Indian occupation and rescuing the Kashmir people from repression. APHC has remained united on the common plank of self-determination and the ultimate aim of *Azadi*, a word that can be translated as freedom or independence. While not involved in militancy, most APHC leaders defended armed struggle because India had closed the political option.

The apparent change in Indian policy of opening a political window did not lead to any reduction in the use of force. Actually, repression was intensified through the formation of a militia of captured Kashmiri militants who, unable to withstand torture, turned into Indian agents. Led by Kuka Parray, they acted as a fifth column against their own kith and kin.

Reacting to Indian atrocities, Kashmiri volunteers from outside IHK, and even former Afghan Mujahideen and members of the Pakistan-based Lashkar-i-Tayyeba, began to enter IHK to join Kashmiri militants. India seized on reports to attribute the 'unrest' and 'secessionist attitude' in Kashmir to 'elements' coming into the valley from the Pakistan side to 'fuel the problem.'[15] The government of Pakistan was accused of providing training and arms to Kashmiri militants. Pakistan denied these accusations saying it provided only political, diplomatic and moral support. The credibility of the denial was undermined, however, by reports that Jehadi groups in Pakistan were recruiting volunteers to join the Kashmiri struggle.

A reputable international journal reported in 1999 that 'about 24,000 people have died in the decade-long insurgency, say the (Indian) police. The militants say 60,000.'[16] Through such brutality, Indian police claimed to have achieved 'pacification.' Yet, 'Srinagar still looks like a city dumped inside a maximum security prison with guns poking through piles of sandbags on nearly every corner.'[17]

Appalled by the world's indifference to the plight of the Kashmiri people, thought in official circles in Pakistan seemed to turn once again to what could be done to attract international attention. The Kargil episode was perhaps a consequence of such a consideration. Kargil was described as 'the latest battle in a conflict that has taken tens of thousands of lives over the last decade.' Summary executions of suspected militants and killings of civilians in reprisal attacks took place. No wonder that Kashmiris 'have no love for the Indian security forces, which human rights groups say regularly ransack and burn villages, torture prisoners and assassinate suspects.'[18]

In the event, Kargil too failed to focus international attention on the need to resolve the Kashmir question. Instead, it provided India with another pretext to intensify repression. The toll continued to mount. An independent international study group reported in November 2002:

> The Indian government officially estimates 30,000 deaths in the last twelve years. Kashmiris, including the All Parties Hurriyat Conference, estimate between 80,000 and 100,000 deaths. Most observers estimate there to have been roughly 60,000 deaths.[19]
>
> The deep sense of insecurity (in IHK) can be directly traced to the thousands of disappearances that have occurred over thirteen years with little accountability. Virtually every one in Srinagar knows someone who has been killed, arrested or tortured, and almost no one has been unaffected by the state of physical insecurity.[20]

Following 9/11, India started accusing Pakistan of sponsoring terrorist attacks in IHK. The 13 December 2001 attack on the premises of the Indian parliament was blamed on Pakistan and without any evidence New Delhi proceeded to curtail diplomatic and communications relations with Pakistan. To raise the tension further, it concentrated the bulk of its armed forces on Pakistan's borders and the Line of Control. Pakistan condemned the attack and decided to ban Harkat-ul-Mujahidin and Jaish-e-Mohammad in January 2002.

The Organisation of the Islamic Conference adopted strong resolutions upholding the Kashmiri right of self-determination and condemning Indian repression. OIC's attempts to obtain access to Kashmir for investigation of the grim situation were, however, blocked by India. Pakistan's efforts to secure official cognisance of the plight of the Kashmiri people by the United Nations Human Rights Commission did not succeed. Too many of the member states of the commission took a restrictive view of its competence, were opposed to international prying into their own record or were disinclined to displease India. Pakistan was obliged to withdraw the draft resolution it had proposed for adoption by the commission in 1994 and 1995.

The United States and some other governments issued statements critical of Indian agencies for arbitrary arrests, torture and deaths in custody. But some of them also criticized Kashmiri militants for acts of a terrorist nature. Pakistan, too, came under adverse notice for police excesses in Karachi, undercutting its credentials for mobilisation of support for Kashmiris.

Formation of a new government in India following the May 1996 elections raised optimism. The manifesto of Janata Dal, the lead party in the coalition government, envisaged discussions with Pakistan to resolve the Kashmir dispute, 'keeping in mind the sentiments of the people of the state.'[21] Also promising was Prime Minister Deve Gowda's statement that he would 'definitely take an initiative to defuse the tension between the two countries.'[22] In a warm letter of felicitations to him, Prime Minister Benazir Bhutto suggested talks 'aimed at the settlement of the issue of Jammu and Kashmir and other outstanding matters between the two countries.' In his response, Gowda made no mention of the core issue. He suggested a 'wide-ranging and comprehensive dialogue' aimed at the realisation of 'a firm relationship of trust, setting aside the difficulties that impede amity and cooperation.'[23] These formulations implying relegation of the Kashmir dispute seemed to throw cold water on hopes for a new beginning in Pakistan–India relations. The Indian decision to organise sham elections in the Indian-held part of the state further corroborated the lack of seriousness of its professions for improved relations with Pakistan.

The Hurriyat Conference boycotted the election for the Indian parliament held in May, and the state elections in September 1996. In the past almost all elections in the occupied state had been rigged but this was the most farcical exercise in history. Independent media reports eloquently depicted scenes of poor villagers driven at gunpoint to polling stations. Hurriyat leaders were placed under detention and anti-poll protest meetings were prohibited. The National Conference, which has historically provided India with a political front for its annexationist aims, agreed to participate in the state election on the basis of secret understandings reportedly given to Farooq Abdullah by the Deve Gowda government. The popular boycott made it clear that elections under the Indian aegis could not be a substitute for a free and impartial plebiscite under UN auspices.

The toll continued to mount as India persisted in repression. By 2004, the APHC said more that 80,000 Kashmiris had died at the hands of the Indian occupation forces.

NOTES

1. *Book of Knowledge—Children's Encyclopaedia*, Lamb, op. cit., p. 304.
2. Statement by Prime Minister Z. A. Bhutto, quoted in Lamb, p. 308.
3. Lamb, p. 331.
4. Justice Burhanuddin Farooqi, *Writ Petition*, p. 30.
5. Farooqi, p. 31, quoting *Current*, Bombay, 26 May–1 June 1990.
6. Amnesty International, *India—Torture, Rape and Deaths in Custody,* (New York, 1992), pp. 20–21.
7. Asia Watch and Physicians for Human Rights, Washington, 1993.
8. *Fédération Internationale des Droigts d'Home*, Paris.
9. Amnesty International, Annual Report, 1994, p. 159.
10. US Depatment of State, Report on Human Rights Situation in India, 30 January 1998.
11. *'Disappearances' in Jammu and Kashmir*, Amnesty International Report, ASA—February 1999.
12. Gautam Naviakha, 'Internal War and Civil Rights, Disappearances in Jammu and Kashmir', *Economic and Political Weekly*, Mumbai, 12 June 1999.
13. Samuel Huntington, 'Clash of Civilizations,' *Foreign Affairs*, Summer 1993.
14. Prominent leaders included Syed Ali Geelani of Jamaat-i-Islami, Yasin Malik of Jammu & Kashmir Liberation Front, Abdul Gani Lone of the People's Conference, and Mirwaiz Umar Farooq of the Muslim Conference.
15. Statement by Prime Minister Narasimha Rao, *The Hindustan Times*, New Delhi, 8 June 1992. (In the detailed account of his life in an Indian prison—*Roodad-i-Qafs*—Syed Ali Gailani, President of All Parties Hurriyat Conference, gives the names of the leaders of the movement for *Azadi* who were detained and murdered by Indian forces.
16. *The Economist*, 22 May 1999, 'Survey India and Pakistan' p. 10.
17. Ibid.
18. *The New York Times*, 21 June 1999, report by Stephen Kinzer.
19. The International Crisis Group, *Kashmir: The View from Srinagar*, 21 November 2002, p. 4, footnote 4.
20. Ibid., p. 11.
21. Quoted in Prime Minister Benazir Bhutto's letter of 3 June 1996 to Prime Minister Deve Gowda, *The News*, Islamabad, 4 June 1996.
22. *Dawn*, Karachi, 1 June 1996, Gowda's statement, reprt by *Reuter & APP*.
23. *The News*, Islamabad, 10 June 1996.

CHAPTER 15

The Afghanistan Civil War, 1990–1998

The Afghan people suffered grievously in the struggle to recover freedom. A million people perished and some six million people had to take refuge outside their country, largely in Pakistan and Iran. The economic and human infrastructure of Afghanistan was devastated on a scale with few parallels. Already one of the least developed countries, it suffered fearful damage to agriculture, irrigation systems, roads, transport, and educational institutions—indeed its entire infrastructure. Nor did its travail end with the withdrawal of the Soviet forces. The regime the Soviets installed under Najibullah fought on for nearly three more years. After the proxy administration finally collapsed in April 1992, a protracted war of succession began among the Mujahideen political parties, founded apparently in the personal power ambitions of their leaders, but progressively exposing its ethnic basis. For their epic sacrifices, the Afghan people deserved a better fate than the long nightmare of internecine fighting, political disintegration and economic collapse.

The Mujahideen started on a hopeful note of unity after Najibullah's fall. At a meeting in Peshawar on 24 April 1992, the Alliance leaders reached an agreement. An Islamic Council headed by Sibghatullah Mojaddedi was installed for two months after which Professor Burhanuddin Rabbani was to become president for four months. A transitional government was then to be formed for two years. Mojaddedi abided by the accord but Rabbani refused to yield power when his term expired. Fighting broke out among the Mujahideen parties.

Brokering the Peshawar accord in concert with Saudi Arabia and Iran, Pakistan worked for unity among the Afghan parties. Gulbadin Hekmatyar, said to be Pakistan's favourite, did not even figure in the new power structure. Actually, he was respected by Pakistan and other supporters of the Afghan insurgency because 'he fielded the most effective anti-Soviet fighters.'[1]

After Rabbani's refusal to hold elections for his successor led to discord and dissension in the country, Pakistan, Iran and Saudi Arabia again joined hands to promote another accord among the Afghan leaders. At a meeting in Islamabad on 7 March 1993, the Afghan leaders agreed on the formation of a government for a period of 18 months, with Professor Rabbani continuing as president and Engineer Hekmatyar becoming prime minister. Although the Afghan leaders reconfirmed the Islamabad accord during visits to Saudi Arabia and Iran, it was not implemented. The composition of the cabinet to be 'formed by the Prime Minister in consultation with the President' was not agreed upon. Hekmatyar felt too insecure to even enter Kabul. The accord soon broke down and Hekmatyar attacked the capital. Though he was repulsed, the attractive city, which had largely escaped destruction during the liberation struggle, was severely damaged as a result of the intra-Mujahideen fighting. The United Nations Representative for Afghanistan made spasmodic efforts to promote reconciliation between the Rabbani government and its opponents. Although little progress was achieved toward unity, a certain calm seemed to have descended over the divided country in 1995. The Tajik-dominated Rabbani government ruled over five of the central provinces, Abdur Rashid Dostum's Uzbek Militia controlled the northern provinces, and a Pushtoon *shura* or council governed the eastern provinces from Jalalabad while the Taliban controlled the southern provinces.

The Mujahideen Alliance failed to establish an effective central administration. The Northern Alliance received assistance from foreign countries to sustain itself in power, but it did little to establish security much less begin economic reconstruction of the ruined country. The absence of a national army, financial resources and administrative reach led to anarchical conditions in the country, with warlords and local commanders trying to impose personal control through intimidation and extortion.

Pakistan's expectations of friendly relations with the government of Islamic Afghanistan received a shock on 6 September 1995 when its embassy in Kabul was sacked by a government-sponsored mob. One employee was killed, the ambassador and forty officials were badly injured and the building, and all official records were burnt. Still, Pakistan exercised patience and prospects of good relations seemed to brighten in May 1996 when a visiting Afghan government delegation acknowledged liability for the reconstruction of the embassy even though it pleaded lack of resources to discharge the responsibility.

The Rise of the Taliban

Graduates and students of religious seminaries, the Taliban played a significant part in the struggle against Soviet occupation but did not have any organisation and played no role in the new power structure under the Mujahideen warlords. The beginning of their rise to prominence was the result of a local incident in a southern village in 1994. Outraged by the offensive social behaviour of a local commander, the villagers approached the local mullah to intercede with the authorities. Mullah Omar led a procession to the office of the local commander. Unable to provide satisfaction or intimidate the angry crowd, the commander fled. The people proclaimed Mullah Omar as leader. Other people in the neighbourhood also yearned for release from the warlords who 'brought sufferings on the Afghans and violated Islamic teachings.'[2] Mullah Omar found himself at the head of a popular revolt. His Taliban supporters were welcomed in other villages. They took the provincial capital of Kandahar without a fight. Warlord commanders did not put up any resistance as the Taliban were invited by people of other provinces. Helmand, Imroz, Uruzgan and Zabul fell one after another.

As the Taliban moved north threatening the Mujahideen-controlled provinces, the Rabbani regime saw a foreign hand behind the popular upsurge. Failing to recognise that the Taliban phenomenon was the indigenous product of popular disgust at the internecine squabbling amongst the warlords, Kabul accused Pakistan of supporting and assisting the Taliban with equipment and manpower. It ignored the historical fact that Pakistan had, throughout the struggle against the Soviets, sought to promote unity among the Mujahideen leaders, and after the fall of the Najibullah proxy regime, also successfully promoted consensus among them for the formation of a government acceptable to them. On two occasions, in 1992 and 1994, Pakistan collaborated with Saudi Arabia and Iran to successfully persuade the Mujahideen to form a unity government. The breakdown of both accords was attributable to the internecine conflict amongst the Mujahideen, with different ethnic leaders ranged against one another for domination of the country.

In September 1996, the Taliban burst forth again. Rapidly, they penetrated the eastern Pushtoon provinces. The *shura* that ruled Jalalabad melted away and the city fell to the Taliban. The Taliban then pushed toward the capital from the east as well as the south. The government forces were by now too demoralised to resist the Taliban. The Rabbani regime, backed now also by Hekmatyar, abandoned the capital. With remarkably little bloodshed the Taliban entered Kabul on the morning of 27 September 1996. Their advance was then halted as Tajik and Uzbek warlords held the northern provinces.

In May 1997, the situation took another dramatic turn as a result of dissension in the Uzbek ranks. Accusing Dostum of pursuing personal power at the expense of the unity of the country, the Uzbek warlord's former foreign minister, General Abul Malik, revolted and invited the Taliban forces to take over Mazar-i-Sharif. It fell to the allies on 24 May. Dostum fled to Turkey. By now Rabbani, the titular president of the country, and Hekmatyar had taken refuge in Iran, and the Taliban controlled some 90 per cent of Afghan territory.

After four days the Taliban lost control of Mazar-i-Sharif. The Uzbek and the Shiite forces balked at the Taliban attempt to centralise power in their hands. Objecting to the order for surrender of arms, the Uzbek force took the Taliban contingent prisoner on 28 May. A few months later, General Dostum staged a comeback, driving out General Malik who fled to Iran. The Northern Alliance was revived. Hopes of restoration of peace and unity appeared to recede as the country became divided along geographic and ethnic fault-lines.

The Taliban succeeded in recapturing Mazar-i-Sharif and most of the northern provinces in 1998. They also extended their control to parts of the Hazara areas. Their repeated efforts failed, however, to dislodge Ahmad Shah Mahsud from his stronghold of the Panjsher Valley and areas to the north of Kabul, with his artillery launching recurrent salvos on the hapless capital.

Meanwhile, the Taliban established better law and order in the territory under their control than the Afghan people had seen for two decades. Their anti-vice squads received popular support. Security conditions improved. Traffic became orderly and their judicial system provided expeditious, if summary, justice. Men of faith and integrity, the Taliban lived austerely so that taxation was light. The vast majority of the people welcomed the Taliban's success in disarming lawless gangs, restoring peace and providing an administration that was religious, modest and uncorrupt.

A simple and idealistic group with only religious education, the Taliban lacked sophistication as well as understanding of international law and world politics. They antagonised the inhabitants of the capital, which had been groomed by the Afghan rulers as an island of modernity in a sea of conservative and tribal countryside. The stringent restrictions they imposed upon women evoked denunciation, more abroad than within.

The narrow and extremist interpretation of Islam by the Taliban chief who was proclaimed head of Muslims (*Amirul-Muslimeen*) offended even Muslim countries who felt mocked and humiliated by the Taliban parody of their great faith. They castigated the Taliban's archaic interpretation of Islam, especially the corporal punishments. Few Islamic countries endorsed the Taliban version of the *Shariah* law. The Islamic Republic of Iran denounced the Taliban for providing another pretext for prejudice against Islam. Tehran's reservations about the Taliban were founded in a number of factors. Like other neighbours of multi-ethnic and multi-sect Afghanistan, Iran had supported a composite government in Kabul with a due share for Tajiks and Hazaras, just as Pakistan hoped for a due share for the Pushtoons and the Uzbeks. Largely Pushtoon and Sunni, the Taliban were perceived to discriminate against the non-Pushtoons and the Shias. The denial of human rights to women, their confinement and ban on employment outside homes, and closure of schools for girls earned worldwide obloquy. The entire international community denounced the demolition of the Buddha statues in Bamiyan, an archaeological heritage of world history and civilisation. Particularly unacceptable in international law was the Taliban complicity in the abuse of asylum by Osama bin Laden and his followers for their terrorist operations.

Opinion in the West was appalled by the stringent interpretation of the *Shariah* laws by the Taliban, in particular the closure of schools for girls and ban on employment for women outside their homes in Kabul.

Moscow's reaction against the Taliban appeared founded in the apprehension that their religious extremism would be exported to the Central Asian republics, posing a threat to the security and stability of the area the fallen great power now termed as 'near abroad.' Some of these republics also feared that the Taliban entertained 'aggressive designs.'[3]

The UN Security Council adopted a Russian-sponsored resolution on 22 October 1996, condemning Taliban discrimination against women and calling for immediate cessation of hostilities, an end to the supply of arms and ammunitions from outside, and resumption of political dialogue among all Afghan parties. The resolution was largely ignored however by the Afghan factions. Efforts by the UN special envoy, Herbert Holl, to promote an intra-Afghan dialogue made little progress.

Proxy War

Objectively, all neighbours of Afghanistan had a common interest in an end to the civil war, and the formation of a broad-based government in Kabul that would ensure the safety of different ethnic and sectarian segments of the population and create conditions conducive to the return of the refugees. Peace and unity, moreover, would facilitate transit and trade, as well as the construction of oil and gas pipelines, to the benefit of all countries of the region, especially land-locked Afghanistan, which would earn substantial amounts in transit fees. Despite the manifest long-term advantages of peace in Afghanistan, the neighbours seemed stuck in a miasma of rivalries and suspicions.

Foreign military assistance to the warring Afghan parties 'continued unabated throughout 1997,' according to the UN Secretary General. In his report[4] to the Security Council, he cited eyewitness accounts of military deliveries in unmarked aircraft to the Northern Alliance and in truck caravans to the Taliban. Bitterly denouncing these activities as 'blatant violations of General Assembly and Security Council resolutions,' he mocked these foreign providers who 'enthusiastically proclaim their support to the UN peace-making efforts' but 'continue to fan the conflict by pouring in arms, money and other supplies to their preferred Afghan factions.' Not surprisingly, their actions 'raised suspicions and worsened relations among the countries in the region.'

Reminiscent of 'proxy wars' of a bygone era, the situation in Afghanistan was tragic for the Afghan people. The 'foreign providers' were said to be engaged in this new 'Great Game' with high stakes in the competition for access to the rich petroleum and gas resources of the Caspian basin. A less Machiavellian explanation could be found in the context of the identical desire of all the neighbours of Afghanistan to save themselves from a further spillover of the Afghan civil war.

Fatal Blunders

Isolated internationally because of their extremist interpretation of Islam, the Taliban invited hostility by their policy of welcoming foreign Muslims, and providing them with military training and arms. Many Arab and Central Asian states, as well as Russia, asked Pakistan to detain and extradite their nationals who engaged in subversive activities, abusing residence or transit facilities in Pakistan. Islamabad was not dismissive of the concerns but was reluctant to intervene in the autonomous tribal areas on its border with Afghanistan. Many of the foreign militants had come to Pakistan to join the jihad against the Soviet forces in Afghanistan. Having developed contacts in the areas along the border, and experts at forging documents and changing addresses, they were difficult to find. Their governments, however, held Pakistan to blame. Algeria and Uzbekistan particularly, made strong and repeated protests.

The Taliban failed to see the writing on the wall and grossly misjudged their capacity to resist. The first sign of the gathering storm was Security Council Resolution 1189 of 13 August 1998 condemning terrorist attacks on US embassies in Kenya and Tanzania, and calling on all states to take effective steps for the prevention of terrorist attacks and prosecution of culprits. Washington blamed Osama bin Laden for the crime. After the terrorist attack on the USS Cole, Security Council Resolution 1267 of 15 October 1999 demanded that the Taliban turn over bin Laden to justice, and imposed sanctions on the Afghan airline. The eight-page Resolution 1333 of 19 December 2000 not only reiterated condemnation of the Taliban and demanded the surrender of bin Laden but also called upon all states to prevent the supply of arms to the Taliban, curtail contacts with their officials, and freeze their assets or suffer sanctions. The Taliban ignored the demands in repeated resolutions of the Security Council under Chapter VII, and merely went on reiterating their demand for evidence, which was implicitly considered sufficient by the Security Council.

Retrospect

A more sinister legacy of the Afghan crisis for Pakistan was the spill-over of extremism and weapons from Afghanistan to which was soon added the influx of narcotics. Modern weapons from Afghanistan proliferated across Pakistan giving rise to a 'Klashnikov culture.'

Dacoits and sectarian extremists now had more lethal weapons than the police. Hundreds of foreign citizens who came to join the jihad stayed behind in Pakistan, and some of them indulged in acts of terrorism. The bombing of the Egyptian embassy in Islamabad in December 1995 was attributed to them. Also, agents of the Rabbani regime in Kabul perpetrated acts of sabotage in Pakistan. A car-bomb explosion in a Peshawar bazaar killed over forty and wounded a hundred innocent people in December 1995.

The glorification of the Mujahideen, however sincere on the part of many in Pakistan, and expedient and cynical on that of the United States with its sole aim of defeating the Soviets, proved equally shortsighted and damaging for both. In Pakistan it encouraged exploitation of religion for the narrow ends of the regime and skewed and vitiated the balance against the modernist vision of its founding father.[5] It sowed seeds that later sprouted extremism and militancy that were to become a nightmare for both countries.

The Russian people were rightly critical of the Soviet invasion of Afghanistan as 'a great mistake.'[6] Afghans can similarly blame their communist leaders for the disaster that befell their country. Pakistanis alone have few scapegoats. They generally approved of President Zia's policy of support for the Afghans. Few foresaw the consequences of involvement, and the grave problems that would emerge in the wake of the conflict. Western supporters of the Afghan struggle, rightly critical of the Afghan warring parties, had themselves to blame for walking away, but had to pay a high price some years later. Pakistan, once praised for 'shouldering great responsibilities for mankind... (and its) courageous and compassionate role,'[7] found itself left in the lurch, saddled with the burden of refugees and the consequences of the strife next door.

Was Pakistan's policy misconceived? In retrospect the answer is easy to give but, alas, humans are not gifted with prescience and policies have to be devised—and can be fairly judged—in the context of the time and contemporary knowledge. Given the history of Soviet expansionism, Islamabad's sense of alarm in 1979 was not a figment of its imagination. Pakistan was neither in a position to challenge the Soviet super-power nor could it ignore the intervention without peril to its security. An alternative to the middle course it pursued seems difficult to conceive even in retrospect. Success and failure can be a measure of policies, but human struggle cannot be appraised in isolation from the nobility of the cause. The Soviet intervention was morally and legally wrong, the Afghan resistance was right. Pakistan's decision in favour of solidarity with the fraternal people of Afghanistan was not only morally right but also based on enlightened self-interest.

Could the consequences of the protracted conflict in terms of the Kalashnikov culture and narcotics proliferation be anticipated and obviated? Surely, these could have been minimised if not precluded. These problems, as well as malfeasance and venality in transactions between the Mujahideen and their friends, surfaced during the struggle in Afghanistan. Priorities and vested interests did not permit timely remedies, however.

Were not the Geneva Accords flawed in that they did not provide for the transition to peace and the formation of a government of unity for Afghanistan? The account that has been given above brings out the fact that, from the beginning, the Geneva negotiations had only the limited aim of getting the Soviets to withdraw from Afghanistan. All the parties agreed that the formation of a government was an entirely internal affair of Afghanistan, and the Afghans alone had the right to decide this matter to the exclusion of the Soviet Union, Pakistan or any other country. The United Nations was understandably reluctant to undertake this task. Until the end of the Cold War it avoided assumption of a role for the promotion of reconciliation or consensus in any embattled country. Moscow and Kabul were at first dismissive of any suggestion for a role for the Mujahideen in the government of Afghanistan except on Kabul's terms. When they later offered accommodation, the Mujahideen rejected any truck with the Soviet puppets. Pakistan as well as other friends and supporters backed the Mujahideen position. President Zia alone changed his view for reasons that remain obscure, though his unjustified and unlawful dismissal of Prime Minister Junejo in May 1988 provides circumstantial evidence of a personal power motivation. In the event, even he was unable to persuade the Mujahideen to meet with Diego Cordovez in pursuit of his mission of promoting a government of unity in Afghanistan.

It was probably too much to expect the Mujahideen leaders to reach accommodation with the surrogate regime after the Soviets withdrew, though a government of unity could have saved the country from fragmentation. More tragic was the rivalry for personal power among the Mujahideen leaders that prolonged the nightmare for the Afghan people. Also, as a result of the anarchy, the Mujahideen themselves were sidelined by new forces in the country. Likewise, the Taliban exclusivism, excess of religious zeal and permission for a foreign adventurer to abuse hospitality sealed their fate.

Pakistan's interest, as indeed that of other neighbours, lay above all in an end to the civil war and restoration of Afghanistan's unity, which were highly desirable objectives also for the Afghan people themselves. Only peace in Afghanistan could relieve Pakistan and Iran of the burden of Afghan refugees. Over two million of them still remained in Pakistan, suffering themselves and burdening Pakistan's economy. Peace was a prerequisite, moreover, for the opening of transit facilities without which cooperation with the central Asian Republics remained blocked.

Could Islamabad influence the Taliban to follow circumspect polices? Not only Tehran but also Washington believed it could. What is obvious in retrospect is the futility of a king-maker role in Afghanistan on the part of any outsider. Like imperial Britain in the nineteenth century, the Soviet super-power failed in its attempt to impose a surrogate government on the Afghans. Pakistan lacked the power and resources to persuade the Taliban to rectify their fatal policies. In contrast, the United States and the West, with their vastly greater resources, would have had a better chance to influence the Afghans. By blaming Islamabad, Washington covered up its own error in walking away from Afghanistan after achieving its Cold War aim, and imposing sanctions on Pakistan to further undermine its capacity to play a significant role in Afghanistan. Not until after 9/11 did the United States rectify its blunder—though at much greater cost.

NOTES

1. Steve Coll, 'This Ghost War: The Secret History of the CIA, Afghanistan and bin Laden', quoted in *Dawn*, Islamabad, 19 November 2004.
2. Mullah Mohammad Omar, Taliban leader, quoted by Rahimullah Yusufzai in *The News*, 4 October 1996.
3. Uzbekistan President Islam Karimov, speaking at the OIC Summit in Ashkabat on 14 May 1997, reported in *The News*, Islamabad, 15 May 1997.
4. UN Secretary General's end-of-the-year Report for 1997 to the Security Council, quoted in a despatch by Anwar Iqbal in *The News*, Islamabad, pp. 1 and 8.
5. Lawence Ziring. *Pakistan: At the Crossroads of History*, Oneworld, 2003.
6. K. M. Arif, op. 327, quoting Eduard Sheverdnadze's statement in *Izvestia* of 19 February 1989.
7. President Ronald Reagan, speech welcoming President Zia to Washington, 7 December 1982, *Documents*, p. 481.

CHAPTER 16

Pakistan–India Disputes and Crises

Despite the pledge in the Shimla Agreement to settle differences by peaceful means, little progress was made towards that objective after 1972. The settlement of Jammu and Kashmir was not even discussed. Other existing disputes continued to fester, and some new ones arose. These disputes and issues are summarised below.

Sir Creek

The demarcation of the line in Sir Creek, at the western terminus of the Pakistan–India boundary in the Rann of Kutch, has remained unresolved since 1969 when the main dispute was settled by an arbitration tribunal. For most of its length, the boundary was demarcated by the tribunal, which did not consider it necessary to take up the question with regard to the 100-km stretch of Sir Creek, because here the boundary between the state of Kutch and the province of Sindh was already delimited by a resolution of the British Indian government in 1914, with the annexed map showing Sir Creek on the Sindh side. Neither side contested that fact before the tribunal. Later, with an eye on the maritime resources, India claimed first that Sir Creek was on the Indian side, and then that the boundary should run in the middle of the creek because it was a navigable channel. The changed Indian stance aimed to substantially reduce the area of Pakistan's economic zone.

Pakistan sought negotiations to resolve the difference, but India said it first wanted to complete an air survey of the area. The surveyors general of the two countries met in May 1989 but could not reach agreement, as India no longer accepted the 1914 resolution map, considered authentic during the proceedings of the tribunal. The stalemate has persisted, to the detriment of poor fishermen on both sides, hundreds of whom are arrested by the coastguard forces of the two sides, charging them with trespass. In 2003, India shot down an

Prime Minister Indira Gandhi, New Delhi, 1981.

unarmed Pakistani aircraft in the area, killing all its crew and passengers.

Siachen: A Dispute within a Dispute

Descending from the lofty Karakorum Range, at elevations of 5,000 meters or more, the Siachen Glacier traverses part of Baltistan in the Northern Areas, whose inhabitants threw off the Maharaja of Kashmir's yoke in 1947. The area was so difficult to access and so inhospitable that no fighting took place here in any of the three wars between the two countries. After the two sides agreed to halt hostilities, an agreement was reached on 27 July 1949 at a meeting of the military representatives of the two countries, under the auspices of the UN Commission for India and Pakistan, on the ceasefire line. In the last sentence, the line was described as: 'Chalunka (on the Shyok River), Khor, thence north to the glaciers.' When delineated on the map, the line terminated at point NJ 9842, some sixty miles south of the Karakorum watershed.

Pakistan exercised control in the glaciated area up to the Karakorum Pass. Following the Sino–Pakistan agreement of 1962, the provisional boundary between the Xinjiang region of China and the Northern Areas of the disputed state of Jammu and Kashmir under Pakistan's control started from the trijunction with Afghanistan in the west to the Karakorum Pass in the east. India's protest against the agreement, claiming that Kashmir was part of its territory, stated that the portion west of the Karakorum Pass was 'under Pakistan's unlawful occupation', implicitly conceding that the pass was under Pakistan's control.[1] Other evidence of Pakistan's control over the region was available in the permits granted by the Pakistan government to mountain climbing expeditions.

After 1965, the two countries agreed to revert to *status quo ante*. During the 1971 war there was no change of control over territory in the region. The terminus of the line of control resulting from the ceasefire of 17 December 1971 remained the same as that of the 1949 ceasefire line.

In the early 1980s, India starting sending army patrols by its high altitude warfare school to the Siachen area. In violation of the explicit provision in the Shimla Agreement prohibiting any attempt to 'unilaterally alter the situation,'[2] a brigade-strength force was sent by India in 1984 to occupy a part of the glaciated area. Apart from protesting against the Indian incursion, Pakistan also dispatched a contingent, which forestalled further Indian advance. Thus arose a new 'dispute within a dispute.' Ever since, the forces of the two countries have fought intermittent duels, losing even more men to frostbite in the highest battlefield in the world.

Of all disputes between the two countries, Siachen is considered as 'arguably the most amenable to a solution that is satisfactory for both sides.' They actually arrived at such a solution following negotiations in 1989 that provided for redeployment of forces to positions conforming with the Shimla Agreement.[3] Prime Ministers Benazir Bhutto and Rajiv Gandhi approved the agreement at their meeting in Islamabad in July 1989, but it has not been implemented.

Differences arose over interpretation, as the Indian side argued that the reference to the Shimla Agreement in the joint statement was to its 'spirit', not to 'positions'. New issues were raised asking for 'authentication' of the existing positions, drawing a line of control in the 'zone of conflict', and demanding the right to establish a 'civil post' even though it did not have one prior to 1984, unlike Pakistan which had maintained an international Himalayan expedition camp in the area.

Salal, Wuller, Baglihar and Kishenganga Projects

The Indus Waters Treaty of 1960 allows the construction of run-of-the-river power plants but forbids the construction of dams on the western rivers in excess of prescribed limits. Whenever India plans projects that interfere with the flow of the rivers, it is obliged by the treaty to provide relevant data to Pakistan. If the magnitude of the dam is considered by Pakistan to violate the treaty provisions, it is entitled to raise the issue in the permanent Indus Commission. If the commission fails to reach agreement, either side can refer the question for consideration at the level of governments. If even they fail to reach agreement, either side can refer the dispute to the World Bank for the appointment of a neutral expert whose verdict is binding on both parties. Four such issues have arisen since 1960.

The first question arose in the 1970s when India decided to build a dam on the Chenab River at Salal. After the Indus Commission failed to settle the issue, it was taken up at the level of governments of the two countries. India then agreed to reduce the height of the dam so as to relieve Pakistan's concerns regarding interference in the flow of the river.

Another question arose in the early 1980s, when the Indian government embarked on the construction of a barrage on the Jhelum River at the mouth of the Wuller Lake, envisaging the creation of storage. Finding it thirty-three times in excess of the prescribed limit, Pakistan raised the issue in the commission in 1985 where no progress was made. In 1987, Pakistan asked India to discontinue construction pending resolution of the question. After some delay India suspended work. India then argued that the barrage could be of mutual benefit. Without entering into a controversy over this argument, Pakistan declined to take part in any discussion that would tinker with the provisions of the treaty, its sanctity being too vital for Pakistan. It asked India to first acknowledge that the project was inconsistent with the treaty. India was unwilling to do so but offered, in 1989, to change the design and operating procedures to eliminate any harmful effects on Pakistan. The two sides then exchanged drafts of a possible compromise. No agreement was reached however, despite numerous meetings at the level of the commission as well as government. After India suspended implementation of the project because of the uprising in Kashmir, the problem lost urgency.

Meanwhile, still another dispute arose when India decided to build a hydroelectric power project on the Chenab River with a dam at Baglihar upstream from the Salal dam. The reservoir was far in excess of the prescribed limit, and would enable India to manipulate the flow of the river in a way that would lead to either complete stoppage for up to twenty-eight days during the critical wheat growing period of December to February, or open the flood gates to inundate the land in Pakistan. At first India did not provide the requisite data about the project in advance and then delayed a visit by the Pakistani experts to the site, as required under the treaty. Negotiations at the level of Indus Commissioners from 2001 to 2004 proved infructuous, as India maintained the design of the dam did not violate the treaty. The matter was taken up at the level of government secretaries in January 2005 but the stalemate remained unbroken. Pakistan offered to continue bilateral negotiation provided India suspended construction work. India rejected the proposal. As work proceeded to complete the first phase of the project by the end of 2005, Pakistan decided to refer the issue to the World Bank invoking the treaty provision that entitles either party to request the appointment of a neutral expert.[4] The World Bank nominated the expert in July 2005.

After learning that India planned to build a power project on the Kishenganaga tributary of the Jhelum River, Pakistan objected on the ground that diversion of the stream would violate the Indus Waters Treaty. The Indus Commission commenced discussion of the issue in 2005.

Consular Missions

Following the resumption of diplomatic relations in 1976, India proposed the reopening also of the consular offices of the two countries, offering to lease Jinnah House in Mumbai for the Pakistan consulate. Since that house, owned by Mr Jinnah until it was taken over by the Indian government as evacuee property, was on lease to the British deputy high commission, and its vacation would entail some delay, India sought permission to open its consulate in advance. Pakistan agreed to this, accepting the Indian promise. The promise was reiterated by the Indian minister for external affairs in parliament on two occasions, affirming: 'The property is at present leased out to the British High Commission and on expiry of the lease in December 1981 it is proposed to lease out this property to the Pakistan Embassy for use by their consulate.'[5] After the house was vacated by the British, Prime Minster Indira Gandhi decided to refuse its lease to Pakistan. Not for the first time was Pakistan to rue its acceptance of an Indian undertaking on trust.

Meanwhile, in August 1980, the Pakistan Embassy in New Delhi sought the permission of the Indian government for the purchase of a plot of land for the construction of the consular office in Mumbai. New Delhi refused the request on the ground that the location was 'not suitable.' Nor was India prepared to help Pakistan acquire an alternative site.

In August 1992, the Pakistan government sent consular staff to open an office in Mumbai. They had to stay in a hotel. Even there, Indian intelligence personnel hounded the Pakistani staff. Pakistan was obliged to close down the office in March 1994. The Indian consulate in Karachi, meanwhile, continued to function even though it was known to the Pakistani authorities that the bulk of its personnel did not belong to the commerce and external affairs ministries of India. After they discovered evidence of subversive activities by the Indian personnel, and their involvement in terrorist activities, the Pakistan government was obliged to order the closure of the Indian consulate in December 1994.

Diplomats of the two countries agreed in 1992 on a bilateral 'code of conduct' for the treatment of the personnel of the missions. This was a superfluous exercise in view of the fact that their privileges and immunities are spelled out in international conventions on diplomatic and consular relations. The problem was not the lack of norms but of the political will to observe international law. Pakistani and Indian governments have repeatedly accused each other of using their diplomatic staff for activities incompatible with their legitimate functions. Apart from vigilance, which is the right of the host government, the authorities have been accused of violating immunities and even resorting to violence against the staff. Whatever the merits of these allegations, it was obvious that instead of contributing to the furtherance of normal relations between the two countries, the consular missions added to bitterness.

Hoping for a new chapter, the two countries agreed, in April 2005, to reopen the consular missions. President Musharraf was reported to have said that India had agreed to lease Jinnah House to Pakistan.

Indian Plan for Attack on Kahuta, 1984

Pakistan received a number of intelligence reports during 1983–85 that India was preparing an air attack on its uranium enrichment plant at Kahuta. Among files reported by the *Hindustan Times* as missing from Prime Minister Indira Gandhi's office was one entitled 'Attack on Kahuta.' Islamabad received information from a friendly country in 1984 alerting it to the imminence of an Indian attack.[6] Apparently, Washington also received similar information from its own sources.[7] Reports indicated that India might act in collusion with an Israeli agency or the Soviet-installed Afghan regime. Washington checked the report with Tel Aviv and informed Islamabad that it was false. As for India, Islamabad took the precaution of informing New Delhi through friendly intermediaries that any such attack would be treated as an act of aggression. Concerns on this account subsided after Pakistan and India agreed informally in December 1985 to refrain from attack on each other's nuclear installations. A formal agreement was later signed which entered into force in 1988.

The Brasstacks Crisis, 1986–87

Another crisis erupted when India decided to hold the largest combined military exercise in South Asian history, code-named Brasstacks, in the winter of 1986–87.[8] Planned by a 'hawkish and flamboyant'[9] Indian army chief, Gen. Krishnaswami Sundarji, the exercise was comparable in scale to the biggest exercises by NATO or the Warsaw Pact. It envisaged the concentration of a quarter of a million troops, nine army divisions, five independent armoured brigades, and 1,300 tanks in western Rajasthan, at places hardly fifty kilometers from the Pakistan border, giving the assembled forces the capability to launch a piercing strike into Pakistan to cut off northern Pakistan from the southern part.

Contrary to an existing understanding, the Indian army chief did not inform his Pakistani counterpart of the location, schedule and scale of the exercise.[10] Specific requests to this effect by the Pakistani GHQ on the 'hot line' and by diplomats in New Delhi were rebuffed. Concerned about the situation, Prime Minister Mohammad Khan Junejo took up the matter with Rajiv Gandhi in their meeting during the SAARC summit in Bangalore in November 1986. He was given to understand that the exercise would be scaled down, which was, however, not done.

As a precaution, the Pakistan army decided to extend its own winter exercises and later, in December 1986, as the crisis escalated, moved some of the formations to forward areas north of the Sutlej river opposite the Indian town of Fazilka and west of the Ravi in Sialkot district. Oblivious to the apprehensions triggered by their own, more massive, force placements in proximity to vulnerable Pakistani border areas, the Indian defence officials termed the Pakistani action provocative. They perceived the Pakistani force dispositions as a pincer posture menacing the security of the troubled Indian state of Punjab, where the Sikh people had been up in arms since the Indian army's assault on the Golden Temple, their most sacred shrine, in 1984.

The crisis peaked in January 1987. The Indian government demanded a pullback of Pakistani forces 'within 24 hours.' Pakistan pointed out that India should first remove the cause of the Pakistan reaction. Both countries placed their forces on alert. Prime Minister Rajiv Gandhi publicly expressed 'tremendous concern'[11]

The defence committee of the Pakistan cabinet, headed by the prime minister, and comprising chiefs of military services, ministers and high officials of defence and foreign ministries, which met frequently during the crisis, held an emergency meeting on 20 January. Although the crisis was not of Pakistan's creation, it was decided not to stand on ceremony and instead take the initiative to try defusing the dangerous situation. Prime Minister Junejo telephoned Rajiv Gandhi and suggested immediate talks, at the level of foreign secretaries, to discuss mutual withdrawal of forces to peacetime locations. The Pakistani delegation arrived in New Delhi on 31 January, and an agreement was signed on 4 February, providing for deactivation of forward air bases and sector-by-sector disengagement and return of forces to their peacetime locations, to commence in the Ravi–Chenab sector in the north. The storm, which had been brewing over several months, passed over within days.

Subsequent studies and research[12] have shown that the Brasstacks crisis brought Pakistan and India closer to the brink of war than any other crisis since 1971. Its basic and direct cause was, of course, the 'mammoth war games'[13] planned by an ambitious Indian army chief. Three wars, chronic tensions rooted in unresolved disputes, inadequate or unreliable intelligence and deep-rooted mutual suspicions fuelled worst-case assumptions. Besides, some Indian planners hoped for the crisis to spiral into actual confrontation and conflict, giving them an opportunity to exploit the disparity of forces. Scholarly research concluded: 'Exercise Brasstacks may have had much larger goals than merely to test the preparedness of the Indian army. These goals appear to have been open-ended.'[14]

To preclude recurrence of unintentional crises, the two sides concluded an agreement in 1991, which specified force thresholds and distances from the border that would require prior notification in the event of exercises or troop movements. Another crisis-prevention agreement concluded in 1991 required advance communication about aircraft flying in proximity to the other side's airspace.

Re-entry to the Commonwealth

Britain's partisan role in the 1971 crisis was disappointing for Pakistan. If media criticism of the excesses committed by Pakistani authorities was understandable on humanitarian grounds, the British failure to censure Indian military intervention was reflective of an expedient and unprincipled policy. London did not even allow a decent interval to lapse before it decided to extend recognition to Bangladesh, persuading several countries of Western Europe, Australia and New Zealand to do so simultaneously. In anger, Z. A. Bhutto decided to pull out of the Commonwealth. A quick analysis revealed that the pullout would not entail any great loss except inconvenience to Pakistani settlers in Britain. National pride would be served by giving a counter-punch to Britain, which looked at the Commonwealth as a source of comfort in its time of decline from a ranking world power status.

If the precipitate decision to quit the Commonwealth was largely Bhutto's, the decision by President Zia to rejoin was no less personal. It was made at the suggestion of visiting British leaders, subject to the condition that re-entry was arranged in an honourable way. For several years Prime Minister Indira Gandhi frustrated the proposal. She vetoed Pakistan's return at the Melbourne summit in 1980, despite pleadings by the Australian prime minister. Her decision was also quite personal, and surprised even the Indian foreign secretary who had earlier told the Pakistani ambassador that India would not stand in the way.[15] Rajiv Gandhi followed his mother's line, justifying the opposition to Pakistan's return to the Commonwealth on the ground that Pakistan was ruled by a dictator. Actually, democratic rule was not a precondition for membership at that time. In any case, India did not abandon its opposition even after elections in 1985, the installation of a civilian government and an end to martial law. Not until after the 1988 election in Pakistan did New Delhi relent. If Pakistan's manner of leaving the Commonwealth in a huff was childish, that of suing for re-entry also did not reflect maturity of decision-making in foreign policy.

War Averted, 1990

Still another crisis erupted in the spring of 1990. As the situation in Kashmir continued to deteriorate, senior military officials in India were reported to have recommended air strikes on targets in Pakistan. Whether their object was to deter Pakistan or intimidate the Kashmiris, the reports triggered anxiety among analysts that Indian adventurism could precipitate war between the two countries which could escalate to the nuclear level. In May 1990, the President of the United States sent Robert Gates, assistant for the National Security Council, to Islamabad and New Delhi. Although sensational reports[16] depicting an actual nuclear threat were discounted, the United States obviously possessed enough information to consider it necessary to launch an exercise in preventive diplomacy.

Disarmament Issues

Chemical Weapons Convention, 1993. Historically supportive of resolutions in the UN General Assembly for general disarmament, and the limitation, progressive reduction and eventual elimination of weapons of mass destruction, Pakistan welcomed the Chemical Weapons Convention (CWC) when it was concluded in 1993. As a country that never had a chemical weapons programme, it was satisfied with the CWC's prohibition on production or acquisition of such weapons and the obligation to destroy existing stocks within ten years. Pakistan did not, however, ratify the CWC until four years later, in October 1997, because of its concern over a provision in the convention regarding verification and inspection. This was unprecedented in its broad scope, giving rise to the apprehension that it might be exploited for intrusion into the country's sensitive nuclear facilities. To neutralise the risk, Pakistan stated in the instrument of ratification that it would not allow abuse of the verification provision to degrade Pakistan's defence capability unrelated to the CWC.[17]

India, too, ratified the CWC. Beside satisfying the principle that Pakistan would not undertake asymmetrical obligations in respect of disarmament and non-proliferation treaties, India's ratification of CWC relieved Pakistan's concerns about the use of such weapons against its security, especially because verification provisions make this convention reliable. The importance of this factor was emphatically illustrated by India's obligatory disclosure pursuant to CWC that it had actually produced chemical weapons, in violation of a bilateral agreement with Pakistan, signed in April 1992, prohibiting chemical weapons. The revelation that India did not actually observe that commitment could not but further undermine the credibility of India's pledges in a bilateral framework.

CTBT. The Comprehensive Test Ban Treaty was conceived in the context of non-proliferation. Its object was to restrict qualitative improvement of weapons technology by the existing, as well as aspiring, nuclear weapons states. The prospects of the treaty looked promising, as all such states appeared to favour the CTBT. India was one of the sponsors.

Pakistan supported the treaty from the day it was proposed. This stance was consistent with its long-standing policy of joining the vast majority of nations that supported limitation, reduction and elimination of weapons of mass destruction. Given Pakistan's preoccupation with security in South Asia, its one and only condition was that such measures should be non-discriminatory. That was, of course, a code word with a region-specific purpose.

Pakistan's stance on the CTBT followed the standard line. It favoured the conclusion of the treaty but declared it would not ratify 'unilaterally'. Pakistan sought to ensure, during negotiations in the UN conference on disarmament, to plug any loopholes India might later exploit to change its mind. To that end, Pakistan successfully sponsored a provision which made CTBT's entry into force contingent on ratification by each and every one of the forty-four nuclear-capable states. Moreover, if any such state later renounced the treaty, that would also entitle other states to review their position.

The prospects of the treaty were suddenly clouded, however, when India opposed the adoption of the treaty by the UN General Assembly, explaining its reversal of stance from sponsorship to opposition on the ground of the refusal of nuclear weapons states to give a timetable for total nuclear disarmament. It became evident that the real purpose behind the idealistic facade was to retain the option to conduct nuclear tests. Prime Minister Deve Gowda's government declared it would not sign the CTBT. Foreign Minister I. K. Gujral candidly said on 15 July that India 'will not allow its nuclear options to be restricted in any manner and would take all necessary measures to cope with any threat that might be posed to its security'.

India's refusal to endorse the treaty sealed its fate. Even the slight hope that India might be persuaded by the United States to change its stance vanished when the United States Senate decided against ratification in 1997.

A suggestion was floated in early 2000 that Pakistan should consider signing the CTBT. Keeping in view the distinction between signing and ratification, and the provision in the CTBT text regarding its entry into force, some[18] in the government felt that Pakistan had little to lose and much to gain by signing the treaty. It would cost nothing because the treaty would not enter into force anyway because of Indian and US refusal to become parties. Many other states, including the United States, had signed the treaty. In doing so, they did not incur any obligation. By signing it, Pakistan, it was argued, could reap considerable benefits. It would deflect and sidetrack international pressures, occupy high moral ground, earn praise for itself, and isolate and expose India. In brief, Pakistan could free-ride known Indian recalcitrance, keep the cake and eat it too. The only problem was that the arguments were too technical and arcane for lay opinion to grasp.

Some of the political parties opposed to the military government sensed an opportunity to exploit the situation by denouncing any unilateral signing. A religious party warned of mass agitation if the government wavered in its resolve. The government, which had never formally approved the suggestion to sign the CTBT anyway, did not pursue the idea.

Although the idea had to be abandoned, its public discussion yielded some benefits. Public opinion in Pakistan became better informed. Foreign governments, especially those of Japan and some EU countries, noted that a section of enlightened opinion in Pakistan favoured a reasoned and rational approach to nuclear issues. The debate also helped soften the impression of a trigger-happy people, generated by popular celebrations in Pakistan (and earlier in India) after the nuclear tests.

FMCT. The Fissile Material Cut off Convention was proposed in the 1980s with the object of limiting nuclear weapon capabilities by freezing the production of enriched uranium and plutonium. Combined with the CTBT, which would restrict qualitatiative improvement of nuclear weapons, FMCT would reduce the dangers inherent in the increasing numbers of nuclear weapons in the arsenals of nuclear states.

An idea supported by a vast majority of states, FMCT has suffered relegation because of the collapse of the CTBT. Since all of the enormous effort invested in negotiating that treaty has gone to waste, members of the Conference on Disarmament are understandably reluctant to embark on another similar endeavour. In particular, the credibility of the United States as a serious negotiator has been undermined by its betrayal of the CTBT. Smaller nuclear-weapons states can now argue even more forcefully that efforts aimed at wider arms limitation should await the reduction of strategic weapons by the two powers with the largest arsenals.

Meanwhile, the United States and Russia have entered into bilateral agreements to reduce the numbers of nuclear weapons and delivery vehicles in their arsenals. From 35,000 or more nuclear bombs in possession of each, they have already reduced the stockpiles to 6,000 and are currently engaged in further reductions to 1,500 bombs.

NOTES

1. R. K. Jain, ed., *China-South Asian Relations*, Vol. 1, p. 197.
2. Shimla Agreement, subparagraph (ii): 'Pending the final settlement of any of the problems between the two countries, neither side shall unilaterally alter the situation....'
3. The joint statement issued in June 1989 read:

> There was an agreement by both sides to work toward a comprehensive settlement based on re-deployment of force to reduce the chances of conflict, avoidance of the use of force and the determination of future positions on the ground so as to conform with the Shimla Agreement and assure durable peace in the Siachen area. The army authorities of both sides will determine these positions.

4. The World Bank was approached on 19 January 2005. For settlement procedure, see section on Indus Waters Treaty, 1960, in Chapter 7.
5. Statements by P. V. Narasimha Rao in parliament on 2 September 1980, and again on 25 March 1982.
6. K. M. Arif, op. cit., p. 362.
7. *New York Times*, 15 September 1984.
8. Bajpai, Chari, Cheema, Cohen and Ganguli l, *Brasstacks and Beyond*, a joint study.
9. Ibid., p. 15.
10. The understanding was reached in letters exchanged between Gen. K. M. Arif and Gen. Sundarji's predecessor. Explaining the omission in an informal conversation at lake Coma sponsored by Steve Cohen in 1995, Sudarji disarmingly told Arif that he was not informed of the 'bloody' exchange of letters!
11. Press conference, 20 January 1987.
12. Apart from the methodically researched *Beyond Brasstacks*, David J. Karl of the Pacific Council on Foreign Policy, University of Southern California, Los Angeles, has written a paper on 'The Impression of Deterrence: Nuclear Weapons and the 1987 Brasstacks Crisis.'
13. Karl, op. cit.
14. Bajpai et al, op. cit., p. viii.
15. The author was the ambassador.
16. Seymour Hersh, 'On the Nuclear Edge' in *The New Yorker*, 29 March 1993.
17. Statement by foreign minister of Pakistan, *Dawn*, Karachi, 26 February 1998.
18. Then foreign minister, the author was the main proponent of the suggestion.

CHAPTER 17

Nuclear Tests

Tests

India conducted multiple nuclear explosion tests on 11 and 13 May 1998. Pakistan, having refrained from testing for over a decade, was suddenly confronted with this surprise development. The popular impulse to test was strong but the government was impaled on the horns of a dilemma. Not to test would jeopardise military security. To test would entail the threat of economic sanctions, which the country could ill-afford, as it was already buried under a mountain of debt,[1] the result of years of fiscal mismanagement and corruption. The US had stopped aid in 1990; now it would also oppose loans by international financial institutions, and Pakistan would be faced with the threat of default.

The security argument was, however, irrefutable. Pakistan had to demonstrate that it, too, possessed weapons capability. Past experience underlined apprehensions that India might again exploit the power imbalance in order to blackmail and browbeat Pakistan. The rumblings of threats and bluster from across the border drowned whatever reservations existed. Indian home minister, Lal Krishna Advani, next in power and influence in the ruling BJP to the prime minister, warned that Pakistan should realise that the Indian nuclear tests had changed the strategic balance. He demanded that Pakistan roll back what he described as its anti-India policy. The minister for parliamentary affairs, Madan Lal Khurana, challenged Pakistan to 'a fourth war.' Pakistan could not ignore the threats. The spokesman for the US Department of State said, 'India is foolishly and dangerously increasing tensions with its neighbours.'

Another factor in Pakistan's decision was the realisation that if it did not respond immediately, international pressures would make it even more difficult to test later. It was recalled that after the 1974 Indian test, the West acquiesced in the *fait accompli* but targeted Pakistan by a policy of denial and discrimination in an attempt to prevent it from acquiring nuclear capability.

Once again in May 1998, Western states focused efforts on preventing Pakistan from following suit. They sent messages and made diplomatic démarches. The United States took the lead. Deputy Secretary of State Strobe Talbot arrived in Islamabad, bringing, the press reported, a lot of sticks and few carrots. President Clinton made several phone calls to Prime Minister Nawaz Sharif, expressing understanding of Pakistan's concerns and promising to review US sanctions and resume economic assistance. But conspicuously missing from the dialogue was the one component most important to Pakistan, namely assurance on the key issue of security.

It became manifest once again that Pakistan had to fend for its own defence. Almost all political parties, political leaders and security analysts, newspaper editors and columnists, the security establishment and public opinion became vociferous in demanding a response to the Indian tests, and a demonstration to adventurists in India that Pakistan too possessed the bomb. The chief editor of a respected newspaper chain was said to have even warned the prime minister that an explosion was unavoidable: the choice was between a nuclear test and his government!

On the afternoon of 28 May 1998, scientists of the Pakistan Atomic Energy Commission (PAEC) and Khan Research Laboratories conducted nuclear explosion tests in a sealed tunnel in the Chaghi Mountain in Balochistan. More were carried out two days later on 30 May, marking the success of a 'truly gigantic endeavour spanning three decades and involving thousands of scientists, engineers, technicians and administrative personnel.'[2]

Motivations. Pakistan's sole motivation for the response to Indian tests was security, which was, in fact, the rationale for its pursuit of the nuclear option. Other than that, Pakistan had no grand design. It entertained no ambition to obtain status and prestige. It did not seek recognition or reward, membership of the nuclear club or a permanent seat on the Security Council. It had no desire to settle scores on account of any resentment against the discrimination implicit in the NPT. Indeed, Pakistan voted for that treaty in 1969 and might have signed it, had it included reliable security guarantees. Similarly, Pakistan voted for the CTBT in 1996 and was willing to sign it, provided India also did so.

In contrast, India's policy and pronouncements as to its nuclear stance were opaque, contradictory and misleading. Its diplomatic stance of denunciation of the discrimination in the NPT and its

demand for time-bound elimination of nuclear arsenals was a
smokescreen to camouflage its own nuclear ambitions. The motivation
behind India's pursuit of nuclear weapons is traceable to its ambition
to strut on the world stage as a great power, project its influence and
power beyond its boundaries and impose domination and hegemony
over less powerful neighbours. That ambition has deep roots in
chauvinism.[3] Having tested the bomb in 1974, the Congress government
did not carry out another test, realising perhaps that the cost-benefit
ratio was adverse. Now, the revivalist Bharatiya Janata Party government
justified the decision in the context of India's two nuclear neighbours.
After the Indian test was criticised internationally, Prime Minister
Vajpayee sent letters to the heads of government of 177 states, justifying
the test in the context of India's two nuclear neighbours. Although
Pakistan had conducted no tests, he called Pakistan 'a covert nuclear
weapon state', and inverting facts, accused Pakistan of having
committed aggression against India three times and continuing to
sponsor terrorism in Kashmir'.

The propagandistic intent of the letters was particularly obvious in
Vajpayee's letters to Western leaders known for their apprehensions
about China, especially the United States which looked upon India as
a champion of democracy against Chinese communism, and a potential
ally for a policy of containment against China. The letter to President
Clinton highlighted the history of India's relations with China—'an
overt nuclear weapon state on our borders, a state which committed
armed aggression against India in 1962.'[4] After China protested,
exposing the Indian pretext by pointing to the substantial progress
toward normalisation since Rajiv Gandhi's visit to China in 1985 and
agreements on military disengagement along the line of actual control
on the disputed boundary, New Delhi back-tracked assuring Beijing
that India did not regard China as a threat.[5] In contrast, the Indian
defence minister, George Fernandes, publicly referred to China as
'threat No. 1'.

International Reaction to Tests. The Indian test was severely criticised
by all major powers. The White House expressed distress and
displeasure, and the US announced sanctions on defence sales,
termination or suspension of some assistance programmes, loans, and
opposition to World Bank and IMF lending. President Clinton was
angry because the test had 'increased the danger of nuclear war on the
subcontinent, dealt a body blow to the global nonproliferation regime,
and dimmed, if not extinguished, the hopes for improving US–Indian

relations.' (This proved to be a hasty reaction in anger, because soon afterwards the US decided to develop a strategic partnership with India, and Clinton embarked on a six-day visit to India—the longest by a US President.[6]

The focus of US policy immediately shifted to 'the more difficult and urgent objective of dissuading Pakistan from conducting its own set of tests.' Deputy Secretary of State, Strobe Talbott, came to Islamabad to make out a case for 'restraint and maturity', believing that 'Pakistanis suddenly had a chance to occupy the high ground in the eyes of a nervous world. They could, literally, cash in by showing restraint. Virtually every dollar of aid that donor countries like the United States and Japan would withhold from India could be offered to Pakistan as a reward for resisting the temptation to test.' Pakistan's response should not have surprised him. Foreign Minister Gohar Ayub 'fidgeted' as Talbott made opening remarks and 'then unleashed a broadside' on India—'habitual aggressor and hegemon'—and on the United States 'a fair weather friend'.[7] A fortnight later, Pakistan conducted the tests.

The world reaction now lumped India and Pakistan together, although the joint communiqué issued by the P-5, permanent members of the UN Security Council, on 4 June 1998 noted that the tests were carried out 'by India and then by Pakistan.' The differentiation was evidently due to the position taken by China noting that India was the first to conduct the tests and Pakistan was obliged to respond, which was appreciated in Pakistan. The Security Council Resolution 1172 of 6 June 1998 failed to make the same distinction.

Resolution 1172 condemned the nuclear tests by India and Pakistan, demanded that the two countries refrain from further tests, weaponisation and development of ballistic missiles, sign the CTBT, and participate in negotiations on the fissile material production cut off treaty (FMCT). Paradoxically, the United States joined this demand although it was one of the killers of the CTBT. The Security Council also urged them to resume dialogue in order to remove tensions and encouraged them to 'find mutually acceptable solutions that address the root causes of those tensions, including Kashmir.'

On 12 June the foreign ministers of P-5 and that of the G-8 group of industrialised states (Canada, France, Germany, Italy, Japan, Russia, UK and USA), issued a communiqué stating that they would work for postponement in consideration of loans by the World Bank and other international financial institutions to the two countries except for basic human needs.

As Pakistan was faced with a grave foreign payments crisis, Saudi Arabia demonstrated its traditional solidarity and agreed to provide 100,000 barrels of oil daily on a deferred payments basis. Valued at over $500 million a year, the assistance over five years was later converted into a grant.

The penalties imposed by Western countries were relaxed a year later. They did not oppose resumption of lending to Pakistan and India by international financial institutions. The International Monetary Fund provided a $1.2 billion credit to Pakistan for structural adjustment. The Paris Club agreed to reschedule some of Pakistan's loans.

Nuclear Restraints

Security Council resolution 1172 of 6 June 1998 prescribed an elaborate agenda of restraints. It is not necessary to agree with every item to say that nuclear restraints are in humanity's interest. Initiatives to stabilise the situation would be consistent with Islamabad's past policy. Pakistan was content with recessed deterrence. It was not the first to conduct an explosion test. It did not weaponise the capability. It was not the first to induct missiles.

Washington, meanwhile, seemed to abandon efforts to restrain India from accumulating an increasing stockpile of fissile material. When the time came for a further supply of enriched uranium fuel for the Tarapur power reactor that the US had supplied to India in the 1960s, Washington asked for no additional safeguards to prevent the reprocessing of the accumulated used fuel, from which India could extract plutonium for possible use for weapons purposes. In doing so, it evaded its own Nuclear Nonproliferation Act of 1978, which prohibited the United States from the export of nuclear materials to a country that did not accept the full-scope inspection and control safeguards of the IAEA. It violated the law, at least in spirit, by arranging for France to provide the fuel.

Moratorium. Immediately after the Chaghi tests, Pakistan announced a moratorium on further tests. It also decided to participate in negotiations for the Fissile Material Cut off Treaty. It was willing to consider compliance with the Security Council's call for refraining from weaponisation, and further development and deployment of missiles, but that required reciprocity at par with India.

The prime ministers of Pakistan and India, in speeches in the UN General Assembly in September 1998, expressed willingness to sign the CTBT by September 1999, when three years would have expired after the treaty was opened for signature and a review conference was scheduled to be held. Their statements of intention were, however, hedged by conditions, Pakistan's in the context of removal of sanctions by the United States, and India's with regard to progress in negotiations on nuclear disarmament. In the event, the plan was derailed. After the Vajpayee government fell, New Delhi decided to postpone a decision on signing the CTBT till after the election in October. On 21 February 1998 Pakistan and India declared in a joint statement that they would continue to abide by their respective unilateral moratoria on conducting further test explosions 'unless either side, in exercise of its national sovereignty, decides that extraordinary events have jeopardised its supreme interests.'

The suggestions in the Security Council Resolution 1172 for restraint by India and Pakistan in regard to weaponisation and development of ballistic missiles had little impact. Both countries claimed they were nuclear weapons states, and accelerated development of missiles.

Impact on Security

As a demonstration of weapons capability, the Pakistani tests helped silence those in India who considered the Pakistan claim to possession of nuclear capability a hoax. Perhaps even the Indian prime minister had been misled into sharing such doubts. Now, in a statement on 28 May 1998, he said the Pakistani tests had created a 'new' situation. Pakistani observers hoped that this realisation might be conducive to a reappraisal of policies of intimidation and use of force.

Even before the May 1998 tests, those familiar with the apocalyptic power of nuclear weapons were outspoken in expressing the view that acquisition of nuclear capability would exercise a restraining influence on jingoism. After overt nuclearisation, the need for caution and restraint in the conduct of Pakistan–India relations was recognised at the level of prime ministers of the two countries. In a joint declaration issued on 12 February 1999, they declared, 'the nuclear dimension of the security environment of the two countries adds to their responsibility for avoidance of conflict.' The two sides also agreed to 'undertake national measures to reduce the risks of accidental or unauthorised use of nuclear weapons' and to provide advance notification in respect of ballistic missile flight tests. The prime ministers also pledged to intensify efforts for the solution of outstanding issues including that of Kashmir.

It was tempting to conclude that the impact of the May tests was salutary. The logic of restraint was strengthened and prospects of peace became brighter. Such optimism was not, however, shared by the chief of the Indian army in 1999, who remarked that 'the possibility of a conventional war cannot be ruled out simply because India had crossed the nuclear threshold.'[8] If militancy in India-held Kashmir 'grows too much', the general added, India could contemplate a conventional war.

'The Root Cause'. Security Council resolution 1172 of 6 June 1998, urged India and Pakistan to remove tensions by finding 'solutions that address the root causes of those tensions, including Kashmir.' The logic of the Security Council's exhortation evoked an apparently positive response. The prime ministers of India and Pakistan, in their declaration of 12 February 1999, not only recognised that 'the resolution of all outstanding issues, including Jammu and Kashmir, is essential' for peace and security but went on to pledge that their respective governments 'shall intensify their efforts to resolve all outstanding issues, including the issue of Jammu and Kashmir.'

The words were not followed, however, with any purposeful action. There was no evidence to suggest that the declaration would mark a departure from the past record of procrastination, obstruction and failure in finding solutions to outstanding issues, in particular that of Kashmir. Over seventy thousand Kashmiris had perished in the freedom struggle in the 1990s and the state continued to bleed. So long as the people of Kashmir were denied the opportunity to exercise their right of self-determination, which was pledged to them by India and Pakistan and in resolutions of the Security Council, relations between Pakistan and India would remain inflammable.

The optimism generated by Resolution 1172 and the Lahore Declaration soon evaporated with the outbreak of the Kargil crisis in May 1999.

Issues and Non-Issues

Non-Proliferation Debate. The academic debate for and against proliferation has necessarily taken place in terms of principles, but few of the participants envisage, advocate or apprehend the spread of nuclear weapons to many additional states. Excluding Argentina and Brazil who decided between them to renounce the nuclear option they were earlier developing, and South Africa, who dismantled the nuclear devices once the white supremacist regime reconciled itself to black-majority rule, only India, Israel and Pakistan, who were not parties to the NPT, acquired nuclear capability. More recently attention has focused on Iran, which denies allegations of pursuing the weapons option, and North Korea, which claims to possess the technology.

Major nuclear powers and some political scientists[9] oppose proliferation basically on the ground that the spread of nuclear weapons would multiply the dangers of their use in war through miscalculation. Medium and small powers, in their view, lack the resources, the mutual learning experience, and the technical safeguards that help the superpowers manage crises. Particularly states in the Third World are considered to be politically unstable and institutionally immature, if not also deficient in prudence and rationality. For these or other reasons, they could lose control over these weapons, imperiling their own people as well as the world community.

Other political scientists, on both historical and doctrinal grounds, do not share the above view, however. Some even argue in support of the efficacy of nuclear weapons as a deterrent to war[10] because nuclear weapons, 'make the cost of war seem frighteningly high and thus discourage states from starting any wars that might lead to the use of such weapons.'[11] Founded in logic, the deterrence argument is also upheld by empirical evidence. Nuclear weapons have helped maintain peace and prevent military adventures in the past, and there is no reason to expect that the future will be different. Even a powerful state is unlikely to resort to aggression if it concludes that the potential gains are not worth the losses it has to risk. Such a conclusion is not obvious in a conventional environment: leaders may contemplate an adventure in a situation which admits of a margin of error in judgment; even if the adventure fails, the consequences may not be suicidal. Margins are eliminated, however, in a nuclear environment.

It is not necessary to conjure up doomsday scenarios of annihilation in a nuclear Armageddon between superpowers to realize that any use of nuclear weapons would entail an 'unmitigated disaster.'[12] Two atomic bombs devastated Hiroshima and Nagasaki, forcing Japan to surrender. It has been estimated that a single 20-kiloton bomb, exploded over a densely populated city, could cause 130,000 instantaneous deaths. In addition, over 200,000 people would suffer blast injuries and radiation burns, and many times more would be condemned to a life worse than death due to ingestion of high doses of radiation and the consequent increase in cancer, abortion and genetic defects. The explosion would also cause destruction of property in a 15-square mile area and incalculable and irreversible damage to ecology and environment that would make the affected area uninhabitable.[13]

The awesome potential for destruction invests nuclear weapons with an unequalled power of deterrence. The possibility that nuclear weapons might be used in desperation by an attacked state should foreclose the thought of resort to war in pursuit of a policy of conquest and expansion. This has been the main rationale for the acquisition of nuclear capabilities by states that lack the conventional power to deter aggression. It is assumed that nuclear weapons 'should be used only if the very existence of the state is threatened by a conventional or nuclear attack.'[14] This 'weapon of defensive last resort' doctrine explained the nuclear policy of Britain and France, although pride and prestige may be a reason for their retention of nuclear weapons now that they face no apparent threat. It was advanced as the principal argument for Ukraine retaining the nuclear weapons it inherited upon the disintegration of the Soviet Union. These weapons, it was argued, were 'the only reliable deterrent to Russian aggression.' A conventional defence would not be viable and Ukraine would otherwise remain 'vulnerable to Russian nuclear blackmail.'[15] The 'last resort' argument was also the Israeli rationale for its nuclear policy, which remains unquestioned by anti-proliferation protagonists and was probably a factor in the American decision to provide prompt and effective assistance to rescue Israel during the 1973 war if when facing defeat it contemplated the use of doomsday weapons.[16]

Arguments against proliferation fail to carry conviction, partly because they are advanced mostly by states that do not themselves practice the precept they preach. Nevertheless, the arguments should be examined on their merits in order to reduce the dangers of proliferation of nuclear weapons, which are too serious to be dismissed or ignored. Miscalculation, for instance, brought the United States and the Soviet Union perilously close to disaster in the Cuban missiles crisis in 1962. Accidental or unintended use is another serious threat. Nuclear powers have to devise and institute agreed precautionary measures to preclude such perils.[17] Procedures need to be tightened to prevent theft and clandestine diversion of nuclear materials. In the past, some states were selective in their vigilance. In the 1960s, 93.8 kilograms of enriched uranium was diverted from a US plant to Israel.[18] In 1968, EURATOM released 200 tons of uranium oxide in the name of a plant in Italy, which ended up in Israel.[19] Neither the USA nor the European community expressed remorse for their collusion. For over a quarter of a century, a Norwegian firm supplied heavy water, directly or through intermediaries, to Argentina, India, Israel and South Africa.[20]

Considering humanity's stake in precluding nuclear dangers, it is obviously desirable that precautions, procedures, and confidence-building measures to reduce the dangers of miscalculation, accidents, and theft developed by more experienced and resourceful states be shared with the others. Similarly, command and control institutions and procedures in the neo-nuclear states should be improved. But the targeting of some 'small' states only for expression of exaggerated fears cannot be constructive. Only 'ethnocentric views' can perceive non-westerners as 'lesser breeds without the law.'[21]

To be sure, nuclear weapons are neither a panacea in every conflict nor within the means of every state. Even with nuclear weapons, a less powerful state 'will face a number of difficult constraints in attempting to construct a survivable deterrent force,'[22] especially if it is condemned to live with short warning time, threat of nuclear decapitation, and lack of resources to develop the requisite infrastructure for a survivable nuclear force. Inadequacy of resources could create dangerous dilemmas if a state ends up with an unsurvivable nuclear capability as well as a degraded conventional force. Unable to deal with a local conflict by conventional means, it might come under pressure to raise the stakes, coming face to face with the fateful 'use or lose' dilemma, cutting into the time for preventive diplomacy and precipitating a nuclear war, which could spell annihilation.

The contingencies warranting a summons to the weapon of last resort should be clearly and carefully defined. Deep penetration of a state's territory by adversary forces, and large-scale attacks threatening to overwhelm and destroy its defensive capability, are types of situations likely to trigger consideration of use of nuclear weapons. What choice a victim of aggression should make between capitulation and annihilation is a cruel question to which only the people of a state can give an answer.

After overt nuclearisation the pristine simplicity of assumptions about nuclear deterrence has given way to a new set of issues even while some of the old ones are surrounded in a fog of confusion. How do we define minimum deterrence? If it cannot be quantified once and for all, what should be the guidelines for dynamic limits to the nuclear arsenal? Is it still possible to induct restraints in South Asia to reduce risks associated with weaponisation and mobile missiles? If not, what measures need to be taken to preclude miscalculation, accident or unauthorised use?

Nuclear Sufficiency. Nuclear powers have built arsenals of diverse sizes. At what level is deterrence realised? Does it remain credible in case of imbalance? To be sure, a nuclear arsenal should not be so small as to be vulnerable to a pre-emptive strike. It is desirable further to have a safety margin for confidence in a crisis and avoidance of panic in response to a false alarm.[23] But neither do the numbers have to be so large as to be unaffordable by a medium state.

Even between superpowers, purely deterrent nuclear forces 'can be relatively modest.'[24] Moreover, nuclear deterrence, unlike a conventional one, is not decisively degraded by quantitative or qualitative disparity. So long as a state's strategic arsenal is sufficient to survive the first strike and still deliver 'unacceptable' damage, it does not have to match the adversary's arsenal.[25] The Soviet Union achieved deterrence when it had 300 nuclear warheads even though the United States then possessed 5,000 nuclear warheads.[26] That the Soviet Union and the United States continued to build stockpiles to peak levels respectively of 45,000 and 32,500 nuclear warheads is explained mainly in the context of 'extended deterrence' involving their responsibility to ensure the security of their allies. Partly, too, the vast build-up is attributed in retrospect to an uncontrolled, but not necessarily uncontrollable, arms race.[27]

Medium nuclear powers have not considered it necessary to build thousands of warheads. Britain and France are said to maintain 200 and 500 nuclear warheads, and China an arsenal of 450. It has been estimated that by 2003, Israel possessed 510-650 kg of plutonium, enough for 110-190 nuclear warheads, India had 330-470 kg of plutonium, enough for 55-115, and Pakistan had 1000-1250 kg of highly enriched uranium, enough for 50-90.[28]

As between medium states, credible deterrence is achieved with a small nuclear arsenal. A scholar has concluded that 'five or six' nuclear warheads should be sufficient.[29] Theoretically, even a smaller number should suffice to deter, provided the weapons can be delivered on targets of high value. It is inconceivable that a responsible government or leader would risk the nuclear devastation of a single metropolis for the satisfaction of vanquishing an adversary.

A deterrence force need not be large but it must be sufficient. The key to the credibility and efficacy of the deterrent is not numbers but the survivability of the nuclear force. If, for instance, five or ten bombs are considered necessary for deterrence, then that number should be sure to survive a surprise attack for delivery and unacceptable destruction of high value targets. If the adversary develops the capacity for pre-emption and interception, the arsenal has then to be correspondingly augmented. If air bases or launch platforms are in danger of being destroyed by a surprise attack, it becomes necessary to build indestructible silos and to develop mobile missiles.

The economic burden of a small nuclear arsenal is not a decisive constraint on a medium state's decision on whether or not to acquire these weapons. The cost of designing, building and testing a plutonium-based nuclear device was estimated in a United Nations study in 1968 at $100 million; the US Arms Control and Disarmament Agency (ACDA) estimated the cost at $51 million in 1976. If a country already possessed the fissile material, the figure according to ACDA dropped to $1 million. While these figures might be two to three times higher in the depreciated dollars of 1994, the expenditures would not greatly strain the budgets of India and Pakistan, each of which spends billions of dollars annually on defence. Moreover, both the countries have already built the infrastructure.

In addition, in judging the burden of a nuclear force, allowance should be made for possible containment of the defence budget because in a nuclear environment the conventional forces do not have to be maintained or equipped for strategic deterrence. Disparity of conventional forces then loses some of its edge: 'if a country was forced to use the nuclear option the moment it seemed to be losing, it would make conventional superiority irrelevant.'[30] In the context of Pakistan and India, General K. Sundarji, former chief of staff of the Indian Army, persuasively argued: 'If a mutual nuclear deterrent exists, I believe there is more scope for both countries to cut back on conventional forces and maintain a lower level balance.'[31]

Minimum Deterrence. From the inception of the programme, Pakistan viewed nuclear weapons as a means of deterring and preventing war, not of fighting one. The sole purpose of acquiring the nuclear option after 1971 was to deter another Indian adventure against residual Pakistan. Nuclear weapons are, in theory and in practice, an effective means for discouragement of aggression. A state or a leader contemplating use of force to achieve perverse ends stands warned against starting a war that might provoke or compel the victim to give a nuclear response. So great is the devastation nuclear weapons inflict that the risk of their use makes an adventure unacceptable.

Every nuclear state determines the size of its defence force according to its own security and economic circumstances. Strategic analysts, who argue in favour of the efficacy of nuclear deterrence, have held the view that nuclear deterrence does not depend on parity of arsenals. This has been the general assumption in Pakistan. Even a smaller arsenal is considered sufficient for the limited purpose in view.

Nuclear deterrence by contrast with the conventional one is not dependent on parity or ratio between arsenals. The Soviet Union possessed deterrent capability during the Cuban crisis even though its nuclear arsenal was a fraction of the size of the United States. The concept of an arms race is, therefore, inapplicable. The US–USSR example is manifestly irrelevant. China, which was once threatened by two superpowers, did not seek to match either, much less both bomb for bomb, missile for missile. Its capability remained fractional. But that is enough for deterrence.

General Krishnaswamy Sundarji, who became a persuasive strategic analyst, once made the memorable remark: 'More is unnecessary if less is enough.' That is an eminently sane view, even though it came under question by hawkish commentators in India who advocate the build-up of a full-fledged strategic arsenal of thermo-nuclear weapons and ballistic missiles of inter-continental range.[32]

Such over-zealous super-patriots misled the United States and the Soviet Union into a race that rational analysts now consider insane. Fuelled by ideological confrontation and power rivalry for global supremacy, the competition got out of control, entailing diversion of enormous resources, which 'ruined' the Soviet Union as Soviet Foreign Minister Shevardnadze later acknowledged. China did not commit the blunder. Informed opinion in Pakistan agreed it, too, must not.

Nuclear Arms Limitation. The logic of complete nuclear disarmament does not appeal to strategic thinkers in the new nuclear-capable states any more than it did in the nuclear-weapons states. Commenting on the proposal for elimination of nuclear weapons, Zbigniew Brzezinski is said to have remarked: 'It is a plan to make the world safe for conventional warfare. I am therefore not enthusiastic about it.'[33] Even after the Cold War, nuclear powers do not consider a nuclear-free world an acceptable idea. The underlying problem persists: how to make the world unsafe for war, conventional or otherwise? Conventional weapons have not historically proved effective in a deterrence role, and deterrence now commands an even higher priority, as 'nations can no longer afford to fight protracted wars.'[34] Great powers may develop high-precision conventional weapons to provide 'strategic' deterrence against conventional weapons.[35] But this option is not in sight of medium powers that lack requisite resources and access to the new weapons.

The ideal of a nuclear-free world will have to await a transformation of the security environment, globally and regionally. Limitation of nuclear weapons or capabilities is, however, a practical proposition. It can serve the interests not only of humankind in general, but also of the states involved, saving expenditures on an unnecessary nuclear arms race and reducing the dangers inherent in nuclear weapons. Such a practical approach would be consistent with the resolutions of the United Nations General Assembly.

The superpowers have set a good example: under START I and II, the Russian Federation and the United States cut their nuclear inventories by some ninety per cent in a decade to 3,000-3,500 warheads. Clearly, the magnitude of the reduction is impressive, even though the two countries still retain over three-quarters of the world's stock of nuclear weapons. Besides, the reduction process is likely to continue. States with large nuclear weapons stockpiles can hardly ignore, much less rebuff, this trend if they are to retain credibility.[36]

Pakistan has supported proposals for a nuclear limitation regime, globally and regionally. Limitation is preferable because it would prevent the unnecessary build-up of nuclear arsenals. A proposal, put forward by the Bush administration in 1990, to consider nuclear and security issues in South Asia at a conference of five states (China, Russia, the United States, India and Pakistan), was accepted by Pakistan but rejected by India. To accommodate India's concern for balance in the conference, the Clinton administration revised the proposal in 1993 to include France, Germany, Japan and the United Kingdom. India, however, turned down that proposal also. Apparently, India wanted an assurance in advance that any limitation proposal would apply to all 'geopolitically relevant' countries, arguing not only that its 'security problems include China,'[37] but also extended to the presence of great power forces in the ocean to its south.

Faced with India's rejection of a regional approach to limitation of nuclear capabilities, Washington gave up and reverted to the Pakistan-specific policy, the Senate apparently wanting Pakistan to roll back its nuclear program, and in effect, give up the nuclear option unilaterally.

Strategic Arms Race. The frequently heard argument of 'an all-out arms race'[38] and its crippling costs is inapplicable to Pakistan because its nuclear capability is, and will continue to be, the smallest of all eight nuclear weapon states. Pakistan has not tried to match India bomb for bomb or missile for missile. India can make many times more bombs, has multiple air-, land- and sea-based launchers and is engaged in serial production of ballistic missiles. A race implies competition in quantity or quality, which has not motivated the Pakistani programme. Driven neither by a craving for prestige nor one-upmanship, the sole purpose of this expensive pursuit has been the need to deter aggression. That aim does not require any nuclear or missile race. Its arsenal is a fraction of India's and will remain so. The guiding principle as to size is that a small nuclear arsenal is enough, so long as it is sufficient and survivable.

Command and Control. Statesmen and scholars knowledgeable about incidents of miscalculation and near-accidents during the Cold War worry about a similar possibility in other countries which lack the resources to put fail-safe mechanisms in place. The concern is not unreasonable. A state in possession of the Doomsday weapon must also develop an appropriate decision-making process to preclude unauthorised use and install built-in technologies to insure against the accidental launch of nuclear weapons.

States with nuclear weapons have learned to address and contain the risks of accidents or unauthorised use. Apart from strengthening command and control, they developed fail-safe mechanisms. Since such arcane technology requires time and expense to develop, Pakistan and India could benefit if the older nuclear states provided relevant information and equipment. At first they were reluctant, because to do so would imply recognition of the nuclear status of Pakistan and India. Emergence of new dangers including that of terrorists gaining access to nuclear materials, and the accidental or unauthorised launch of dispersed strategic weapons persuaded the United States to reconsider its policy for nuclear threat reduction measures for India and Pakistan. It has been reported that the US 'may' have provided such assistance ranging from 'guards and gates' around nuclear facilities to 'permissive links' which act as locks on nuclear weapons to prevent unauthorised use.'[39] Meanwhile, both countries kept warheads separate from delivery systems to prevent accidents.[40]

In the United States and Russia the presidents are vested with the authority to take the fateful decision. Also, they carry Black Boxes and only they can give the coded signals without which nuclear weapons cannot be armed for explosion. Every other nuclear state, too, must develop a system of command and control to obviate the inherent risks. Not every field commander can be given authority to fire off the bomb.

Benefiting from the experience of other nuclear states, Pakistan also decided to vest final responsibility for a decision regarding the use of nuclear weapons in the head of the government. At the same time, the decision making process would involve advisers and experts, not merely from the armed forces and military intelligence, but also top professionals from the foreign ministry. Taking into account that a surprise attack on the capital could decapitate the command structure, the command system also envisages devolution of responsibility.

No-First-Use. The Soviet Union first proposed this idea during the Cold War. NATO rejected the idea because its defence doctrine was predicated on use of nuclear weapons to deter Moscow from exploiting conventional force superiority in Europe.

A state with truly peaceful intentions should renounce first-use of not only nuclear, but also conventional weapons. India trumpets the no-first-use of nuclear weapons but reserves for itself the right to use conventional force. It is obviously illogical to seek to keep the cake and eat it too. China's commitment to peace is manifest from its policy of renunciation of first-use of nuclear weapons as well as a policy of peace toward neighbours.

Over-dependence on strategic deterrence. Whilst strategic weapons provide unmatched deterrence, they do not eliminate the need for adequate conventional defence capability to cope with situations short of general war. If conventional capacity is eroded, even a local and low-intensity conflict might be misperceived as commencement of general hostilities. Inherent in such a situation is the terrible danger of making the weapon-of-last-resort a weapon-of-first-resort. A responsible nuclear state has an obligation to its own people, as well as the world, to ensure maximum possible delay before invoking the strategic option.

Clandestine Acquisition of Technology. India's polemical approach to nuclear issues was manifest in its attribution of Pakistan's achievement of nuclear capability to the transfer of technology from outside. The propaganda ignored the capacity of Pakistani scientists to assimilate knowledge in the public domain fifty years after the nuclear bomb was invented and the efforts of its engineers to indigenously replicate and develop nuclear and missile technologies, not to mention the prodigious material sacrifices Pakistan has made due to the imposition of sanctions. Indian spokesmen and others who joined this chorus exposed their bias by shutting their eyes to the fact that India was the first developing country to receive massive transfers of nuclear technology and equipment from foreign countries. They were either duped by Indian professions of peaceful intentions or led by power politics to assist India's pursuit of nuclear ambition. Thousands of Indian scientists were trained in Britain, Canada, France, the Soviet Union and the United States.

'Islamic Bomb'. Not only Indian but other foreign commentators sought to stroke atavistic prejudices by describing the Pakistan programme as a plan to produce an 'Islamic bomb.' The instigation became all the more sinister after 9/11 when the world was alarmed that terrorists might gain access to nuclear materials and technology or even mini nukes. Alive to the terrible danger, Pakistan has joined the world community in tightening custodial controls to prevent leakage or theft of technology and sensitive materials.

Unauthorised Technology Transfer. Reports surfaced in 2003 that a transnational underworld network of manufactures and suppliers from a number of Asian, European and African countries was engaged in clandestine trade in nuclear materials and technology. Dr A. Q. Khan, head of the uranium enrichment programme for 25 years until 2001, and some of his colleagues, were accused of involvement with clandestine manufacturers and traders from a number of countries, including Britain, Switzerland, Malaysia, South Africa, Turkey and the United Arab Emirates. Iran, Libya and North Korea were reported to have received centrifuges.[41] Evidence in support of the allegation included centrifuges and drawings for a crude explosive device handed over to the United States by Libya after President Moammer Qaddafi renounced the clandestine nuclear programme.[42] Similarly, when IAEA learned that Iran was engaged in uranium enrichment research, the Khan network was alleged to be involved in the supply of technology.[43]

Pakistan acted expeditiously to contain the damage by agreeing to cooperate in the investigation of allegations. A. Q. Khan and some of his subordinates were interrogated. He issued a confession taking personal responsibility for the lapse. Considering that he was popularly regarded as a national hero, the president granted him a pardon and the government declined to permit any foreign agency to interrogate him. However, the Pakistan government itself obtained the relevant information through the interrogation of accused individuals. Investigation confirmed that he and some of his subordinates had indulged in the sale of technology.[44] The inquiry also concluded that the government had not authorised any transfer, and that the sale was on account of the personal greed of a few persons. The United States acknowledged that it had received 'the information we need to break up the network.'[45] Pakistan also agreed to give parts of its old centrifuges to IAEA for technical examination for purposes of comparison with centrifuges sold by the underground network.

Fortunately, the US concerns were anticipated, and President Pervez Musharraf's government took measures both before and after 9/11 to streamline command and control and strengthen custodial security of strategic assets. Also, it appointed new chief executives of organisations dealing with nuclear and missile programmes. Still, the apprehensions were not completely allayed. Involvement of Pakistani scientists in the underground international network of suppliers and traffickers of nuclear equipment and technology, and recurrent incidents of extremist violence, kept Pakistan in the limelight.

Appreciation of Pakistan's key role in the war on terrorism fortunately fostered a predisposition in the West to credit the findings of its official investigation about the infamous technology traffickers. The prestigious Washington-based Institute for Science and International Security concluded, after investigations, that 'the Pakistani government was not directing this network.' The United States evinced understanding of the leakage and accepted the result of the official inquiry.[46] Perhaps it recalled that a similar lapse had taken place in the United States a decade earlier.[47]

Although Pakistan took effective measures to prevent any further leakage of technology, the lapse continued to provoke international concerns about Pakistan's capacity to ensure foolproof custodial safety.

Doubts continued to surface in research articles in the international media, and also in official statements, of persisting concerns about the security of Pakistan's strategic assets, the danger of terrorists gaining access to nuclear materials, and even about political stability and the contingency of radicals gaining control of the assets. During his visit to Pakistan in April 2005, Japan's Prime Minister Koizumi expressed 'serious concern' regarding international black market networks. Earlier the Japanese ambassador told the media that Tokyo wanted more information about the alleged transfer of enrichment technology to North Korea.

In January 2005, influential Senator John F. Kerry (the defeated Democratic nominee for president) expressed concerns about Pakistan's refusal to allow interrogation of A. Q. Khan and the danger of Pakistani nuclear assets falling 'in the hand of a radical Islamic state.'[48] Secretary of State-designate Condoleezza Rice said, 'We are getting the information that we need to deal with the A. Q. Khan network.' As for the danger of weapons or material falling into the hands of extremists, she did not discuss the subject in the open but acknowledged, 'We have noted this problem, and we are prepared to try to deal with it.' After her visit, Pakistan decided, in March 2005, to provide parts of old and discarded centrifuges to IAEA for comparison with the centrifuges Iran had bought on the underground market. The comparison confirmed Iran had received centrifuges of Pakistani origin. That also substantiated Iran's claim that the enriched uranium IAEA had found in Iran was not produced by Iran.

Researchers believe the United States has been in the grip of an obsession since 9/11 about lethal nuclear material and technology falling into the hands of al Qaeda.[49] Finding no defence against the catastrophic contingency once the terrorists gained possession, US experts were said to have conceived a plan for simultaneous global covert and overt assault on all nuclear facilities that were regarded 'either unintentionally unsecure or intentionally hostile.' The uncertainty concerns mounted after a dirty bomb consisting of radioactive Cesium 137 was found in a park in Moscow. Suspecting Chechens of planting the bomb, concerns now focused on the Central Asia Republics, Iran, Libya and Pakistan where, analysts feared, Muslim extremists might gain access to nuclear weapons and radioactive materials. To guard against such danger of leakage or transfer, the experts suggested the US seek verifiable evidence that known stockpiles had been secured. Furthermore, they wanted the United States to be prepared for a pre-emptive strike on unsecured facilities with a new generation of precision-guided, small-yield nuclear weapons that could penetrate down into underground bunkers. Another investigative journalist, who highlighted the US and Israeli preoccupation with Iran's nuclear programme, reported that influential people in Washington believed, 'the war on terrorism would be expanded.'[50]

Ballistic Missiles: The Threat of Destabilization

As force-multipliers, missiles enhance both offensive and defensive capability. Armed with nuclear warheads, missiles make deterrence more credible as they are more difficult to intercept than aircraft. Also, missiles greatly increase the first strike capability of a state, degrading the survivability and therefore the credibility of the adversary's nuclear deterrent. What was sufficient before would become insufficient after the missiles enter the scene, creating new dilemmas connected with threats to the survivability of a small nuclear force. To guard against such an eventuality, the threatened state would be faced with the necessity of the enlargement and dispersal of its nuclear arsenal and launchers, making more problematic the safety and security of nuclear weapons and command and control over them, and adding to dangers of custodial leakages and accidents.

Such a threat arose for Pakistan as a result of India's extensive missile programme, reflecting its 'desire to seek or enhance international prestige and be an important player in world developments.'[51] Apart from short-range surface-to-air missiles like *Trishul* and *Akash* and the anti-tank *Nag*, India deployed *Prithvi*, which, with its range of 150-250 kilometers makes 'Pakistan's entire territory vulnerable to its lethal attack.' Also, it has developed long-range *Agni*, with a range of 1,000-2,500 kilometers 'or more if necessary.'[52] Equipped with inertial guidance and protected against electronic countermeasures as well as high re-entry temperatures, *Agni* was said to have been 'developed mainly to strike China.'[53] It is capable of delivering nuclear warheads as far away as Beijing, Jakarta, Riyadh, and Tehran. It also gives India capability to launch these missiles against Pakistan from distant sites. Another missile under development by India is a polar space launch vehicle with intercontinental range capability. More directly relevant to Pakistan's concern is the Indian programme to produce an anti-ballistic-missile system, for which it has received technological assistance from Russia and Israel.

Gravely concerned, Pakistan responded to the situation with missiles of its own. Since indigenous production would take time, Pakistan first approached China for supply of missiles and received a small number of short-range tactical missiles in the late 1980s. Learning about the transfer, the United States raised vociferous objections. China and Pakistan explained that international law did not prohibit trade in missiles. Although China was not a party to the Missile Technology Control Regime, the missiles it sold to Pakistan were within the range and payload criteria of the MTCR. More surprising for Pakistan was the fact that Washington did little to restrain India from inducting missiles into South Asia.

Pakistan also launched a missile research and development programme of its own. Over the years, it has indigenously produced a variety of ballistic missiles. These include liquid-fuel *Ghauri* and solid-fuel *Shaheen,* with ranges from 180 to 2000 kilometers as well as the anti-aircraft *Anza* and the anti-tank *Baktar Shikan.* 'Based on the highest scientific and technological standards and incorporating highly refined guidance and control systems,'[54] some of these missiles can be launched from mobile platforms. In August 2005, Pakistan also tested a cruise missile.

Even with conventional warheads, ballistic missiles represent a qualitative leap in weapons systems. Traversing distances in minutes they strike with little notice, and they are almost impossible to defend against. If used to bomb urban areas, they are an instrument of intimidation and terror; they can spread panic and demoralise the population. Secondly, missiles can be used to deliver knockout punches at airfields, arms and ammunition depots, petroleum storage facilities, communication junctions, etc. Attack by such missiles can thus undermine the victim's will and capacity to resist aggression.

Tests of missiles have to be conducted for validating the technology and also for development and improving accuracy. But matching the adversary test for test and missile for missile is neither necessary for the credibility of deterrence, nor is it affordable for Pakistan. Both theory and experience of other nuclear states lead to the same conclusion: sufficiency, not parity, is the precondition for the efficacy of deterrence.

NOTES

1. The international debt had doubled from about $18 billion in 1988 to $36 billion in 1998.
2. Dr Ishfaq Ahmed, op. cit.
3. For statements of Indian National Congress leaders, see under Retrospect in Chapter 21.
4. Strobe Talbott, *Engaging India: Diplomacy, Democracy and the Bomb*, excerpt published in *Dawn*, Islamabad, 23 January 2005.
5. Cheng Ruisheng, 'China-India Relations', a paper presented at a forum sponsored by the UNESCO School of Science for Peace, Como, 20-22 May 1999.
6. Strobe Talbott, op. cit.
7. Ibid.
8. *The Asian Age*, New Delhi, 11 February 1999, reported Gen. V. P. Malik to have said that 'the possibility of a conventional war cannot be ruled out simply because India had crossed the nuclear threshold.' Gen. Malik was quoted to have added that 'Nuclear deterrence only restricts an all-out war employing weapons of mass destruction' and that 'As a military strategist, I will say that if militancy (in Jammu and Kashmir) grows too big, both the initiator, i.e. Pakistan and the affected nation, i.e. India, are tempted to use nuclear weapons.'
9. Lewis A. Dunn, *Containing Nuclear Proliferation*; Steven E. Miller, 'The Case Against a Ukrainian Deterrent', *Foreign Affairs, No. 72*, (Summer 1973); Scott D. Sagan, 'The Perils of Proliferation', *International Security* 18 (Spring 1994) and others listed by Sagan, p. 67, footnote 5.
10. Kenneth N. Waltz, *The Spread of Nuclear Weapons: More may be Better*, Adelphi Papers, no. 171 (London, 1981); John J. Mearsheimer, 'The Case for a Ukrainian Nuclear Deterrent', *Foreign Affairs* No. 72 (Summer 1973); Barry R. Posen, 'The Security Dilemma and Ethnic Conflict', *International Survival* 35, (Spring 93) and others listed by Scott D. Sagan, himself an opponent, in Sagan, op. cit., p. 66 and footnote 4 on p. 67.
11. Kenneth N. Waltz, op. cit. p. 3.
12. Robert McNamara, former U.S. secretary of defense.
13. S. Rashid Naim, 'Aadhi Raat Ke Baad (After Midnight),' in Stephen P. Cohen, *Nuclear Proliferation in South Asia* (Boulder, CO: Westview Press, 1991).
14. Panofsky, et. al., 'The Doctrine of the Nuclear-Weapon States and the Future of Non-Proliferation', *Arms Control Today* (July/August, 1994), p. 6. This doctrinal surmise is based on *Strategic Views from the Second Tier: The Nuclear Weapons Policies of France, Britain and China*, University of California Institute on Global Conflict and Cooperation, January 1994.
15. Mearsheimer, *loc. cit.*, p. 50 *et seq.*
16. 'The circumstances could not possibly have been worse,' says Golda Meir in *My Life* (New York: G. P. & Putnam Sons, 1975), p. 427, when the Israeli forces were suffering heavy casualties and the Egyptians advance into the Sinai during the first three days of the war. According to Special Report on 'How Israel Got the Bomb' in *Time* of 12 April 1976, p. 39, she gave Defence Minister Moshe Dayan permission to activate Israel's Doomsday weapons. (The Israeli panic appears to have been premature. The war was still confined to occupied Arab territories, with no evidence yet of a threat to Israel's integrity and existence.)
17. Robert S. McNamara, *The Changing Nature of Global Security And Its Impact On South Asia* (Washington, DC: Washington Council on Non-Proliferation, 1992), p. 7.
18. Seymour M. Hersh, *The Samson Option* (New York: Vintage Books, 1993), pp. 242–243. Zalman Shapiro was, according to Hersh, 'an active member of the Zionist Organization of America' who 'organized a publicly owned nuclear fuel processing firm....'
19. Davenport, et. al., *The Plumbat Affair* (London: Andre Deutsch, 1978). The book describes at length how an Israeli agent in West Germany ordered the uranium ore on behalf of an Italian chemical company in Milan, the approval of the sale by EURATOM, its shipment in 560 drums marked PLUMBAT aboard a ship which was purchased with Mossad funds, the

transfer of the material to an Israeli vessel in the Mediterranean after a mock hijacking, and the sweeping of the affair under the rug by EURATOM. For a summary reference to this affair, see Hersh, op. cit., p. 180–181.

20. *International Herald Tribune*, 7 October 1988, p. 6, report entitled '3 Scandals Oslo Must Put to Rest' by Gary Milhollin, director of Wisconsin Project on Nuclear Arms Control, and *Der Speigel* of 17 October 1988. In 1959, Norway permitted export of 20 tons of heavy water directly to Israel for use in the Dimona reactor for 'peaceful purposes.' Again, 1 ton was exported to Israel in 1970 through an intermediary. In 1983, Norway authorised sale of 15 tons of heavy water through the West German firm of Alfred Hampel to Romania, which was airlifted instead to Switzerland and thence to Mumbai. Hampel was alleged also to have exported 70 tons of heavy water from China to Argentina and India.

21. Waltz, op. cit., p. 11.

22. Steven E. Miller, *loc. cit.*, p. 73.

23. Waltz, op. cit. p. 22. The remark was made by former US defense secretary, Harold Brown.

24. Waltz, op. cit. p. 15.

25. Robert S. McNamara, *Blundering Into Disaster* (New York, NY: Pantheon Books, 1986), p. 44.

26. McNamara, op. cit.

27. Peter Gray, *Briefing Book on the Nonproliferation of Nuclear Weapons* (Washington, DC: Council for a Livable World Education Fund), p. 7. Also figures about the nuclear arsenals of other countries are taken from this source.

28. Figures estimated by the Institute for Science and International Security, Washington, *Dawn*, Islamabad, 12 October 2004.

29. Rodney W. Jones, *Small Nuclear Forces and U.S. Security Policy* (Lexington, MA: Lexington Books, 1984), pp. 243–256.

30. Gupta, et, al., op. cit.

31. Ibid.

32. Protagonists of such a view included Brahma Chellaney, a frequent commentator on strategic issues. Former foreign secretary Maharajakrishna Rasgotra said in *The Hindustan Times* of 14 April 1999, that 'to sign the CTBT and to desist from testing, developing and deploying missiles, without which there can be no credible deterrence... is a recipe for making India a nuclear eunuch.' Lt. Gen (Retd) Pran Pahwa advocated in *The Tribune*, Chandigarh, of 11 February 1999: 'The size of the minimum deterrent should be such that after absorbing the first strike, the number of its weapons that are likely to survive would be larger than those that would still remain with the enemy... Assuming that the enemy has 300 and fires 280 in the first strike, then India should have at least 140 so that if 80% are destroyed, it would still have 22 weapons.'

33. McNamara, op. cit., p. 87.

34. Keith Suter, *Visions for the 21st Century*, p. 28.

35. Paul Nitze ('Is It Time To Junk Our Nukes?', *The Washington Post*, January 16, 1994) recommends that the United States should convert 'its principal strategic deterrent from nuclear weapons to a more credible deterrent based at least in part upon smart conventional weapons... (because they) are safer, cause less collateral damage and pose less threat of escalation than do nuclear weapons.'

36. Declaration of the Non-Aligned Summit, 1992.

37. *The Washington Post*, 7 July 1994, p. A12, despatch entitled 'U.S. Efforts to Curb Nuclear Weapons in Peril as India Insists on Limits for China' by Thomas W. Lippman, quoting a senior Indian official.

38. Strobe Talbot, op. cit. He makes the point that testing by India and a response by Pakistan 'could trigger an all-out arms race....'

39. US Congressional Research Service Report, *Dawn*, Islamabad, 14 March 2005.

40. Ibid., *Dawn*, Islamabad, 14 March 2005.

41. Report by Institute for Science and International Security, Washington; *Dawn*, Islamabad, 3 March 2005.

42. The prestigious Washington-based Institute for Science and International Security concluded in an investigative report, 'The Pakistani government was not directing this network.' The network included nationals of a dozen countries. Operating over two decades, it was 'essentially a criminal operation... spread throughout the world.' Discarded centrifuges and weapon designs were smuggled out, some of the components were procured from suppliers in Europe, manufacturing was done in workshops in Malaysia, Turkey and South Africa, and equipment was shipped via Dubai. Libya was said to have received 20 centrifuges of Pakistan origin and bought about 200 from the network, and components for about 500 centrifuges went to Iran. The IAEA was trying to determine whether Iran and North Korea also received nuclear weapons information. *Dawn*, Islamabad, 13 & 14 October 2004.

43. A CIA report to US Congress charged: 'A. Q. Khan network provided Iran with designs for Pakistan's older centrifuges as well as designs for more advanced and efficient models, and components.' Summary of the report posted on the CIA website, *Dawn*, Islamabad, 26 November 2004.

44. Pakistan's Information Minister, Sheikh Rashid Ahmed said, 'He (A. Q. Khan) had given centrifuges to Iran.' *Dawn*, Islamabad, 11 March 2005.

45. Condoleezza Rice, secretary of state-designate, during a confirmation hearing at the Senate Foreign Relations Committee, *Dawn*, Islamabad, 20 January 2005.

46. While acknowledging the Pakistan government's cooperation in dismantling the network, a US State Department spokesman said, 'We certainly don't see any connection with the leadership of Pakistan', *Dawn*, Islamabad, 20 March 2005.

47. The US itself had experienced a similar embarrassment. Note 18 above.

48. Senate Foreign Relations Committee, Secretary of State Condoleezza Rice confirmation hearing, 17–18 January 2005.

49. George Friedman, founder of *Stratfor* journal, 'America's Secret War', Doubleday, New York, 2004.

50. Seymour H. Hersh, *The New Yorker*, New York, 18 January 2005.

51. The phrasing in the paragraph is based on a draft paper contributed by an Indian scholar at the Shanghai workshop in February, 1994. For report on the workshop, see Stone, op. cit.

52. Chengappa, op. cit., p. 38, quoting A. Kalam, head of India's 10 billion rupees ($330 million) defence research programme.

53. Ibid., p. 39.

54. Inter-Services Public Relations, after another test, *Dawn*, Islamabad, 13 October 2004. Shaheen-II tested on 19 March 2005 had a range of 2000 kms, *Dawn*, Islamabad, 20 March 2005.

CHAPTER 18

Increasing Isolation, 1990–2001

If, in the 1980s, Pakistan rose from isolation to a position of international respect and admiration for its courageous role in support of the Afghans struggle against Soviet intervention, the turn of the decade reversed the trend. The process started with a return of the international limelight on Pakistan's nuclear programme and the imposition of sanctions by the United States. The world community, which initially blamed India for repression and gross violation of human rights in Kashmir, became increasingly critical also of Pakistan's interference in the state. Islamabad's declarations that its role was limited to political, diplomatic and moral support for the liberation struggle were openly questioned. Washington took the lead by considering inclusion of Pakistan in the list of states accused of sponsoring terrorism. As the only state that recognised the Taliban regime, Pakistan was saddled with the responsibility for their policies. Poor governance, reckless international borrowing and rampant corruption added to Pakistan's increasing loss of prestige. Stringent international sanctions imposed after the 1998 nuclear tests aggravated the economic plight. The Kargil episode projected Pakistan as an 'irresponsible' state. Intervention by the army and the overthrow of an elected government in October 1999 attracted 'democracy sanctions' that tightened the financial squeeze. To cope with the challenge, General Pervez Musharraf's government began the process of rescuing the state from international isolation. It began with earnest internal reforms and stringent austerity that averted further borrowing even before the government's decision to cooperate with the United States in the war on terrorism after 9/11 rehabilitated the state in the international mainstream.

US Sanctions Again

No sooner did the Soviet forces complete their withdrawal from Afghanistan in 1989 than the nuclear issue began once again to dominate Pakistan–US relations. Washington asked Islamabad to discontinue the weapons research programme. When it declined, the Pressler Amendment was activated. Adopted by the Senate in 1985, it required the US president to provide an annual certificate that Pakistan did not possess a nuclear weapon, failing which economic and military assistance to Pakistan was prohibited. So long as the Soviet forces were in Afghanistan, President Ronald Reagan had issued the certificate without much fuss. President George Bush did the same in 1989 but then the US became intrusive and demanding about the research the US knew Pakistan had been carrying on for many years, and the president declined to issue the certificate in 1990. The US immediately cut off $700 million in assistance it was pledged to provide to Pakistan annually during 1988–94. It also declined to permit the transfer of F-16 aircraft and other military equipment for which the US had earlier cleared commercial contracts with manufacturers and Pakistan had paid a billion dollars in cash. An embargo was even ordered on the return of Pakistan-owned equipment sent to the United States for repairs with costs paid in advance. Predictably, the US decision revived the bitter memories of Pakistan's past grievances of US refusal to honour commitments. It was manifestly wrong for the United States to renege on the six-year agreement for economic and military assistance. The injustice of refusing to deliver the F-16s for which Pakistan had paid was not rectified until 1995 when President Clinton finally acknowledged it was unfair to keep both the equipment and the cash, and ordered reimbursement of the payments Pakistan had made as well as the return of Pakistan's own equipment which lay aging in the United States.

Fortunately, international financial institutions and bilateral donors, especially Japan, which was providing $500 million a year, did not follow the US example. Still the economy suffered a severe jolt and the predicament continued to aggravate as the government failed to adjust budgetary policies and was progressively caught in a debt trap.

Support for the Taliban

Pakistan's recognition of the Taliban government in May 1997 provoked international disapproval and criticism, although the decision was not without justification. This included the necessity of conducing official business with the authorities in power in Kabul on matters of travel and trade between people of common ethnicity on both sides of the border. The return of refugees required negotiations with the Taliban who controlled three-quarter of Afghanistan's territory. Many of them, having lived in refugee camps in Pakistan, evinced goodwill and friendship. Islamabad also hoped to influence the Taliban. It could not have foreseen that the Taliban would prove unreasonable and rigid and commit one blunder after another, provoking international outrage.

Islamabad failed to foresee that the Taliban were internationally perceived to be the creation of Pakistan. A Pakistani minister was on the record for calling them 'our boys'.[1] The Tajik, Uzbek and Hazara parties in Afghanistan denounced Pakistan. International opinion believed Pakistan was involved in assisting the Taliban in the internal struggle for control and domination. Uzbekistan was not alone in criticizing Pakistani recognition as 'external meddling'[2] while ignoring interference by other countries that not only continued to recognise the rump government but also provided large assistance in cash and arms to the opposition factions, thus fuelling the civil war in Afghanistan. As the only friend of the Taliban, Pakistan was blamed for their policies.

Pakistan tried to persuade friendly countries to recognise the Taliban regime but with little success. Not just the United Nations, even the OIC and the ECO refused to accept the Taliban regime. Saudi Arabia and UAE recognised the Taliban but found their anachronistic interpretation of Islam unacceptable. Iran not only denounced Taliban extremism but also enhanced assistance to the opposition warlords. Arab and Central Asian neighbours were antagonised by the encouragement, training and assistance the Taliban gave to their dissident nationals.

Already blamed for alleged political and military support to the Taliban, Pakistan came under mounting US censure for its perceived failure to prevent the Taliban from giving asylum to Osama bin Laden and his followers who, Washington believed, were engaged in planning and perpetrating terrorist attacks against the United States. The fact that Pakistan lacked the means and the leverage to influence the Taliban, and the United States itself did little to influence the Taliban, were ignored.

Pakistan, anxious as always to maintain cooperative relations with Afghanistan and cognisant of the Taliban's friendly disposition toward Pakistan, proffered counsel and advice for moderation, which would have helped save them from the predictable consequences of their policies. The first such intercession, suggesting the Taliban restrain

Osama Bin Laden, was made by Prime Minister Nawaz Sharif's government in 1998 but with little effect. Convinced of their rectitude and impervious to the remonstrations of other Islamic countries, the Taliban leadership was dismissive of criticism and persisted in its suicidal course. Instead of heeding the Pakistan government's advice, they relied on religious parties in Pakistan for support, and even exported their obscurantist views by influencing Pakistani counterparts, giving shelter to extremists and proclaimed offenders, and facilitating cross-border criminal activities in Pakistan.

Again after 9/11, Pakistan suggested that the Taliban expel Bin Laden. Their refusal to heed the world community's outrage sealed their fate. Within days of the commencement of the coalition attack, the Taliban lost control of the country.

Declining Prestige

Another issue that undermined international goodwill for Pakistan was corruption at high levels. Transparency International, a monitoring organization in Germany, declared Pakistan as the second most corrupt country in the world.[3] Poor governance, fiscal extravagance, mounting budgetary deficits and an escalating debt burden pushed Pakistan to the brink of insolvency. By 1999, the accumulated burden of foreign debt amounted to $38 billion and the annual cost of servicing it to over $5 billion. With exports stagnant at $8 billion, the payments gap widened and recurrent scams and defaulted loans of nationalised banks raised the spectre of a deep economic crisis and financial crash.

Nuclear Tests

Pakistan alone was not the target of sanctions after it followed India to carry out tests in May 1998, but its economy was more vulnerable to the aid cut off by countries that had continued to provide loans after the US terminated assistance in 1990, including Japan which was extending yen credits of $500 million a year. The government resorted to a freeze of $11 billion in foreign currency deposits which the state had attracted by the solemn pledge of transferability. The deposits could now be cashed only in devalued rupees, involving a loss of 30 percent to account holders expecting payment in foreign currency. The default antagonised hundreds of thousands of people who had trusted the government. Remittances from Pakistanis abroad nose-dived.

Pakistan–India Dialogue, 1997–99

Dialogue between Pakistan and India, suspended in 1994 because it proved sterile, was reopened in February 1997 at the level of foreign secretaries. The Indian emphasis was, as usual, on normalisation of trade and travel, though it was willing to discuss all issues. Pakistan underlined the centrality of the Kashmir issue. The gap between the two positions was not bridged when prime ministers Nawaz Sharif and I. K. Gujral held a meeting at Male in May 1997. Gujral reportedly pleaded that his minority government was too weak to make a bold policy shift. Sharif countered by saying that no government in Pakistan, however strong its majority in parliament, could ignore popular opinion in the country.

For the first time since the Kashmir dispute arose, a *hartal* was called by the All Parties Hurriyat Conference in Kashmir when the prime ministers met. A Kashmiri spokesman explained that while the Kashmiri people welcomed these talks, the dispute involved three parties, {and} any attempt to strike a deal between two without the association of the third, would fail to yield a credible settlement.[4] He also appealed that the world community should promote an initiative toward settlement of the Kashmir dispute in order to end the bloodshed and suffering of the Kashmiri people, eliminating regional tensions and the risk of a nuclear war between India and Pakistan.

In June 1997, the foreign secretaries of the two countries met in Islamabad and agreed to recommence dialogue on all outstanding issues of concern to the two sides, and to set up working groups for the purpose. The prime ministers met three months later on the sidelines of a UN summit in New York and exchanged mutual expressions of determination to renew and reinvigorate efforts for durable peace.

Lahore Summit. The prime minister of India, Atal Bihari Vajpayee, visited Pakistan from 20-21 February 1999, travelling to Lahore on the inaugural run of the Delhi–Lahore bus service. He and Prime Minister Nawaz Sharif concluded the most prolific, if not successful, summit with three documents.[5] In a declaration, the two leaders agreed to undertake 'immediate steps' for reducing the risk of accidental or unauthorised use of nuclear weapons and discuss concepts and doctrines, and in a memorandum of understanding, pledged to 'continue to abide by their respective unilateral moratoria on conducting further nuclear explosions unless either side, in exercise of its national sovereignty decides that extraordinary events have jeopardized its supreme interest.' The two sides further undertook to provide each other with advance notification in respect of ballistic missile flight tests.

The Lahore documents were comprehensive and covered the whole gamut of issues of bilateral interest ranging from commitment to 'intensify their efforts to resolve all issues, including the issue of Jammu and Kashmir', to 'condemnation of terrorism in all its forms and manifestations' and to 'undertaking national measures to reduce the risks of accidental or unauthorised use of nuclear weapons.'

The summit was a grand if ephemeral success. Neither the beginning nor the end of the summit proved auspicious, however. It was greeted with vociferous protests in Lahore against India's brutal repression in Kashmir. On return to New Delhi, the Indian leaders downplayed the importance of the commitment to resolve the outstanding issues. In Pakistan, influential sections of opinion criticised the emphasis on bilateral negotiations and the failure to mention even the United Nations' principles for governing bilateral relations (as in the Shimla Agreement). The 'Lahore process' glorified by the two sides was considered to provide a convenient alibi to world opinion, and especially influential powers, to abdicate responsibility to promote a just settlement of the Kashmir question.

Particularly insensitive was the reference to the 'sanctity' of the Line of Control. It invested this temporary line with a characteristic that applies to international boundaries and departed from Pakistan's view which maintained that the Line of Control 'resulting from the ceasefire of 17 December 1971' was, like the 1949 ceasefire line, a temporary arrangement to be respected by both sides pending a final settlement of Jammu and Kashmir.

The Kargil Crisis, 1999

A grave crisis erupted following intrusion of armed personnel from Pakistan into the Kargil heights in Kashmir in May 1999. Islamabad denied the facts and attributed the fighting to Kashmiri freedom fighters, recalling that after promising, at the Lahore Summit, to intensify efforts to resolve all issues, including Jammu and Kashmir, Indian leaders in statements on their return to Delhi portrayed insincerity and absence of serious intent. It recalled also that the UN Security Council's call in its resolution of June 1998 for the resumption of dialogue to remove the root causes of tensions, including Kashmir, was not followed up, and that Indian Home Minister Lal Krishna Advani had embarked on a 'proactive' policy, intensified repression in Indian-held Kashmir, resorted to recurrent violations of the Line of Control forcing closure of the Neelum Valley road in Azad Kashmir and subjected the villages to fierce artillery bombardment.[6] Few foreign countries credited Pakistan's disclaimer, however. Statements issued by the G-8, the United States, Britain and Germany implicitly blamed Pakistan for the 'intruders' in Kargil.

As armed men penetrated the Kargil–Dras sector and seized high ground threatening the Srinagar–Leh road, an artery in the summer months for stockpiling supplies for Indian garrisons in Ladakh and Siachen, India denounced the operation as a violation of the Shimla Agreement and retaliated with a massive air and army operation to dislodge the guerillas. Describing them as Islamic militants, Taliban and regular army personnel, India accused Pakistan of aggression.

Indian bombardment targeted not only the Kargil Heights on the Indian side of the Line of Control but also the alleged supply bases on the Pakistan side. Also, duels raged elsewhere along the Line of Control. In an attempt to defuse the situation, the Pakistani foreign minister was sent to New Delhi on 12 June for diplomatic efforts for de-escalation and dialogue. He was accorded a frigid and hostile reception. India took a rigid, no-negotiation stance, insisting on Pakistani withdrawal of personnel from Kargil before discussion on any other issue. Briefing the press after the meeting, the Indian foreign minister used the word 'demand' three times in one minute.

Meanwhile, concern mounted internationally that the fighting in Kargil might escalate and lead to a general war between Pakistan and India, now declared nuclear states. The Group of Eight (industrialised countries) considered 'infiltration of armed intruders' as 'irresponsible'.[6] The European Union called for 'the immediate withdrawal of infiltrators.' Washington asked Pakistan to withdraw 'its forces' and 'restore status quo ante'. Only the OIC backed the Pakistani position by asking for de-escalation and dialogue. China did not criticise Pakistan and called on both India and Pakistan to 'respect the Line of Control.'

Prime Minister Nawaz Sharif sued for the US President's intercession to defuse the crisis. Clinton received Sharif for an emergency meeting on Sunday, 4 July—US Independence Day. He discussed the situation with Prime Minister Vajpayee over the 'phone and persuaded Sharif to agree to a joint statement which provided for immediate cessation of hostilities, concrete steps to be taken for the restoration of the Line of Control in accordance with the Shimla Agreement, and resumption of a Pakistan–India dialogue as begun in Lahore in February 1999 for resolving all issues dividing India and Pakistan, including Kashmir. President Clinton promised to take a personal interest in encouraging an expeditious resumption and intensification of the bilateral efforts, 'once the sanctity of the Line of Control has been fully restored.' Military officers of Pakistan and India later agreed on steps for disengagement. The Pakistani personnel withdrew from Kargil by 16 July.

Reading into the Washington joint statement a US pledge of effort to promote settlement of the Kashmir question was not only a spin aimed at misleading public opinion but a self-deception. From authoritative clarifications given by US administration officials it became clear that all that the president had promised, after careful prior clearance with New Delhi, was 'personal interest' in promoting the 'Lahore process.'

A US official compared Sharif's dash to Washington to Yahya Khan's request for US help in the face of a rapidly deteriorating situation in the 1971 war.[7] Henry Kissinger had then remarked that the US was asked to be in at the crash-landing when it was not in on the take-off! If Pakistan was mercifully spared that biting sarcasm this time, it was partly because all that it asked was the proverbial fig leaf to cover retreat from an impulsive adventure undertaken without forethought.

Most commentators blamed the Pakistan government for losing sight of strategy in a tactical bid to awaken international attention to the festering Kashmir dispute. Given the power disparity, a military solution was obviously out of question. A war that could escalate to the nuclear level was considered inconceivable. One eminent journalist castigated the government saying, '...the original political blunder of approving a strategically flawed and unsustainable plan of guerilla action was compounded first by diplomatic and domestic mishandling and then by a sudden and inadequately explained policy *volte face*.'[8] A provident policy had to steer clear of extremes of bravado and soul-destroying capitulation.

Prime Minister Nawaz Sharif and Chief of Army Staff General Pervez Musharraf were held 'responsible for approving this misconceived operation.'[10] While some described the operation as 'tactically brilliant' others considered it 'a complete fiasco.' A spokesman of the All Parties Hurriyat Conference of Jammu and Kashmir described the Pakistan government's policy as 'unpredictable.'[9] Another APHC leader said, 'First we were excluded, then betrayed.'[10]

Inconsistent and contradictory statements undermined Pakistan's credibility. Its spokesmen disclaimed knowledge of the Mujahideen operation in Kargil one day and accepted responsibility for their withdrawal the next day. Shallow thinking was manifest also in pendulum swings from naive bus diplomacy to the Kargil gamble, from glorifying bilateral negotiations in the Lahore declaration to self-deceiving claims of success in inducting American interest in resolving Kashmir. Politics of corruption and crass calculation of immediate political advantage was diagnosed as the main reason for the shallow and myopic policies of the ruling families, along with the absence of long-term thinking and institutional decision-making.

Autopsies of the Kargil crisis by Pakistani commentators underlined agonising dilemmas that Pakistan faced in regard to the Kashmir issue. If it did not act, India claimed to have achieved a final solution; if it did, it incurred the risk of war. Similarly placed were the Kashmiri people: if they did not struggle for freedom, they were considered to have acquiesced in India's illegal annexation; if they did, they were subjected to savage repression, killings, torture and other excesses no human being should have to suffer in a civilised world.

Misconceived policies and actions not only isolated Pakistan internationally, they also gravely damaged the heroic freedom struggle of the Kashmiri people. Focus shifted from indigenous agitation for self-determination to Indian allegations of its Pakistani sponsorship, from inhuman Indian excesses in Kashmir to restraint in limiting response to its side of the Line of Control, from brutality of Indian forces against the Kashmiri people to bravery on the Kargil Heights.

If the Kargil episode exposed Pakistan to international censure it also opened a breach between the prime minister and the Army hierarchy. Nawaz Sharif was reported to have blamed the army for keeping him ignorant of the plan for the Kargil operation. A few months later Sharif dismissed Chief of Army Staff General Pervez Musharraf while Musharraf was on his way back from a visit to Sri Lanka, and ordered refusal of landing facilities to the PIA airliner on which Musharraf was a passenger. Musharraf, however, refused to be diverted to another destination and the Karachi corps commander intervened to save the passengers and crew as the plane ran low on

US Secretary of State Colin Powell, Washington D.C., 2001.

fuel. On return, the chief of staff took over the government in a bloodless coup.

Coping with Isolation

General Pervez Musharraf, chief executive of the new government, focused efforts on improving governance and rectification of Pakistan's fiscal predicament. A decision was taken to stabilise the debt burden, which had grown by $3 billion a year during the 1990s to $38 billion.[15] Since foreign aid was cut off, exports were stagnant at $8 billion and remittances had declined, the debt-servicing burden of over $5 billion a year necessitated austerity and belt-tightening. None of the ministers in the 16 member cabinet asked for replacement of old cars. Even some development projects had to be postponed. Priority attention was given to accountability and recovery of defaulted loans. By the end of June 2001, efforts had yielded a measure of success; exports increased by 10 per cent growth, tax revenues increased and foreign debt remained stable.

Meanwhile, friendly countries maintained solidarity with Pakistan. Saudi Arabia was generous in economic assistance. China and Kuwait provided balance of payments support. Premier Zhu Rongji visited Pakistan in 2001 and announced cooperation in the construction of Gwadar port. Sultan Qaboos of Oman visited Pakistan in April 2001 and extended substantial assistance for economic development apart from taking a 50 per cent share in a joint investment fund. Also, the government's performance persuaded some countries to review sanctions. Prime Minister Yoshiro Mori paid an official visit to Pakistan, announced resumption of suspended aid for development projects and invited the foreign minister to visit Tokyo. The United States appreciated Pakistan's assistance for confidential contacts with the Taliban. President Clinton did not omit Islamabad during his tour of South Asia. The US used its influence for containment of Pakistan–India tension and its officials made a valuable contribution to avert the danger of conflict.[11] The International Monetary Fund agreed to provide a loan for balance-of-payments support to Pakistan.

Bound by its rules, the Commonwealth suspended Pakistan's membership but maintained contacts. A Commonwealth ministerial action group delegation was the first to visit Pakistan at the end of October 1999 to meet with the new leadership, if only to encourage them to move towards the restoration of democracy. Privately, some of them recognised the baneful effects of corruption. In a meeting with the C-MAG in September 2000 in New York, the Pakistan delegation urged the UK to join in efforts to reform bank secrecy laws which encouraged corruption, undermined good governance and siphoned off scarce capital. More than lectures on democracy, reform of these laws in countries like the UK, Switzerland, and Luxembourg would help address the root cause of political instability in developing countries like Pakistan. Despite United Nations and World Bank recognition of the problem of corruption, and the adoption of an international convention on cooperation against corruption in 2004, progress towards rectification of bank secrecy laws remained meagre, however.

The Agra Summit

On New Year's Day, 2001, Prime Minister Atal Bihari Vajpayee wrote an article highlighting the need for India to address two outstanding issues, namely, Kashmir and the Babri Mosque in Ayodhya. Regarding Kashmir, he went on to suggest a meeting with the Pakistani president. After a delay of nearly four months, evidently a result of internal debate, he sent an invitation for the two leaders to meet at Agra on 15 and 16 July.

The two leaders held several exclusive meetings. They recognised the need to transform the fifty-year-old confrontation into good neighbourly cooperation. To that end, President Musharraf urged earnest efforts to resolve the Kashmir dispute. Around noon on 16 July they called in the foreign ministers and informed them of the understanding they had reached to resume dialogue which should be the basis of a declaration to be issued later that day.

Working on the draft[12] already prepared by the foreign secretaries, the two ministers agreed on a declaration text to be recommended to the leaders. President Pervez Musharraf approved it promptly. On the Indian side, the draft was considered in the cabinet committee on political affairs.[13] The meeting lasted over two hours, after which External Affairs Minister Jaswant Singh sought a meeting with his Pakistani counterpart at 6 p.m. to discuss an amendment to the one-line paragraph on Kashmir. After a short and amicable discussion, the foreign ministers agreed to the substance of the amendment desired by the Indian cabinet committee with a slight modification. The apparent hitch thus removed, the Indian conference services officials started making arrangements for the signing ceremony as the Indian minister hoped to obtain formal final approval in 'five minutes'. Once again the cabinet committee held a long meeting. At about 9 p.m. the Pakistan side was informed that the agreement would not be signed. Held in a blaze of global multimedia coverage, the summit ended on an anticlimactic note to the surprise of the media people and the disappointment and frustration of the Pakistan delegation.

Before departing Agra for Islamabad, the Pakistani president was told by the Indian prime minister that it had not been possible to reach agreement in the cabinet committee. He did not explain what the disagreement was about, adding only that 'the time was not favourable' and that he would visit Pakistan later to finalise the proposed agreement.

The prospect of another summit helped contain disappointment. Both sides tried to relieve the gloom. President Musharraf declared, 'I came back empty-handed but the Summit was not a failure.'[14] Prime Minister Vajpayee also underlined the progress that was made 'towards bridging the two approaches in a draft joint declaration.'[15] In the same vein, Jaswant Singh said, 'I do not characterise [the summit] as a failure. I do term it as yet another step in our march towards finding lasting peace, amity and cooperation between the two countries', adding, 'We will pick up threads from the visit of the President of Pakistan.'[16] The Pakistani foreign minister gave a similarly positive appraisal: 'The Agra Summit was 'natamam, not nakam' (inconclusive, not a failure).'[17]

The optimism did not last long, however. The Indian side soon started backtracking on the agreed draft. A spokesperson of the ministry of external affairs said, 'No agreement was reached. There was no closure of an agreement and no subscription by signature.'[18] A week later, Vajpayee said in the parliament: 'Obviously India's concerns in vital areas—such as cross-border terrorism—will have to find place in any document that future negotiations endeavour to conclude.' Actually, this point was already covered in the draft declaration.

Meanwhile, observers on both sides speculated about what had prevented agreement at the summit. Some identified President Musharraf's breakfast meeting with Indian media luminaries on 16 July as having offended the Indian leaders. The videotape of the question–answer meeting telecast by an Indian commercial channel projected Musharraf's persuasive views on the need to address the Kashmir dispute to a spellbound audience in both countries. The Indian side was said to be angry that he had stolen a march over the Indian prime minister. Actually, there was little new in what he said.

He had expressed the same view many times previously. Hours after the telecast the Indian side had not raised the issue with the Pakistan side, and even agreed to finalise the draft of the declaration.

As for the Pakistani president's reference to Kashmir as the principal obstacle to normalisation of Pakistan–Indian relations, that was no more than a statement of the obvious. Quite apart from the experience of Pakistan and India, normalisation has seldom taken place between pairs of countries with serious disputes and differences. Recent examples of the causal link include the Portugal and Indonesia, over East Timor, Japan and Russia over the Northern Islands, and USA and Cuba over ideological differences.

Another explanation was later given by Prime Minster Vajpayee in a statement in parliament on 24 July, saying, 'Eventually, however, we had to abandon the quest for a joint document because of Pakistan's insistence on the settlement of the Jammu and Kashmir issue as a pre-condition for the normalisation of relations.' This was factually incorrect, as the text of the draft declaration confirms. At no point in the negotiations did Pakistan present any 'pre-condition.' Similarly unfounded was the allegation that Pakistan's approach was 'unifocal.' The draft provided for dialogue on all issues of concern to both sides, including terrorism.

More interesting was the question as to who in the Indian cabinet committee had objected to the draft. Not until months later did a clue appear in the Indian press. A usually well-informed journal attributed responsibility for obstructing agreement to the deputy prime minister, L. K. Advani, dubbing him 'the saboteur of Agra.'[20] When Vajpayee was asked at a press conference to comment on the report, he did not give a direct reply.[25] Four years later, President Musharraf publicly blamed Advani for the failure of the summit. Advani, however, attributed the failure to Pakistan's refusal to agree 'to the clauses on terrorism in the draft suggested by India.'[21] The contention was incorrect: terrorism was included among subjects for sustained dialogue at the political level in paragraph 3 of the agreed draft.

Considering that Vajpayee had conceived and canvassed the initiative for dialogue with Pakistan on Kashmir, he was probably disappointed by the outcome and it can be assumed that he was sincere in his intention to visit Pakistan at a more favourable time to finalise the agreement. In retrospect it would have been better for the fulfilment of his ambition to improve relations with Pakistan had he asserted leadership to persuade the one or more members of the cabinet committee who vetoed the declaration.

Another opportunity to change the course of Pakistan–India relations was missed as one more agreement fell victim to internal political battles.[22] Three months later, terrorists carried out attacks in New York and Washington that transformed the global situation.

NOTES

1. Cabinet Minister Nasirullah Babar made this factually incorrect remark after the Taliban helped rescue a convoy of Pakistani trucks held up by Afghan warlords.
2. Iran and the Northern Alliance in Afghanistan were similarly critical.
3. Transparency International's report is said to be based on surveys of business houses, etc.
4. Ghulam Nabi Fai, Director, Kashmir Center, Washington, in 'Why the world should care?' in The News, Islamabad, 21 May 1997.
5. The documents were the Lahore Declaration, Joint Statement and Memorandum of Understanding.
6. The G-8 summit statement of 20 June 1999, read: 'We are deeply concerned about the continuing military confrontation in Kashmir following the infiltration of armed intruders which violated the Line of Control. We regard any military action to change the status quo as irresponsible. We therefore call for the immediate end of these actions, restoration of the Line of Control and for the parties to work for immediate cessation of fighting, full respect in the future for the Line of Control and the resumption of the dialogue between them in the spirit of the Lahore Declaration'.
7. Shirin Tahirkheli, The News, Islamabad, 13 July 1999.
8. Maleeha Lodhi, Newsline, Karachi, July 1999.
9. Comments by Air Marshal (Retd.) Noor Khan, Lt. Gen. (Retd.) Asad Durrani, Lt. Gen. (Retd.) Kamal Mateenuddin and Gulam Nabi Safi, The News, 18 July 1999.
10. The News, 18 July 1999.
11. Undersecretary of State Thomas Pickering played a key role on contacts with Islamabad while Deputy Secretary of State Strobe Talbott was in contact with New Delhi.
12. The text of the draft is given at Appendix IV.
13. Members of the Committee, chaired by the Prime Minister, were Ministers of Commerce, Defence, External Affairs, Finance, and Home Affairs. Portfolios of Defence and External Affairs were held by one minister.
14. President Pervez Musharraf, Press Conference, 20 July 2001.
15. Prime Minister A. B. Vajpayee, statement in the Indian Parliament, 24 July 2001.
16. External Affairs Minister of India Jaswant Singh, press conference, 17 July 2001.
17. Foreign Minister Abdul Sattar, press conference, 17 July 2001.
18. Report by AFP quoted in Dawn, Islamabad, 21 July 2001.
19. India Today, November 2001.
20. When a Pakistani journalist asked in an interview with Prime Minister Vajpayee on 1 January 2004 if the agreement was sabotaged by some elements in the Indian cabinet, Vajpayee said 'the draft was written by the two foreign ministers, but it had not had the governmental approval'. Dawn, Islamabad, 2 January 2004.
21. Report from New Delhi, Dawn, Islamabad, 14 March 2005.
22. The two countries agreed, for instance, that the question of the accession of the State of Jammu and Kashmir would be decided through the democratic method of a free and impartial plebiscite, and that the commitment was sanctified in resolutions adopted by the UN Security Council in 1948 and 1949. Later, India gave the resolutions unilateral interpretations and came up with novel explanations to renege on its obligation. The Shimla Agreement and the Lahore Declaration suffered a similar fate.

CHAPTER 19

Post-9/11 Policy

The terrorist attacks on the World Trade Centre and the Pentagon on 11 September 2001 triggered a transformation of world politics as profound and far-reaching as the television images of hijacked airliners crashing into the symbols of American military and economic power were surreal. With three thousand people killed and material losses amounting to a hundred billion dollars or more, the unprecedented and never-imagined assault on the US mainland was not merely more destructive than the attack on Pearl Harbor in 1941, it traumatized the American nation. Its pride and confidence deeply hurt, the United States seethed with anger and the urge for revenge.

The world community reacted with shock. All condemned the attack, and expressed condolences and solidarity with the American people. The president of Pakistan issued a strong statement of condemnation and sympathy. Also, he affirmed Pakistan's readiness to join the United States in the fight against terrorism.

As the US media instantly pointed a finger of accusation at Osama bin Laden, naming him as the mastermind behind the terrorist attacks, implicated the Taliban and speculated about likely US action against them, a sense of crisis and foreboding dominated the air in Islamabad. Because of its geographical location and being the sole supporter of the Taliban, Pakistan was bound to face painful choices in the days ahead.

Policy Planning by Pakistan

President Musharraf, who was on tour in Karachi, returned to Islamabad on the evening of 12 September and immediately attended a high-level meeting to discuss the grave crisis and its implications for Pakistan. Until then there had been no contact or communication between the governments of Pakistan and the United States. It was not difficult, however, to surmise that the United States would take military

Pervez Musharraf (President of Pakistan, 2001–).

action against the Taliban. Two years earlier, attributing the attacks on US embassies in East Africa to Osama bin Laden and his followers, the US had fired missiles from ships at sea to bomb suspected terrorist camps in Afghanistan, without asking Pakistan for permission to fly over its territory. It was presumable that the US would react with even greater force now. What should be Pakistan's response if the US asked for permission not merely for overflights but also made other, more problematic demands? The question required anticipation and consideration of Pakistan's options. Whilst it was obvious that Pakistan had to avoid opposition to US policy, and a refusal to cooperate would not only be ineffectual but might also provoke US hostility, it was necessary to evolve a strategy of approach, keeping in the forefront both the national interest and the need for a realistic assessment of the obtaining environment.

It was assumed that major powers would extend cooperation to the United States in punishing the terrorists. None would oppose a likely US decision to mount an attack against the Taliban. No proof would be asked, or considered necessary, of Taliban complicity with bin Laden. Already, a year earlier, the Security Council had condemned and imposed sanctions on the Taliban precisely because they provided bin Laden with sanctuary and a base for terrorist activities. In the new, more grave circumstances, the Security Council would be even more sympathetic to the United States. Some of the major powers might even join in the attack, and the Arab countries and Central Asian neighbours of Afghanistan would probably agree to allow use of landing facilities for US aircraft. India, already canvassing Indo–US cooperation against terrorism, was likely to provide assistance.

The Security Council resolution of December 2000 had imposed sanctions against the Taliban under Chapter VII requiring compulsory compliance. Pakistan had cooperated by closing Taliban-controlled banks and curtailing official contacts. In the graver situation now, a defiant policy course was out of the question. The horizon was dark with dangers. Pakistan might be bracketed with the Taliban, declared a 'terrorist state' and its territory subjected to attacks to neutralise resistance. Pakistan's vital interests would be in jeopardy if India was given a free hand against Pakistan. The Kashmiri freedom struggle might be labelled as a terrorist insurgency. Azad Kashmir and Pakistan territory could be attacked under the pretext of eliminating terrorist bases. It was known that in the 1980s, India had pondered an attack on Kahuta. It might again entertain thoughts of targeting Pakistan's nuclear assets.

Objective analysis of the situation pointed to an obvious conclusion: Pakistan had to pursue a strategy that would reduce risks to Pakistan's own security and strategic interests. It had to steer clear of defiance and avoid offence to the United States. The question was not whether Pakistan could exploit its strategic location for economic or political benefits from the United States, the weightier and decisive factor was the predictable cost of non-cooperation. At the same time, long term considerations and cultural and geographical bonds with Afghanistan precluded any actions that might offend the interests or sensibilities of the Afghan people.

The crisis called for a policy that balanced global and regional constraints, immediate imperatives and long-term interests, national priorities and the norms of an international order based on principles of international law. Cautious cooperation in a UN-approved action against the Taliban emerged as the only feasible alternative. Its components would include: (a) Pakistan should join the global consensus; (b) it could not and should not oppose US attacks on targets in Afghanistan; and (c) in the event of US request for Pakistan's cooperation, it should indicate a generally positive disposition and negotiate details later. Such a 'Yes-but' approach would allow Pakistan tactical flexibility. It could then also seek modification of US policy and its expectations of Pakistan.

It should be noted that Pakistan's strategy was decided, in broad outline, on the evening of 12 September—still forenoon in Washington—on the basis of objective analysis of contingencies and anticipation of the likely course of events, and before, not after, any specific requests were received from the United States. Until then US leaders had said little. Public statements by President Bush and administration officials on 12 September were heard in Islamabad either late that night or on 13 September, due to the time difference with Washington.

US Policy

The clairvoyance of Pakistan's analysis was soon borne out by the events, as world consensus solidified in favour of the United States. The Security Council and the General Assembly adopted unanimous resolutions on 12 September, which condemned the terrorist outrage, extended condolences to the United States, and called for bringing the perpetrators, sponsors and organizers to justice. NATO invoked the treaty provision for joint defence. Canada, UK, Germany, France and Denmark offered military contingents for a coalition force to attack the Taliban. China, Japan and Russia expressed solidarity with the coalition. Turkey and the states of Central and South Asia, including India, Bangladesh and Sri Lanka indicated willingness to provide logistic facilities, as did several Arab countries.

Soon the contours of US policy began to emerge. On 12 September, President George W. Bush spoke of a 'monumental struggle of good versus evil.'[1] Secretary of State Colin Powell announced that the US expected 'the fullest cooperation' of Pakistan. In another statement on 13 September, President Bush said those who harboured terrorists would be treated as terrorists. Asked whether he had made any progress in obtaining cooperation from Pakistan, Bush replied, 'We will give the Pakistani government a chance to cooperate.'[2] The note of warning was unmistakable.

US records that became available three years later confirmed the apprehensions Pakistan had anticipated. In a restricted National Security Council meeting chaired by President Bush on 11 September, Secretary of State Powell said, 'the United States had to make it clear to Pakistan, Afghanistan, and the Arab states that the time to act was now.'[3] Also, the NSC Principals Committee, on 13 September, 'focused on Pakistan and what it could do to turn the Taliban against al Qaeda (and) concluded that if Pakistan decided not to help the United States, it too would be at risk.'[4]

On 13 September, US deputy secretary of state, Richard Armitage, summoned the ambassador of Pakistan, (and the director general of Inter-Services Intelligence, then on a visit to Washington) for a meeting to convey the list of seven steps the United States wanted Pakistan to take. He was reported to have painted a stark picture: the situation was black or white. Pakistan had a choice to make. Either it was with the US or it was not. There were no half measures. There was no room for manoeuvre. 'The future starts today.' The 'seven steps' were:

- to stop al Qaeda operations at its border and end all logistical support for bin Laden.
- to give the United States blanket overflight and landing rights for all necessary military and intelligence operations.
- to provide the United States with intelligence information.
- to provide territorial access to US and allied military intelligence and other personnel to conduct operations against al Qaeda.
- to continue to publicly condemn the terrorist acts.

- to cut off all shipments of fuel to the Taliban and stop recruits from going to Afghanistan.
- if the evidence implicated bin Laden and al Qaeda, and the Taliban continued to harbour them, to break relations with the Taliban government.[5]

Having decided on its strategy in advance, Islamabad was in a position to give a prompt and generally positive response, when the US request was received,[6] with details on some points to be worked out later. The impression that Pakistan had 'totally' acquiesced in US 'demands' was incorrect. Actually, Pakistan's role was to be within acceptable limits. Still, Pakistan made substantial concessions and President Musharraf made that point in his response, suggesting that the people needed to see Pakistan was benefiting from the decision.[7] As the US requests were examined in detail, a couple of points required no action: Pakistan had already condemned terrorist attacks, and it had not provided logistic access to bin Laden. Some misguided *imams* (preachers) in the border areas had encouraged simple youths to go to Afghanistan to fight on the side of the Taliban but this was never approved or encouraged by the government. Diplomatic relations with the Taliban were to be cut off only if bin Laden was implicated and the Taliban still continued to harbour him. The extent of logistic support to US forces was to be worked out, as was territorial access. Pakistan later allowed the use of three landing strips for logistic purposes and provisions for the coalition forces in Afghanistan were sent via Pakistani ports. However, US war operations were conducted from naval ships or distant bases, not from Pakistan territory. Pakistan did not participate in US military action in Afghanistan.

Consultation with Opinion Leaders

Over a period of about two weeks, the president held lengthy and interactive discussions with a dozen groups of prominent people from various walks of national life, including leaders of political parties, the intelligentsia, media luminaries, *ulema and mashaikh*, influential persons from areas adjoining Afghanistan, labour leaders, women, youth and minorities. He gave them a candid analysis of the costs and benefits of the policy options. Their response was reassuring. They were realistic in their assessment of the gravity of the situation and the need for circumspection. Most—some 90 per cent—agreed with the president's conclusions.

Only the *ulema* (religious scholars) differed. A majority of them opposed cooperation with the US, arguing that right was on the side of the Taliban, and therefore, religious duty required Pakistan to support them, regardless of costs and consequences. The deductive reasoning was obviously flawed. Moreover, other religious scholars put forward convincing refutation by citing instances from early Islamic history, showing that a leader had the duty to take into account the countervailing circumstances in specific situations before deciding a policy in the best interest of the community. Particularly weighty and relevant were the sagacious decisions of the Prophet (PBUH) to enter into a treaty with the Jews of Medina after the *Hijrah*, and the Hudabia peace agreement with the non-Muslim rulers of Mecca despite the objection of some eminent *Sahaba* (companions).

After the US-led coalition attacked Afghanistan on 6 October, Pakistani religious parties called for demonstrations. Assessing the situation intelligently, the public doubted the wisdom of protest, and participation was limited to a narrow section of opinion. As in other Muslim countries, so also in Pakistan, most people realised that the Taliban had provoked the attack and rejected the argument that the war on terrorism was a war against the Muslim world. Islam disapproves and abhors the killing of even a single innocent person. Extremism and violence was not acceptable to the vast majority. That assessment was soon validated by the declining numbers of people who participated in street demonstrations.

The US and the West applauded the Pakistan government for enlightened leadership, and manifested their solidarity by visits to Pakistan. Never before had so many leaders come to Pakistan as in the months after September, one on the heels of the other and sometimes on the same day.[8] They included heads of government of the UK, Germany, Belgium and the Netherlands, US secretaries of state and defence, foreign ministers of Japan, UK, France, Germany, Greece and Norway and the Troika delegation of the European Union. Also the president of Turkey, prime minister of Lebanon, and foreign ministers of Saudi Arabia, Egypt, Iran, Turkey and Oman came on visits. Other dignitaries included the UN Secretary General, UNDP Administrator, UNHCR, and UN High Commissioner for Human Rights, OIC secretary general and a number of special envoys.

Economic Cooperation and Assistance

Although Islamabad did not bargain for a quid pro quo, it was not unmindful of the value and importance of its contribution to the fight against terrorism, and hence of Pakistan's entitlement to reciprocity by the US and other Western countries. It made known its expectation of the termination of the so-called non-proliferation and democracy sanctions, and the resumption of support and assistance. They evinced understanding of Pakistan's hardships on account of past mismanagement and corruption, the rise of international debt and loss in exports due to the destabilising effect of the military action in Afghanistan, and their response became progressively more forthcoming.

Appreciating Pakistan's key role as a 'frontline State' in the war on terrorism, the United States, the European Union and Japan dismantled nuclear and democracy sanctions and resumed assistance to Pakistan. The Brownback-II amendment authorized the US President to annually waive 'democracy sanctions' and the Akerman amendment in 2004 waived the nuclear sanctions for five years. By March 2002, Pakistan had received over one billion dollars in aid and debt write-offs.[9] More substantial was long-term relief in debt servicing as a result of the Paris Club's decision to reschedule $12 billion in bilateral debt at lower interest rates and extended maturities, effectively reducing the burden by 30 per cent.

Apart from immediate fiscal relief, improvement of relations with major countries yielded long-term aid and trade benefits as well as an empathetic political environment conducive to the maintenance of peace in the region.

USA. Resumed in late 2001, US economic and military assistance to Pakistan amounted to $1,766 million by 2003.[10] In 2004, the US announced a five-year package of $3 billion in grants for economic and military assistance. Also, the Bush administration extended low-interest credits for the purchase of airliners for PIA, expanded trade access with long-term benefits for Pakistan's exports that rose to nearly three billion dollars in 2004, and agreed to sell C-130 transport planes, P-3 Orion marine surveillance aircraft, TOW anti-tank missiles and other equipment for defence, valued at $1.2 billion. In March 2005, the United States further decided to sell F-16 aircraft to Pakistan.

EU. The European Union reflected its appreciation of Pakistan's policy in its decisions regarding economic assistance and market access. It joined the US-led efforts to prevent a Pakistan–India war in 2002. Also its stance on Kashmir reflected recognition of the root cause of the protracted agitation and violence in the disputed state.

Japan. Not misled by false assumptions, Japan had neither exaggerated Pakistan's capacity to influence the Taliban nor adopted a hard stance toward Pakistan after nuclear tests in May 1998. It even considered resumption of development assistance, if Pakistan signed the CTBT. Prime Minister Yoshiro Mori was the only Western leader, apart from Clinton, to visit Pakistan between October 1999 and September 2001. Japan also made an exception to the suspension of aid by providing a loan for the second phase of the Kohat tunnel.

After 9/11, Japan, like most Western countries, welcomed the change in Afghanistan and appreciated Pakistan's cooperation against terrorism. It decided to provide $300 million as grant assistance and supported Pakistan's case in the IMF and the Paris Club. Prime Minister Junichiro Koizumi invited President Musharraf to visit in March 2002, and accorded him a warm reception. Japan's support in the Paris Club for rescheduling bilateral debt brought substantial relief, as with $5 billion Japan was the biggest creditor of Pakistan. In April 2005, Koizumi announced recommencement of official development assistance that had been suspended after Pakistan conducted nuclear tests in 1998. Until then Japan's ODA amounted to $500 million a year.

China. The 'all weather friendship' between Pakistan and China, and Beijing's characteristically profound understanding of Islamabad's motivations, had ensured continuity of cooperation between the two countries, despite its reservations over Islamabad's support for the Taliban. Equally mature was China's reaction to Pakistan's decision to join the US-led war on terrorism after 9/11, despite the arrival of US-led forces in Afghanistan close to China's border. Pakistan, on its part, took care to keep Beijing informed of the cross services agreement it signed with the United States, for logistic facilities for the US military operation in Afghanistan. China endorsed the UN-led Bonn process and the installation of a transitional regime in Afghanistan. In 2002, China joined the US and the EU efforts to prevent a possible war between Pakistan and India. Secretary of State Powell later praised China's 'very helpful' role.[11]

Pakistan–China friendly cooperation gathered momentum as Pakistan's economy progressed toward stability. Apart from agreeing to roll over the deposit of $500 million to support Pakistan's balance of payments, during 2000–02 China committed $700 million for projects under implementation and $800 million for new projects. A Chinese company won the tender for the revival and management of the Saindak copper mine in Baluchistan. Another Chinese company was invited to join Pakistan for development of the Lakhra coalmines in Sindh and for the generation of electric power. During Prime Minister Shaukat Aziz's visit to China in December 2004, an agreement was signed to expand trade. A credit of $150 million was pledged for the Chashma-II nuclear power plant. China's cumulative loans and investments in Pakistan amounted to $4 billion.[12] Two-way trade in 2004 totalled 2.1 billion dollars.

The visit of Premier Wen Jiabao to Pakistan on 5-6 April 2005 marked a new stage in the burgeoning relations between 'good friends, good neighbours and good partners' whose friendship has 'withstood the test of time and international vicissitudes.' Wen and Shaukat Aziz signed the Treaty of Friendship, Cooperation and Good Neighbourly Relations, pledging mutual support in defence of sovereignty, independence and territorial integrity. Also, twenty-one other agreements were signed to promote closer trade and economic ties, whilst deepening mutually beneficial cooperation across the board. China increased to $350 million the credit for a second 340-MW nuclear power plant at Chashma. Joint manufacture of JF17 Thunder fighter aircraft was set to commence during 2005 and Pakistan signed a framework agreement for the construction of four modern frigates by China for an estimated $175 million each.

US Commitment. If Pakistan nourished historical grievances about fluctuating US commitment, it now seemed to be the turn of officials in high places in the Bush administration to entertain doubts about Pakistan's reliability for sustained support to the United States. The Chairman of the key House Appropriations Committee, that recommends budgetary allocations for financial assistance, questioned the degree of Pakistan's cooperation.[13] Deputy Secretary of State Armitage thought Pakistan had agreed to cooperate because it had little choice, implying it might back out.[14]

No longer was Pakistan alone in hankering after durable commitment. Washington, too, seemed to have recognised the need to contain the volatility that has characterised its past relations with

People's Republic of China, Prime Minister Zhu Rongji, Beijing, 2001.

Prime Minister of Japan, Yoshiro Mori, Tokyo, 2001.

Pakistan. This was welcome news to people in Pakistan, who place great emphasis on sincerity, as much in inter-state relations, as inter-personal ones, a reflection no doubt of the nation's culture that invests *dosti* with characteristics of *ishq*, and expects a friend to be constant, faithful, selfless and sacrificing. Only those with knowledge of international relations recognise that such an expectation ignores history. Protection and promotion of the strategic and economic interests of state is the guiding factor in foreign policy.

Nevertheless, a British statesman's adage 'We have permanent interests but not permanent friends' is only partly correct, for interests, too, are subject to change with evolution of the environment, and friends are always an asset, especially in adversity. Such a transition of understanding took place in Washington after 9/11. It was realised that the sudden termination of support for Pakistan in 1990, and US neglect of Afghanistan after the Soviet withdrawal, had been a flawed policy. Washington's termination of cooperation with Afghan leaders made them insensitive to its protests about the presence of foreigners hostile to the United States. Pakistan's limited capacity to influence the Taliban was undermined as a result of US sanctions and aid cut off. An objective appraisal of the prevailing situation in the region, marked by tension and instability, poverty and insecurity that have bred extremism and terrorism, called for a long-term policy and sustained attention on the part of the sole superpower.

After 9/11, US spokesmen repeatedly sought to assure the nations in the region of the durability of their country's new policy, emphasising especially the continuity of US cooperation with Pakistan. The priorities of the Bush administration during its second term were a 'further broadening of the bilateral relations with Pakistan in economic and security fields,' said the deputy secretary of state, Richard Armitage, on his visit to Islamabad after the re-election of President Bush. He noted that Pakistan enjoyed 'broad-based and solid support' in the United States. The 9/11 Commission recommended that the United States should make 'the difficult long-term commitment to the future of Pakistan sustaining the current scale of aid to Pakistan.'[15] The US Congress passed an act in December 2004 with provisions assuring continued assistance after the expiry of the five-year package in 2009. 'Pakistan has become a vital ally with US in the war on terror,' said Secretary of State Condoleezza Rice. Recalling that 'at one time in our history we did not maintain and continue deep relations with Pakistan after having shared strategic interests during the Cold War,' she assured her Pakistani audience during her visit to Islamabad, 'The US will be a friend for life.'[16]

Iran and the Central Asian Republics. The fall of the Taliban lifted the shadow on Pakistan's relations with Iran. Both countries welcomed the installation of a consensus government in Afghanistan. Islamabad kept Tehran informed of the limited logistical facilities it provided for the coalition forces, abating its concerns rooted in the hostility of the United States since the overthrow of the Shahanshah. The dominant position acquired by the Western countries in Afghanistan had the effect of eliminating Pakistan–Iran rivalry for influence in Afghanistan. Improvement of relations that began in 2000 after Pakistan agreed to facilitate the construction of a pipeline for the supply of natural gas from Iran to India picked up momentum. After a gap of many years, the President of Iran paid a visit to Pakistan in 2003.

Arab, Central Asian and other foreign countries appreciated the measures taken by Pakistan to extradite or expel their nationals who abused their stay in Pakistan for militant and subversive activities against their own countries. Muslim as well as other states applauded Pakistan's ban on militant and extremist organisations and its advocacy of enlightened moderation.

New Afghanistan

The US-led coalition's military intervention in Afghanistan resulted in much suffering. Not only Taliban fighters, but also many foreign volunteers were killed, wounded or taken prisoner. They included some thousands of Pakistanis who were misled by religious preachers into joining the self-proclaimed jihad. Also, a very large number of innocent civilians became casualties of the war.

Pakistan cooperated with the world community for an end to civil war, promotion of peace and reconciliation among the different ethnic communities, and political stability in Afghanistan. Valuing its knowledge of Afghanistan, the United Nations and major coalition partners sought consultations with Pakistan on the formation of a balanced multi-ethnic government.

Pakistan and Saudi Arabia prepared a joint working paper, recommending a three-pronged political, military and economic strategy for the promotion of reconciliation, unity and cooperation among Afghans, a fair and equitable sharing of power among different ethnic communities, and reconstruction of the country. Foreign Minister Saud Al Faisal presented the paper to the leaders of the United States and Britain. Fair and objective, the information and suggestions that Pakistan shared with others, were perhaps of some value. The Security Council resolution of 14 November 2001, the Bonn Agreement of 5 December, and the commitment of over four billion dollars for the reconstruction of Afghanistan by donors at the Tokyo meeting in December 2001 opened the door to a better future for the Afghan nation. A silver lining appeared on Afghanistan's horizon that had long been dominated by the dark clouds of foreign intervention and civil war. The shadow of divisive and obscurantist ideological politics was lifted and the nation could now hope for reconstruction and unity.

The UN-chaired Bonn conference of prominent Afghans endorsed a multi-phase formula that provided for (1) formation of an interim administration, with a well educated, multi-lingual Pushtoon leader, Hamid Karzai as chairman, (2) a *loya jirga* to confirm the appointment of the chairman and election of members of a commission to draft the constitution, (c) another *loya jirga* for approval of the draft constitution, and (4) a general election for the presidency. The Afghan parties also agreed to the return of former King Zahir Shah to his country, though not the restoration of the monarchy. The interim authority combined cultural authenticity with commitment to a democratic future for all Afghans.

Chairman-designate Hamid Karzai and members of the interim administration appreciated Pakistan's prompt recognition and its decision to send a delegation led by the foreign minister to participate in the installation ceremony on 22 December 2001. Members of the administration, Pushtoon as well as non-Pushtoon, including those from the Northern Alliance, greeted the delegation warmly. Expressing lasting gratitude for Pakistan's role in the liberation of their country and its hospitality to millions of refugees over many years, they joined the Pakistani guests in looking to a future of cooperation between the two countries bound by ties of geography, history and culture.

The Tokyo meeting of donors agreed to a multi-year aid package for reconstruction of the ruined economy of Afghanistan. Pakistan pledged $100 million, out of which an amount of $10 million was paid in cash to enable the new administration to meet urgent needs.

President Hamid Karzai's decision to include Pakistan among the countries he visited soon after assuming his office, and the president of Pakistan's return visit to Kabul on 2 April 2002 illustrated the desire of both sides to reconstruct close friendly relations between the two countries. Pakistan's policy of strong support for the peace, unity and territorial integrity of Afghanistan, strict non-interference in its internal affairs, expansion and extension of the international security assistance force, and advocacy of international assistance for the reconstruction of Afghanistan helped to restore mutual confidence and goodwill. The rise of Afghanistan from the ashes of a protracted war was a blessing for its neighbours, especially the people of Pakistan, who look forward to the revival of links across their borders, development of trade and the construction of pipelines for gas and oil, and access for the people of Pakistan to their civilisational hinterland.

An emergency *loya jirga* held in 2002 approved the composition of the interim government. Another *jirga* in 2003 reached a consensus on the constitution of the Transitional Islamic State of Afghanistan. In November 2004, Chairman Hamid Karzai became the first-ever popularly elected president in the history of his country, receiving 55.4 per cent of the vote, with solid support in the Pashtun east and south, as well as a comfortable majority in the multi-ethnic west and urban centres, including Kabul. The high voter turnout, absence of the widely feared disruption by Taliban remnants, the orderly conduct of the ballot by the electoral management body, and the certificate of an international UN-selected team, lent credibility to the result. Younus Qanuni with the next highest vote (16.3 per cent), who received the bulk of his votes from the Panjshir province, Abdul Rashid Dostum from the Uzbeks and Haji Mohammad Mohaqqeq from the Hazaras, gracefully accepted the election results.

Elections held in September 2005 provided political representation to all Afghan ethnic and sectarian components of the population in the parliament which would exercise a check on the relatively strong presidency.[17]

Meanwhile, improvements in internal security and the very substantial assistance provided by the world community created conditions conducive to the return of a significant number out of the three million refuges in Pakistan. Also bilateral trade increased to a record $500 million in 2004.

Political stability, the establishment of law and order, and continued economic progress in Afghanistan will be crucial to hopes of resolving problems of narcotics production and trafficking, and smuggling across the Pakistan border that have magnified since the fall of the Taliban. Also prospects will open up for the expansion of trade and transit between Pakistan and the Central Asian Republics.

NOTES

1. President George Bush, 12 September 2001.
2. At a Press conference on 13 September 2001, Bush was asked: 'Have you made any progress?' in obtaining needed cooperation from Pakistan and Afghanistan 'which have not necessarily done so in the past'. He replied, 'Won't we? We will give the Pakistani government a chance to cooperate and to participate as we hunt down those people who committed this unbelievable despicable act on America.'
3. *The 9/11 Commission Report*, W. W. Norton & Co., New York, p. 330.
4. Ibid., p. 331.
5. Ibid., p. 331.
6. Ibid., p. 332. Whether the US request reached Islamabad on 13 or 14 September is unclear. Armitage made the requests on 13 September—i.e. already 14 September in Islamabad. However, Powell in said to have informed the NSC Principals' Committee on 13 September, 'President Musharraf had agreed to every US request for support in the war on terrorism.' Footnote 38 on p. 558 of the *Report* refers to the US embassy, Islamabad, cable of 14 September.
7. Ibid., p. 331. The US embassy cable reported, 'Musharraf said the GOP was making substantial concessions on allowing use of its territory and that he would pay a domestic price. His standing in Pakistan was bound to suffer. To counterbalance that he needed to show that Pakistan was benefiting from his decision.'
8. UK prime minister, Tony Blair, Netherlands prime minister Wim Kok, German chancellor Gerhard Schroeder, and Belgium prime minister Guy Verhofstadt.
9. The USA provided $600 million in cash, $145m in aid for F'2002 and $1 billion debt write-off; Japan offered a $300m grant payable over two years; the UK $75m; Canada $285m in loan swap for aid; Italy $85m and the EU $31m for SAP, $22m for livestock services and market access for textiles with 15 per cent reduction in tariffs on clothing. In 2003, the USA wrote off a further $495 in debt.
10. US assistance to Pakistan (Source: K. Allan Kronstadt, *Pakistan–US Relations*, Issue Brief for Congress no. IB94041, Congressional Research Service, Washington, 2 March 2005):

						(million dollars)
	2001	2002	2003	2004	2005 (Estimate)	2006 (Proposed)
Economic support*	0	625	188	200	298	300
Military sales	0	75	224	75	149	300
Misc.	91	851	201	136	91	98
Total	91	1,152	513	411	538	698

* FY 2003 & 2004 support funds were used to cancel $988m & $495m of outstanding debt.

11. US Secretary of State Colin Powell said in an interview: 'Besides urging New Delhi and Islamabad to show restraint, Washington also appealed to China to use its influence on Pakistan to prevent a possible war.' *Dawn*, Islamabad, 14 November 2004.
12. *Dawn*, Islamabad, 16 December 2004.
13. Jim Kolby, Chairman of the House Appropriations Committee, referred to 'disturbing' reports that Pakistan had 'balked' at the US request for its forces to go into its border areas, released the extremists arrested after the president's 12 January ban on militant organizations, and although the degree of cooperation was appraised highly, the subsequent release of the detained extremists was considered inconsistent with the announcement.
14. Armitage told the House Appropriations Committee on 18 April 2002: 'I think they (Pakistanis) have thrown their lot in. I don't think they have a choice.'
15. *The 9/11 Commission Report*, p. 369.
16. Interview on Pakistan TV, reported in *Dawn*, Islamabad, March 18, 2005.
17. International Crisis Group report, *Afghanistan: From Presidential to Parliamentary Elections*, 23 November 2004.

CHAPTER 20

Terrorism

Pakistan has been of one voice with the rest of the world community in condemning terrorism, and supporting international cooperation to eradicate the scourge in all its forms and manifestations by eliminating its root causes—alien occupation, state oppression and repression, and gross violations of human rights. The government enacted laws to ban extremist and militant groups that organised or participated in acts of violence in and outside the country. After 9/11 Pakistan became a frontline state in the 'war on terrorism', and intensified its pursuit of foreign militants. Many of them were brought by the CIA to assist the Afghan Mujahideen in their liberation struggle, but continued to reside in the mountainous terrain of the tribal areas and later participated in the civil war in Afghanistan. Members of extremist movements in their countries of origin and terrorists, they were led by Osama bin Laden. In 2003, Pakistan deployed over seventy thousand armed forces personnel in the border areas adjoining Afghanistan to ferret out the foreign extremists and their local supporters, incurring heavy costs in lives during the protracted campaign (over 300 killed by mid-2005, a number much higher than the casualties suffered by the international Security Assistance Force in Afghanistan). Meanwhile, with US financial assistance, Pakistan procured modern equipment and strengthened the training of police and security personnel to upgrade their capacity for vigilance, investigation of terrorist crimes and bringing perpetrators to justice.

The president of Pakistan urged world leaders to promote a just resolution of international issues, many of which had brought protracted suffering to Muslim peoples and generated resentment. Pakistan was disappointed at the lack of a salutary response. Few of the influential states seemed disposed to adopt effective policies and measures to restrain states that allowed their armed forces to resort to terror and repression against civilian populations seeking respect for their human rights. Negotiations in the UN General Assembly on a comprehensive international convention against terrorism were stalled because of disagreements on the definition of terrorism, with a group of states resisting the distinction between terrorism and freedom struggle.

The events of 9/11 marked what Secretary General Kofi Annan called a 'seismic shift in international relations.' Some states began to use the lable of terrorism 'to demonise political opponents, to throttle the freedom of speech and the press, and to de-legitimise political grievances... States living in tension with their neighbours make opportunistic use of the fight against terrorism to threaten or justify new military action on long-running disputes.'[1]

Ironically, some nations that justified resort to violence against the ruling powers during their own freedom struggle, condemned the same means when others under their yoke took to militant struggle. Such a striking contradiction characterised the Indian stance. When Bhagat Singh was hanged for assassinating a British police officer and throwing a bomb in the colonial legislature in New Delhi in 1930, the Indian National Congress described him as a 'great martyr', and seventy years later the Indian government issued a postage stamp to honour him as a national hero; purblind to the irony, it described the Kashmiris who attacked the Indian parliament building as terrorists.

The Universal Human Rights Declaration, two human rights conventions, and covenants on crimes against humanity, war crimes and genocide, have not restrained states from suppressing popular protests for freedom and other human rights, allowing their agencies to terrorise people by resort to indiscriminate violence, torture, custodial killings, destruction of homes and businesses, molestation and rape, and thus driving people to despondency and desperation to the point that even death seems preferable to life. President Jacques Chirac rightly called terrorism 'a feverish expression of suffering, frustration and injustice.'

Oppressive policies of states against people have historically been a main generator of terrorism.[2] No state has contributed more than Israel to the generation of suffering and outrage among Muslims in recent history. As Ken Livingstone, Mayor of London has said: 'Israel's expansion has included ethnic cleansing. Palestinians who had lived in that land for centuries were driven out by systematic violence and terror. The methods of groups like the Irgun and the Stern gang were the same as those of the Bosnian Serb leader Karadzic.'[3] Mr Livingstone more forthrightly castigated Ariel Sharon for continuing seizures of Palestinian land, military incursions and denial of the rights of Palestinians. Recalling that Israel's own Kahan commission found that

Sharon shared responsibility for the Sabra and Shatila massacres, Livingstone noted that more than 7,000 Palestinians were in Israel's jails.

Since its birth, Israel has enjoyed the strong support of the Western countries with influential domestic Zionist lobbies. The United States has provided large budgetary support, allowed tax exemption for private donations, facilitated market access, supplied the latest military weapons, and abused its veto power in the Security Council to shield Israel from resolutions condemning its actions, thus emboldening the Jewish state to persist in its iniquitous policies in flagrant violation of international law and the human rights of the Palestinian people. US policy has provoked deep resentment in the Arab world, Pakistan and other Muslim countries sympathetic to the just cause of the Palestinians. It has also fuelled rage and the rise of extremism responsible for terrorist attacks on US targets. The US political elite, however, conspicuously ignored this root cause as Zionist lobbies exploited the popular outrage against terrorism, and Ariel Sharon's government resorted to demonisation. 'Initial targets were and have now become Muslims.'[4]

Islam Targeted

As the Soviet Union collapsed, Zionists, born-again Christian priests and political lobbyists in the United States supplanted Islam in place of communism as the new threat to the West, insidiously stoking prejudices rooted in medieval crusades[5] to plant seeds of Islamophobia. Bernard Lewis,[6] a Jewish 'authority' on Islam, coined the phrase 'clash of civilisations' which was further developed by Harvard professor Samuel Huntington in an article in the prestigious Foreign Affairs in 1993. The slogan attracted worldwide publicity and influenced powerful political circles in the US, spreading fear that the Judeo-Christian civilisation forever faced a 'hostile Islamic world hell-bent on the conquest and conversion of the West'.[7] Even though the perpetrators of the 9/11 outrage were not religious men and their motivations were political, the anti-Islamic activists exploited the crime to stoke anti-Islamic hysteria. Daniel Pipes, an American–Israeli political activist, relied on 'quotes taken out of context, guilt by association, errors of fact, and innuendo' to whip up hatred against Islam. He had earlier launched the Campus Watch website dedicated to monitoring alleged anti-Semitic, anti-Israel, pro-Palestinian and/or

Islamist bias in teachers of Middle East studies at US colleges and universities.'[8] Out-of-context quotations from the Quran and incorrect translations were used to whip up hate campaigns against Muslims.

The projection of Islam as an enemy of the West was a preposterous fabrication, as objective observers of the global strategic reality know.[9] The predominant political thought in the Muslim world does not regard the West as an adversary. On the contrary, it recognises the desperate need for cooperation in order to end centuries of stagnation, by benefiting from the undeniable progress the West has made in all fields of knowledge, including political, economic and social sciences. As a perceptive US panel observed, 'Muslims do not "hate our freedoms", but rather they hate our policies.' It blamed the government for characterising the new threat of Muslim militancy in a way that offended most Muslims.[10]

UN Secretary General Kofi Annan decried 'the distortion of Islam by a wicked few' and urged the vital need to expose 'those who wrongly claim that Islam justifies the callous murder of innocents to give this rich and ancient faith a bad name.'[11]

Islam. The word meaning peace, Islam emphasises coexistence. Murder is a crime under Islamic law. Islam upholds the sanctity of human life and abhors the killing of even a single innocent person. The Quran ordains: 'Whosoever kills a human being for other than manslaughter or corruption in the earth, it shall be as if he killed all mankind, and whosoever saves the life of one, it shall be as if he saved the life of all mankind.'[12] 'The Holy Prophet (PBUH) said: 'A believer remains within the scope of his religion so long as he does not kill another person illegally.' Islam teaches the noble precept of human fraternity, and abhorrence of discrimination on grounds of race or colour, language or national origin, wealth or gender. 'There is no compulsion in religion.'[13]

All OIC countries joined in condemning the 9/11 outrage and several of them have also provided logistic support for the fight against terrorists in Afghanistan. Enlightened leaders in the West were also anxious to avoid besmirching Islam and alienating the large Muslim world. President Bush and Prime Minister Blair took the trouble to quote from the Quran to emphasize that Islam was a religion of peace. They were not oblivious to the value and importance of Pakistan's support, not only because of its location, but also because, as a large Muslim nation, its decisions would influence other Muslim nations.

Osama bin Laden exploited the concept of jihad in pursuit of his self-proclaimed mission against the government of his country—Saudi Arabia—and later against the United States. But his influence owed much to his role, with the encouragement and even the instigation of the United States, in the Afghan liberation struggle against Soviet occupation. Supporters of the struggle, including Pakistan, Saudi Arabia and the United States, were not averse to the invocation of jihad by the Mujahideen alliance to fight Soviet expansionism. The CIA reportedly recruited some twenty-five thousand Arabs to join the war. After the war was won, some of these and other foreigners skilled in making bombs joined bin Laden and al Qaeda. The United States was not their only target. Pakistan, Saudi Arabia and Egypt were also their victims.

Examples are not lacking where secret agencies recruited, trained and sustained terrorists, and at times even allowed them to raise funds through narcotics trafficking. Justifying their tactics by 'resort to a vulgar pragmatism—it is right because it works,' they raised an infrastructure of terror which later turned on its masters.[14]

The Islamic doctrine of jihad is too often mis-translated as 'holy war'. Actually the word means individual or collective struggle by thought, word and action against evil. States, too, have historically used the term in the same sense as the doctrine of 'just war' developed by Hugo Grotius. However, there is no warrant in Islamic law for the use of the term Jihad by an individual to proclaim violence against another person or community. Terrorism has been rightly equated to 'privatisation of war',[15] which has no sanction under any system of law.

Muslims Victimised. Politically motivated exploitation of acts of militancy and violence by an extremist fringe among Muslims unleashed a wave of Islamophobia in countries with significant Muslim immigrant populations, especially the United States, France, Germany and the Netherlands. Muslim citizens, residents and visitors to the United States were exposed to economic and social discrimination, exclusion and discriminatory surveillance. Doors began to close for the admission of Muslim students to institutions of higher education. Discrimination in employment deprived immigrants of jobs in business and industry. In the United States 'profiling criteria came to include ethnicity, national origin and religion, a heightened scrutiny and harassment at airports (and) selective enforcement of visa regulations.'[16] Muslims became targets of FBI interrogations while their mosques came under surveillance, creating a state of fear.[17] Uncounted numbers of innocent Muslims, including a large number of Pakistanis, suffered detention without charge, loss of jobs, deportation and discrimination, not to mention those who were subjected to humiliation. Some of the other Western countries known for religious tolerance were beset with an eruption of hostility towards Islam. France prohibited the use of *hijab* in public schools. In the Netherlands, Muslim immigrants and settlers, already suffering discrimination, were exposed to a new campaign of hate after the brutal murder by a Muslim of Dutch film producer Theo van Gogh in November 2004.

The Muslim World's Response. Muslim countries realised the need to project a correct understanding of their faith.[18] The OIC called for an extraordinary meeting of the Islamic Conference of Foreign Ministers (ICFM). Held in Doha on 10 October 2001, the 57-member ICFM reiterated condemnation of the 11 September outrage, cooperation in bringing perpetrators to justice for deserved punishment, and willingness to contribute to the elimination of the scourge of terrorism. It also underlined Islamic teachings that uphold the sanctity of human life, prohibit the killing of innocent people and emphasise tolerance, understanding and coexistence among people of different faiths.

Another important conference to highlight harmony among civilisations was convened by Turkey in February 2002. Held in Istanbul, the crossroads of continents, in a land which witnessed over the millennia interaction of great civilisations, the colloquium attended by foreign ministers of OIC and EU members provided a unique opportunity for better mutual understanding. Participants rejected the perverse thesis of 'clash of civilisations.' They emphasised instead the history of mutually beneficial interaction among civilisations. Participants recalled that Muslim scholars recovered Greek literature from oblivion, and translated and transmitted it to Europe. Over recent centuries, hundreds of thousands of students from Africa and Asia travelled to Europe and America in pursuit of knowledge. Benefiting from the West's advances in science and technology, philosophy and politics, they contributed, on their return, to the progress of their own societies.

The need was also recognised to combat the extremist fringe within Muslim societies. Pakistan and Saudi Arabia adopted policies to denounce such elements. Both suffered numerous attacks by terrorists. Three times in 2003 and 2004, President Musharraf was personally targeted. Refusing to be intimidated, he courageously embarked on an energetic promotion of 'enlightened moderation' emphasising the need 'to replace the institutions of hate, anger and militancy' with a correct projection of Islam that stands for 'peace, harmony, justice, equality and brotherhood.'[19]

Terrorism and Religion

Religion has long been abused to justify wars and campaigns of terror. As far back as the first century AD, a Jewish sect of Zealots targeted fellow Jews suspected of aiding the Romans. Extremist interpretations of Christianity misled medieval Christendom to unleash the crusades against Muslims. The 'Assassins', an extremist sub-sect of Muslims, waged a campaign of terror against other Muslims during the twelfth and thirteenth centuries. In the fifteenth century, Muslims were liquidated in Spain and the Inquisition carried out brutal burnings of alleged heretics at the stake. The Spanish clergy subjected the indigenous people in Central and South America to a veritable genocide starting in the sixteenth century. Millions of people perished in the Thirty Years War between Catholic and Protestant Christians in the seventeenth century.[20]

State Terrorism

State terrorism has an equally long history. To deter resistance to his ambition of conquering the world, Alexander burned and razed Persepolis in 325 BC. Roman emperors Tiberius and Caligua executed people to terrorise the opposition. During the French Revolution, the Jacobins officially proclaimed the 'Reign of Terror' in 1793 to ensure their power in the face of opposition. Medieval invaders routinely ordered arson and slaughter in cities that resisted their attacks. As recently as the twentieth century, Britain, France and Portugal unleashed terror against freedom movements in their colonies. India has used even more savage, if modern, methods to suppress the Kashmiri struggle for freedom, and as a result of indiscriminate killings and arson of houses and shops, the number of victims since 1989 is estimated at 60,000–100,000.

The Need for a Comprehensive Strategy

The demonisation of Islam, or Palestinians and Kashmiris and Chechens, represents uncivilised responses to an objective problem that calls instead for a comprehensive strategy combining preventive and deterrence measures with redress of root causes. The High-Level Panel on Threats, Challenges and Change appointed by the UN Secretary General in 2003 recommended such an approach. 'Terrorism,' it said, 'attacks the values that lie at the heart of the United Nations: respect for human rights, the rule of law, rules of war that protect civilians, tolerance among peoples and nations, and the peaceful resolution of conflict.' Noting that the war on terrorism, too, 'has in some instances corroded the very values that terrorists target: human rights and the rule of law,' it recommended:

1. Dissuasion, working to reverse the causes or facilitators of terrorism, including through promoting social and political rights, the rule of law and democratic reform, working to end occupations and address major political grievances, combating organised crime, reducing poverty and unemployment, and stopping state collapse.
2. Efforts to counter extremism, including through education and fostering debate.
3. Development of better instruments for global counter-terrorism cooperation, all within a legal framework that is respectful of civil liberties and human rights.
4. Building state capacity to prevent terrorist recruitment and operations.
5. Control of dangerous materials and public health defence. [21]

The High Level Panel emphasized the need to resolve 'long-standing disputes which continue to fester and to feed the new threats we now face. Foremost among these are the issues of Palestine, Kashmir and the Korean Peninsula.' Otherwise, it warned, 'no amount of systemic changes to the way the United Nations handles both old and new threats to peace and security will enable it to discharge effectively its role under the Charter.' [22]

Kofi Annan has outlined a similar five-point global strategy for fighting terrorism, comprising dissuasion of disaffected groups from choosing terrorism as a tactic to achieve their goals, denial of means for terrorists to attack, deterring states from supporting terrorists, developing state capacity to prevent terrorism, and defending human rights and the rule of law. He criticised repressive tactics, saying, 'Terrorism is in itself a direct attack on human rights and the rule of law. If we sacrifice them in response, we are handing victory to the terrorists.'[23]

Annan also endorsed the panel's recommendation for the United Nations to agree on a universal definition of terrorism that would stress the fact that no cause or grievance, no matter how legitimate, could justify the targeting of civilians in order to intimidate a population or influence government policy.[24]

NOTES

1. Tiburg University, 21 November 2002.
2. Sri Lankan President Chandrika Kumaratunge made a statement to this effect at the SAARC summit at Katmandu in 2002.
3. *The Guardian News Service/Dawn*, Islamabad, 5 March 2005.
4. Ibid.
5. Manifest in a 'slip of tongue' by President George W. Bush.
6. Professor Bernard Lewis, author of the essay *The Roots of Muslim Rage*.
7. Quoted by Anjum Niaz in her Sunday column in Dawn, 7 November 2004.
8. Jim Lobe, 'Anti-Muslim activist plants new seeds of hatred', *InterPress News Service/Dawn*, Islamabad, 27 February 2005.
9. Zalmay Khalilzade, *Strategic Appraisal—1996*, pp. 13–14. He does not even mention the Muslim world as one of the important features of the current international environment.
10. US Defense Science Board report, *Dawn*, Islamabad, 26 November 2004.
11. Message to the antiterrorism conference in Riyadh, *Dawn*, Islamabad, 10 February 2005.
12. Al Quran, 5:32.
13. Al Quran, 2:256.
14. Mahmood Mamdani, *Good Muslim, Bad Muslim: America, the Cold War & Roots of Terror*, Vanguard Books, Lahore.
15. The term was first used by President Musharraf in a speech on 12 March 2005.
16. US Commission on Civil Rights, quoted in report, *Dawn*, Islamabad, 18 November 2004.
17. Report on Convention of American Muslim Voice, San Francisco, *Dawn*, Islamabad, 5 October 2004.
18. Crown Price Abdullah of Saudi Arabia called for the establishment of an international centre. *Dawn*, Islamabad, 7 February 2005.
19. Convocation address at the International Islamic University, Islamabad, *Dawn*, Islamabad, 12 March 2005.
20. For an informative study of the abuse of religion for violence and war, see Shahwar Junaid, *Terrorism And Global Power Systems*, Oxford University Press, 2005. Among the examples, the author recalls are: Jewish Zealots targeted other Hebrews in the first century. The Assassins belonged to a secret sub-sect of Muslims who conducted a campaign of terror against other Muslims in the twelfth century in what is Syria. Medieval Christendom launched the notorious Crusades against Muslims to conquer the Holy Land. In the fifteenth century, the Spanish Inquisition tortured and executed Christians they considered heretics. In the Thirty Years War in the seventeenth century Catholics and Protestants visited death and destruction on each other. In the 1930s and 1940s, Nazi Germany perpetrated the

Holocaust. Millions of Muslims, and Hindus and Sikhs were killed in politically-motivated riots before and after the independence of India and Pakistan in 1947. Even as recently as 27 February 2002, Hindu extremists in the Indian state of Gujarat killed two thousand innocent Muslims after the bigoted state chief minister Narendra Modi blamed Muslims for the train fire at Godhra—a charge that was found false by the Justice U. C. Banerjee Committee.

21. *Report of the High-Level Panel on Threats, Challenges and Change*, UN General Assembly document, 29 November 2004, p. 41.

22. Ibid., pp. 1, 41 and 42,

23. Address to International Conference on Terrorism, Madrid, AFP report, *Dawn*, Islamabad, 11 March 2005.

24. Report to Security Council, 21 March 2005.

Chapter 21

Pakistan–India Relations, 2001–05

Retrospect

The roots of the antagonism between Pakistan and India can be traced to the history of Hindu–Muslim relations and contention between the Indian National Congress and the Muslim League. But the religious factor is often exaggerated. The evolution of relations between the states of South Asia since Independence is better understood in the secular paradigm of a conflict of aims between a more powerful state seeking domination and less powerful neighbours aspiring to protect their rights. Forgetting its own struggle for independence, India ignored the legitimate aspirations of its smaller neighbours for relations based on the principle of sovereign equality. Stepping into Britain's imperial shoes, India imposed unequal treaties on the Himalayan kingdoms of Hindu Nepal and Buddhist Bhutan. Sikkim was forcibly occupied and annexed despite the treaty India had signed recognising its separate and autonomous status. Sri Lanka, too, did not escape Indian hegemonic pressure and became the victim of interference and intervention during the 1980s and 1990s.[1]

India's imperial attitude is partly inherited from the predecessor British Raj[2] but its roots are traceable to great power ambitions cultivated in the minds of the Indian political elite by leaders of the Indian National Congress since the late nineteenth century. They conjured up and asserted India's title to world power status long before the country became independent. It was not merely an aspiration to greatness which every nation has a right to cherish; their dream envisaged the aim of domination over neighbours.

As far back as 1895 a committee chairman of the annual session of the Indian National Congress, Rao Bahadur V. M. Bhide declared: '[India] is destined under providence to take its rank among the foremost nations of the world.'[3] In 1919, the Congress claimed a right to attend the Paris Peace Conference and even appointed an uninvited delegate. Justifying the claim, Gangadhar Tilak argued, in a letter to President Georges Clemenceau: 'With her vast area, enormous resources, and prodigious population, she [India] may well aspire to be a leading power in Asia.'[4] Jawaharlal Nehru, the mentor of the post-Independence generations of Indian strategic thinkers, considered India as a world power, which 'will have to play a very great role in security problems of Asia and the Indian Ocean, more especially in the Middle East and South Asia.' He envisioned India as 'the pivot of Western, Southern and Southeast Asia.'[5] His ambition for an Indian sphere of influence extended from Bab el Mandeb to the Straits of Malacca. Hegemonic in his narrow nationalistic drive, on the eve of Independence Nehru even urged the proclamation of an Indian Monroe doctrine with respect to Asian countries.[6]

If India could not impose its will on Pakistan immediately upon Independence, Nehru looked forward to a time when it would be able to do so. In a confidential letter he wrote on 25 August 1952, later declassified, Nehru said:

> We are superior to Pakistan in military and industrial power. But that superiority is not so great to produce results in war or by fear of war. Therefore, our national interest demands that we should adopt a peaceful policy towards Pakistan, and at the same time, add to our strength. Strength ultimately comes not from the armed forces but the industrial and economic background behind them. *As we grow in strength, as we are likely to do so, Pakistan will feel less and less inclined to threaten or harass us, and a time will come when, through sheer force of circumstances, it will be in a mood to accept a settlement that we consider fair, whether in Kashmir or elsewhere.*[7] [Emphasis added]

Commenting on Nehru's writings before India achieved independence a commentator observed:

> Firstly, the goal pursued by this ambitious Nehru is the establishment of a great empire unprecedented in India's history. The sphere of influence of this great empire would include a series of countries from the Middle East to Southeast Asia and far surpasses that of the colonial system set up in the past by the British Empire . . .
>
> Secondly, this ambitious Nehru believes that . . . the small nation state is doomed, it may survive as a culturally autonomous area but not as an independent political unit. In a word, it can only be a vassal in Nehru's great empire. . . .
>
> After India's independence, the Indian ruling circles headed by Nehru inherited and have tried their best to preserve the bequests of the British colonial rulers; they have become increasingly brazen in carrying out their

chauvinistic and expansionist policy. India is the only country in Asia that has a protectorate.[8]

The drive to impose its own preferences on less powerful neighbours in utter disregard of the principles of justice and international law has been manifest in India's insistence on the bilateral settlement of differences and disputes, which allows it to exploit power disparity for duress. To that end India has refused to utilise the other peaceful means for settlement of disputes evolved by the community of states through centuries of experience. Article 33.1 of the UN Charter provides:

> The parties to any dispute, the continuance of which is likely to endanger the maintenance of international peace and security, shall, first of all, seek a solution by negotiation, enquiry, mediation, conciliation, arbitration, judicial settlement, resort to regional agencies or arrangements, or other peaceful means of their own choice.

Developments

Assuming, after 9/11, that Pakistan would be bracketed with the Taliban, New Delhi tried to paint Pakistan into the terrorist corner. Exploiting worldwide outrage against terrorism, Indian leaders accused Pakistan of sponsoring terrorism, bracketed it with the Taliban and adopted the pose that India, too, was a victim of terrorism. Pakistan pointed out that India was not a victim, but a perpetrator of state terrorism. The Indian propaganda line failed because Pakistan adopted a provident policy that made it a frontline ally in the fight against terrorism.

Soon after 13 December 2001, when armed men entered the premises of the Indian parliament and clashed with security personnel, the shadows lengthened to darken the Pakistan–India horizon. Without any evidence, the Indian government charged Pakistan with responsibility for the attacks. Exploiting the international condemnation of the terrorist act, New Delhi escalated pressure on Pakistan. It downgraded diplomatic relations, suspended train and air services, and moved its forces, including strike formations, forward to the border with Pakistan and the Line of Control in Kashmir. It further demanded that Pakistan hand over twenty Indian and Pakistani nationals who were alleged to have hijacked Indian airliners and committed other acts of terrorism in India over the previous twenty years. Faced with the threat of aggression, Pakistan moved its troops to forward defensive positions. For a year the two armies stood 'eyeball to eyeball' and on more than one occasion the two countries came dangerously close to the brink of war.

Fortunately for both nations, the danger of a conflict was averted due to an unprecedented combination of factors. Pakistan's capacity for self-defence acted as a restraint. The risk of escalation to the nuclear level was a powerful deterrent. Moreover, all major powers from the United States to the European Union, Russia, China and Japan, counselled restraint. After nearly a year, having incurred colossal expenditure and exposed Pakistan to a similar burden, India decided to begin withdrawal of its forces towards peacetime positions.

Meanwhile, New Delhi followed a single-track policy of threatening Pakistan, demanding an end to what it called 'infiltration' and labeling the Kashmiri freedom struggle as a 'terrorist' movement. Pakistan responded with restraint and reason, refraining from diplomatic brick batting. Once again Islamabad proposed reactivation of UNMOGIP to monitor alleged violations of the Line of Control by infiltrators, and proposed a dialogue to discuss an extradition treaty.

In April 2003, Prime Minister Vajpayee announced a reversal: high commissioners would be assigned again, overflights would be permitted, cricket would be allowed, and dialogue resumed. Pakistan reciprocated by announcing a ceasefire on the LOC and withdrawing the ban on overflights.

Prime Minister Vajpayee met President Musharraf on 6 January 2004 during his visit to Islamabad for the SAARC summit, and the two leaders announced an agreement to recommence the composite dialogue, expressing confidence that it would lead to 'peaceful settlement of all bilateral issues, including Jammu and Kashmir.' At a press conference, Vajpayee emphasized that 'violence, hostility and terrorism must be prevented' and Musharraf reassured him stating he 'will not permit any territory under Pakistan's control to be used to support terrorism in any manner.'

Progress was made at meetings held in 2004 at ministerial, foreign secretary and senior official levels to discuss the components of the bilateral dialogue, with greater success on normalisation issues than on resolution of disputes. President Musharraf and Prime Minister Manmohan Singh met in New York on 24 September and agreed on a number of normalisation measures including resumption of bus and rail links on old and new routes.

A bus service was inaugurated on the Muzaffarabad–Srinagar road in early April 2005 before the two leaders met again in New Delhi on 17–18 April and 'determined that the peace process was now irreversible.' The two sides decided to open also the Poonch–Rawalakot road, and reopen the Khokharapar–Munabao rail link. On Siachen and Sir Creek, their officials would reopen discussions 'immediately with a view to finding mutually acceptable solutions expeditiously.' The two sides 'addressed the issue of Jammu and Kashmir and agreed to continue their discussions in a sincere and purposeful and forward-looking manner for a final settlement…and expressed their determination to work together to carry forward the process and to bring the benefit of peace to their region.'[9]

In public statements the Pakistani president advocated flexibility on both sides in their stated positions. While the Indian side no longer laid claim to the entire state of Jammu and Kashmir as an integral part of India, the Pakistani side no longer insisted on a plebiscite to determine the accession of the state, still emphasising, however, that a settlement must be in conformity with the wishes of the Kashmiri people.

Peace in Kashmir

Writing in 1966, Joseph Korbel, a Czechoslovak member of the UNCIP, concluded his book with the following perceptive observations:

> The people of Kashmir have made it unmistakably known that they insist on being heard…The accession of the State of Jammu and Kashmir to India cannot be considered as valid by canons of international law…The issue itself cannot be sidetracked. The history of the case has made it clear that time has only aggravated, not healed the conflict; that neither the Pakistanis nor the Kashmiris will accept the status quo as a solution…No high hopes should be entertained that bilateral negotiations will lead to a settlement… The United Nations has a principal responsibility to seek a solution….[10]

Korbel's assessment has stood the test of time. Fifty years of Indian occupation and repression has steeled the will of the Kashmiri people. Their heroic struggle and sacrifices have demonstrated their resolve to win freedom. Nor has India's threat or use of force intimidated Pakistan to acquiesce in India's usurpation of Kashmir. Meanwhile, relations between Pakistan and India remain strained, and prospects of normalisation as distant as ever. Bilateral negotiations have proved sterile in the past. Hopes of success will remain elusive so long as India persists in its policy of denying or circumventing the right of the Kashmiri people to self-determination.

The Security Council has not resumed consideration of the Kashmir question since the early 1960s, and although in its resolution after the nuclear tests in 1998 it implicitly recognised the 'root cause' of the tension between Pakistan and India and the threat it poses to the maintenance of international peace and security, the prospect of its addressing the issue remain bleak in the foreseeable future.

Although diplomacy remains stuck in a blind alley, the people of Kashmir have taken their destiny into their own hands. Their heroic sacrifices in the protracted struggle for *Azadi* are a guarantee that the cause will endure. By contrast, India's savage repression has exposed the colonial nature of its stranglehold over occupied Kashmir. Civilised opinion in the world, and in India itself, cannot fail to recognise the inevitability of conceding to the Kashmiri people their aspiration to *Azadi*. Translatable as liberation, independence or freedom, their goal transcends differences among political parties over the ultimate aim of the struggle.

Hurriyat leaders have pointed out that the question of whether Jammu and Kashmir should accede to Pakistan or become independent is premature. So long as India is not prepared to honour its pledge that the people of the state have the right to determine their own destiny, a debate over alternative options can only divide and weaken their struggle.

Debate on Options. In October 2004, President Musharraf called for a public debate on options—alternatives to a statewide plebiscite—for settlement of Jammu and Kashmir. Airing his own ideas, he said (a) the state had seven geographical regions with different religions, sects and languages, (b) some should remain with one side or the other, and (c) the others could become autonomous, be placed under UN trusteeship or a condominium or divided between the two countries.[11] Some of the alternatives were novel while others had been bruited about earlier.

The alternatives to a statewide plebiscite, such as regional plebiscites or one only in the valley, partition, status quo, independence, condominium and UN trusteeship, were bruited in the past, too, in Pakistan or India, mostly unofficially, or by individuals or political parties. None was acceptable to all three parties—the people of Jammu and Kashmir, Pakistan and India. A statewide plebiscite remained the only formula bearing the imprimatur of Security Council resolutions for determination of the future of Jammu and Kashmir by its people.

The regional alternative was first conceived in 1950 by UN mediator Owen Dixon. Concluding, after talks with the leaders of the two countries, that it was extremely unlikely that any proposal for a plebiscite of the kind suggested by the UN Commission for India and Pakistan would ever bear fruit, Dixon explored a 'fresh approach' based on regional plebiscites and the allocation of 'each section or area according to the results of the vote therein.' Alternatively, his plan envisaged a plebiscite only in 'the Valley of Kashmir and perhaps some adjacent country' assuming that some areas were certain to vote for accession to Pakistan and some for accession to India.

Prime Minister Jawaharlal Nehru, according to Dixon, was prepared to discuss the second alternative of a plebiscite in the valley alone. Apparently he calculated that Sheikh Abdullah, then at the helm in Indian-held part of the state, could swing or manipulate the vote in the valley in India's favour. Since India had earlier rejected proposals for demilitarisation and a UN administration to ensure a free and impartial plebiscite, Pakistan was not unaware of the risk of rigging under Abdullah. Besides, the regional plebiscite idea was little to Prime Minister Liaquat Ali Khan's liking because it would amount to a deviation from the Security Council resolution.

Sheikh Abdullah floated the idea of independence after New Delhi's interference in Kashmir's administration convinced him that his friend Nehru was intent on maintaining Indian occupation and had no intention of allowing a fair and impartial plebiscite. Realising he had been deceived and Nehru had merely used him to give the appearance of legitimacy to the Indian grab of the state against the principle of the partition, he belatedly started protesting. Thereupon he was dismissed and jailed in 1953 and remained there for twelve years.

The only serious Pakistan–India dialogue on Kashmir took place after the Sino–Indian border clash in 1962. At the urging of Britain and the United States, the two countries agreed to talks specifically focused on Kashmir alone. Six rounds were held between delegations led by Z. A. Bhutto and Swaran Singh. At first, the Indian side appeared open to discussion of the idea of partitioning the state on the basis of the presumed wishes of its people, but it back-tracked as soon as the Chinese forces withdrew to the pre-war lines. Swaran Singh then spoke of the possibility of only minor adjustments in the ceasefire line.

India formally put forward the idea of not only freezing the status quo but converting the ceasefire line into an international border at the Shimla Conference in 1972, proposing, 'Minor adjustments to the line of peace in Jammu and Kashmir or the rest of the international border considered necessary by both sides to make the border more rational and viable may be made by mutual agreement.' The 'line of peace' was thus to be a part of the 'international border'. Pakistan resolutely resisted the Indian proposal and, despite terrible pressures following the 1971 disaster, refused to barter away the right of the Kashmiri people to self-determination. Acceptability to the Kashmiri people has remained an explicit premise for any settlement formula, as the Pakistan government has reiterated again and again.

While media analysts have long talked about some of these alternatives to a statewide plebiscite, there has been no sign of flexibility from the Indian side. In a speech in November 2004, Prime Minister Manmohan Singh ruled out any redrawing of borders or further division.[12] As a result, public debate on alternatives lost relevance or utility. Confident that in the emergent era of human rights the people of Kashmir will prevail, Pakistan could best support them by maintaining the bottom line: to be acceptable to Pakistan a settlement must conform to the aspirations of the people of Kashmir.

Mirwaiz Umar Farooq, leader of the All Parties Hurriyat Conference, endorsed the peace moves between Pakistan and India. He also underlined 'the fact that the people of Kashmir have made immense sacrifices and . . . (CBMs) have to lead to a situation where can address the (Kashmir) problem politically . . . We are looking at a permanent solution to the dispute . . . In Jammu and Kashmir we have more than 450,000 military and para-military troops and it is a virtual military camp.'[13] However, the new stance created a division of opinion in IHK. After the 18 April 2005 joint statement, veteran Hurriyat leader Syed Ali Shah Geelani expressed disappointment that the agreements between the Indian and Pakistani leaders brought no relief to the Kashmiri people.[14]

Prospects

Pakistan is well aware that it has to ensure its own security, and formulate an effective strategy for peace and progress. More than ever before, it has to rely on its own resources, political will and defence capacity. Fortunately, the nation has the scientific talent and the political and economic resilience necessary to overcome technological barriers and cope with external pressures and penalties.

Better fiscal management and provident policies have rescued Pakistan from the deepening fiscal crisis of the 1990s and improved the State's capacity to sustain adequate allocations for defence as well as enhance allocations for economic growth and social development, thus reconciling the demands of the present with the imperatives of a better future. The combination of strategic and conventional defence forces has enabled the nation to improve security without excessive demands on fiscal resources. Budgetary allocations for defence have increased at a rate lower than that of economic growth. As a proportion of GDP, defence expenditure declined from 6.5 per cent in 1990 to 3.8 per cent in 2002-03.[15] Meanwhile, development, education, health and poverty alleviation receive a substantially higher share.

History, it has been said, abhors determinism. The future can and should be different from the past. But the past is surely a guide to the future. It has lessons to offer for dealing with the challenges that continue to hover over Pakistan's security horizon.

NOTES

1. The report of the Jain Commission, set up by the Indian government to investigate the assassination of Rajiv Gandhi 'minutely details the nature of support provided by the Government of India to the LTTE, a fact which has blown the lid off India's claims of non-intervention as well as its global stand against international terrorism'. Aunohita Mojumdar, *The Statesman*, Delhi, 5 December 1997.
2. 'Progressively, but inescapably, Indian leaders since independence have assumed the mantle of the British raj.' George K. Tanham, *Indian Strategic Thought*, RAND, Santa Monica, 1992, p. vi.
3. A. Moin Zaidi and Shaheda Zaidi, *The Encyclopaedia of the Indian National Congress* (New Delhi, S. Chand and Co.), Vol. II, p. 506.
4. R. Palme Dutt, *India Today* (London, Victor Gollance, 1940), p. 549.
5. J. Nehru, *Selected Works* (Delhi, Oxford University Press), Second Series, Vol. 1, p. 406.
6. *Selected Works of J. Nehru*, Vol. 3, p. 133. J. Nehru, op cit., Vol. 19, p. 322.
7. J. Nehru, op cit., Vol. 19, p. 322.
8. Commentary by *People's Daily*, Beijing, 27 October 1962.
9. R. K. Jain, op. cit. p. 215.
10. Joseph Korbel, *Danger in Kashmir*. p. 351-52.
11. The President made the suggestion informally at an *iftar* dinner on 25 October 2004. Later he clarified that his statement should not be understood to give up Pakistan's recognised position on the issue.
12. The statement was made on 21 November 2004.
13. Interview report in *Dawn*, Islamabad, 10 April 2005.
14. *Dawn*, Islamabad, 19 April 2005.
15. Ishrat Hussain, Governor, State Bank of Pakistan, *Dawn*, Islamabad, 8 October 2004.

CHAPTER 22

The UN and International Cooperation

The Millennium Summit

Heads of state and governments assembled at the United Nations in New York from 6 to 8 September 2000, to adopt the Millennium Declaration, reaffirming faith in the organisation and its Charter as the indispensable foundation for a more peaceful, prosperous and just world. They recognized collective responsibility to uphold human dignity and equity at global level, pledged efforts to strengthen respect for the rule of law in international as well as national affairs, free peoples from the scourge of war, strengthen security and promote disarmament, and renewed support for the resolution of disputes by peaceful means and in conformity with the principles of justice and international law.

The declaration was notable for its emphasis on development and poverty eradication, and the setting of goals to be achieved by 2015 including the halving of poverty, primary education for all children, reduction of maternal mortality by two-thirds, and halting and reversing the spread of HIV/AIDS. The summit also called for efforts to spread the benefits of globalisation, protection of the environment and promotion of human rights, democracy and good governance, and for strengthening of the United Nations.

Progress towards the realisation of the Millennium Development Goals during the first five years fell short of its targets. Only the momentum of economic growth in China, India and a few other countries of Asia and North Africa contributed to the reduction of the proportion of people in extreme poverty from 30 to 21 per cent. In sub-Sahara Africa poverty was intensified and HIV/AIDS took an increasing toll. The world's population continued to grow at an excessive rate, especially in low-income countries, and was projected to increase from 6.4 billion in 2004 to 9 billion by 2050. In Pakistan, the high population growth rate posed a serious obstacle to the reduction of unemployment, despite the acceleration of economic growth.

Development assistance by affluent countries remained inadequate. Only five of the twenty-two most affluent countries met the UN-endorsed target of 0.7 per cent of GDP for official development assistance and only six of the rest promised to do so by 2015. Meanwhile, global military expenditure began to gallop in 2002, rising nearly 40 per cent to approach the colossal total of one trillion dollars.[1]

Reform of the United Nations

Failing states in the Third World (e.g. Somalia and Ethiopia), genocide in Rwanda[2] in 1994, 'ethnic cleansing' in Bosnia[3] in 1995, proliferation of poverty, environmental degradation, the rise of terrorism and recurrent crises in international relations raised a demand for reform of the United Nations to strengthen its capacity to deal effectively with these and other transformations. Also, a proposal for enlargement of the Security Council surfaced in the early 1990s, as membership had increased greatly since 1965 when the Charter was amended to add four non-permanent seats. Also Japan, Germany and other major states asserted claims to permanent seats.

The Millennium Declaration called for efforts to make the United Nations a more effective instrument for pursuing global priorities. Whilst reaffirming 'the central position of the General Assembly as the chief deliberative policy-making and representative organ', the summit called for 'a comprehensive reform of the Security Council in all its aspects.'

The terrorist attacks on the United States on 11 September 2001, and the US attack on Iraq in 2003, ignoring the Security Council's rejection of its proposal for authorisation of the use of force, further underlined the need for reform.

Recognising that the 'past year has shaken the foundations of collective security and undermined confidence in the possibility of collective responses to our common problems and challenges,' Secretary General Kofi Annan appointed a 16-member high-level panel to recommend 'clear and effective measures for ensuring effective collective action.' The panel's report, released on 1 December 2004, put forward a vision of collective security that would address all major threats to international peace and security. Its recommendation on terrorism, pre-emptive use of force, and enlargement of the Security Council attracted special attention. Notably, the panel's letter transmitting the report to the Secretary General stated:

...The members of the Panel believe it would be remiss of them if they failed to point out that no amount of systemic change in the way the United Nations handles both old and new threats to peace and security will enable it to discharge effectively its role under the Charter if efforts are not redoubled to resolve a number of long-standing disputes which continue to fester and to feed the new threats we now face. Foremost among these are the issues of Palestine, Kashmir and the Korean Peninsula.[4]

Based on the recommendations of the high-level panel and the plan of action prepared by experts, Kofi Annan presented a plan for reform focusing on the three pillars of freedom from want, freedom from fear and freedom to live in dignity.[5]

Prior to the summit meeting in September 2005, emphasis shifted to the scandal of corruption in the management of the funds accumulated by the UN from export of oil by Iraq. Secretary General Kofi Annan was exposed to embarrassment because of his son's role in the award of contracts. The General Assembly was bogged down in disagreement over controversial issues, including enlargement of the Security Council, funding for implementation of the Millennium Development Goals approved in 2000, and criteria for the preemptive use of force in humanitarian emergencies such as genocide. The summit meeting held in September 2005 had to be content with the minimum common denominator acceptable to member states.

Enlargement of the Security Council. Discussion on the enlargement of the Security Council began in the General Assembly in 1993. Recalling that in view of the increased membership of the United Nations since 1945, the Security Council was enlarged in 1965 to add four additional non-permanent seats, and that membership of the organisation had since greatly increased again, a demand arose for further enlargement of the Security Council. At the same time, Germany and Japan staked claims to permanent seats on the grounds of their rise in economic power and large contributions to the UN budget. That led to demands for regional balance in the permanent category by addition of other states from Africa, Asia and Latin America. Meanwhile, a group of like-minded states known as the Coffee Club, including Argentina, Mexico, Italy, Pakistan and the Republic of Korea, joined together in support of a democratic and accountable Security Council in which they advocated the addition of non-permanent seats only.

As consensus eluded the General Assembly and the Millennium Summit, the Secretary General appointed a high level panel for advice on enlargement of the Security Council and other UN reform issues. It too was divided and suggested two alternative models for enlargement. Model A provided for the addition of six new permanent seats without veto power, and model B for the creation of a new category of eight four-year renewable-term seats. In electing states to these seats it would be for the General Assembly to take into account Article 23 of the Charter, that provides for 'due regard being specially paid, in the first instance, to the contribution of Members of the United Nations to the maintenance of international peace and security.' The criteria, the panel suggested, should include: (a) increasing 'the involvement in decision-making of those who contribute most to the United Nations financially, militarily and diplomatically' and those developed countries that make substantial progress towards 0.7% contribution in overseas development aid, (b) bringing in countries that are 'more representative of the broader membership, especially the developing world', and that (c) enlargement should not impair the effectiveness of the Security Council.

After Germany, Japan, Brazil and India formed a group (G-4) to canvass for model A, the Coffee Club also became more active in support of model B. The latter's argument against permanent seats was founded on Article 24.1 of the Charter in which UN members 'agree that in carrying out its responsibilities the Security Council acts on their behalf.' The only way of ensuring that the Security Council actually does so is to make its members accountable to the General Assembly, and to achieve that aim the accepted method is periodic elections. To have a chance for election or re-election, aspirants to seats on the Security Council should have to be accountable to the electorate.

The existing permanent members of the Security Council, each of whom can veto an amendment of the Charter, took divergent positions. France and UK endorsed the G-4, the United States backed only Japan and was joined by Russia in opposing veto power for new permanent members, and China preferred to await the emergence of consensus. After Kofi Annan proposed that a decision should be made by a vote in 2005, China and the United States disagreed, saying a decision should await formation of a broad consensus and that there should no forced timeline. The Coffee Club supported the consensus approach. In the hope of expediting a decision, the G-4 circulated a draft resolution in May 2005 providing for expansion of the Security Council to 25 members with six additional permanent seats without the right of veto, and four non-permanent seats. If pressed to a vote, the proposed amendment of the Charter would require the affirmative vote of nine out of the fifteen members of the Security Council, including the votes of the permanent members, and a two-thirds majority in the General Assembly.[6]

UN Summit, September 2005 Held on the 60th anniversary of the founding of the United Nations, the 2005 Summit provided an opportunity for decisions on core issues of reform of the organisation, progress on implementation of the Millennium Development Goals, promotion of human rights and threats to international peace and security. One hundred and fifty heads of state or government reaffirmed a strong and unambiguous commitment to achieve the Millennium Development Goals and pledged an additional $50 billion a year to fight poverty. Some of the major affluent states however resisted commitment to 0.7 per cent of GDP for official development assistance.

The summit resolution voiced unqualified condemnation of terrorism 'in all its forms and manifestations, committed by whomever, wherever and for whatever purposes' and affirmed the resolve to push for a comprehensive convention against terrorism within a year.

Deciding to enhance the relevance, effectiveness, efficiency, accountability and credibility of the United Nations, the leaders pledged collective action, in a 'timely and decisive manner', through the Security Council and in accordance with the Charter, to protect populations from genocide, war crimes, ethnic cleansing and crimes against humanity, when peaceful means prove inadequate and national authorities are manifestly failing to do it. The leaders agreed to replace the Commission on Human Rights with the Human Rights Council and requested the General Assembly president to conduct open and transparent negotiations to decide on the new body's functions.

No agreement was reached on the enlargement of the Security Council due to the opposing approaches of 'dividing for privilege' and 'uniting for consensus.' Those who sought to force through a resolution for the addition of six permanent seats were checkmated largely because of opposition by the United States, which opposed the enlargement idea on grounds of its effect on efficiency, and China which supported the group of 'Uniting for Consensus' states, arguing against an immediate decision by vote.

Also no agreement was reached on disarmament and nuclear proliferation due to the refusal of the big powers with the largest nuclear arsenals to commit themselves to reduction of stockpiles.

The summit's meagre achievements were largely due to disagreement among big powers that sought tighter control over the organisation and the majority of states seeking to strengthen collective decision-making to address issues of fundamental concern to humanity. The attempt to focus on terrorism and 'new threats' to international peace and security failed to inspire consensus because it ignored wars of aggression and failed to provide for more effective action to resolve festering disputes in conformity with the principles of justice and international law.

Human Rights

Humanity has coveted, craved and struggled for equal rights since the dawn of civilisation. People have sought to curtail and eliminate distinctions and discriminations based on race and colour, and to supplant the arbitrary powers of rulers with a system of laws to protect civil and political rights. Islam promulgated values and laws to sanctify human rights to life, human dignity and equality without distinction of race, language, gender, or religion and promoted social justice. The Renaissance movement in Europe built up the philosophic rationale for civil and political rights; these were then embedded in the constitutions of democratic states. But it was not until after the Second World War that the world community embarked on concerted efforts to set international standards of human rights.

The United Nations Charter reaffirmed faith in fundamental human rights, in the dignity and worth of the human person, and in the equal rights of men and women. It also envisioned higher standards of living and full employment, and international cooperation for the realisation of human rights and fundamental freedoms. The Universal Declaration of Human Rights, adopted unanimously by the UN General Assembly on 10 December 1948, with only the apartheid regime of South Africa and communist states abstaining, codified as well as extended general concepts. It commenced with the inspiring proclamation 'All human beings are born free and equal in dignity and rights, without distinction as to race, colour, sex, language, religion, political or other opinion, national or social origin, birth or other status'.

The process of binding state parties to respect and require observance of human rights began with the adoption of two international covenants in 1966, one on economic, social and cultural rights and the other on civil and political rights. Common to both these covenants is Article 1 affirming, 'All peoples have the right to self-determination.' Both covenants have established monitoring committees which receive reports from state parties on the measures adopted by them to give effect to the rights, with the capacity to promote observance of the obligations. (Pakistan has signed the first but not the second covenant.)

The process of broadening and enlarging human rights has since been accelerated, with the adoption of numerous covenants and conventions on the elimination of all forms of racial discrimination, the rights of women and children, and the prohibition of torture and inhuman and degrading punishments. Of course, older than any of these are conventions on the rights of workers promoted by the International Labour Organisation.

The Human Rights Commission came under strong criticism by the United States and other Western countries alleging it had been politicised. Some of them sought to prescribe qualifications for election to the commission so as to exclude states with a poor human rights record. In the end, the summit meeting agreed to replace the Commission with the Human Rights Council. Its forty-seven members are to be elected by the General Assembly.

Pakistan's record. The constitution of Pakistan requires the state to ensure observance of fundamental rights, including the rights to life and liberty, dignity and inviolability of privacy, freedom of religion, speech, association and assembly, and provides safeguards against arrest and detention, forced labour and traffic in human beings, etc. The state is also party to most of the human rights treaties and has been endeavouring to raise standards of compliance by additional legislation. Some of these, especially the abuse of Hudood[7] and blasphemy laws, however, have exposed the country to severe criticism at home and abroad. The government responded to legitimate concerns by amendments to these laws in 2004–05 to protect innocent people from the excesses resulting from inefficient implementation. More problematic are social practices prevalent among traditional tribes living in a time warp, such as 'honour killings,' (*karo kari*) and discrimination against women, which have proved difficult to eradicate despite the laws in force. The spread of education and enlightenment has proved the only effective remedy in human societies.

International Financial Institutions (IFIs)

For the promotion of economic and social progress for all people, the world community has established a number of international agencies to facilitate international cooperation for economic development, expansion of trade, monetary stability and the provision of multilateral and bilateral assistance to developing countries.

The International Bank for Reconstruction and Development—better known as the World Bank—was established at Bretton Woods in 1944 for the purpose of providing financial assistance for the reconstruction and development of war-shattered economies. Later, it became the primary source of assistance to developing countries. In 2003, it was operating in over a hundred countries and provided $ 18.5 billion in assistance.

The International Monetary Fund (IMF)—the other Bretton Woods institution—was established to promote international monetary cooperation, help establish a multilateral payments system, lend out of its resources, under adequate safeguards, to needy member states to maintain adequate exchange reserves, and facilitate expansion of international trade. Unlike the World Bank, the IMF is not a provider of economic assistance; like the World Bank, it provides loans under adequate safeguards. Both expect the recipient states to follow agreed programmes and conditions.

Economics being a developing science, the strategies followed by IFIs have evolved over time, conceding that some past policies were flawed. However, criticism of IFIs for imposing preconceived agendas on borrowers misses two essential points: first, they provide funds only upon application; secondly, like any provident lender, they try to ensure that the borrower will utilise the loaned funds for the agreed purpose in a manner that will enable it to repay the loan within the agreed period. Neither writes off defaulted loans.

Foreign Assistance. Like other developing countries, Pakistan has over the decades received substantial amounts in concessional loans from foreign countries and IFIs. Of the total foreign debt of $38 billion in the year 2000, bilateral debt was $12 billion and the bulk of the rest was owed to World Bank, Asian Development Bank, Islamic

Development Bank and the International Monetary Fund. Development banks usually provide long-term loans for infrastructure projects at interest rates that are lower than the market rate. A significant part of the loans are interest-free and repayable over up to forty years. In the decade of the 1990s, Pakistan resorted to borrowing from commercial banks, supplier-credit and foreign currency bonds at usurious rates. Most of such high-interest debt was retired by 2004.

Pakistan's dependence on foreign loans has declined as a result of increased earnings through exports and remittances by Pakistanis abroad (amounting to $14 billion and $4 billion respectively in 2005), and increased inflow of foreign private investment and higher domestic revenues. Meanwhile, the end of multiple sanctions and resumption of bilateral assistance have facilitated inflows while debt rescheduling has reduced the annual debt-servicing burden from over $5 billion to less that $3 billion. With the country out of the debt-trap, the government no longer resorts to borrowing at high interest rates.

Globalisation. Globalisation, resulting from the gathering momentum of mass media, instant radio and video communications, horizontal spread of multinational corporations, expansion in international trade in goods and services and ease of movement of people across international borders has knitted the world together and made humanity more interdependent than ever before.

As the Millennium Declaration of the UN General Assembly noted in September 2000, 'While globalisation offers great opportunities, at present its benefits are very unevenly shared, while its costs are unevenly distributed.' Developing countries particularly faced special difficulties in responding to this central challenge. The Declaration therefore called for broad and sustained efforts to create a shared future for humanity through international cooperation for development and poverty eradication, protection of the environment, promotion of human rights, and strengthening the United Nations. Included among measures to be taken in order to realise the objectives were commitment to good governance within each country, and at the international level, transparency in financial, monetary and trading systems, enhanced programmes of debt relief, and more generous development assistance.

International trade, aid and capital for investment and negotiations for an orderly legal framework for enhancing their smooth flows have become an increasingly important part of international diplomacy since the mid-twentieth century. So also servicing the expatriate communities in foreign countries. Of course, public diplomacy to inform and influence opinion abroad has been an expanding field.

Corruption. IFIs and the United Nations have recognised corruption as a major obstacle to economic development. In 2004, the UN General Assembly adopted an international convention on cooperation to eliminate corruption. When it comes into force, after the requisite number of states have ratified it, the parties will be required to assist one another in the prosecution of persons charged with crimes of corruption, seizing their assets and returning illicit funds to their countries. Countries that have historically attracted deposits into secret accounts are expected to reform banking laws. Meanwhile, the process of recovering illicit funds remains subject to numerous obstacles including denial of access to information, expensive litigation and interminable delays in court proceedings.

WTO. International trade, increasing 12-fold between 1948 and 1995, has contributed significantly to faster economic growth across the globe. The World Trade Organisation plays an increasingly important role in the promotion of fair and free trade based on binding rules, ensuring transparency and predictability, liberalisation and reduction in tariffs on industrial products, and the smooth implementation of existing agreements on trade in agricultural products, textiles and clothing, services and intellectual property, and settlements of disputes.

Expiry of the Multi-Fabric Agreement and reversion of international trade in textiles and garments to normal General Agreement on Tariffs and Trade (GATT) rules from 1 January 2005, was of special importance to Pakistan, as this category accounts for some 60 per cent of its exports. Open international competition was expected to present Pakistan and other major exporters of textile products with an opportunity as well as a challenge.

Two principles that govern all trade-related agreements are 'most-favoured-nation' and 'national treatment'. Both proscribe discrimination, the former in the rate of customs duty and the latter between national and foreign persons. Members of a group may, however, agree to special rates and rules governing intra-group trade.

The latest round of trade negotiations that began in 2001 covers the Doha Development Agenda, focusing on concerns regarding the implementation of existing agreements, especially relating to agriculture and textiles, technical barriers, and improvement of dispute settlement mechanisms, etc. With the industrialised countries continuing to provide massive support for domestic agriculture, estimated at $400 billion a year, and to build new barriers, developing countries desire the phasing out of market-distorting price support and export subsidies, and improvement in market access for their goods. Central to the strategy for promoting a level playing field is a fair regime for trade in agricultural products and elimination of non-tariff measures such as import quotas, domestic support, and especially any subsidies on the export of agricultural products.

Regional Cooperation. Pakistan has also been engaged in efforts to develop regional cooperation with countries to its west and, more recently, in the South Asian region. ECO and SAARC are expected to become significant new components in the acceleration of development, although cooperation among developing countries is inherently problematic because their product range is limited and their exports are often more competitive than complementary. ECDC and TCDC— economic and technical cooperation among developing countries— have so far proved to be of limited value. Even in the ASEAN region intra-trade remained a small fraction of their global exports[8] until economic development led to a broadening and sophistication of products that opened up possibilities for profitable exchange.

SAARC—South Asian Association for Regional Cooperation

The idea of cooperation among the South Asian countries was late to be conceived and has been slow and faltering in evolution. Impulses toward cooperation in South Asia have been historically weak, primarily because of political discord and the existence of bitter disputes among the states of the region. Neither a common threat perception, such as that which actuated states of Western Europe to abandon old patterns of conflicts, nor the shared vision of security through cooperation that motivated countries of South-East Asia, has existed in South Asia. Fears founded in the political experiences of the peoples of the region are compounded by asymmetries of resources. India, the largest and the most industrialised country in the region, accounts for nearly three-quarters of its economic production and trade. Conscious efforts have therefore to be made to ensure mutual and balanced exchange of costs and benefits.

In 1980, Bangladesh formally proposed that South Asian states begin negotiations for forming a regional forum of cooperation. Actively supported by Nepal and Sri Lanka, the idea was greeted with reservation by Pakistan. Islamabad was apprehensive lest the forum be used by India to realise its dream of hegemony over the region. Surprisingly, India, too, appeared unenthusiastic. Its spokesmen apprehended the danger that the neighbours might 'gang up' against India. Actually, New Delhi was quite pleased about opportunities for expansion of its exports of industrial products to the markets of the neighbouring countries, but decided to assume a calculated posture of reluctance[9] in order to undercut the argument that India would be the principal beneficiary of the proposal. In the end, Pakistan decided to defer to the preference of friendly countries in order both to avoid offence to proponents and to mould the proposal so as to preclude damage.

The first meeting of the foreign secretaries of the South Asian countries, held in Colombo in April 1981, endorsed the view that regional cooperation in South Asia was 'beneficial, desirable and necessary.' They also 'noted the need to proceed step by step, on the basis of careful and adequate preparations.' It was agreed that decisions should be taken on the basis of unanimity. At India's suggestion it was further agreed that bilateral and contentious issues should be excluded from the scope of the regional forum.[10]

Lengthy preparatory work went into the identification of areas for fruitful cooperation. The list was progressively expanded to encompass agriculture, rural development, telecommunications, meteorology, health and population activities, science and technology, education and tourism etc. Significantly, cooperation in trade and industry was relegated in early years. Some of the countries of the region wanted to gain experience, and in particular, to study the implications of cooperation in trade so that their economies would not be swamped.

After four years of intensive preparation, the South Asian Association for Regional Cooperation was formally launched at a summit meeting at Dhaka in December 1985. The SAARC charter defined its aims of accelerating economic growth, social progress and cultural development in the member states and strengthening collaboration in international fora on matters of common interest. It also elaborated on the principles and the organisational structure of the association and the mandates of its various committees.

Although trade is by definition mutually beneficial, intra-regional trade was not included in the scope of the association until 1993.

Experience in other regions testified to the fact that trade cannot prosper if relations between countries are abnormal. Tensions obstructed trade between the western and socialist countries during the Cold War. Trade between Arab countries and Israel remained abnormal for decades due to the Palestine question. The USA has used trade as a foreign policy lever against China, Cuba, Iran, Libya, Sudan and Syria.

Besides, the trade policies of the countries of South Asia were at odds. India, the biggest exporter in intra-regional trade, followed a restrictive import policy. Its long-time emphasis on autarchic development, or self-sufficiency, excluded the import of consumer goods generally. This policy denied access to the Indian market for the primary manufactures produced by the other countries of the region. On the other hand, with its wide range of products, India sought to penetrate the markets of neighbouring countries. As a result, trade with India evinced the colonial characteristics of exchange between raw materials and manufactured goods. Consequently, trade relations among countries of South Asia have not been significant historically, averaging less than 3 per cent of their global trade.[11]

Pakistan spent a million dollars in 1981 on participation in the Indian trade fair in New Delhi. The pavilion exhibiting almost the entire range of Pakistani products attracted record crowds of curious visitors. Export sales were, however, a big zero.

It was evident that implementation of a programme for economic cooperation in South Asia was 'fraught with very grave and daunting difficulties.'[12] Not until 1993 did leaders agree to include trade in the ambit of SAARC. An embryonic system of preferences was instituted after the members agreed to establish the South Asian Preferential Trading Area (SAPTA), envisaging reciprocal exchange of concessions in customs duties. However, it achieved little progress in substance. In 1997, the SAARC leaders evaluated the results of regional cooperation as disappointingly meager.

SAFTA. At the SAARC summit in January 2004, members decided to establish the South Asian Free Trade Area (SAFTA) through exchanging concessions. The framework envisaged a graduated programme for the promotion of trade and economic cooperation through exchanging concessions, with the Least Developed Countries (LDCs)—Bangladesh, Bhutan and Maldives—to be allowed a longer period for the realisation of the objective. Starting from 1 January 2006, members would begin reducing tariffs. Non-LDCs would bring down the rate to 20 per cent in two years and LDCs to 30 per cent. They would further reduce tariffs to between 0-5 per cent, non-LDCs in five years, i.e. by 1 January 2013, and LDCs in eight years, i.e. by 1 January 2016. The agreement provided for each country to maintain a sensitive list of goods for which tariff reductions would be subject to negotiations.

The agreement on SAFTA provided a practical framework with differentiated timetables for free trade. It recognised that trade liberalisation has to be achieved in a manner beneficial to all members. Still it remains to be seen whether it can be implemented smoothly. Unless SAARC can assimilate the experience of other regional cooperation groups, and adopt measures to level the playing field and safeguards to protect, assist and subsidise states that might face problems owing to their unequal stages of development, its progress will remain slow. Assimilation of lessons in other regions would facilitate a realistic solution.

To enable less developed countries to adjust to integration, the European Union developed well-considered safeguards to preclude shocks to their economies. Subsidies were agreed for agriculture and particular care was taken to shield, assist and strengthen states with vulnerable economies. Greece, Portugal and Spain, for instance, were allowed sufficient lead time during which they enjoyed unilateral duty-free access to the markets of the more advanced countries. Similarly, aid has been pledged to countries of Eastern Europe admitted to the EU in 2004, taking into account their dependence on customs duties for revenues to finance budgetary expenditures for the transitional period.

ECO—Economic Cooperation Organization

The difficulties of promoting economic cooperation among developing countries have been illustrated in the excruciatingly slow progress of the Economic Cooperation Organization. Originally established by Iran, Pakistan and Turkey in 1964 as Regional Cooperation for Development (RCD), it was renamed ECO in 1985 and expanded to include Afghanistan and six Central Asian republics (CARs)— Azerbaijan, Kazakhstan, Kyrgyz Republic, Tajikistan, Turkmenistan and Uzbekistan. The ten nations share bonds of history and culture, and ECO meetings are distinguished by fraternal cordiality and a unanimous desire for economic integration through the progressive removal of trade barriers and development of infrastructure for intra-regional trade. The seven new members are particularly keen for development of communications and transport links giving them access to the sea.

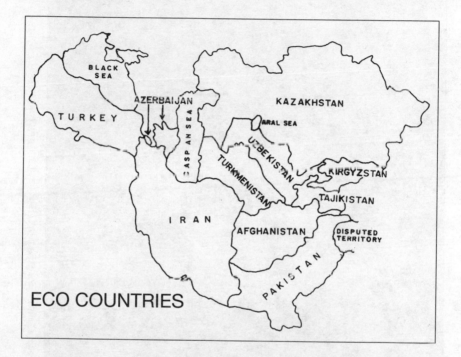

ECO COUNTRIES

The first summit meeting of the expanded ECO, held in Tehran in February 1992, endorsed the goal of 'ultimate elimination of all tariffs and non-tariff barriers' among the members, and underlined the importance of the development of cooperation in transport and communications, energy, industry and agriculture. Progress towards the agreed goal has been slow mainly due to lack of investment capital.

Earlier decisions placed a high priority on communications, transport, oil and regional linkages in energy and minerals. In February 1993, the Quetta Plan of Action elaborated proposals for enlarged cooperation. Agreements on transit trade and visa simplification were signed at the Islamabad summit in March 1995.

The first major step towards integration was the launching of the ECO Trade Agreement in 2003. Upon its entry into force, requiring ratification by five members, the highest tariff rates will be reduced from 15 to 10 per cent in five years.[13] In 2002, intra-regional trade

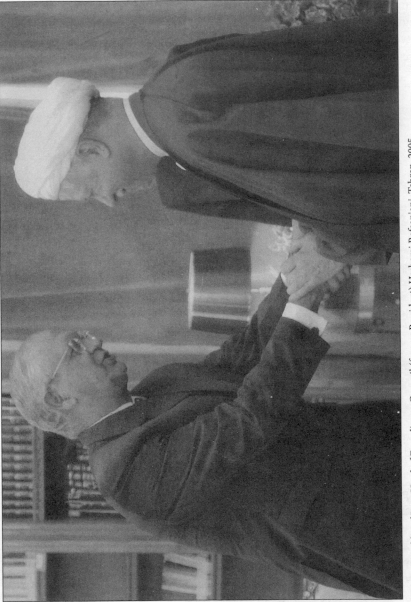

Islamic Republic of Iran. Head of Expediency Council (former President) Hashemi Rafsanjani, Tehran, 2005.

amounted to $11 billion, or 5.6 per cent of their global trade, and comprised mainly of petroleum products.

With sizeable natural and human resources, the region has a promising potential. Turkey, benefiting from commitment to modernisation and market access to Europe, has achieved rapid progress in industry. Iran, too, is self-reliant, and has made productive use of its large oil revenues for economic development. Kazakhstan has begun to receive enough revenue from oil exports to become a middle-income country. Azerbaijan, a traditional oil exporter, and Turkmenistan, with vast reserves of natural gas, should also achieve better living standards.

Turkey, with a GDP of $173 billion, has the biggest economy in the ECO region and the highest per capita income of $2,520. Iran stands next with a GDP of $113 billion, and a per capita annual income of $1,720. Pakistan's GDP of $95 billion comes next in size of the economy but its per capita income is lower than that of Kazakhstan and Azerbaijan. Afghanistan, Uzbekistan, Kyrgyztan and Tajikistan are even poorer.[14]

The Central Asian Republics (CARs) have good communication and transport links to the north. Also, China has connected its rail system with the Central Asian network. Iran completed the Meshad–Sarakhs–Tagen rail link with the Central Asian railway network via Turkmenistan to Uzbekistan and Kyrgyztan to Kazakhstan, providing access for the Central Asian republics to international trade via Bandar Abbas on the Persian Gulf, and the establishment of a Trans Asian Railway main line from Almaty to Istanbul for passenger and freight traffic via Syria and Turkey to Europe.

Meanwhile, the plan to connect the Iranian and Pakistan railways, first agreed under the RCD, remains on paper. Iran has not built the Kerman–Zahidan link nor has Pakistan improved the track from Quetta. As a result, Pakistan remains unconnected to Central Asia and Europe. For the benefit of through trade to Central Asia and Europe, Pakistan would also need to develop rolling stock to facilitate transfer of wagons off wheels for the direct transport of goods and passengers without unloading.

Potentially, the shortest and most economical route to and from Central Asia is via Afghanistan and Pakistan, but the requisite resources are not in sight for the construction of roads from Gwadar to the north, not to mention the construction of railways in Afghanistan. Also, the economy of the Karakorum Highway for trade access for the CARs to Pakistani ports is highly problematic. Passing through high mountains, transport via this route would incur heavy freight costs. In the short term, progress on the Torkham–Jalalabad, Kabul–Mazar-i-Sharif and Kandahar–Spin Baldak roads will relieve the problem.

Financially, the most feasible projects for early implementation are gas pipelines. An Iran–Pakistan–India pipeline is under active consideration since Pakistan decided in December 1999 to allow transit. Also, the proposal for the construction of a gas pipeline from Turkmenistan to the south, conceived in 1996, was reactivated after the end of the civil war in Afghanistan. Investment capital is shy however, and revival of the project is dependent on assessments of political stability in the region. When the projects are implemented, the transit countries will earn substantial transit fees.

In addition to global efforts to eliminate restrictive trade practices and reform structural inequities in the global system, groups of states have established regional cooperation to promote trade and economic cooperation. A favourable global and regional environment is an important factor in accelerating economic progress, though there is no substitute for appropriate national policies, which explains the rapid economic growth in states like China, South Korea, Malaysia, Thailand and India in recent decades. Increased investment in the development of natural and human resources, expansion of manufacturing industries for production of quality goods at competitive prices and ballooning exports, especially to the industrialised countries of North America and Europe, have been key components of their success. Pakistan, too, has embarked on the assimilation of proven growth strategies; in 2005, it achieved a record 8.3 per cent growth.

NOTES

1. UN Report on Social Development, 2005, The InterPress News Service Summary, *Dawn*, Islamabad, 11 September 2005.
2. An estimated 800,000 people of the minority Tutsi and moderate Hutu tribes were massacred.
3. Tens of thousands of Bosnian Muslims were liquidated. A Serb militia segregated 8,000 Muslim men and boys in Sreberenica and massacred them in cold blood.
4. UN General Assembly document dated 29 September 2004, p. 2.
5. Report to the Security Council, 21 March 2005.
6. Article 27.3 of the UN Charter.
7. Hudood laws relate to crimes of extra-marital sex and consumption of alcohol by Muslims.

8. Intra-ASEAN trade was estimated to amount to a quarter of their global trade. This figure includes, however, intra-regional re-exports (from Singapore) and petroleum, each about 10 per cent.

9. Years afterwards, an Indian foreign secretary told the author that New Delhi had assumed the posture of calculated reluctance mainly to undercut Pakistan's (correct) assumption of Indian enthusiasm.

10. *From SARC to SAARC*, Vol. 1, SAARC Senatorial, Kathmandu, p. 9.

11. Dr Ashfaque H. Khan, 'Trade and Regional Economic Cooperation', *The News*, 13 April 1998.

12. Vernon L. B. Mendis, *SAARC—Origins, Organization & Prospects*, p. 124.

13. These improved targets were agreed at the Dushanbe summit in September 2004. The 2003 agreement provided for reducing tariffs to 15 per cent in eight years.

14. GDP—Turkey $173b (Per capita income $2,490), Iran $ 113b ($1720), Pakistan $95b ($635), Kazakhstan $23b ($1,520), Uzbekistan $8b ($310), Kyrgyztan $1.4 ($290), Afghanistan $5-6b ($200).

CHAPTER 23

Policy in a Changing World

Sabaat ek taghayyur ko hai zamaney mein.[1]
Allama Iqbal

As a means to an end, a state's foreign policy adapts, as it must, to the flux in world affairs in order to safeguard independence and integrity, protect the right of the nation to live in peace and security, promote the legitimate aspirations of its people to economic and social progress, and attain a position of dignity and honour in the comity of nations. Past evolutions in Pakistan's foreign policy reflected adjustments to the imperatives of the changing global and regional environment. The process can be expected to continue as the world power structure changes and nations rethink their priorities.

Pakistan emerged as an independent state two years after the founding of the United Nations, in an era full of hope of durable international peace and security based on principles of justice and international law, respect for human rights, and international cooperation for economic development and social progress. As the age of colonialism drew to a close, fifty-three new States emerged by 1960 and another fifty-six by 1990. A palpable exuberance was in the air as the emergent nations sought to build a new international order.

The post-war optimism fell victim to the realities of the Cold War and the contest for power and conflict of ideologies between the two most powerful states of the time. The Soviet Union, successor to czarist Russia, historically a victim of invasions from the west, sought security by perpetuating its hold over East European countries. The United States led the policy of containment of communism because of the challenge it posed to the existing international order by its aggressive promotion of revolution and overthrow of non-communist governments.

The Cold War triggered the formation of opposing alliances, each trying to contain the other. Although few of the emergent nations were inclined to take sides, they did not escape its consequences. The world was polarised and focus shifted away from their agenda of consolidation of independence, acceleration of economic and social progress, and support for struggles against colonialism and imperialism.

The high hopes of the emergent nations were disappointed by the realities of a divided world. Freedom struggles were distorted. As the UN Security Council became paralysed by the abuse of the veto by the USA and the USSR, the UN was rendered ineffective in settling disputes and promoting peace; the Palestinian and Kashmir issues festered; Algeria and Vietnam suffered protracted agony; proxy wars were fought in Southern Africa; Afghanistan was destroyed by Soviet intervention.

Most developing countries were wracked by the difficulties of the struggle for economic, social and political progress on account partly of the inequitable economic and political international order, and in many cases, failure to build domestic consensus and establish good governance.

'End of History'

The sudden and spectacular, if totally unforeseen, collapse of the Soviet system brought the ideological contest that dominated the twentieth century to a conclusion in 1991, triggering a strategic transformation in world affairs. The communist–totalitarian system was discredited, liberal democracy emerged as 'the end point of mankind's ideological evolution... (and) the final form of human government.'[2] The economic collapse of the Soviet Union hastened the triumph of the free market as the best economic system for producing material prosperity.

Seminal in scope, the transformation reverberated worldwide. Tensions abated as the fear of an Armageddon and Doomsday apocalypse was relieved. Fifteen nations formerly under Soviet rule recovered sovereignty. Germany was reunited. Proxy wars ended in Afghanistan, Southern Africa and Central America. Protagonists of apartheid reversed policy and South Africa emerged as a new leader on the continent.

With the lapse of confrontation, USA and Russia agreed on further reduction of their strategic arsenals. The UN General Assembly approved the CTBT. Expecting sharp reductions in military budgets, the developing world hoped that affluent countries would set aside a part of the 'peace dividend' for the alleviation of poverty.

It seemed that the UN Security Council could now fulfil its envisioned role of safeguarding international peace and security.

Prospects brightened for harmony and cooperation among major powers, with each playing a role in international affairs in proportion to its economic and military power.

The New Power Structure

The United States, with a GDP of 11 trillion dollars—one-quarter of the world total—and unrivalled capacity to project power globally, became the 'sole superpower' with an unprecedented opportunity to influence the world community's response to the old and new challenges to international peace and progress.

The European Union, comparable to the United States in global trade, and with Germany, UK, France, Italy and Spain among the top ten states with the largest economies as its members, is potentially another economic colossus. Sharing strong ties of history and civilisation across the Atlantic, the EU is a strategic partner of the United States, with convergent international policies. The 15-member bloc decided in 2004 to admit ten new states from Eastern Europe. It also agreed to strengthen coordination for a common foreign policy and enhance the role of the European parliament.

Japan, with a GDP of 4.5 trillion dollars, remains at second place among states by size of economy. A part of the West by virtue of its economic and political system, it maintains close security links with the United States, and remembering the disastrous consequences of competing for dominance in the Pacific in the 1930s, consciously avoids a high profile foreign policy.

China, ranking sixth at present, is on the way to taking third place in the world hierarchy by GDP, thanks to political stability, development of human resources and sagacious demographic and economic policies. Committed to priority for economic development, it pursues a foreign policy of peaceful coexistence. While eschewing rivalry with other powers, it has opposed hegemony in international affairs. A sought-after partner in trade and investment, it has broken out of the ring of containment that its erstwhile adversaries sought to erect in the past. In 2000, Colin Powell said China was 'not a strategic partner' but 'a competitor and potential regional rival.' [4] However, in 2004, he acknowledged that the Chinese leadership had been 'very helpful' in working with the US to resolve multilateral disputes.'[5] Still, the containment lobby in the United States has advocated policies aimed at the build up of rivals to check China's rising power.

The Russian Federation, the largest state by territory and a superpower with the second largest arsenal of strategic weapons, and producer and exporter of modern military equipment, is at sixteenth place in the world by economic size, below Canada, Mexico, South Korea, India, Brazil, the Netherlands, and Australia. Several developing countries have succeeded in raising per capita annual income to above $2,000; they include Brazil, Chile, Malaysia, Mexico and Thailand. Most Third World countries remain trapped in low income and low growth. Extreme poverty blights many countries in Africa and Asia.

India's rise in economic, technological and military power has added to its international importance and influence. By 2005 it was twelfth in the world hierarchy by GDP, with the potential of rising higher. With a per capita income of $500, it has achieved considerable reduction in the proportion of population living below the poverty line. Retaining its traditional cooperative relations with Russia, India has also pursued a policy of normalisation of relations with China. India's relations with the United States have continued to improve since the 1980s. In the strategic dialogue in the 1990s, the two sides discussed cooperation for security of the sea-lanes for oil tankers from the Gulf. After 9/11, India underlined a commonality of interests with the West in opposing 'Islamic fundamentalism.' In March 2005, senior American officials said the US would 'help India become a major world power in the twenty-first century.' An analyst saw the rationale of this policy in 'preserving a stable balance of power in Asia through the presence of strong states on China's periphery.'[6] In July 2005, President Bush reversed sanctions on the export of civilian nuclear technology and sophisticated weapons to India.

Setbacks to an Emergent Era of Peace

The prospects of an emergent era of peace and harmony suffered several setbacks in quick succession. Dissolution of the Soviet Union lifted the lid on unresolved ethnic tensions: Armenia occupied the enclave of Ngorno–Karabach in Azerbaijan; Georgia was convulsed with separatism; Particularly sanguin was the suppression of Chechnya's demand for autonomy.

Humanitarian Emergencies. The eruption of ethnic tension and strife in former Yugoslavia in the early 1990s culminated in a savage 'ethnic cleansing' by the Serbs. Finally, the United States intervened to bring an end to the travails of the Muslim people of Bosnia and Kosovo. The UN Security Council proved powerless to enforce its resolutions. It suffered further loss of prestige because of its failure to take timely action to prevent the genocide of a million ethnic Tutsis in Rwanda.

Palestine. For a time the Palestinian–Israeli conflict seemed to be moving towards a solution. The Palestinian Liberation Organization (PLO) recognised Israel's right to exist in 1988. In 1993, President Bill Clinton mediated a successful meeting between President Yasser Arafat and Prime Minister Yitzhak Rabin in Washington, laying the foundation for the Israeli–Palestinian peace accords and the Oslo Declaration of Principles on Interim Self-Government Arrangements. Rabin, Arafat and Foreign Minister Shimon Perez were awarded the Nobel Peace Prize and Arafat returned to Palestine in 1994. Clinton convened another summit in December 2000 at Camp David to promote agreement on the final status of Jerusalem but Ehud Barak obstructed a compromise.

Barak's successor, Ariel Sharon, a right-wing leader who 'shared responsibility for the Sabra and Shatila (Palestinian refugee camps) massacres' in the early 1970s, and had sabotaged negotiations with the PLO by his provocative visit to the al-Aqsa Mosque, re-embarked on Israel's old policies of expansion and ethnic cleansing by systematic violence and terror.[7] The Israeli army's re-entry into Palestinian towns, suicide attacks by desperate Palestinians and massive Israeli retaliation, confining Arafat to his small compound in Ramallah in 2001, halted the political process. In 2003, the EU, UN, Russia and USA worked out a 'roadmap' aiming to restore the peace process but, despite agreeing to the outline, Israel violated its basic provisions and started to build a 'security fence' on Palestinian land. Following Israeli cut off of talks with Yasser Arafat, the US called him an 'obstacle' to peace.

Following Arafat's death in November 2004, President Bush agreed to recommence efforts for a settlement hoping to see an independent Palestinian state before the end of his second term. Israel also signalled readiness to resume peace negotiations. In February 2005, Ariel Sharon and Mahmud Abbas agreed on a ceasefire, and Sharon announced a decision to dismantle Jewish settlements in Gaza and release 500 of some 8,000 Palestinians from Israeli jails. These commitments were later implemented.

War on Iraq

The US–led war on Iraq launched on 20 March 2003 marked a black day in the history of the United Nations. For the first time since the end of the Cold War, a superpower, founder of the United Nations and a permanent member of the Security Council, resorted to use of force not only without authorisation by the Security Council, but in defiance of its manifest opposition. The main question before the Security Council was whether Iraq was in breach of Resolution 1441 of November 2002, which warned of serious consequences if it did not cooperate with the UN Monitoring, Verification and Inspection Commission charged with the task of ascertaining elimination of weapons of mass destruction. All members agreed Iraq must comply and a majority were of the view the UN Commission should be given the time it needed to confirm compliance. Hans Blix, the chief UN inspector, expressed confidence that given time the commission could complete the mission. However, the United States argued that Iraq was obstructing inspections and continued to defy the ban on its WMD programme.

In February 2003, US Secretary of State Colin Powell presented intelligence reports and documents as evidence before the Security Council purporting to prove Iraqi possession of prohibited weapons. The US further argued that authorisation for the use of force already existed in Resolution 1441 and no new resolution was needed. Most other members disagreed. Even the UK, a declared US ally, differed with the US view, and persuaded the US to move a resolution to seek Security Council authorisation for use of force. A draft resolution was then floated giving Iraq two days to prove it no longer possessed any of the banned weapons, implicitly conceding that Resolution 1441 did not provide the requisite authorisation. When the Security Council was found disinclined to approve the ultimatum, the US did not formally introduce the resolution; instead, it decided to act unilaterally and go ahead with the preconceived plan of war.

Approaches of major powers. Although a majority of the permanent members of the Security Council were opposed to the war on Iraq, none adopted a posture of confrontation. France, China and Russia exercised restraint in their criticism. Other major powers likewise sought to limit, if not prevent, damage to their bilateral relations. Germany spoke in sorrow more than anger. '[A] world order cannot function when the national interests of the most powerful nation are the defining criteria for the deployment of that nation's military might.'[8] The United States, unaccustomed to criticism, at first reacted with anger, but soon embarked on damage-limitation and reconciliation, obviously keen to preserve traditionally friendly relations with former allies.

The Roles of Medium and Small States. The non-permanent members, too, evinced a mature recognition of the power realities. Realising that responsibilities for restraining one major power lay primarily with other major powers that possessed the material means for influence, they played restrained roles, exercising extraordinary care to avoid unnecessary offence to the United States or the United Kingdom. Pakistan and Chile were under pressure to support the US–UK resolution giving a two-day ultimatum to Iraq preparatory to the war, but resolutely, if quietly, maintained their positions based on respect for principles of international law. Few of the Third World states supported the war on Iraq but, at the same time, all exercised restraint in comments, evidently realising the limits of their influence, individually as well as collectively.

Particularly indefensible was the conduct of the Iraqi president. Saddam Hussein courted disaster by pursuing policies that isolated him and his country in the community of nations. Despotic rule and crimes against his own people made him a detested ruler. His war on Iran in the 1980s resulted in a heavy toll of life and colossal loss of assets, also for Iraq. Use of chemical weapons against Iraqi Kurds earned him abiding international obloquy. Aggression against Kuwait outraged the entire world, and provoked the first US intervention. Delay in compliance with the Security Council demand for elimination of weapons generated an impression of defiance. Iraq was totally isolated. Not a single state spoke to defend the Iraqi government.

Apart from joining the majority of other members of the Security Council in taking a position of principle, Pakistan did not agree even to post-war requests to send troops to Iraq and deferred consideration of the question of whether it should participate in a UN peacekeeping force until after a decision by the Security Council.

World's Concern at Setbacks. While the United Nations had increasingly come to mirror the frailties and foibles of its members, the world community was shocked by the setbacks to humanity's hopes to outlaw war and civilise the use of force. Decent opinion was outraged by the conduct of the United States. Less powerful states were particularly concerned about US statements claiming the right to resort to 'preemptive war.' The threat of forcible 'regime change' prompted premonitions of primeval insecurity and neo-imperialism.

Massive anti-war protest demonstrations erupted in major cities in the United States and Europe. New York witnessed a five-kilometer long march with protesters chanting 'No Blood for Oil',[9] Nobel laureates advertised their protest, and celebrities ridiculed President Bush at the Academy Awards function in Hollywood.[10] A large majority of the people even in countries that joined the US in the war on Iraq, especially UK, Spain[11] and Italy, opposed the decision of their governments. The Pope voiced distress.

A Better Future

The setbacks to the emerging international order disappointed humanity but are unlikely to reverse the march of civilisation. Idealism has moved human hearts throughout history. The Hobbesian 'state of nature' with brute force as the arbiter of relations between people runs against human nature. Humanity yearns for a society based on law and justice. The progress of civilisation is measured by the extent to which might has been supplanted by right. Laws and norms have been developed by human communities to regulate hierarchies and provide for impartial determination of disputes. At the level of states the trend is intermittent but clear over the millennia.

The United Nations Charter embodies humanity's aspiration for civilising inter-state relations to save the world from the scourge of war, maintain international peace and security, and promote settlement of disputes by peaceful means in conformity with the principles of justice and international law.

Over the decades the UN has served to advance its purposes. Where its successes have fallen short of expectations, the causes are to be found in the lack of political will on part of the sovereign members of the organisation. Especially on issues involving international peace and security, the United Nations is dependent on agreement among permanent members of the Security Council. Militarily powerful states are the pillars of the international system and their cooperation is a prerequisite for further progress towards an international order based on law.

Persuading sovereign states to accept the supremacy of law has been historically a difficult and slow process. But the world community is irrevocably committed to peace and the rule of law. The process is accelerating. Globalisation is knitting humanity together and building up popular pressure on governments to join in building a just international order. People stage massive demonstrations against war, against international financial institutions for their perceived failure to relieve poverty-stricken nations of heavy debt, and against the WTO for the existing trade order that protects big farmers and corporations in rich countries at the expense of the poor. States that indulge in aberrant behaviour and wilful defiance of law and equity pay a price in international prestige, as do their leaders. People are a growing force for peace and justice.

New directions and dynamism in foreign policy in recent years have helped pull Pakistan out of isolation into the international mainstream. Pakistan is a participant in efforts to propel the world towards a future better than the past. It is making a significant contribution to UN peace-keeping operations and has played an active part in the reform of the United Nations in order to promote international peace and progress. While continuing to consolidate existing friendships and develop cooperative relations with the rest of the world, the state has also reduced tensions in the region and expanded cooperation with countries near its western and eastern borders. Tension has abated in Pakistan's relations with India and prospects for SAARC are more promising. After a quarter century, Afghanistan is on its way to peace and reconstruction that will enable it to assume its key role as a bridge among the fraternal states of the ECO region.

At home, too, improvements are writ large on every facet of national life. Provident fiscal management and efficacious development strategy combined with improved implementation and containment of corruption have pulled Pakistan back from the brink of bankruptcy. The country has extricated itself from the debt trap into which poor governance, corruption, and irresponsible international and domestic borrowing had pushed the nation in the 1990s. The external debt that had doubled in that decade has since been stabilised and even reduced. Exports and remittance receipts have nearly doubled and dependence on foreign aid has been substantially reduced. Hopefully, the past alternation between demagogic politics and military interventions may also become a thing of the past though breaking the feudal hold and the nexus between money and elections, assimilating a democratic and pluralist culture and building good governance are bound to require great effort.

Trapped in the 1990s in trends towards religious extremism and sectarian violence, Pakistan has successfully reversed direction and reverted to the founding fathers' vision of a moderate, liberal and progressive Islamic polity committed to reform and modernisation of political and social thought. The scientific method, as Muslim philosophers pointed out centuries earlier...,[12] is the only sure way for extension and deepening of human knowledge. Allama Iqbal, recognising the need for reconstruction of religious thought in view of the altered conditions of modern life, recommended resort to *Ijtihad* through *Ijma* or assembly of elected representatives for review of the legal systems compiled by the classical scholars.[13]

Quaid-i-Azam Mohammad Ali Jinnah set an inspiring example of intellectual dynamism and integrity and commitment to the service of the people. The principles he enunciated remain of enduring value for the nation to realise its aspiration to a productive, fulfilling and respectable place in the world community.

NOTES

1. 'Nothing endures but change.' Heraclitus.
2. Fukuyama, Francis, *The End of History And the Last Man*, pp. xi–xiii.
3. According to figures for 2003, USA with GDP of $10,946 billion, nearly one quarter of the world total, was in first place, followed by Japan ($4,390 b), Germany ($2,085 b), UK ($1,680 b), France ($1,523 b), China, ($1,417 b) and Italy ($1,243 b). With its higher growth rate, China is projected to overtake Germany and the UK. World Bank, *A Better Investment Climate for Everyone*.
4. Statement by Secretary of State-designate, Colin L. Powell, Senate Foreign Relations Committee, 17 January 2001.
5. *Dawn*, Islamabad, 14 November 2004.
6. Background briefing by senior US officials, 25 March 2005. Carnegie Endowment *Policy Brief*, by Ashley Tellis, May 2005.
7. Ken Livingstone, Mayor of London. *The Guardian News Service,Dawn*, Islamabad, 5 March 2005.
8. German Foreign Minister Joshca Fischer said, 'US power is a decisive factor for world peace and security. But a world order cannot function when the national interests of the most powerful nation are the defining criteria for the deployment of that nation's military might. There must be the same rules for the big, the middle-sized and the small countries.' Interview published in *Der Spiegel* of 24 March 2003, as reported by AFP and carried by *Dawn*, Islamabad, of the same date.
9. *Dawn*, Islamabad, 24 March 2003.
10. BBC radio report heard in Islamabad at 0800 A.M., 24 March 2003.
11. Polls found 91 per cent of Spaniards opposed to the war.
12. With the discontinuation of prophecy and revelation, humankind was thrown on its own resources for addition to existing reservoir of knowledge, and that was possible only through observation, experiment and induction. For scholarly discussion of the point see Allama Mohammad Iqbal, *The Reconstruction of Religious Thought in Islam*, Sang-e-Meel Publications, Lahore, pp. 114–119.
13. Ibid., pp. 150–153.

Appendix I: The Shimla Agreement, 1972

The Government of India and the Government of Pakistan are resolved that the two countries put an end to the conflict and confrontation that have hitherto marred their relations and work for the promotion of a friendly and harmonious relationship and the establishment of durable peace in the sub-continent, so that both countries may henceforth devote their resources and energies to the pressing task of advancing the welfare of their peoples.

In order to achieve this objective, the Government of India and the Government of Pakistan have agreed as follows:

(i) That the principles and purposes of the Charter of the United Nations shall govern the relations between the two countries.

(ii) That the two countries are resolved to settle their differences by peaceful means through bilateral negotiations or by any other peaceful means mutually agreed upon between them. Pending the final settlement of any of the problems between the two countries, neither side shall unilaterally alter the situation and both shall prevent the organization, assistance or encouragement of any act detrimental to the maintenance of peaceful and harmonious relations.

(iii) That the pre-requisite for reconciliation, good neighbourliness and durable peace between them is a commitment by both the countries to peaceful co-existence, respect for each other's territorial integrity and sovereignty and non-interference in each other's internal affairs, on the basis of equality and mutual benefit.

(iv) That the basic issues and causes of conflict which have bedevilled the relations between the two countries for the last 25 years shall be resolved by peaceful means.

(v) That they shall always respect each other's national unity, territorial integrity, political independence and sovereign equality.

(vi) That in accordance with the Charter of the United Nations, they will refrain from the threat or use of force against the territorial integrity or political independence of each other.

Both the Governments will take all steps within their power to prevent hostile propaganda directed against each other. Both countries will encourage the dissemination of such information as would promote the development of friendly relations between them. In order progressively to restore and normalise relations between the two countries step by step, it was agreed that:

(i) Steps shall be taken to resume communications, postal, telegraphic, sea, land, including border posts, and air links including overflights.

(ii) Appropriate steps shall be taken to promote travel facilities for the nationals of the other country.

(iii) Trade and cooperation in economic and other agreed fields will be resumed as far as possible.

(iv) Exchange in the fields of science and culture will be promoted.
(v)   In this connection delegations from the two countries will meet from time to time to work out the necessary details.

In order to initiate the process of the establishment of durable peace, both the Governments agree that:

(i)   Indian and Pakistani forces shall be withdrawn to their side of the international border.
(ii) In Jammu and Kashmir, the line of control resulting from the ceasefire of December 17, shall be respected by both sides without prejudice to the recognized position of either side. Neither side shall seek to alter it unilaterally, irrespective of mutual differences and legal interpretations. Both sides further undertake to refrain from the threat or use of force in violation of this line.
(iii) The withdrawals shall commence upon entry into force of this agreement and shall be completed within a period of 30 days thereof.

This agreement will be subject to ratification by both countries in accordance with their respective constitutional procedure and will come into force with effect from the date on which the instruments of ratification are exchanged.

Both Governments agree that their respective Heads will meet again at a mutually convenient time in the future and that, in the meanwhile, the representatives of the two sides will meet to discuss further the modalities and arrangements for the establishment of durable peace and normalisation of relations, including the questions of repatriation of prisoners of war and civilian internees, a final settlement of Jammu and Kashmir and the resumption of diplomatic relations.

(Signed) Indira Gandhi   (Signed) Zulfikar Ali Bhutto
Prime Minister, Republic of India   President, Islamic Republic of Pakistan.

FINAL INDIAN DRAFT
(2 July 1972)

Agreement on bilateral relations between the Government of India and the Government of Pakistan

1. The Government of India and the Government of Pakistan are resolved that the two countries put an end to the conflict and confrontation that have hitherto marred their relations and work for the promotion of a friendly and harmonious relationship and the establishment of durable peace in the sub-continent, so that bath countries may henceforth devote their resources and energies to the pressing task of advancing the welfare of their peoples.

In order to achieve this objective, the Government of India and the Government Pakistan have agreed as follows:

(i)   That the principles and purposes of the charter of the United Nations shall govern the relations between the two countries.

(ii) That the two countries are resolved to settle their differences by peaceful means through bilateral negotiations or by any other peaceful means mutually agreed upon between them. Pending the final settlement of any of the problems between the two countries, neither side shall unilaterally alter the situation and both shall prevent organization, assistance or encouragement of any acts detrimental to the maintenance of peaceful and harmonious relations.

That the pre-requisite for reconciliation, good neighbourliness and durable peace between them is a commitment by both the countries to peaceful co-existence, respect for each other's territorial integrity and sovereignty and non-interference in each other's internal affairs, on the basis of equality and mutual benefit.

That the basic issues and causes of conflict which have bedevilled the relations between the two countries for the last 25 years shall be resolved by peaceful means.

That they shall always respect each other's national unity, territorial integrity, political independence and sovereign equality.

That they will refrain from the threat or use of farce against the territorial integrity or political independence of each other:

2. Both Governments will take all steps within their pawed to prevent hostile propaganda directed against each other. Both countries will encourage the dissemination of such information as would promote the development of friendly relations between them.

3. In order progressively to restore and normalise relations between the two countries step by step, it was agreed that:

(i)   Steps shall be taken to resume communications, postal, telegraphic, sea, land, including border pasts, and air links, including over-flights.
(ii) Appropriate steps shall be taken to provide travel facilities to the nationals of the other country.
(iii) Trade and co-operation in academic and other agreed fields will be resumed as far as possible.
(iv) Exchange in the fields of science and culture will be promoted.

In this connection delegations from the two countries will meet from time to time to work out the necessary details.

4. In order to initiate the process of the establishment of durable peace, both the Governments agree that:

Indian and Pakistani forces shall be withdrawn to their side of the international border.

In Jammu and Kashmir, the line of control resulting from the ceasefire of December 17, 1971 shall henceforth be respected by both sides as a Line of Peace. Neither side shall seek to alter it unilaterally, irrespective of mutual differences and legal interpretations. Both sides further undertake to refrain from the threat or the use of force in violation of this Line.

Minor adjustments to the Line of Peace in Jammu and Kashmir or the rest of the international border considered necessary by both sides to make the border more rational and viable may be made by mutual agreement.

A joint body composed of an equal number of representatives, nominated by each Government, shall be appointed to establish ground rules and to supervise the effective observance of the Line of Peace and the rest of the border between the two countries. The withdrawals shall commence upon entry into force of this Agreement in accordance with the ground rules evolved by the above-mentioned joint body and shall be completed within a period of 30 days thereof.

5. This agreement will be subject to ratification by both countries in accordance with their respective constitutional procedures, and will come into force with effect from the date on which the Instruments of Ratification are exchanged.

6. Both Governments agree that their respective Heads will meet again at a mutually convenient time in the future and that, in the meanwhile, the representatives of the two sides will meet to discuss further the modalities and arrangements for the establishment of durable peace and normalization of relations, including the questions of repatriation of prisoners of war and civilian internees, a final settlement of Jammu and Kashmir and the resumption of diplomatic relations.

(Indira Gandhi)	(Zulfikar Ali Bhutto)
Prime Minister Republic of India	President, Islamic Republic of Pakistan

1972 INDIAN DRAFT - I
(29 June 1972)

Draft Treaty for Reconciliation, Good Neighbourliness and Durable Peace between the Republic of India and the Islamic Republic of Pakistan

The Government of India and the Government of Pakistan

DETERMINED to put an end to the conflict and confrontation that have hitherto marred the relations between India and Pakistan and work for the promotion of a friendly and harmonious relationship between the two countries and their peoples with a view to the establishment of durable peace in the sub-continent;

CONVINCED of the undesirability of diverting resources from development to defence, and of the need to devote their resources and energies principally to the pressing task of advancing the welfare of their peoples;

UPHOLDING their firm faith in the principles of peaceful cooperation and co-existence between States, non-interference in each other's internal affairs and respect for sovereignty, national independence and territorial integrity of each other;

DECLARING their firm resolve to restore normal and peaceful relations between their countries and to work jointly and unceasingly for maintaining a climate of reconciliation and understanding between their peoples;

HAVE AGREED as follows:

ARTICLE I

The Government of India and the Government of Pakistan attach supreme importance to maintaining a climate for durable peace and preventing the development of any situation capable of causing exacerbation of their relations.

ARTICLE II
The Government of India and the Government of Pakistan affirm their resolve to respect the independence, sovereignty and territorial integrity of each other and refrain from interfering in each other's internal affairs.

ARTICLE III
The Government of India and the Government of Pakistan regard as totally inadmissible recourse to war for the solution of international problems, and hereby renounce the threat or use of force in their mutual relations. In pursuance of this pledge, they undertake to settle all issues between them bilaterally and exclusively by peaceful means.

ARTICLE IV
The Government of India and the Government of Pakistan shall refrain from organising or encouraging the formation of irregular forces or armed bands, including mercenaries or volunteers howsoever named, for incursion into the territory of the other'

ARTICLE V
In order to concentrate their energies on economic and social development and avoid diversion of resources from development to defence, the Government of India and Government of Pakistan agree to a balanced reduction of their defence forces facing each other and of their stationing and development in areas mutually specified so as to eliminate the possibilities of a sudden outbreak of hostilities.

The Government of India and the Government of Pakistan further agree that joil inspection teams shall be established to ensure effective implementation of agreement entered into pursuant to this Article. The joint inspection teams will submit their repol1 from time to time to the two Governments.

Both sides agree to enter into a Protocol for the implementation of this Article which shall be an integral part of this Treaty.

ARTICLE VI
The Government of India and Government of Pakistan agree that in order to create and maintain a climate of peace, friendship and understanding between the peoples of the two countries, it is essential that all hostile propaganda directed against each other shall cease. They further agree that both countries shall actively encourage the dissemination information to promote the development of friendly relations and cooperation in various fields between the two countries.

ARTICLE VII
The Government of India and Government of Pakistan undertake to identify develop areas of cooperation and common interest between their two people. In order achieve this objective, they shall establish joint commissions or their joint bodies so that areas of cooperation may develop on a firm and long-term basis for mutual benefit. For this

purpose, both sides agree to enter into Protocols which shall be integral parts of this Treaty.

ARTICLE VIII

The Government of India and the Government of Pakistan regard commercial, economic and cultural ties as an important and essential element in the strengthening bilateral relations. They agree to promote the growth of such ties.

ARTICLE IX

The Government of India and the Government of Pakistan agree to facilitate visits of nationals of one country to the other through mutually agreed routes for personal, commercial, religious, cultural and other reasons.

ARTICLE X

The Government of India and the Government of Pakistan agree that with a view to the effective implementation of this Treaty, periodic consultations shall be held between the two countries at appropriate levels.

ARTICLE XI

This Treaty shall enter into force upon signature. It shall continue to be in force for a period of ten years in the first instance. It shall continue to be in force thereafter until it is terminated by either party by giving to the other six months' notice in writing.

IN WITNESS WHEREOF, the representatives duly authorised by their respective Governments have signed this Treaty in two original texts, each of which is authentic.

DONE on this the......... day of........

For the Government of India   For the Government of Pakistan

Note

As agreed earlier, the question of Jammu and Kashmir will be discussed separately. To complete the text of the Treaty, the agreement reached at such discussion shall be incorporated in the form of Articles at an appropriate place in this Treaty, and shall constitute an integral part of this Treaty.

PAKISTANI DRAFT
(30 June 1972)

Agreement on bilateral relations between the Government of India and the Government of Pakistan

The Government of India and the Government of Pakistan are resolved that that the two countries put an end to the conflict and confrontation that have hitherto marred their relations and work for the promotion of a friendly and harmonious relationship with a view to the establishment of durable peace in the sub- continent, so that both countries m henceforth devote their resources and energies principally to the pressing task of advancing the welfare of their peop

In order to achieve this objective, the Government of India and the Government Pakistan have agreed as follows:

The two Governments reaffirm the universal and unconditional validity of the purposes and principles of the Charter of the United Nations as the basis of relations between the two countries, and declare that the breach of these principles cannot be justified in any circumstances whatsoever.

2. The two Governments shall in their bilateral relations adhere to the principles set out in the Declaration on the Strengthening of International Security adopted by the United Nations General Assembly on 16 December 1970, and which was accepted by both India and Pakistan. In accordance with that Declaration, they reaffirm that they will:

(i)   respect each other's national unity, territorial integrity, political independence and sovereign equality;
(ii) refrain from the threat or use of force against the territorial integrity or political independence of each other;
(iii) not interfere in any manner whatsoever in each other's internal affairs; and
(iv) fulfil in good faith the obligations assumed by them under the United Nations Charter.

3. Any dispute between India and Pakistan or any situation the continuance of which is likely to endanger peace between them will be settled by peaceful means such as negotiation, inquiry, mediation, conciliation, or, should these methods prove unavailing, by arbitration or judicial settlement.

4. In order to concentrate their energies on economic and social development, the two Governments will, as far as possible, avoid diversion of their resources from development needs to defence purposes, keeping in view the principle of equal security.

5. Hostile propaganda directed against each other shall cease. Both countries will encourage the dissemination of such information as would promote the development friendly relations between them.

6. The two Governments will progressively normalise their relations step by step by:

(i)   resuming communications, postal, telegraphic, sea, land and air links, including over flights, in accordance with bilateral agreements entered into by the two Governments in the past and relevant international Conventions and Agreements;
(ii) opening of border posts;
(iii) providing adequate travel facilities to the nationals of the other country;
(iv) resumption of trade and cooperation in economic and other agreed fields as far as possible; and exchanges in the fields of science and culture.

In this connection, teams of experts from the two countries will meet from time to time to work out the necessary details.

7. This Agreement will be subject to ratification by both countries and will come into force with effect from the date on which the Instruments of Ratification are exchanged. The President of Pakistan has declared that this Agreement will require ratification by the National Assembly of Pakistan.

In the meantime, both Governments will take immediate steps to implement Resolution No.307 (1971) of the United Nations Security Council by:

(i)   withdrawing all armed forces to their respective territories and to positions which fully respect the Cease Fire Line in Jammu and Kashmir supervised by the United Nations Military Observers' Group in India and Pakistan, and
(ii)   repatriating all prisoners of war and civilian internees in each other's custody in conformity with the Geneva Conventions of 1949.

Also, the two Governments will resume diplomatic relations as from an agreed date.

(Zulfikar Ali Bhutto)   (Indira Gandhi)
President, Islamic Republic of Pakistan   Prime Minister, Republic of India

INDIAN DRAFT II
(1 July 1972)

Agreement on bilateral relations between the Government of India and the Government of Pakistan.

The Government of India and the Government of Pakistan are resolved that the two countries put an end to the conflict and confrontation that have hitherto marred their relations and work for the promotion of a friendly and harmonious relationship and the establishment of durable peace in the sub-continent, so that both countries may henceforth devote their resources and energies to the pressing task of advancing the welfare of their peoples.

In order to achieve this objective, the Government of India and the Government of Pakistan have agreed as follows:

(i)   That the principles and purposes of the Charter of the United Nations shall govern the relations between the two countries.
(ii)   That the two countries will not use force for the settlement of any differences between them and resolve them exclusively by peaceful means through bilateral negotiations or by any other peaceful means mutually agreed upon between them. Pending the final settlement of any of the problems between the two countries, neither side shall unilaterally alter the situation and shall prevent the organization, assistance or encouragement of all acts detrimental to the maintenance of peaceful and harmonious relations.

(iii) That the pre-requisite for reconciliation, good neighbourliness and durable peace between them is a commitment by both the countries to peaceful co-existence, respect for each other's territorial integrity and sovereignty, non-interference in each other's internal affairs and cooperation on the basis of equality and mutual benefit.

(iv) That the basic issues and causes of conflict which have bedevilled the relations between the two countries for the last 25 years shall be removed bilaterally and by peaceful means.

(v) That they shall always respect each other's national unity, territorial integrity, political independence and sovereign equality.

(vi) That they shall always refrain from the threat or use of force against the territorial integrity or political independence of each other.

Hostile propaganda directed against each other shall cease. Both countries will encourage the dissemination of such information as would promote the development of friendly relations between them.

In order to progressively restore and normalise relations between the two countries, it was agreed that:

(i) Steps shall be taken to resume communications, postal, telegraphic, sea, land and air links, including over-flights.

(ii) Steps shall be taken for the opening of border posts.

(iii) Adequate travel facilities to the nationals of the other country will be provided.

(iv) Trade and cooperation in economic and other agreed fields will be resumed as far as possible.

(v) Exchange in the fields of science and culture will be promoted.

In this connection, teams of experts from the two countries will meet from time to time to work out the necessary details.

This Agreement will be subject to ratification by both countries in accordance with their respective constitutional procedures, and will come into force with effect from the date on which the Instruments of Ratification are exchanged.

Both Governments agree that their respective heads will meet again at a mutually convenient time in the future and that, in the meanwhile, the officials of the two sides will meet to discuss further the modalities and arrangements for the establishment of durable peace and normalisation of relations, including the question of Jammu and Kashmir, repatriation of prisoners of war and civilian internees, withdrawal of an armed forces to their respective territories and the resumption of diplomatic relations.

Indira Gandhi
Prime Minister, Republic of India.

Zulfikar Ali Bhutto
President, Islamic Republic of Pakistan

Appendix II: Composite Dialogue 1997–98

Joint Statement by Foreign Secretaries, Islamabad, 23 June 1997
(Extracts)

'As decided at their meeting in New Delhi in March 1997 and as directed by their respective Prime Ministers, the Foreign Secretaries of India and Pakistan continued their wide-ranging and comprehensive dialogue on all outstanding issues between the two countries with each side elaborating its respective position. The discussions were held in a cordial and constructive atmosphere. It was also agreed that that both sides would take all possible steps to prevent hostile propaganda and provocative actions against each other.

'With the objective of promoting a friendly and harmonious relationship between Pakistan and India, the Foreign Secretaries have agreed as follows:-

(i) to address all outstanding issues of concern to both sides including inter alia:

> Peace and security, including CBMs
> Jammu and Kashmir
> Siachen
> Wullar Barrage Project/Tultbul Navigation Project
> Sir Creek
> Terrorism and drug-trafficking
> Economic and Commercial Cooperation
> Promotion of friendly exchanges in various fields.

(ii) to set up a mechanism, including working groups at appropriate levels, to address all these issues in an integrated manner. The issues at (a) and (b) above will be dealt with at the level of Foreign Secretaries who will also coordinate and monitor the progress of work of all working groups.'

Joint Statement by Prime Minister of Pakistan and Prime Minister of India after meeting in New York on 23 September 1998
(Extracts)

'The discussions covered the whole range of bilateral relations. The two Prime Ministers also carried out a detailed review of new developments in the region during the past few months.

'They reaffirmed their common belief that an environment of durable peace and security was in the supreme interest of both India and Pakistan, and the of the region as a whole. They expressed their determination to renew and reinvigorate efforts to secure such an environment. They agreed that the peaceful settlement of all outstanding issues, including Jammu and Kashmir, was essential for this purpose.

'The two Prime Ministers noted with satisfaction the agreement reached between the Foreign Secretaries on operationalizing the mechanism to address all items in the agreed agenda of 23rd June 1997 in a purposeful and composite manner. They directed the Foreign Secretaries, accordingly, to resume the dialogue on the agreed dates.'

Appendix III: Lahore Declaration, 21 February 1999

(Extracts)

The Prime Ministers of Pakistan and India:-

<u>Sharing</u> a vision of peace and stability between their countries, and of progress and prosperity for their peoples;

Have agreed that their respective governments:-

- shall intensify efforts to resolve all issues, including the issue of Jammu and Kashmir.
- shall refrain from intervention and interference in each other's internal affairs.
- shall intensify their composite and integrated dialogue process for an early and positive outcome of the agreed bilateral agenda.
- shall take immediate steps for reducing the risk of accidental or unauthorized use of nuclear weapons and discuss concepts and doctrines with a view to elaborating measures for confidence building in the nuclear and conventional fields, aimed at prevention of conflict.
- reaffirm their commitment to goals and objectives of SAARC and to concert their efforts towards the realization of the SAARC vision for the year 2000 snf beyond with a view to promoting the welfare of the peoples of south Asia and to improve their quality of life through accelerated economic growth, social progress and cultural development.
- reaffirm their condemnation and terrorism in all its forms and manifestations and their determination to combat this menace.
- shall promote and protect all human right and fundamental freedoms.

Memorandum of Understanding
Lahore, 21 February 1999
(Extracts)

The Foreign Secretaries of Pakistan and India:-

Reaffirming the continued commitment of their respective governments to the principles and purposes of the UN Charter:

Have on this day, agreed to the following:-

1. The two sides shall engage in bilateral consultations on security concepts, and nuclear doctrines...
2. The two sides undertake to provide each other with advance notification in respect of ballistic missile flight tests, and shall conclude a bilateral agreement in this regard.
3. The two sides are fully committed to undertaking national measures to reducing risks of accidental or unauthorized use of nuclear weapons under their control. The two sides further undertake to notify each other immediately in the event of any accidental, unauthorized and unexplained incident that could create the risk of a fallout with adverse consequences for both sides, or an outbreak of a nuclear war between the two countries, as well as adopt measures aimed at diminishing the possibility of such actions, or such incident being misinterpreted by the other. The two sides shall identify/establish the appropriate communication mechanism for this purpose.
4. The two sides shall continue to abide by their respective unilateral moratorium on conducting further nuclear test explosions unless either side, in exercise of its national sovereignty decides that extraordinary event have jeopardized its supreme interests.
5. The two sides shall conclude an agreement on prevention of incidents at sea in order to ensure safety of navigation by naval vessels, and aircraft belonging to the two sides.

Joint Statement
Lahore: 21 February 1999
(Extracts)

2. Prime Minister Vajpayee 'visited Minar-e-Pakistan, Mausoleum of Allama Iqbal, Gurdawara Dera Sahib and Samadhi of Maharaja Ranjeet Singh...

'3. The two leaders held discussions on the entire range of bilateral relations, regional cooperation within SAARC, and issues of international concern. They decided that

a) The two Foreign Ministers will meet periodically to discuss all issues of mutual concern, including nuclear issues.
b) The two sides shall undertake consultations on WTO related issues with a view to coordinating their respective positions.
c) The two sides shall determine areas of cooperation in Information Technology, in particular for tackling the problems of the 21st century.
d) The two sides will hold consultations with a view to further liberalizing the visa and travel regime.
e) The two sides shall appoint a two-member committee at ministerial level to examine humanitarian issues relating to civilian detainees and missing POWs.

Appendix IV: Agra Declaration, 2001— Draft Agreement

Having met at their retreat in Agra on 15-16 July 2001 and held wide-ranging discussions on Pakistan-India relations, particularly on Jammu and Kashmir and having affirmed their commitment to addressing each other's expressed concerns, creating an environment conducive to the establishment of peaceful, friendly and cooperative ties, for the welfare of the peoples of the two countries.

Agree to the following:

1. Progress towards settlement of Jammu and Kashmir issue would be conducive towards normalization and will further the establishment of a cooperative relationship in a mutually reinforcing manner.
[Before the amendment the sentence read: Settlement of the Jammu and Kashmir issue would pave the way for normalisation of relations between the two countries.]

2. There was progress in the discussions towards an understanding of each other's viewpoints. There was also recognition of the requirement of keeping the door open for future dialogue. There was agreement on continuing the process of dialogue.

3. The two sides will resume a sustained dialogue at the political level on:
    (a) Jammu and Kashmir;
    (b) Peace and Security, including both conventional and nuclear CBMs;
    (c) Terrorism and Drug Trafficking.

4. The following will be addressed at the appropriate level of officials of the two countries:
    (a) Economic and Commercial Cooperation;
    (b) Siachen;
    (c) Wullar Barrage/Tulbul Navigation Project;
    (d) Sir Creek;
    (e) Promotion of friendly exchanges in various fields.

The progress on these issues would be reviewed by the Foreign Minister of Pakistan and the External Affairs Minister of India at their meetings.

5. The President and the Prime Minister further agreed and directed that all these issues be addressed purposefully, constructively and in an integrated manner, with a sense of urgency.

6. There was also agreement on the following dialogue structure:
   (a) Annual Summit level meetings;
   (b) Bi-annual meetings between the Minister of Foreign Affairs of Pakistan and Minister of External Affairs of India;
   (c) Foreign Office consultations at the level of Foreign Secretaries.

7. The two sides will support reactivation of the SAARC process and the holding of the Eleventh Summit on a date convenient to the host country and other Member States of the Association.

8. The President of Pakistan invited the Prime Minister of India to visit Pakistan. The invitation was accepted. Dates would be fixed through diplomatic channels.

9. The President and the Prime Minister also agreed to meet again in New York in September 2001 during the session of the UN General Assembly.

The President of Pakistan thanked the Prime Minister of India for the warm reception and gracious hospitality extended to him and his delegation during their stay, as well as for the excellent arrangements for the visit.

Appendix V

PRESIDENTS, PRIME MINISTERS AND FOREIGN MINISTERS OF PAKISTAN

Head of State/Government	Foreign Minister
Quaid-i-Azam Mohammad Ali Jinnah Governor General, 1947 to 11-9-48	Mohammad Zafrullah Khan 1947-54
Liaquat Ali Khan, Prime Minister 1947 to 16-10-51	
Khawaja Nazimuddin Governor General, 1948-51 Prime Minister, 1951-53	
Ghulam Mohammad Governor General, 1951-55	
Iskander Mirza Governor General, 1955-56 President, 1956-58	
Mohammed Ali (Bogra) Prime Minister, 1953-55	
Chaudhri Muhammad Ali Prime Minister, 1955-56	Hamidul Haq Chowdhury 1955-56
Huseyn Shaheed Suhrawardy, Prime Minister, 1956-57	Malik Firoz Khan Noon 1956-57
Ismail I. Chundrigar Prime Minister, Oct.-Dec. 57	
Malik Firoz Khan Noon Prime Minister, 1957-58	
Muhammad Ayub Khan President, 1958-69	Manzoor Qadir, 1958-62 Mohammad Ali Bogra, 1962-63 Zulfikar Ali Bhutto, 1963-66 Syed Sharifuddin Pirzada, 1966-68

Agha Mohammad Yahya Khan
1969-71

Mian Arshad Hussain
1968-69

Zulfikar Ali Bhutto
President, 1971-73
Prime Minister, 1973-77

Aziz Ahmed, 1972-77

Fazal Ilahi Choudhry
President, 1973-1977

Mohammad Ziaul Haq
President, 1977-88

Agha Shahi, 1978-82
Sahabzada Yaqub-Khan,
1982-87

Mohammad Khan Junejo
Prime Minister, 1985-88

Zain Noorani
Minister of State, 1985-88

Ghulam Ishaq Khan
President, 1988-93

Sahabzada Yaqub-Khan, 1988-91

Benazir Bhutto
Prime Minister, 1988-90

Mian Mohammad Nawaz Sharif
Prime Minister, 1990-93

Mohammad Siddique Khan Kanju
Miniter of State 1991-93

Benazir Bhutto
Prime Minister, 1993-96

Sardar Assef Ahmed Ali
1993-96

Farooq Ahmad Khan Leghari
President, 1993-1997

Mian Mohammad Nawaz Sharif
Prime Minister, 1996-99

Gohar Ayub Khan, 1996-98
Sartaj Aziz, 1998-99

Muhammad Rafiq Tarar,
President, 1998-2001

Pervez Musharraf
Chief Executive, 1999-2001
President, 2001-

Abdul Sattar
1999-2002

Muhammad Zafrullah Khan Jamali
Prime Miniser, 2002-2004

Mian Khurshid Mahmud Qasuri
2002-

Shaukat Aziz
Prime Minister, 2004-

Bibliography

Ahmed, Aziz, *Manuscript* (Foreign Policy, 1958-65).

Ali, Chaudhri Muhammad, *The Emergence of Pakistan*, Columbia University Press, New York, 1967.

Ambedkar, B. R, *Thoughts on Pakistan*, Thacker & Co., Bombay, 1947.

Arif, K., ed., *America-Pakistan Relations-Documents*, Vanguard Books, Lahore, 1984.

Arif, K.M., General, *Working With Zia*, Oxford University Press, Karachi, 1995.

Azad, Abul Kalam, *India Wins Freedom*, Orient Longman, New Delhi, 1959.

Bajpai, K., et al., *Brasstacks and Beyond*, Manohar Publishers, New Delhi, 1995.

Bajwa, Farooq Naeem, *Pakistan and the West*, Oxford University Press, Karachi, 1996.

Bhatty, Maqbool A., *Great Powers and South Asia: Post-Cold War Trends*, Institute of Regional Studies, Islamabad, 1996.

Bhutto, Zulfikar Ali, *The Myth of Independence*, Oxford University Press, Karachi, 1969.

Burke, S.M., and Lawrence Ziring, *Pakistan's Foreign Policy*, Oxford University Press, Karachi, Second Edition, 1990.

Campbell-Johnson, Alan, *Mission with Mountbatten*, Atheneum, New York, 1966.

Cordovez, Diego, and Harrison, Selig, *Out of Afghanistan-The Inside Story of the Soviet Withdrawal*, Oxford University Press, New York, 1995.

Choudhury, G.W., *Pakistan's Relations with India, 1947-66*, Pall Mall Press, London, 1967.

Farooqi, Bahauddin, 'Writ Petition' in *Kashmir Holocaust-The Case Against India.*, ed., Khalid Hasan, Dotcare, Lahore, 1992.

Fukuyama, Fracis, *The End of History and The Last Man*, The Free Press (Macmillan Inc.), New York, 1992.

Gauhar, Altaf, *Ayub Khan: Pakistan's First Military Ruler*, Sang-e-Meel Publications, Lahore, 1994.

Geelani, Syed Ali, *Roodad-i-Qafs* (My Life in Prison), Institute of Policy Studies, Islamabad, 1993.

Hasan, Khwaja Sarwar, *Documents on the Foreign Policy of Pakistan*, Institute of International Affairs, Karachi, 1986.

Hyder, Sajjad, *The Foreign Policy of Pakistan, Reflections of an Ambassador*, Progressive Publishers, Lahore, 1987.

Jinnah, Mohammad Ali, *Speeches as Governor General, 1947-48*, Ferozsons, Karachi.

Kadeer, A.A., and Tahir, Naveed A., eds., *Pakistan-Europe Ties*, University of Karachi, 1988.

Kennedy, Paul, *The Rise and Fall of Great Powers*, Random House, New York, 1987.

Khalilzad, Zalmay, *Strategic Appraisal 1996*, RAND, Santa Monica, 1996.

Khan, Air Marshal M. Asghar, *The First Round–Indo-Pakistan War*, Islamic Information Services Ltd., London, 1979.

Khan, Riaz M., *Untying the Afghan Knot*, Progressive Publishers, Lahore, 1993.

Kissinger, Henry, *The White House Years*, Little Brown, 1979.

Kux, Dennis, *India and the United States: Estranged Democracies,* National Defense University Press, Washington, DC, 1993, and *United States and Pakistan, 1947-2000 – Disenchanted Allies,* Woodrow Wilson Center Press, Washington, D.C., 2001.

Lamb, Alastair, *Kashmir-A Disputed Legacy,* Oxford Books, UK, 1991, reprinted by Oxford University Press, Karachi, 1992.

Longer, V., *The Defence and Foreign Policy of India,* Sterling Publishers, New Delhi, 1988.

Malik, Hafeez, *Soviet-Pakistan Relations and Post-Soviet Dynamics,* Macmillan Press, London, 1994.

McMahon, Robert 1., *The Cold War on the Periphery-The United States, India and Pakistan,* Columbia University Press, New York, 1994.

Mendis, Vernon LB., *SAARC-Origins, Organization and Prospects,* Indian Ocean Centre for Peace Studies, Perth, 1991.

Nehru, Jawaharlal, *Selected Works,* Second Series, distributed by Oxford University Press, New Delhi, 1984.

Nixon, Richard M., *The Memoirs of Richard Nixon,* Warner Books, New York, 1978.

Perkovich, George, *India's Nuclear Bomb,* University of California Press, Berkeley, 1999.

Raina, Asoka, *Inside RAW,* Vikas Publishing Co., New Delhi, 1981.

Roy, Oliver, *Islam and Resistance in Afghanistan,* Cambridge University Press, Cambridge, 1986.

Rubin, Barnett R., *The Search for Peace in Afghanistan-From Buffer State to Failed State,* Yale University Press, New Haven, 1995.

Sattar, Abdul, 'Reducing Nuclear Dangers in South Asia—A Pakistani Perspective' in *The Non-proliferation Review,* Monterey, Winter 1995.

Schlesinger, Arthur M., Jr., *A Thousand Days,* Fawcett Publications, Greenwich, 1965.

SAARC Secretariat, *From SARC to SAARC,* Katmandu, 1995.

Shahi, Agha, *Pakistan's Security and Foreign Policy,* Progressive Publishers, Lahore, 1988.

Salik, Siddiq, *Witness to Surrender,* Oxford University Press, Karachi, 1977.

Sisson, Richard, and Rose, Leo E., *War and Secession-Pakistan, India, and the Creation of Bangladesh,* University of California Press, Berkeley, CA. 1990.

Spector, Leonard S., and Smith, Jacqueline R., *Nuclear Ambitions,* Westview Press, Boulder, CO. 1990.

Stephens, Ian, *Horned Moon,* Chatto and Windus, London, 1954.

US Policy Documents, US Government Publications, Washington, DC.

Yunus, Mohammad, *Reflections on China,* Wajidalis, Lahore, 1986.

Ziring, Lawrence, et. al., *Pakistan: The Long View,* Duke University Press, Durham, 1977.

Zaidi, A Moin, and Zaidi, Shaheda, eds., *The Encyclopedia of Indian National Congress,* S. Chand & Co., New Delhi, 1976-1981.

Index

A

Abbas, Ghulam, 24
Abbas, Mahmud, 298
Abdul Malik, 180
Abdul Sattar, 134
Abdullah, Farooq, 169, 170, 175
Abdullah, Sheikh, 22, 23, 24, 27, 28, 29, 90, 91, 93, 169, 72; 27, 28, 29
Abdurrahman, Amir, 154
Abdus Salam, 145-146
Acheson, Dean, 36, 63, 123n
Advani, Lal Krishna, 201, 231, 238
Afghanistan crisis, 60
Afghanistan, 13, 18-19
Afridi tribesman 23
Afro-Asian summit conference, See Bandung Conference.
Agartala Conspiracy, 113
Agni, 220
Ahmad, Tajuddin, 114
Ahmed, Aziz, 65, 80, 84, 87n, 92, 93, 102, 124, 125 129, 131, 134, 141
Ahmed, G., 82
Al Aqsa Mosque, 110
Al Qaeda, 244, 245, 260
Ali, Amjad, 46, 47
Ali, Chaudri Muhammad, 49, 55, 59
Ali, Ghazanfar, 35
Ali, Mir Laik, 37, 39, 42
Ali, Muhammad, 56
Aligarh Muslim University, 2
All Jammu and Kashmir Muslim Conference, 22
All Parties Hurriyat Conference (APHC), 173, 174, 176, 229, 233
Amin, Hafizullah, 155
Amnesty International, 171, 172
Andropov, Yuri, 161, 163
Annan, Kofi, 257, 259, 263-264, 276, 277, 278
Arab nationalism, 49
Arafat, Yasser, 298
Argonne Laboratory School of Nuclear Science and Engineering, 151
Armed Forces Special Powers Act, 171
Armitage, Richard, 244, 249, 251

Asia Watch and Physicians for Human Rights, 171
ASPARA, 151
Aswan High Dam, 55
Ataturk, Mustafa Kemal, 12, 18
Atomic Enegery Research Committee, 150, 151
Atoms for Peace, 151
Attlee, Clement (Prime Minister), 27, 33
Auchinleck, Field Marshal, 24
Ayub Khan, See Khan, Ayub
Ayub, Gohar, 204
Azad Kashmir 23, 24, 26
Aziz, Shaukat, 249

B

Babri Mosque, 236
Badaber Base, 49, 85, 107
Baghdad Pact, 18, 48-49, 53
Ball, George, 65, 82
Bamiyan, 181
Bandung Conference, 51, 68, 69, 83
Barak, Ehud, 298
Beg, Mirza Afzal, 93
Ben Bella, Ahmed, 84
Bhaba, Homi, 150
Bharatiya Janata Party, 170, 203
Bharka Dam, 73
Bhide, Rao Bahadur, 266
Bhutto, Benazir, 175, 190
Bhutto, Zulfikar Ali 87n, 101, 113, 114, 125, 139, 140, 148, 196, 78, 82, 84, 102, 108, 144, 86n, 103-104, 147, 154, 155, 124, 133, 139, 145
Bin Laden, Osama, 181, 183, 227, 228, 240, 242, 244, 245, 256, 260
Black, Eugene, 65, 73
Blair, Tony, 259
Blix, Hans, 299
Bogra, Mohammad Ali, 29, 43, 46, 48, 51, 58, 68, 77
Bonn Agreement, 253
Border Security Force (BSF), 170
Boundary Commission, 16; Punjab, 22
Bowles, Chester, 44, 61, 67n, 80

Brezhnev, Leonid, 84, 161, 167
British Atomic Energy Commission, 151
British Indian Act, 21
British Labour Party, 33-34
Brownback-II amendment, 247
Brzezinsky, Zbigniew, 149, 159, 213
Bulganin, Nikolai, 51, 57
Bunch, Ralph, 104n,
Bush, George W., 152, 214, 226, 244, 247, 251, 259, 297, 298
Byroade, Henry A., 43

C

Cabinet Mission Plan, 36
Campus Watch, 258
Carter, Jimmy, 149, 158, 167
CENTO, 49, 50, 52, 58, 83, 85, 97, 107
Central Reserve Police Force (CRPF), 171
Chashma-II, 249
Chemical Weapons Convention 1993, 197
Chernenko, Konstantin, 162
Chib, Ashik S., 134
Chidambaran, R., 151
China, 96, 97
Chirac, Jacque, 257
Chowdhury, Hamidul Haq, 56
Churchill, Winston, 36
CIA, 158, 256, 260
CIRUS, 151
Clay, Lucius, 80
Clinton, Bill, 152, 202, 204, 214, 226, 231, 232, 235, 298
C-MAG, 236
Coffee Club, 278
Cold War, 27
Commission on Human Rights See Human Rights Council
Comprehensive Test Ban Treaty (CTBT), 197-199, 204, 206, 248
Cooper, John Sherman, 61, 62
Cooperation Agreement (1959), 107
Cordovez, Diego, 161, 162, 163, 166

D

D' Estaing, Giscard, 149
Dal, Janata, 175
Dalai Lama, 63
Daoud, Sardar Mohammad, 154
De Cuellar, Perez, 161
De Gaulle, Charles, 83
Dhar, D.P., 124, 125, 129, 139, 140, 141
Divide-and-quit, 5

Dixon, Owen (Judge), 28, 78, 272
Doha Development Agenda, 284
Dostum, Abdur Rashid, 178, 180, 254
Dubs, Adolph, 158
Dulles, John Foster, 43, 44, 46, 47, 56, 58, 62
Durand Line, 18, 66n, 154

E

ECDC, 285
Economic and Political Weekly, 172
Economic Cooperation Organization (ECO), 227, 285, 289
Eden, Anthony, 44, 46
Egypt, 18, 53, 55
Eisenhower, Dwight D., 43, 44, 45, 58, 63
Engineering Research Laboratories, 147
Enlai, Zhou, 51, 68, 69, 71, 75, 81, 82, 86, 118
EURATOM, 210

F

Faisal bin Abdul Aziz (King), 143
Farooq, Mirwaiz Mohammad, 93
Farooq, Mirwaiz Umar, 173, 273
Fatima Jinnah, See Jinnah, Fatima
Fédération Internationale des Droigts d'Homme, 172
Fernandes, George, 203
Fissile Material Cut off Treaty (FMCT), 199, 204, 205
Foreign Assistance for Pakistan, 282-283
France, 12
Freemen, John, 92

G

Galbraith, John Kenneth, 67n, 75, 80
Gandhi, Indira, 115, 116, 119, 124, 125, 133, 139, 140, 141, 157, 169, 192, 193, 196
Gandhi, Mahatama, 6, 15, 17, 22, 40n
Gandhi, Rajiv, 150, 169, 190, 194, 196
Gates, Robert, 196
Geelani, Syed Ali Shah, 273
General Agreement on Tariffs and Trade (GATT), 284
Geneva Accords, 163, 164, 165, 166, 167, 185
Ghauri, 221
Gibraltar Operation, See Operation Gibraltar
Gilgit Scouts, 24
Gilgit, 24
Global Food Aid Programme
Goa, 65, 75
Gogh, Theo van, 261

Gorbachev, Mikhail, 162, 163, 164, 167
Gowda, Deve, 175, 198
Gracy, General, 24, 26
Graham, Frank P., 28
Gromyko Andrei, 84, 163
Grotius, Hugo, 260
Gujral, I.K., 198, 229

H

Haig, Alexander, 160
Haksar, P.N., 126, 128, 129, 132
Hari-Singh. *See* Maharaja of Kashmir
Harkat-ul-Mujahidin, 174
Harriman, Averell, 61, 78, 80
Hazara, 181
Hazaribagh, 23
Hazratbal shrine, 89
High-Level Panel on Threats, Challenges and Change, 263
Hikmatyar, Gulbuddin, 164, 165, 177, 178, 180
Hilaly, Agha, 46, 109
'Hindi-Roosi bhai bhai', 57
Hindustan Times, 193
Holl, Herbert, 182
Hua, Huang, 118
Human Rights Commission, 281
Human Rights Council, 279
Human rights in Pakistan, 281-282
Huntington, Samuel, 258
Hunza, 71
Hurriyat Conference, 175
Hussein, Saddam, 300
Hyderabad, 21, 31; Nizam of, 21

I

Ikramullah, M., 39, 42
Indian Air Force, 150
Indian Defense Committee, 23
Indian Military Intervention, 48
Indian National Congress, 3, 8, 15, 22, 266
Indian-held-Kashmir (IHK), 170, 173, 174, 273
Indonesia, 18
Indo-USSR Friendship Treaty, 115-120
Indus Commission, 190, 192
Indus River, 73
Indus Waters Treaty 1960, 190, 192
Institute for Science and International Security, 218, 224n
International Atomic Energy Agency (IAEA), 144, 205, 218, 219

International Bank for Reconstruction and Development, 282
International Court of Justice, 137
International Monetary Fund, 205
International Monetary Fund, 235, 282
Iqbal, Allama, 4, 7n, 11
Iran, 12, 18, 159-160
Iraq War, 300
Iraq, 18
Islamic Bomb, 217
Islamic Conference of Foreign Ministers (ICFM), 261
Ispahani, M.A.H., 35, 37
Israel, 258
Iyenger, P.K., 151

J

Jaish-e-Mohammad, 174
James, Maurice, 92
Jammu 16, 17, 127
Janata, Bharatiya, 152
Jiabao, Wen, 249
Jinnah, Fatima, 56
Jinnah, Mohammad Ali, 4, 8, 112, 303; views on foreign policy, 11-13, 36; views on human rights, 13-15
Johnson, Lyndon, 63, 64, 82, 85, 93, 98, 100, 106,
Joint Resolution to Promote Peace and Stability in the Middle East, 57, 58
Junagadh, 21, 31
Junejo, Mohammad Khan, 164, 185, 194, 195

K

Kahuta, 147, 149, 150
Karadzic, Radovan, 257
Kargil, 174
Karmal, Babrak, 155
Karzai, Hamid, 253, 254
Kashmir Publicity Committee, 94
Kashmir, 45, 71, 127
Kashmiri Hizbul Mujahidden, 170
Kaul, T.N., 126, 131
Kennedy, John F., 51, 61, 62, 63, 64, 75, 76, 77, 79, 80, 81, 82; efforts to promote a Kashmir settlement, 64-65
Kennedy, Mrs (Jacqueline?), 64
Kerry, John F., 219
Khan of Kalat, 72
Khan Research Laboratories, 202
Khan, A.Q., 147
Khan, A.Q., 217, 218, 219, 224

Khan, Abdul Ghaffar, 18
Khan, Amir Amanullah, 19
Khan, Asghar, 102
Khan, Ayub, 43, 44, 45, 46, 48, 49, 50, 58, 62,
   63-64, 69-70, 77, 78, 81, 82, 83, 85, 86n, 91,
   93, 94, 96, 97, 98, 99, 100, 101, 102, 113,
   145
Khan, Liaquat Ali, 8, 25, 24, 28, 35, 37, 38, 39,
   272
Khan, Mohammad Hashim, 18
Khan, Munir Ahmad, 146, 150
Khan, Nur, 102
Khan, Sardar Abdul Qayyum, 23
Khan, Sardar Mohammad Ibrahim, 23
Khan, Syed Ahmed, 11
Khan, Yahya, 106, 109, 113-114, 116, 117
Khan, Zafrullah, 8, 12, 25, 26, 43, 46, 47, 65
Khruschev, Nikita, 51, 57
Khurana, Madan Lal, 201
King Zahir Shah See Shah, Zahir
Kissinger, Henry, 98, 114, 117, 118, 146, 148,
   152n, 232
Knowland, William, 61
Koizumi, Junichiro, 219, 248
Korbel, Joseph, 270
Korean War, 41
Kosygin, Alexei, 84, 99, 100, 101, 106, 154
Kushk-Kandahar road, 57
Kuznetsov, Vasily, 119

L

Lahore Declaration, 207
Lahore Summit, 229-230
Lashkar-i-Tayyeba, 173
League-Congress relations, 3-5
Lewis, Bernard, 258
Liaquat Ali Khan, See Khan, Liaquat Ali
Lilienthal, David, 73
Line of Control, 138, 139, 141, 230, 231, 232,
   239, 268, 269
Line of Peace, 133, 134, 273
Lippman, Walter, 85
Livingstone, Ken, 257, 258
Lone, Mushtaq Ahmad, 172

M

Macmillan, Harold, 81
Maharaja of Kashmir, 21, 22, 31
Mahsud tribesman, 23
Mahsud, Ahmad Shah, 180
Mainstream, 139

Majrooh, Syed Bahauddin, 163
Malhotra, Jagmohan, 169, 170, 171
Malik, Akhtar Hussain, 94, 95,
Mangla dam, 74
Manila Conference, 46
Manila Pact, 107
Matchpolitik, 65
McConaughy, Walter P., 80
McGhee, George, 41
McMahon Line, 74, 75
McMahon, Henry, 74
McNaughton A.G.L.,, 78
Menderes, Adnan, 48
Menon, Krishna, 45, 66
Menon, V.P., 23
Middle East Defence Organization (MEDO),
   42, 43
Militia, Uzbek, 178
Millennium Declaration, 275, 276, 283
Millennium Development Goals, 275, 277,
   279
Milliken, Max, 61
Mirza, Iskander, 49
Missile Technology Control Regime, 221
Mohammad, Bakshi Ghulam, 89
Mohammad, Ghulam, 41, 43, 44
Mohaqqeq, Haji Mohammad, 254
Mojaddedi, Sibghatullah, 177
Moo-e-muqaddis, 89
Mori, Yoshiro, 235, 248
Mossadegh, Mohammed, 42, 49
Motherland, 152
Motilal Nehru Report See Nehru Report
Mountbatten, Lord Louis, 6, 16, 21, 22, 23, 24,
   42
Mujahideen, 161, 162, 173, 177, 184, 185;
   Afghan, 150, 256; Alliance, 163, 164, 165,
   178, 179, 260
Mukti Bahini, 115, 117
Mullah Omar, 179
Multi-Fabric Agreement, 284
Murtagh River, 71
Musharraf, Pervez, 193, 218, 225, 232, 233,
   234, 236, 237, 238, 240, 245, 261, 269, 271
Muslim Conference, 24
Muslim League Conference, 22
Muslim League, 3, 12, 14, 36, 112, 122n, 266;
   struggle, 4, 8; Sindh 5
Mutual Defence Assistance Act, 46
Mutual Defence Assistance Agreement, 46,
   51
Mutual Security Act, 46

N

Najibullah, Mohammad, 163, 177
NAM, 162; Coordinating Bureau, 157
Narayan, Jayaprakash, 90, 92-93,
Nasser, Gamal Abdul, 42, 49, 55, 56, 98-99
National Conference, 22, 28, 175
National Security Council, 44
NATO, 216, 243-244
Nawaz, Begum Shah, 36
Nazimuddin, Khawaja (Prime Minister), 39, 43
Neguib-Nasser government, 49
Nehru Report, 4
Nehru, Jawaharlal, 5, 16, 22, 24, 25, 27, 29, 31, 40n, 43, 45, 53, 64, 65, 66, 67n, 69, 75-76, 78, 79, 88, 89, 90, 91, 151, 267, 272
New Delhi, 24
New York Times, 39
Nishtar, Sardar Abdur Rab, 56
Nitze, Paul, 42
Nixon, Richard, 45, 108, 114, 116-117, 118, 119, 120, 147
No-First-Use, 216
Non-Aligned Movement (NAM), 156-157
Non-aligned Movement, 52
Non-Proliferation Treaty (NPT), 145, 148, 202
Noon, Feroz Khan, 37, 56, 62
Northern Alliance, 178, 180, 182
Nuclear Nonproliferation Act 1978, 205
Nuclear Suppliers Group, 146, 152

O

Operation Gibraltar, 102, 107
Organization of Islamic Conference (OIC), 157, 162, 174, 227, 231, 259, 261; summit, 142, 143
Osama Bin Laden, See Bin Laden, Osama
Oslo Declaration of Principles on Interim Self-Government Arrangements, 298

P

Pacific Settlements of Disputes, 26
Pact of Mutual Cooperation, 48, 49
Pakistan Atomic Energy Commission (PAEC), 144, 146, 147, 149, 152n, 202
Pakistan Consortium, 85
Pakistan Institute of Nuclear Science and Technology (PINSTECH), 144, 150
Pakistan People's Party, 113
Pakistan Plan, 5

Pakistan Resolution, 5
Pakistan-India War, 1965, 48, 113
Pakistan-US Agreement on Cooperation, 50
Palestine, 18
Palestinian Liberation Organization (PLO), 298
Parray, Kuka, 173
Partition Plan (3rd June), 21
Patel, Sardar, 15
Pentagon, 50
People's Democratic Party of Afghanistan (PDPA), 154, 155, 157, 163
Perez, Shimon, 298
Permanent Indus Commission, 74
PIA, 81, 247
Pipes, Daniel, 258
Point Four Programme, 39
Powell, Colin, 244, 248, 299
Pressler Amendment, 226
Pressler Law, 173
Prithvi, 220
Pukhtoonishtan 18-19, 57, 154
Pushtoon, 181

Q

Qaddafi, Moammer, 217
Qanuni, Younus, 254
Quaid-i-Azam. *See* Jinnah, Mohammad Ali
Quetta Plan of Action, 289

R

Rabbani, Burhanuddin, 164, 177, 178, 179, 180, 184
Rabin, Yitzhak, 298
Radcliffe, Cyril, 16, 22
Radhakrishnan, Sarvepalli, 81
Radio Cairo, 53
Rahman, Amir Abdur, 19
Rahman, Sheikh Mujibur, 113, 143
Raja Ramanna, 151
Rann of Kutch, 88, 103, 187
Ravi (river), 17
Raza, Rafi, 125, 126
Reagan, Ronald, 150, 160, 226
Regional Cooperation for Development (RCD), 291 (*See* Economic Cooperation Organization)
Republic of Ireland, 66
Research and Analysis Wing (RAW), 113, 114
Rice, Condoleezza, 219, 251
Rongji, Zhu, 235

Roosevelt, Franklin D., 36
Rostow, Walt, 61
Rusk, Dean, 65, 80, 108

S

Said, Nuri, 48
San Francisco conference, 39
Sandys, Duncan, 78, 79
Sangh, Jana, 152
Sarabhai, Vikram, 151
Saud Al Faisal, 253
Saudi Arabia, 18
Saur Revolution, 155
Saxena, Girish, 171
Sayeed, Mufti Mohammad, 170
Scenario Paper, 163
SEATO, 46-48, 51, 58, 66n, 68, 69, 83, 97, 147
Security Council, 26, 243, 277; on Kashmir,
    25-31, 51, 65-66, 90, 96, 271; resolution,
    88, 117, 119, 130, 181, 183, 204, 205, 206,
    207, 231, 242
Sethna, Homi, 150
Shah, G.M., 169
Shah, Mohammad Zahir (King), 154, 163,
    253
Shahanshah, 49
Shaheen, 221
Shahi, Agha, 110, 156
Shao-chi, Liu, 105
Sharif, Nawaz, 228, 229, 231, 232, 233
Sharon, Ariel, 257, 258, 298
Shastri, Lal Bahadur, 91, 92, 100
Sheikh Mujibur Rahman, 113
Shevardnadze, 164, 213
Shimla Agreement, 189, 190, 231, 232;
    amendments to the Final Draft, 133-135;
    Conference, 273; Indian objectives, 136;
    Kashmir, 138-139; Pakistan's objective,
    136
Shindad military airfield, 57
Shoaib, Mohammad, 103
Sindh Muslim League, 5
Singh, Bhagat, 257
Singh, Charan, 157
Singh, Jaswant, 236, 237
Singh, Manmohan, 269, 273
Singh, Swaran, 272
Singh, Swaran, 78, 129
Sino-Indian conflict, 61, 64, 71, 72, 79
Sino-Pakistan Agreement 1962, 189
Sir Creek, 270
Six Points, 113
Soekarno, Ahmed, 86, 98

South Asian Free Trade Agreement (SAFTA),
    287-288
Soviet Union, 12, 30, 57
Sri Lanka, 13
Srinagar, 23, 29, 30
Stalin, Joseph, 35, 40n, 61
Stevenson, Adlai, 29, 61, 90
Stevenson, Adlai, 65
Strategic Arms Race, 215
Suez Canal Company, 55
Suez Crisis, 53, 55-57, 60
Suhrawardy, Huseyn Shaheed, 49, 56, 59
Sultan of Oman, 72
Sultan Qaboos, 235
Sundarji, Krishnaswami, 194, 212, 213
Sunday Standard, 152
Sutlej (river), 17
Swaran, Sardar, 101,
Symington and Glenn Amendments to the
    Foreign Assistance Act, 148, 160

T

Tajik, 181
Talbot, Philips, 36, 65, 67n
Talbot, Strobe, 202, 204
Taliban, 180, 183, 186, 240, 242, 245, 246, 252,
    254, 268
Taraki, Nur Muhammad, 155
Tarbela dam, 74
Tashkent Conference, 100
Taylor, Maxwell, 75, 82, 83
TCDC, 285
Technical Cooperation Agreement, 51
Tehrik, 170
Ten Principles of Peaceful Coexistence, 83
Thant, U., 96
The New York Times, 153n
The Washington Post, 66, 150, 153n
Tibet, 69
Tibet-Xingiang road, 74
Tilak, Gangadhar, 266
Tirah, 23
Transparency International, 228
Treaty of Friendship, Cooperation, and Good
    Neighbourly Relations, 249
Treaty of Peace, Friendship and Cooperation,
    109
Trivedi, Vishnu, 151
Truce Agreement, 27
Truman, Harry (President), 27, 35, 36, 37, 65,
    67n
Turkey, 18
'Two Chinas' Policy, 72

U

UN Monitoring, Verification and Inspection Commission, 299
UN resolutions, 30, 31; General Assembly, 158
UN Summit (September 2005), 279
Unauthorised Technology Transfer, 217
UNCIP, 26-28
United Front, 112
United Muslim Front, 170
United Nations Charter, 8, 30, 137, 138, 268, 278, 280, 301, in Shimla Agreement, 127, 128, 133
United Nations Human Rights Commission, 174
United Nations Military Observers Group, 130; in India and Pakistan (UNMOGIP), 134-135, 269
United Nations, 19, 25, 27, 29, 30, 38, 227
United States policy to reduce nuclear threat, 215-216
United States, 12, 18, 29, 30, 41, 45, 49, 247; 'Seven steps', 244-245; during 1965 war, 93, 97-98; public law, 63; 9/11 Commission, 251
Uniting for Peace, 118, 156
Universal Human Rights Declaration, 257, 280
US Arms Control and Disarmament Agency (ACDA), 212

US Department of State, 172
US State Department, 27

V

Vajpayee, Atal Behari, 139, 152, 203, 206, 229, 232, 236, 237, 269
Vance, Cyrus, 148
Vernon, Mount, 64
Vitro International, 151
Vorontsov, 165, 166

W

Warren, Avra, 67n
Waziristan, 23
Wilson, Harold, 77, 80, 97, 99
World Bank Consortium, 93
World Bank, 63, 73, 74, 190, 191, 204

Y

Yi, Chen, 97
Yusuf, Mirwaiz Mohammad, 24

Z

Zedong, Mao, 72
Ziaul Haq, 149, 154, 155, 159, 164, 165, 185, 196